John Paradise *and*
Lucy Ludwell

The Ludwell-Paradise House in Williamsburg, Virginia.

Photograph by Nivison.

John Paradise *and* Lucy Ludwell

of London and Williamsburg

BY

ARCHIBALD BOLLING SHEPPERSON

AN OFFICIAL PUBLICATION
OF COLONIAL WILLIAMSBURG

THE DIETZ PRESS, *Incorporated*
Publishers
RICHMOND, VIRGINIA
1942

*To John Paradise
and all lovers of Liberty
then and now.*

CONTENTS

PROLOGUE. A BRIDGE BETWEEN TWO WORLDS . . .   I

   I. COLONIALS AT "HOME"   II

  II. NON INCAUTUS FUTURI 36

 III. THE PARADISE HOUSE IN LONDON 60

 IV. SCHOLARSHIP FOR DELIGHT 80

  V. THE VAST PRESENCE OF DR. JOHNSON . . . 100

 VI. ACCOMPLISHED JONES 120

 VII. CITIZEN PARADISE 139

VIII. AN INTERNATIONAL ACCIDENT 158

 IX. LEVÉE PARADISIAC 181

  X. EXCELLENCY MEETS MAJESTY 195

 XI. A HARPSICHORD FOR MONTICELLO 212

 XII. ELOPEMENT À LA MODE 245

XIII. A PASSAGE THROUGH AMERICA 273

XIV. MR. JEFFERSON'S GREAT YOUNG MAN 308

 XV. PUBLIC ENEMY AND PRIVATE FRIEND 351

XVI. JOHN PARADISE—LOST 399

EPILOGUE. THE PARADISE HOUSE IN WILLIAMSBURG . 433

THE FAMILY CONNECTIONS OF
    LUCY LUDWELL PARADISE 451

ACKNOWLEDGMENTS 457

SELECTIVE BIBLIOGRAPHY 461

CHAPTER REFERENCES 467

INDEX 485

ILLUSTRATIONS

THE LUDWELL-PARADISE HOUSE IN WILLIAMSBURG,
VIRGINIA . . . . FRONTISPIECE

Facing Page

BENJAMIN FRANKLIN 30
Painted in 1762 to the order of Philip Ludwell III, father-in-law of John Paradise.

ARCHITECTURAL DRAWING OF GREENSPRING . . . 42
Made in 1797 by the architect B. H. Latrobe for a proposed remodelling.

CAVENDISH SQUARE, LONDON 60
The neighborhood of the Paradise house at No. 28 Charles Street.

SIR JOSEPH BANKS 64
President of the Royal Society of London.

DOCTOR JOHNSON 108

SIR WILLIAM JONES 120
Oriental scholar.

DR. SAMUEL PARR 127
Classical scholar and divine.

JOSEPH PRIESTLEY 142
Scientist and Liberal.

HIS EXCELLENCY THOMAS JEFFERSON 196

HIS MAJESTY GEORGE III 197

THE LUDWELL PLANTATIONS IN VIRGINIA 274
A map showing the principal Ludwell properties.

CHIPPOKES, SURRY COUNTY, VIRGINIA 276
Inherited by Mrs. Paradise from the Ludwells.

JEFFERSON, THE PRIDE OF AMERICA 312

LETTER FROM JOHN PARADISE TO DR. WARREN . . 400
Physician to Dr. Johnson, Boswell and Paradise.

EASTERN LUNATIC ASYLUM, WILLIAMSBURG, VIRGINIA 446
America's first hospital for the insane, where Mrs. Paradise died.

John Paradise *and*
Lucy Ludwell

PROLOGUE

A Bridge Between Two Worlds

O UR knowledge of the past is largely governed
by our ability to dramatize and classify the
facts of history which have been brought to
our attention. We remember little enough as it is and
would remember still less without the simplifications
and generalizations that are employed by all historians.
Lives of great men would remind us of nothing at all if
their biographers, and we ourselves as their unconscious
biographers, did not use the mnemonics of symbolism
to pin the facts about them to our fickle memories; the
irony being that posthumous fame should depend so
little upon the importance of achievement and so much
upon the vividness of the symbol. One man can single-
handed preserve all Europe from invasion by the Turks
and become half forgotten within a century, while a
contemporary will be remembered forever because he
made a foolish, but picturesque gesture with a cloak.
Memorable events, as a disillusioned Oxford don has
put it, are events you can remember.

Facts, once in our minds, must like the books in a
large library, be arranged and classified in some sort of
searchable order. But this classification, in providing
the only hope for clarity, often proves a barrier to a
true understanding of what has been so carefully put in
order. Events and personages, reigns of kings, wars
and revolutions, political reforms, literary and artistic
upheavals are identified according to "movements" and
"ages," frequently to the detriment of reason and con-

tinuity. These ages or periods, or whatever the division may be, are permitted to be bounded in our minds by fortuitous circumstances and artificial associations which in actual fact did not bind them at all. The understanding thus becomes the victim of the very process by which knowledge has been secured and we lose much of the flavor, the significance, and even of the didactic value of our knowledge and contemplation of the past; our reserves of information are segregated in neat compartments with little or no communication between them, where communication ought to be. Who, for example, recalls without some deliberate effort that while Henry the Eighth of England was divorcing and beheading his unfortunate wives, the Sistine Chapel and the tombs of the Medici were being decorated by Michael Angelo and that at the same time Hernando Cortez was imposing the will of Spain upon the Aztec Indians in Mexico? Who can realize without something of a shock that Milton's epics and Pepys's diary were written within the same decade and the same city? Or that the Empress Eugénie lived to hear that Warren G. Harding was elected President of the United States? We require liaison agents of the mind to keep communication clear between our little armies of fact; else with all our getting of knowledge we will get but little understanding.

An undeniable remoteness exists in the minds of many people between the America of Franklin and Jefferson and the England of Dr. Samuel Johnson. America was moving rapidly forward with eyes and mind upon her future of industrial democracy; England, while moving in the same direction, was moving fitfully and reluctantly, with nostalgic eyes upon the agricultural squirearchy behind her. In America, liberalism was predominant, while in England it was still fighting a losing fight against a stubborn king and a reactionary ministry. The America of Franklin and Jefferson was a world of political and economic reform; the England of Dr. Johnson was one of leisurely scholarship, literature, and comfortable dining. The fact that Dr. Franklin and Dr. Johnson should have lived for many years together in the comparatively small world of intellectual London and should, so far as is known, never actually have met, is as significant as it is surprising. Significant, too, is the fact that a few months before Franklin and Jefferson affixed their signatures to the Declaration of Independence, the Great Lexicographer published his "Answer to the Resolutions and Address of the American Congress," a pamphlet entitled *Taxation no Tyranny*, which breathed such "extreme violence" and "appeared to me," said Boswell, "so unsuitable to the mildness of a christian philosopher . . . that I was sorry to see him appear in so unfavorable a light." It is true that Franklin knew and understood the England of his time; nevertheless, he did as much as any one man to make permanent the separation of England and America. Jefferson did not know the English and certainly did not sympathize with them. His one brief visit to England, during which at a royal levee the Monarch turned his back when Jefferson was introduced, made him detest them even more than he had done before. "I am willing to love all mankind," said Dr. Johnson, *"except an American"* and his "inflammable corruption bursting into horrid fire, he 'breathed out threatenings and slaugh-

ter'; calling them 'Rascals—Robbers—Pirates'; and
exclaiming, he'd 'burn and destroy them.'" Franklin
and Jefferson, as long as they bore any part in British
politics, were both of course ardent Whigs. "And I
have always said," quoth Dr. Johnson, "the first Whig
was the Devil."

The violent differences between such individuals as
these were naturally reflected in the people by whom
they were surrounded and in the separate worlds in
which they moved. Between the world of Franklin and
Jefferson on the one hand and that of Samuel Johnson
on the other there would appear to have been fixed a
gulf so wide that none could cross it. And yet upon the
bridge of friendship one man at least did cross it, passing back and forth between those two worlds whose
differences were so violent and so dramatic as to blind
both those who lived in them and us who view them
now to the overwhelming stock of tradition and racial
character which they had in common.

Stand in imagination upon the Duke of Gloucester
Street in Williamsburg, Virginia, in front of a house
which exists there in reality. Built in the second decade
of the eighteenth century, this house for two generations belonged to one of the richest and most influential
families in the Colony. The name, however, which has
been associated with it for more than a century is that
of a man who never owned or occupied it, who was
born in Macedonia, lived most of his life in London,
and spent only a few months of his fifty-two years in the
country of which he became a citizen before he had
crossed the Atlantic. As you stand before the house,
gaze about you at the Raleigh Tavern, the Colonial
Capitol, and the other buildings which give evidence

that you are in the heart of Colonial and Revolutionary Virginia. Cross its threshold and pass from Jefferson's Virginia into Dr. Johnson's London; for the house which you have entered bears the name of John Paradise, who, although he was a friend and *protégé* of both Franklin and Jefferson and moreover was a Whig, an American, and a benefactor of the Revolution, was also, incongruously and simultaneously, a beloved and respected member of that great circle of friends who surrounded the Leviathan of English literature. John Paradise—a scholar who never wrote a book, a Fellow of the Royal Society who never recorded an experiment, a widely reputed linguist who spoke imperfectly the language of the country in which he lived, a Doctor of Civil Laws of Oxford who knew but little of the law, a philosopher whose domestic life was a tragic failure, and a lover of Liberty who was the slave of his environment and his wife. A man who thought intelligently and yet acted ineptly or not at all. A man who numbered among his closest friends many of the greatest statesmen of England and America and who probably had a wider acquaintance among the intellectuals of continental Europe than any Englishman of his day, but who offered in return no more than gracious hospitality, personal charm, and a genius for friendship. A man who traded worldly ambition for intellectual companionship, of which he was at long periods deprived by hypochondria and a shrewish wife. Such was he who more than any other private individual served as a link between two unfriendly, but inherently similar worlds. His life, although it was one of tragic unfulfillments, can show how two hostile peoples were held together even while they were being torn asunder.

It can make more evident those cultural and traditional bonds which still hold them—frequently to the resentful dismay of them both—closer together than any other two politically separate nations.

There were two ties which bound the British John Paradise to America. One of them was his political liberalism, out of which grew a sympathy for the cause of American liberty shared by so many of his fellow Englishmen before, during, and after the Revolution: Horace Walpole, Dr. Richard Price, James Boswell, Edmund Burke, and Joseph Priestley, to name but a few of them. It seems remarkable, on looking back to that time of bitter feelings, to learn that, just as in America there were many who saw things from the British point of view, so there were in England many who very articulately and with some danger to themselves embraced the cause of the Americans. Among these, John Paradise was not the least.

Although there can be no question of the sincerity of his political views, there was another and more practical reason for the stand he took. He was married to an American wife who was born in Virginia and owned a share in one of the greatest properties there. Lucy, daughter of the third Philip Ludwell of Green Spring, near Williamsburg, is the last person to have borne that distinguished name. In 1760, at the age of nine, she sailed for England in the company of her father and sisters[1] and did not return for a permanent stay until 1805. However, she never for an instant forgot, nor allowed anyone else to forget, that she had been born a Ludwell of Virginia and that she was an American, not only in fact but in feeling. Her attitude in London during the Revolution caused her to be described as a "strenuous American republican" and by her speech and actions she well deserved the description.

Madam Paradise, as Williamsburg knew and has continued to remember her, was a woman small in stature but great in personality and will power. Her extraordinary beauty and her elegance in dress and manners were acknowledged even by her feminine adversaries. In her the Ludwell family traits of pride, possessiveness, and a violent, stubborn temper, were present in a marked degree. She inherited from them also her charm of manner, (when her temper was unruffled), and the untiring interest in public affairs which had helped to win for them a position of the first prominence in the Colony of Virginia. What she lacked was the ability, and especially the opportunities, which made them so conspicuously successful.

Her great-grandfather, the first of the three Philip Ludwells, and his brother Thomas were both close friends of the "tyrant," Sir William Berkeley, and both supported him in the war against Bacon. Giles Bland, one of Bacon's followers, nailed Thomas Ludwell's glove to the door of the State House at Jamestown with the legend "That the Owner of that glove was a son of a whore, mechanic fellow, puppy, and a coward."[2] At the end of the Rebellion, Philip had revenge for this insult to his brother and his family by capturing Giles Bland and bringing him to Jamestown to be hanged. When the Rebellion had been quelled and Governor Berkeley recalled to England by the angry Charles II for having overdone his revenge, the opposition to the new Governor was led by Philip Ludwell, whose "rash and fiery temper," so his enemies declared, was the main cause of a renewal of the conflict. On a certain occasion, having drunk "part of a Flagon of Syder which he was pleased to call for," Ludwell declared that Governor Jeffreys was a perjuror who had delayed justice and committed injustice, that he was a "worse rebel than Bacon," and that he was a "pitiful Little Fellow with a perriwig." In spite of an appeal to the Lords of Trade and Plantation in England, this tirade cost Philip Ludwell his place on the Council and a fine of £500.[3] He was soon restored to the Council at the unanimous demand of the members, but another quarrel with another Governor, Lord Howard of Effingham, lost his place for him again. This time, as a protest by his friends he was elected to the House of Burgesses, but, like "Liberty" John Wilkes a century later, he was not allowed to take his seat. The Burgesses then sent him to England to present their petition against Lord Howard to the King. He returned with a reward of £250 for his "indefatigable and prosperous endeavours."

In 1694, Ludwell resigned his Hotspur rôle to his son and retired to England where he lived until his death in 1716.[4] The grandfather of Lucy Paradise, Philip Ludwell II, followed his father in being an harasser of Royal Governors.[5] For more than a decade he fought beside Commissary Blair, his brother-in-law, in the interests of the College of William and Mary and in opposition to Governor Nicholson and like his father he was dismissed from his membership in the Council, owing to a quarrel with Governor Spotswood. But, as with his father, this caused no permanent damage to his career and he died full of honors.

Lucy Paradise's father, the third Philip Ludwell,

fell heir to a position second to none in the Colony of Virginia, now truly in the summer of her golden age. The mantle of leadership which descended upon him from his father and grandfather became him better than it had them, since he had been fortunate enough to inherit what they had been obliged to win by hard blows. Unlike them he bore no marks upon him of the struggle. Moreover, his nature was gentler and more lovable than theirs; no single incident is recorded in which he displayed the famous "Ludwell temperament," so notorious in his ancestors and unhappily so conspicuous in his daughter, Lucy Paradise. Above all he possessed a kindliness that came from being in harmony with the life around him and a spirit of democracy which is the hallmark of the true aristocrat.

Perhaps the extraordinary devotion which Lucy Paradise evinced for her father and for his memory can partly be explained by the law of contrasts. We know her to have been spirited, headstrong, and high-tempered from the moment she burst into the letters and memoirs of her time and the legend that grew up about her in Williamsburg after her death shows that these traits increased rather than diminished throughout her life. There are some people in whom the instinct for possessiveness is so strong that even the intangible and ideal appear as real and solid objects to be acquired and stored away. Such was Lucy Paradise, and as such she was doomed to the aching disappointment and unsatisfied craving that always torture a nature like hers; for in finding, she lost, and in seeming to possess she discovered that she held the shadow without the substance. The love of her husband and children, the friendship of great men and women, even social position and personal charm—all these things were within her grasp but evaded her grasping reach. Though death released her body, her implacable ghost has never yet been laid. Unsubdued in life, her strident spirit is unconquered in death and her possessive ghost still claims its own. For Madam Paradise still haunts the Duke of Gloucester Street, the Bruton Parish Church, those great outlying estates which her family once owned—Green Spring, Rich Neck, Chippokes across the James—and most of all the Paradise House itself, as restless, as shrill, as vivid, as possessive as she was when she died almost a century and a half ago.

CHAPTER I

Colonials at "Home"

ON May 18, 1769, "was married John Paradise, Esq. of Rathbone-place, to Miss Ludwell, of the same place."[1] This announcement in *The London Chronicle* was repeated a little later by *The Virginia Gazette* in Williamsburg. It is not likely that the marriage caused any great stir in London, outside of the colonial society in which the Paradises and the Ludwells moved, but in Virginia it was great news for it meant that one of the wealthiest heiresses in the Colony had endowed with her riches, not a fellow Virginian, as might be hoped and expected, but an unknown Englishman with an oddly picturesque name. No doubt the usual puns were made on "Paradise" and no doubt there was a good deal of laughter at the expense of the egregious William Lee, who had married Lucy Ludwell's elder sister two months before and, as everybody knew, was looking forward a little too eagerly to the division of the huge Ludwell estate. Certainly his brother, Philip Ludwell Lee of Stratford Hall, who had little cause to love him, must have chuckled at the notion that William could now no longer hope to boss the proceedings alone but must act with the unwelcome assistance of "Miss Lucy's" husband. There was no news which stimulated a more animated interest in eighteenth-century Virginians than that of a wealthy marriage and it can be taken for granted that demands for further details soon reached Arthur Lee in London, who was the bride's first cousin as well as the brother

of her sister's husband. He could give his correspondents all the information they desired. He could,
and no doubt did tell them that John Paradise was
a wealthy man in his own right, that he was a
native of Salonica, and that he was the only son of an
English father and a mother who was half English and
half Greek. He could tell them, for he was well acquainted with Paradise, that he was a young man of a
retiring nature and extremely scholarly tastes who had
studied at the University of Padua and who had, about
the time of his marriage, been "created" M. A. of the
University of Oxford.[2] He could add that in all probability the marriage had been arranged by Col. Ludwell before his death, for in his will he had appointed
John and Peter Paradise as two of the three guardians
of his daughters' interests in London.

The story behind this marriage, which may have
been intended as one of convenience but which certainly proved to be one of the greatest inconvenience to all
concerned, is the story of two British colonial families
who arrived in London about the same time, one from
Virginia and one from Macedonia. Like most Americans and colonials before and since, the Paradises and
the Ludwells huddled together for warmth against the
coldness of English formality. Philip Ludwell and
Peter Paradise were both actively interested in the
importation of tobacco into England and it is quite
probable that they had business dealings together.
Moreover, there is a possibility that the two families
were akin. John Paradise's maternal grandfather was
named Lodvill, a name which was pronounced, and
sometimes spelled, Ludville; his Christian name was
Philip. It may be the purest coincidence, but Philip

Lodvill was buried at the parish church of St. Mary at
Stratford-le-Bow, which is also the resting-place of the
father and the great-grandfather of Lucy, both of
whom were named Philip Ludwell.[3] But whether there
was any kinship or not, the heads of the two families
became close friends and the marriage of the son of one
to the daughter of the other was, in the eighteenth
century, a most usual consequence.

Lucy Paradise brought not only more wealth to her
marriage than did her husband, but also more social
prestige. It is true that in London the social prestige of
a mere colonial did not count for much, but of that
Lucy Paradise was quite unconscious. She knew, even
if the world around her chose to ignore it, what it
meant to be a Ludwell of Virginia, and this knowledge
was to dominate her relationship to other people
throughout her life.

First of all it meant her birthplace, Green Spring,
with its background of ease and plenty and its wealth
of associations. Even as early as 1760 this "first great
house of the American Colonies," already more than a
century old, had accumulated tradition and history
enough to fire the imagination of the nine-year-old girl
whose home it was. She no doubt learned from her
father how it had been built by Virginia's fiery Royalist
Governor, Sir William Berkeley, upon land which had
been granted to him by Charles I, and how it had
derived its pleasant name from "a very green spring
that is upon the land." It was constructed in part during Berkeley's bachelor days and here he had entertained the Cavalier refugees who came to Virginia
after 1649. Later on another group of visitors had been

less hospitably entertained; these were the rebel Bacon
and his men, some of whom were detained, not in the
house itself but in the barred brick jail which still
stands near its ruins. Three of these intruders were
hanged on Green Spring trees. It was at Green Spring
that the Virginia Assembly had for a time held its
meetings after Bacon burned the State House in Jamestown, three miles away. Here too the spirited Lady
Berkeley had rebuffed the King's Commissioners, sent
to undo her husband's wrongs, and speeded them to
Jamestown in a carriage driven by the common hang-
man.[4]

Not long after this, on the death of her second husband, Lady Berkeley had married Lucy Paradise's
great-grandfather, the first Philip Ludwell, who had
himself already married and lost a wife.[5] His son,
Philip Ludwell II, was the only surviving male descendant of these four marriages and he inherited the
greater part of the property that accumulated from
them, consisting of the plantations of Green Spring,
Rich Neck, and Chippokes, each of which was made
up of several farms. Early in the eighteenth century
he had extended the grounds at Green Spring and
added to its buildings, and Lucy Paradise could remember a house a hundred and sixty feet in length and
fifty-two in width, its upper half-story broken by
dormer windows, with an ell at its north end, and a
terraced boxwood garden extending toward the James
River and flanked by two serpentine walls, each leading
to a brick pavilion. The house itself was of brick and
the traditions regarding it as well as the dimensions of
the existing foundation indicate that it was one of the
most splendid in colonial America. Its lower story was

fronted by an arcade running the entire length of the house, above which was a gallery ten feet wide, reached by a high flight of steps. Adjoining the gallery were the three principal rooms of the main floor. The house was mainly of Jacobean architecture with a Tudor arch rising above its entrance and two clusters of chimneys at either end of the main structure. Like Bacon's Castle, it bore but little resemblance to the Georgian houses which were later built in Virginia in such great numbers.

In the middle years of the eighteenth century, when Lucy Paradise's father was its master, Green Spring was at the peak of its development. Like the other two plantations, it was economically all but self-sufficient. The principal crop was of course tobacco, both dark and light, which was grown, stemmed, tied, and then prized into hogsheads. The hogsheads were rolled to her father's wharfs on both banks of the James where they were packed into vessels belonging to his "dear and ffaithful friends," Messrs. Cary, Moorey and Welch, merchants of London and Virginia. In London the tobacco was exchanged for farming implements, household furniture, harness, clothing, wines and liquors, and such articles of food as could not be produced in Virginia. The surplus value of the tobacco, then as now Virginia's principal money crop, was left as credit in the hands of the merchants who handled it, or else it was invested in the funds of Great Britain. Green Spring was exceptional in producing large quantities of indigo, of which but little was raised elsewhere in Virginia. Wheat, Indian corn, and other grains were produced upon the three plantations in sufficient quantities to supply malt liquors and bread, as well as feed

for the cattle. The grain was ground in mills owned
and operated by Col. Ludwell. Green Spring alone
possessed two hundred sheep, the same number of
horned cattle, and twenty-three horses. Both cotton and
flax were grown and these were spun and woven by
the slaves and made by them into garments for their
own use.

The several hundred slaves on the Ludwell estates
formed a valuable part of the property, but they were,
as many Virginians had begun to realize, an ever-increasing source of enervation and destruction. Colonel
Ludwell, like every other plantation owner, was confronted with the problem of the runaway slave. A man
was valued at about sixty pounds, a woman at about
fifty. The running away of a slave meant not only the
loss of a considerable sum in the value of the slave
himself, but also payment for the damage that was only
too likely to be inflicted by the refugee upon the property of others. It reflects some credit on Lucy Paradise's
father, Colonel Ludwell, that of the innumerable ad-
vertisements of runaways during his life in Virginia
only three are from his hand and all of these are for the
same slave. This was "a tall slim young Fellow hollow
Eye'd" by the name of Anthony.[6] He ran away twice
in one year, the second time committing a robbery in
the neighborhood of Williamsburg. He did not escape
again for seven years. Still "hollow Eye'd," he was
wearing this time "a blue cotton jacket and breeches
and a fine white Linen Shirt."[7] The only other slave of
Col. Ludwell's of whom there is special mention is a
woman named Cress. When Lucy Paradise's mother
died, Lucy was two years old and her sister Frances
three. According to their father, Cress was "faithful

and never varied" in her care of them; she went with
them to England and finally sacrified her life in their
service.[8] As a reward, Col. Ludwell promised Cress
that he would free her own two daughters, Jane and
Sarah, and this promise he performed by directing in
his will that they should be brought to England and
there manumitted.

The orchards at Green Spring, three in number,
were famous throughout Virginia and grafts from the
fruit trees there were much in demand. Lucy Paradise's friend Thomas Jefferson was proud to note that
the golden wilding apples which he planted in his
garden at Monticello were from these orchards.[9] There
were also groves of white mulberry trees, planted by
Col. Ludwell in an unsuccessful attempt to cultivate the
silkworm, and a kitchen garden from which he supplied his friends in Williamsburg with early asparagus
and green peas. In 1751, the year in which John Blair
recorded Lucy's birth in his diary, he also noted that
her father and he had gathered oranges together on a
"fair but windy" afternoon in March in the orangery
at Green Spring.[10]

In Lucy's childhood the stables at Green Spring were
rivalled only by those at Westover and Newmarket.
Almost a hundred years before, they had been installed
by Governor Berkeley, who was passionately fond of
horse-racing. Lucy's father, like the good Virginian
that he was, had kept the stables up; but after his death
his frugal son-in-law William Lee became convinced
that race horses were "realy useless" and consumed "a
vast deal of corn."[11] In consequence the bay mare
"Ruby," the two sorrels "Skim" and "Sterling," and

the two famous stallions "Young Breton" and "Partner" went under the hammer and the Green Spring stables were no more.[12]

Of all Lucy Paradise's early memories of Virginia, that of her father and all that he had been and represented was the one which most dominated her thoughts in after years. The comparative obscurity of the closing years of his life in London by no means dimmed for her the glory that had been his. Col. Philip Ludwell was, like his father, the only surviving male heir and was the third of his name to become a member of the House of Burgesses, of the vestry of Bruton Church—named for the parish in Somerset from which the Ludwells originally came[13]—and of the Governor's Council. His career, compared with those of his father and grandfather, was a peaceful one, partly owing to his milder nature and partly to the fact that during his lifetime Virginia was freer from outside interference than she had been for a hundred years or ever was to be again. In such public crises as did occur he conducted himself with distinction, but on the whole he was content with supporting the fortunate rôle of an eighteenth-century Virginia gentleman.

He was born at Green Spring on December 28, 1716,[14] the year of his cantankerous grandfather's death, and was by eighteen years the youngest of his parents' three surviving children. The eldest was Lucy, for whom Lucy Paradise was named, and the second was Hannah Philippa—named Hannah for her mother, who was a Harrison of Surry, and Philippa for her father. Of the youngest Ludwell's youth nothing is

known except that at the age of twenty, after the death
of both his parents, he was a student at the College of
William and Mary. It was in his final year as a college
student that he published one of those eloquent appeals
for the restoration of lost property that often give us
the only knowledge we have of the private lives of
eighteenth-century Virginians:

Lost, in *Williamsburg*, on *Monday* last, a Gold
Mourning Ring, having, on a Lozenge, a black
enamel'd Cross, between 4 small Sparks; and round the
Hoop these Words: *H. Ludwell, vd. Ob. 4 Aprilis,
1731. Æt. 52.*
Whoever will bring the said Ring to me at the
College, or to the Printer hereof, shall have Half a
Pistole Reward.   *Philip Ludwell.*[15]

Six months before he reached his majority, on July
29, 1737, he was married to Frances Grymes, eldest
daughter of Col. Charles Grymes, "a young Lady of
great Merit, and Fortune." Within a little less than five
months, on December 21, a child was born—a daughter
—to whom was given the name Hannah Philippa.[16]
Apparently this lapse on the part of the two young
people, (which was certainly atoned for promptly),
was completely forgiven them, for there is no surviving
reference, either facetious or otherwise, to the telltale
proximity of these two dates. In 1750, after a sequence
of tragic births and deaths, another daughter was born,
who was named Frances. On November 8, 1751, Philip
Ludwell's friend, John Blair of Williamsburg, made
the following laconic entry in his diary: "Cart^d Wine
&c. Mr Nicholas's Benefit Night. Col. Ludwell's
Daught^r Lucy Baptised."[17] Lucy Ludwell, afterwards
Lucy Paradise, was destined to be the youngest member

of her family; two years later, her mother died and her
father did not marry again.

In the year of Lucy's birth her father received the
highest honor but one within reach of the colonial
Virginian—appointment to the Governor's Council.[18]
One of his first official acts was to take part in welcoming a king of the Cherokee Indians, who came as ambassador to Williamsburg, accompanied by eight nobles
and thirty other attendants to negotiate a treaty of
peace and commerce between the Government of the
Colony and the Emperor of Choto. The meeting took
place in the Market Square and after the preliminary
formalities had been gone through, the President of the
Council began a speech in which he attempted to explain to the Indians "the Happiness and Advantages
the Christians enjoy, in the Hopes and Assurance of a
blessed Immortality." At this most inopportune of
moments there suddenly arrived in town a large party
of the Nottoways. Although the new arrivals were
marching under a white flag, the Cherokees, as yet
unaffected by the Hon. President's harangue, immediately gave the signal for attack. Col. Philip Ludwell
was among the "several Gentlemen" who with much
difficulty prevented a conflict and persuaded the two
hostile tribes to smoke the pipe of peace and join together in song, to the great entertainment of a crowd
of townspeople in the Square.[19]

This was but one of a number of formal occasions in
which Col. Ludwell was called on to officiate. A year
before, he had been among those delegated to meet the
new Governor, Robert Dinwiddie, on the road between
York and Williamsburg and deliver to him an address
of welcome from the Colony.[20] He was also present at

the subsequent meeting of the General Assembly to
hear the Governor speak of his zeal for the good of the
Colony as a "Spring of Pleasure in his Breast" and
urge the Assembly to pursue friendly relations with
the Indians and to prevent "our European neighbors"
(meaning the French) from settling the interior parts
of America.[21] Ludwell became Governor Dinwiddie's
most valued assistant in his negotiations with the Indians and accompanied him to Winchester on a mission
of friendship to the tribes of the Ohio.[22] When the Earl
of Loudon arrived as Commander in Chief of His
British Majesty's Forces in America, Dinwiddie appointed Col. Ludwell to travel to New York to greet
him and to urge upon him the necessity of aid from
England against the French and Indians. This commission he performed successfully and on his return
was able to report a favorable reply from Loudon.[23]

Perhaps Col. Ludwell's most notable service with
respect to Indian affairs was an indirect one. Being one
of the few prominent Virginians who remained on
friendly terms with Dinwiddie, he possessed an influence over him which he used effectively in gaining
for George Washington the appointment as Commander of the Virginia forces. The following letter was
written shortly after Braddock's defeat and a few weeks
before Washington was appointed:

Williamsburgh Au^{gt} 8, 1755
Dear Washington
I most heartily congratulate your safe return from so
many Dangers & fatigues; & by this Time I hope you
are well enough recovered to give us ye pleasure of
seeing you here which all your Friends are extremely
desirous of.

The House has voted 1200 Men but it is very probable they will determine at last for 4000. In conversation wth ye Govr about it, I said if this should be done, I supposed his Honour would give ye Command of them to Col; Washington for I thought he deserved every thing that his Country cou'd do for him. The Govr made a reply much in y^r Favour; tho' I understand there is ano^r warm Sollicitation for it; & if we cou'd be so happy as to have you here at this Time, & that it were known you were willing to take such a Command; I believe it wou'd greatly promote ye Success of our Endeavours with the Assembly. Mine, as they have allways been, uniformly continue to procure for such eminent Merit, ye utmost Encouragement: for, Dear Col^o whilst I am serving so deserving a Man I think with pleasure that I am serving my Country as well as testifying the Sincerity with which I am

Sir

Your most Obed^t Servt

Phi: Ludwell[24]

This service of Col. Ludwell to his much younger friend was to be returned many years later in kindness to John and Lucy Paradise when they visited Washington at Mount Vernon.

Lucy Paradise's aunt, the blue-eyed, fair-haired Lucy Grymes, is reputed to have been the "Lowland Beauty" whom George Washington had ardently but unsuccessfully courted when he was but fifteen years of age. She was later won by Henry Lee and her marriage to him took place at Green Spring, when Lucy Paradise was a child of two. Col. Ludwell's letter, written not long after the wedding, shows him in a kindly, humorous light which was characteristic of his social relationships.

Dear Harry

I shoud have been glad to have heard from you ye agreeable news of yours & Lucy's Health but I can easily suppose that ye busy Scenes y^t attend a recent Wedding may prevent my having rec^d this Pleasure which will be allways one to me. When I speak of Mrs Lee's Health I do not mean to exclude ye salutary interruption of it y^t ought to be expected & shoud not be wished against.

I shall be very much oblidged to you for sending me a good Bundle of Grafts of each of the following sorts. P. H. Russett. White Russett. Pierces Russett & ye Maryland Russett. & the character each sort deserves. Your Burgesses must be at ye Assembly which opens ye 14th of next month. & by them you may favour

Your affect^e Friend
& Servt
Phi: Ludwell[25]

Jan: 23. 1753.

P. S. The Widow Taliaferro was married to Mr George Nicholas last Sunday Night.

There was still another close tie between the Ludwells and the Lees. Henry Lee's brother, Thomas Lee of Stratford Hall, married Col. Ludwell's sister Hannah Philippa. When their daughter Alice Lee was left an orphan, Col. Ludwell took her with him to England in order that she, along with his own daughters, might have the benefit of an English education.[26]

The decision to leave Virginia could not have been an easy one for Philip Ludwell to make. It was hardly a question of retiring there, as his grandfather had done, for he was only forty-six years of age and in the prime of a successful life. Ill health and the lack of satisfactory medical attention in Williamsburg was probably his chief reason. "Col: Ludwell is, I think, in a declining way; he is at present in London," one of his friends wrote George Washington about a year after the Ludwells left.[27] Since this was still six years before his death, the illness, whatever it was, could not have been a very serious one. His other motive was to provide a proper education for his two younger daughters, Frances and Lucy. The eldest, Hannah Philippa, was twenty-two, but she had had the benefit of her mother's training while the others had been all their lives under the supervision of Cress, who could hardly be expected to give them the graces and accomplishments that were thought necessary. It must have been Lucy in particular who brought her father to realize the need for a more disciplined environment. The Ludwell traits of high temper and a stubborn will were no doubt being too well cultivated in a child who had the freedom of a big plantation, with only a Negro nurse to curb her and a host of Negro playmates to scold and bully. Such a situation was common enough with the children of slaveowners and at least one other family in the Ludwell connection had solved the problem by moving to England.[28]

So it was that, late in the spring of 1760 when John Paradise was an unsuspecting youth of seventeen, the ship which bore his stormy destiny sailed eastward from Virginia, slipping between the forested banks of the muddy, silent, almost tropical James into Hampton Roads and out through the Capes toward England.

At about the same time that Lucy Ludwell, a child of nine, arrived in London, bearing in her tenacious memory the best traditions of the New World, her future husband, John Paradise, arrived there from Italy, richly laden with the learning and culture of Europe and the Near East. The civilizations of ancient Greece and Rome and of the Levant met and mingled in Salonica, the city of young Paradise's birth and he, equipped with a brilliant mind and a most impressionable nature, absorbed freely what they had to offer. At the time of his birth, Salonica was a teeming commercial city in which the French, the English, the Dutch, and the Venetians were rivals in trade and with whom the older residents, the Turks, the Spanish Jews, and the Greeks, commingled to make it one of the cosmopolitan centers of the world. As a child and a youth, Paradise became familiar with many of the languages spoken there—modern Greek, English, French, Italian, Turkish. Moreover, he formed friendships with continental Europeans both there and in Italy that were to have far-reaching effects on his life in London and on that of his Virginia-born wife.

He was born in April, 1743.[29] Almost nothing is known about his parents. The only remark he made concerning them was to the effect that his father was English and that his mother was Greek.[30] Actually his mother was only half Greek, for her father was the English-born Philip Lodvill. John's father, Peter Paradise, was thirty-nine years of age in the year of his son's birth and had for two years been acting as the British consul at Salonica, although official confirmation of his appointment did not take place until seven years later, in 1747.[31] At this time the appointment of consuls was in the hands of the Levant Company, which controlled all British interests in Macedonia. The

Levant Company was an ancient one, having been
founded in 1581 by Edward Osborne with the aid of
Queen Elizabeth, who had supplied a part of its capital
from silver acquired by Sir Francis Drake and had
granted to Osborne and his associates the exclusive right
to trade with Turkey and the privilege of using the royal
arms of England with a red cross upon their flag.[32] At
the time when Peter Paradise became connected with it
the successful rivalry of the French had succeeded in
reducing its sphere of operations to Greece and Macedonia. The factory at Salonica was never very large,
but it reached its maximum number, the consul and five
factors, during the incumbency of Peter Paradise. As
consul, it was his duty to superintend the exchange of
English manufactured products for tobacco, cotton, and
Oriental rugs.

Although the consuls were forbidden to trade on
their own account, it seems likely that this command
was as lightly regarded by them as it was by the nabobs
of the East India Company. Certainly Peter Paradise
retired to England with a good fortune, which it seems
unlikely he could have accumulated from his salary of
a thousand dollars a year. The Levant Company demanded that its consuls live in elaborate style, so as to
outshine their rivals the French, and it probably gave
tacit permission for them to take advantage of the
golden opportunities that came their way.

Besides his knowledge of languages, John Paradise
brought with him from Salonica a taste for scholarly
and antiquarian research by which his whole life was
affected. This was probably developed in him by his
Lodvill grandfather. Lodvill was a clergyman and a
scholar and the translator of the first authoritative work

in English on the doctrines and practices of the Eastern
Church. The Levant Company played a large part in
developing the knowledge of Englishmen in such matters. Each one of its factories had attached to it an
English chaplain, of whom John Paradise's grandfather was one, and the monasteries of Mount Athos
and other places were eagerly ransacked of their treas-
ure of ancient manuscripts. The monks were for the
most part ignorant men who were willing enough to
part with manuscripts of the greatest antiquity and
value for only a few pounds or shillings. The interest
in antiquarianism which began to stir in England in the
early eighteenth century had for one of its principal
objects the study of Near Eastern civilization, and
Lady Mary Wortley Montagu was only one among a
great number of English travelers there who returned
with knowledge both practical and historical. When
John Paradise was elected to the Royal Society, three
of his five sponsors were scholars who had traveled or
resided in the Levant.

On his retirement to England, Peter Paradise secured a house in Charlotte Street, Rathbone Place, in
what was then a new and fashionable quarter of London's West End. His means permitted his son to
continue at Oxford University the education that had
already been so well begun and he was soon enrolled
as a student at St. Mary Hall.[33] Here he gained a
brilliant reputation as a scholar, especially as a linguist,
and here also he formed lasting friendships with men
of learning. Oxford became then, and ever afterward
remained for him a spiritual sanctuary, where during
the periods of despondency which so often assailed him
in later life he could revivify himself in the compan-

ionship of friends whose tastes and interests were his
own: Churchill of Corpus Christi; Page of Christ
Church; Jackson, later the Dean of Christ Church;
Cleaver, later Bishop of Chester; and especially Dr.
Nowell, the principal of St. Mary Hall. Literally to
his dying day he remembered the pleasure which he
had received from the society of those Oxford men and
the "useful instruction" which they had given him.[34]

The friendship that developed between John and
Peter Paradise and Col. Philip Ludwell of Virginia
must have begun in the early seventeen-sixties, soon
after the arrival of the two families in London. The
Ludwell household consisted of the Colonel's three
daughters and his niece, Alice Lee. Two of Alice's
brothers, Arthur and William, were also in London
and they too were in a measure under their uncle's
protection. After the death of Thomas Lee of Stratford
Hall, these three, the youngest of a large family of
children, had been obliged to turn to Col. Ludwell for
assistance in getting possession of their rightful inheritance. Philip Ludwell Lee, the eldest of the family, was
administrator of the estate and had proved to be a most
dilatory one.[35] There was a family lawsuit and a delay
of eight years and even then, as William complained,
they received only the "refuse" of their father's property. Their education had been scandalously neglected
and their uncle, who had been their friend from the
beginning, was now helping them to secure in London
the opportunities they had failed to receive in Virginia.
Arthur was sent to the University of Edinburgh to
study medicine. William was launched on the career

of commission merchant for Virginia planters. After
two years Alice was advantageously married off to
William Shippen of Philadelphia, a fellow student of
Arthur's. The marriage took place at the church of St.
Mary le Strand, Middlesex, with William and Col.
Ludwell as witnesses.[36] Shippen took his wife to Phila-
delphia, where he inaugurated the first school of sur-
gery in the United States and later on became Chief
Surgeon of the American Revolutionary Army. Arthur
Lee attempted to practice medicine in Williamsburg
but this proved a failure and he soon returned to
London and took up the study of law at one of the
Inns of Court.

William Nelson of Yorktown, also a student of law,
and William Reynolds of the same place and George
Flowerdewe Norton, who carried on his family's business in London, were three other young Virginians who
swam in the Ludwell orbit. Dr. Johnson's friend,
William Strahan, and Sir John Pringle, President of
the Royal Society, were also members of their circle, as
well as the famous surgeon, Sir John Hunter, and Dr.
Home and his daughter Anne, whom Sir John fell in
love with and married. Anne Home was Alice Lee's
most intimate friend. She was a beautiful woman with
a charming voice and became famous as the composer
of the popular song, "My Mother Bids Me Bind My
Hair." The Quaker physician and botanist, Dr. John
Fothergill, was a friend with whom Col. Ludwell
shared his interest in horticulture. Fothergill lived at
Ham House near Stratford-Langton in Essex. His
garden there rated as the second botanical garden in
Europe, consisting of five walled acres with a crescent-
shaped canal and hothouses containing many thousands

of botanical specimens. There were five Virginia cedars
in it, the first of their kind to be planted in England,
and many other trees and shrubs sent to him by the
American botanist John Bartram: tulip trees, mag-
nolias, butternuts, locusts and "liquid amber" trees.[37]

In London Philip Ludwell had established his family in a house in Cecil Street.[38] It was a street containing
only twenty or thirty houses, and ran from what was
then the Strand down to the Thames. Col. Ludwell's
house was on the west side of the street, which was in
the parish of St. Martin's in the Fields and in the
neighborhood of St. James's. Not far away at No. 36
Craven Street, which also led off from the Strand,
lived Benjamin Franklin, who was near the end of his
second visit to London when the Ludwells arrived there
and was already distinguished for his scientific researches. Col. Ludwell, in his pride at his fellow-countryman's achievements, commissioned Mason Chamberlain to paint him. This was the portrait of himself that
Franklin liked best; it was reproduced in mezzotinto,
and he was long accustomed to distribute copies among
his friends. He remarked that it "has got so French a
Countenance, that you would take me for one of that
lively Nation."[39] It pictures him seated in an arm chair
before a window, outside of which a violent thunder-
storm is seen to be in progress. At his right is his
recently invented lightning detector toward which he is
glancing with an expression of skepticism. Franklin
became an intimate in the Ludwell household and on his
return to Philadelphia he sent his "best wishes to Miss
Ludwell and the other ladies."[40] Many years later in
Paris he befriended John Paradise and gave him all

BENJAMIN FRANKLIN.
Painted in 1762 to the order of Philip Ludwell III, father-in-law
of John Paradise.

Portrait by Mason Chamberlain. Reproduced with the permission of the
Metropolitan Museum of Art.

the assistance he could in regaining possession of his wife's Virginia estate.

One of the few surviving letters by Col. Ludwell was written soon after his arrival in London. It is to Emmanuel Jones, the son of his friend by the same name, who had added to his duties as Usher at the College of William and Mary and Master of the Indian School, that of the management of the Ludwell estates. The ease and cordiality of his relationship with younger men, and indeed the flavor of his entire personality, are reflected here.

London November 8. 1760.

The 25th of July last I saluted my Dear Mr Jones: & by his Favour of ye 18th I had the Pleasure to find that I was no less in his Thoughts at the same Time.

People are sadly prone to pervert ones words as well as ones Deeds or else they would never so willfully have mistook what I said about my Goods which was only that if they were all taken off at once by ye Invoice unopened & remittance directly made [I] woud desire no more than the first Cost.

Your Tenderness suppressed ye Particulars of Mr Rowes abuse which I shoud be glad to know. Not as an incentive to Resentment but as a cautionary Information. Resentment God knows I truly endeavour to divest my self of. It is a troublesome Inmate & a treacherous Councellour. But an higher Consideration is, that it is made the Condition of our Remission sicut et nos remittimus Debitoribus nostris.

I hear many disagreeable things from Virginia; as the Battle of the Scholars, [illegible] Regiments laying down their Arms &c. but none with more concern than that the Com[issar]y was presented by the Grand Jury for drunkenness. How sad a wound does Religion receive like Cæsar from those who by all Tyes are bound to be her best Friends & Supporters!

I am much oblidged to you for your kind Intelligence about my Affairs. I hope I shall find my Confidence well placed in Cary [Wilkinson] whose Honesty I allways had a great Opinion of. I hope he will have your friendly advice & assistance and I am extremely thankfull to you for that you have already given him on my Acc'. How many Bucks have you slain? or do you choose rather to sport among the Does? I hope you have made sure of one: Virginis Os, habitum que gerens qua pulchra faciat Prole Parentem.

I wish you had [not] asked Pardon with s[uc]h a formal Countenance for "The Trouble you gave, and the Freedom you took in writing so long an Epistle"— But perhaps it was a hint to me not to be too tedious as old Fellows are very apt to be & you might justly fear I shoud from ye great Pleasure I have in your Company which writing to you is a kind of Succedaneous enjoyment of.

Well, a Word to ye Wise is enough: and so to let you see that I woud willingly be thought to deserve the Proverb; I most respectfully withdraw with a thousand Apologies for the great Trouble I have given you by such a long Intrusion. However I cannot do it before I have heartily said Amen to your kind Prayer that we may meet again in the happyness of Green Spring

I am Dear Sir
Your affect^e Friend
And humble Servant

Phi: Ludwell

P. S. Tho' I coud not with any Decency go on with my Letter; I might, after the Example of many great Writers run on in the Postscript as long as I woud. However I rather choose to present you with the News Papers themselves than copy them. You will see by them what is to[o] serious a subject of Mourning to be fond of transcribing.

Pray present mine and the Young Ladies particular

Compliments to Mr Allen & his good Lady whom I
hope are now blessed with a fine Son & Heir. I will
send your Seeds by ye next Ship. I have not yet rec^d
'em from a country Seedsman recommended to me by
my friend ye famous Miller. There is no depending on
what is sold in & about Town. It will be ye greatest
Pleasure in ye world to me to serve you.[41]

The "serious subject of Mourning" was the death of
George II, which had occurred in October. Col. Ludwell's reluctance to record it bespeaks a loyalty which
was then shared by all Americans and so is no indication of what his attitude would have been at the time
of the Revolution. There can be little doubt that his
family's traditionally independent attitude, his own
interests, and the influence of his family and friends
would have placed him on the side of the Colonies as
one of the leaders of their cause.

The death of Philip Ludwell on March 25, 1767,[42]
marks the end, not only of one of Virginia's greatest
colonial families, but of a great era in Virginia history.
The Ludwells of three generations had performed, a
little more brilliantly than the majority, the typical
cycle of a Virginia colonial family, the pattern of their
development being almost identical with that of the
Carters, the Lees, the Byrds, the Fitzhughs, the Corbins, the Burwells, and many others. The first Philip
Ludwell had come to Virginia in the mid-seventeenth
century, the younger son of a good English county
family, determined to establish in a new land a family
dynasty modeled on those with which he was familiar.
This purpose he very successfully accomplished by

personal enterprise and industry, by two good marriages and by inheritance from a brother who had been
as fortunate as himself. He set for his son and for his
grandson an example of assiduous service in public
affairs, in the church, in education and in social life.
This example had been followed ably by his son and no
less ably by his grandson, until ill health had required
him to retire.

Nothing could reflect better the blithe confidence of
one who had lived in a homogeneous, well-ordered
society than do the terms of Philip Ludwell's will.[43]
Having stated his wishes regarding the disposition of
his properties, he appointed as his executors in Virginia
his "Dear and worthy ffriends" the Hon. Richard
Corbin, Esq., his Majesty's Receiver General; Robert
Carter Nicholas, Esq. Treasurer of Virginia; and John
Wayles and Benjamin Waller, Esquires, Attorneys at
Law in Virginia. He desired the three parts of his
estate, which he had left to his three daughters, to be
made equal in value "by the most Convenient and beneficial Methods for the Interest of my Children by adding part of one Division either Land or other Estate to
another or by any better Method (if my Trustees above
named can find a better for the purpose Expressed
afore . . .)." In a codicil directing what was to be done
in the interval between his death and the coming of age
of his two younger daughters, he declared it to be his
"Express Will that my Death Shall make no Alteration
in the Oeconomy of my Affairs but that the whole
Estate Shall during that time be kept together Just as
I leave it and Conducted and made the most of by my
Stewards and Overseers and People in Virginia and
the Tobacco and other Annual Produce Shipped to . . .

London and . . . be accounted for and Issued as my said Executors think fit. . ." The three daughters were to share equally in the income "Just as it is now in my lifetime while we are all together, my Meaning and Intention and Desire being that my Death be no Disturbance or the Cause of any Disorder whatever, but that everything Should go on in the Same regular Quiet Orderly Course as now that I am alive."

Concerning all his executors, including William Dampier and John and Peter Paradise in London, he said: "Whereas to Give Legacies Expressive and in any Degree equal to the Esteem Confidence and Affection with which I Consider these my Dear and Worthy ffriends . . . would Exceed my Ability and their own happy Affluence would make a trifle rediculous, I therefore only beg the ffavour of each of them to Accept an handsome Ring of the value of five Guineas."

The three daughters of Philip Ludwell continued for a time to reside in the house in Cecil Street under the supervision of their London guardians. The estate in Virginia was administered by the trustees there, no doubt in the manner which their father had desired. The second eldest daughter, Frances, died unmarried a year and a half after her father and was buried near him at the church of St. Mary, Stratford-le-Bow. Not long after, two events occurred which interrupted the "Quiet Orderly Course" of the Ludwell family affairs in such a way that that course was never to be restored. Hannah Philippa was married to her father's nephew, William Lee, and Lucy was married to John Paradise, the native of Salonica who had now become a scholarly gentleman of leisure in London.

CHAPTER II

Non Incautus Futuri

THE story of the Ludwell estate in Virginia from the time that the death of Col. Ludwell placed it in the hands of his daughters until the American Revolution temporarily deprived them of it is chiefly the story of the acquiesence of John Paradise and the acquisitiveness of William Lee. The two men were placed in almost identical situations. Lee had married the elder Ludwell heiress in March and Paradise had married the younger the following May, and by the law and custom of the time both men were thrown in complete control of their wives' estates. Neither of them had ever seen the lands in their possession, and both were obliged to manage them with the aid of persons who lived three thousand miles away.

William Lee possessed a number of advantages which Paradise did not. His wife had been a grown young lady when she left Virginia and she had many friends there who were willing to assist her for her own sake. Morover, she was of age at the time of her marriage, while Lucy was less than eighteen, and this gave her husband greater authority in saying what should be done concerning her property. William Lee's greatest advantage over Paradise was that he had been born and brought up at Stratford Hall and so had been able to observe the operation of a large Virginia estate at first hand. More than this he was a professional man of business with years of the most valuable sort of experience behind him—that of carrying on trade in London with Virginia planters.

Paradise was totally ignorant of Virginia and possessed not a single friend or acquaintance there. It is true that his wife was closely related to men of power and influence, but the only interest which they could be expected to take in her affairs grew out of the fact that she had been one of Col. Ludwell's little girls. Paradise was completely without experience in business. Brought up in Macedonia and Italy as the only child of a prosperous father, he had been encouraged to indulge his taste for the impractical arts of philosophy and literature. It was thought that his only concern with financial matters would be to collect the interest on the government bonds with which his father expected to endow him.

In view of all this, it seems nothing short of amazing that Paradise should have succeeded so well and Lee so badly. Apparently, however, the whole matter can be reduced to one of personalities and it was here that Paradise distinctly had the better. Actually neither of the men could hope to do very much in the direct control of their estates as long as they remained in London. Except for disposing of the Virginia tobacco when it arrived, they were entirely dependent on the honesty and good will of Robert Carter Nicholas, the most active of the trustees, and of the estate's manager, Cary Wilkinson. This was a situation which William Lee could never bring himself to realize. His wife's property was his, he felt, and he was determined to have the final word on every detail. His efforts to dictate soon came to be looked on in Virginia as interference and almost from the first he incurred the dislike and the ill will of those on whom he was dependent. Even his brothers at times lost patience with him. He had enough knowledge of conditions to make him feel competent to direct them and yet not really enough to make his instructions of value. Consequently his brothers were often forced to carry out orders which local circumstances had made unnecessary or positively harmful. Paradise was Lee's direct opposite in all this. He knew nothing and he had enough judgment to realize that he knew nothing. He threw himself entirely on the good disposition of the men whom Col. Ludwell had appointed to control the estate's affairs, and accepted what they told him without question. The only positive course he ever took was to insist on following strictly the instructions set down in the will. In this he was opposed by Lee but supported by the majority of the trustees. Thus he obtained coöperation while Lee provoked opposition. By putting the Virginians on their honor, Paradise won from them the best service that they could possibly render him.

Almost all that is known concerning the Ludwell estate at this time comes from the carefully preserved papers of William Lee. These reflect the difficulties and disappointments of his absentee managership and they also tell all there is to know about the Paradises' Virginia affairs at this time. The similarity of the two men's interests is so great that a good deal about Paradise's problems can be deduced from a knowledge of those of his brother-in-law.

William Lee was a man who had a grievance all his life. His disposition invited bad treatment. The injustice of his eldest brother toward him over his inheritance left its mark and he was ever afterward distrustful of his fellow men and excessively jealous of his own interests. Richard Corbin characterized him well: "He is a man of Sense, frugal and Industrious in whom My Lord Bacons observation will be verified, that he Never knew a younger Brother unfortunate, except where the eldest has been disinherited."[1] In Lee the desire to succeed was almost a disease.

Several years before his marriage he had begun a career in London which was to take him along a very different path from that traveled by John and Lucy Paradise. His business brought him into close contact with the City merchants of London and among them he formed his associations and friendships. It was not long before he became prominent in City politics. In 1767 he stood for Parliament as the Whig candidate for the borough of Bridgport, and was defeated.[2] By 1769 he and his brother Arthur were deep in the ranks of the supporters of "Liberty" John Wilkes and in that year they were among those who presented a petition to the King for the repeal of the Stamp Act. The political activities of the two brothers were not very favorably viewed by their fellow Virginians. It was considered that the merchants among whom they had cast their lot had been cajoled into quiescence by the King and that they had done the cause of American liberty more harm than good by their support of the notorious Wilkes. William Nelson wrote disparagingly enough of them from London[3] and George Flowerdewe Norton was even more outspoken:

. . . The American Dr. [Arthur Lee] lately re-

nown'd for his pretended patriotism has fallen greatly
to *Leeward* of his (I believe) sanguine expectations,
my scurrility is thrown out chiefly against him, & his
mercantile Brother [William Lee] but will leave him
for an abler hand to cudgel than myself. . .[4]

This was hardly fair. Arthur and William Lee were
not pretended patriots but very real ones, and although
they were both of them fractious and over-suspicious of
other people, none of their enemies was ever able to
prove a case of dishonesty or double dealing against
them.

It was after his rich marriage that William became
successful as a City politician. In 1774 he was made a
sheriff of London and shortly afterwards "William
Lee, Haberdasher" defeated "William Baker, Weaver"
by a vote of 73 to 40 and was elected Alderman of
Aldgate Ward. He held this position almost to the end
of the Revolution, despite the fact that he was known
to be an ardent American patriot and was, during the
last two years of his incumbency, America's official
emissary to Belgium and Germany. He was the only
American ever to be an Alderman of the City of London. He was famous for his parsimony and the compiler of the "Mottoes for Alderman" applied to him
Dryden's satirical couplets on Slingsby Bethel:

> . . . His shrieval board
> The grossness of a City feast abhorred:
> His cooks with long disuse their trade forgot;
> Cool was his kitchen, though his brains were hot.[5]

In the early part of 1769, William Lee was planning
to go to India on a commercial venture. However, his

plans were suddenly altered for on March 7th he was
married. ". . . Our brother William . . . has changed
his voyage to India, in the Princess of Wales, to one to
the land of matrimony in the Miss Ludwell," Arthur
wrote to Richard Henry. "As a warm climate suits not
with him, I hope he will find a temperate one in the
place of his destination."[6] William himself was quite
unable to conceal his satisfaction and announced his
marriage to his Virginia friends in terms which show
him to have been a man of more sense than sensibility.
"The 7th inst: made me happy in the possession of Miss
H. P. Ludwell," he told the Hon. Richard Corbin
of Laneville.[7] "The 7th instant compleated the full
measure of my felicity by puting me in un-rivaled
possession of the dear & amiable Miss Ludwell," he
wrote his brothers.[8] Everyone concerned must have
been well aware that the "dear & amiable Miss Ludwell" was the heiress to half her father's estate, (which
was still reputed to be one of the largest in Virginia),
yet William Lee was not a man to leave anything to
chance, and he announced that important fact in each
of his letters.

Much of his satisfaction over his marriage arose
from his belief that his "possession" of Miss Ludwell
was to be "un-rivaled." Soon afterwards, however, events
began to take a turn which disturbed him very much
indeed. His wife's sister Lucy, instead of remaining in
Cecil Street as she might naturally have been expected
to do, elected to move to the home of her guardian,
Peter Paradise, in Rathbone Place. The disturbing
factor in this was that Lucy would be thrown into

intimate contact with John Paradise, a young man of
excellent prospects and suitable marriageable age. The
marriage of Lucy to John Paradise or to anyone else at
this time meant that William Lee would be obliged to
share the delightful responsibility of settling the Ludwell property with another man. If the division could
only be made before, and not after, this possible marriage he would be in a far more advantageous position.
He urged the trustees in Virginia to act at once. He
told his brothers there that he was very much afraid
that the trustees might divide against his inclinations
and begged them to see that his wishes were carried out
at the earliest possible moment. His wife's share of her
deceased sister Fanny's part must be selected as near as
possible to the Green Spring plantations, which were
already in her possession. He was sure that it would be
immaterial to "Miss Lucy" which part was allotted to
her since her principal estate was divided from all the
rest by the James River. He said that he did not want
any share in the houses in Williamsburg and that these
must be given to Lucy and he expressed himself a little
too often as being sure that there would not be any disadvantage to her in this.[9]

All these schemes went for naught, for long before
the division could possibly have been made the dreaded
marriage of Lucy and John Paradise took place. This
was a hard blow for the ambitious William and he
received it almost as a personal affront. Try as he
might, and he undoubtedly did try at times, he was
never able to forgive the man who married his wife's
sister and so thwarted his desire to be in control of one
of the handsomest fortunes in the New World.

Even after the Paradise marriage, Lee continued to

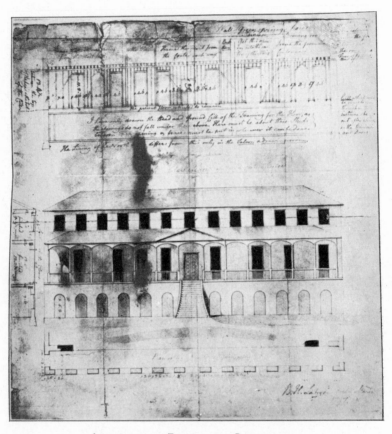

ARCHITECTURAL DRAWING OF GREENSPRING.

Made in 1797 by the architect B. H. Latrobe for a proposed remodelling.

Reproduced from an article by W. G. Stanard in the *Virginia Magazine of History and Biography*, Volume 37.

try to hurry the trustees into dividing the estate. He told his brothers, Richard Henry and Francis Lightfoot Lee, to insist on its being done immediately and that if the trustees refused his brothers were to "take such methods as you shall think proper to compell them to do it."[10] He was almost as importunate with the trustees themselves and more than that he was tactless enough to keep imploring them to do him justice, a demand that served no other purpose than to show that he distrusted them. His impatience must have been extremely annoying to men engaged in so difficult and thankless a task. The division was postponed from October to November and at length, in March 1770, Lee received word that it had not yet taken place.[11] The trustees blamed the delay on the Lee brothers and Richard Henry blamed it on the trustees. Francis Lightfoot gave still another reason: Mr. Paradise had written that he intended to come to Virginia and the trustees considered it proper to await his arrival.[12] In his desperation William wrote letters of clumsy diplomacy to each one of the trustees,[13] but to his brothers he continued to insist bluntly on a speedy division, at the same time demanding that all the "remaining refuse" of the estate, such as books and furniture, should either be sold or equally divided: "I have already, you know, suffered by old coaches & other lumber, you'll please also to remember what I have already twice wrote you about the Houses in W^msburg. From ye situation of affairs between M^r. Paradises Family & mine you must be very sensible how extremely Irksome it is to have any connection with them, wch must unavoidably be the case as long as ye estate continues as it is, therefore I beg you will exert y^rselves to have ye division finally com-

pleated in ye course of ye year."[14] It is evident that the
first of his many quarrels with the Paradises had taken
place, although the particular circumstances must remain a mystery.

Eventually in June 1770 the division took place, with
the trustees and Richard Henry Lee present.[15] To
make an equitable division was almost inconceivably
difficult. In his will, Col. Ludwell had divided property into three parts. The Green Spring house and
plantations went to Hannah Philippa; the Rich Neck
property, which was made to include Archer's Hope
and the lots and houses in Williamsburg, were to have
gone to Frances; and the Chippokes plantation, which
possessed an overseer's dwelling but no "mansion," went
to Lucy. The task of the trustees was to give to the
two remaining daughters the share that had been assigned them by the will and to divide between them
that of their deceased sister Frances. If the thing were
to be done fairly, the Green Spring and Chippokes
parts would have to be evaluated, with all their appur-
tenances such as slaves, stock, farming implements,
timber etc. etc., and then, in accordance with this
evaluation, Frances' share must be disposed in such a
way that in the end, each of the surviving sisters would
have exactly half of her father's estate. In estimating
the value of land, its productivity had to be considered;
also what proportion was in timber, whether there were
orchards, what kind of crops could be produced, and
the value of these. Another consideration was the distance from Williamsburg, particularly of the timbered
property; this would govern the expense of transporta-
tion to the market and consequently the profit to be
derived. Perhaps the most difficult problem of all was

the slaves. The sex and age of these made a great difference in their value and consequently still further complicated the division.

The trustees set about their task by first evaluating Green Spring and all that went with it by the Ludwell will, and also Chippokes. It was discovered then that the disproportion between the sisters was so great in favor of Mrs. Lee that it would be necessary to give Mrs. Paradise all of the land formerly assigned Frances, to make the two parts even. This still left out of account the houses in town. Richard Henry Lee considered it necessary for his brother to have a part of the Rich Neck land and brought about a compromise by which Mrs. Paradise received some of the Green Spring slaves in exchange for 1,100 acres of wooded land near Williamsburg. The town property was divided into two presumably equal parts and the ownership of them was determined by chance. Mrs. Paradise received a number of houses and some vacant lots; the Ludwell town residence, among other things, went to Mrs. Lee. Richard Henry Lee wrote his brother that as far as the town property was concerned, fortune had favored him. It was further arranged that the division was not to take effect until the end of the year 1770, and that until then the two estates should continue to be operated as one.[16]

William Lee was obliged to be satisfied, much as he desired for the division to be effective at once. The fact that the two properties were continued as one prevented him from discovering for more than a year a thing that was extremely disturbing. It was not until the spring of 1770, after the accounts for his estate for 1771 had been made up and compared with Paradise's, that he realized that Paradise's income was considerably larger than his own. In answer to his indignant inquiry he was informed by Richard Henry Lee and also by Robert Carter Nicholas that the division had in reality been entirely fair. It was pointed out by them both that because of the close proximity of much of Paradise's land to Williamsburg, his income would at first be larger. That had been made up for in the division by the trustees having assigned to Lee the larger share of young negroes. In time, they contended, Lee's income would equal to Paradise's and probably exceed it.[17] William Lee maintained a discontented silence for another year. At the end of that time he again drew up a comparison of accounts and to his horror and indignation discovered that Paradise's income for 1772 had exceeded his own by more than £400: he had received only £329/15/1 and Paradise had received £736/3/9.[18] He again contended to Nicholas and to his brothers that the division had been unfair and that he had been so informed by several persons in Virginia who had his interests at heart.[19] Both Richard Henry Lee and Nicholas again remonstrated with him and tried to explain on the same grounds as before that matters would eventually adjust themselves.[20] It was in vain; William Lee never believed them. Unfortunately the Revolution so impaired the productivity of both estates that there was no opportunity of proving whether the division had been unfair or not. Certainly, as far as things had gone, it was not fair to William Lee; but it is impossible to say what would have transpired regarding it if conditions had remained normal.

Some of William Lee's greatest difficulties with his Virginia estate were due to his relationship with his local manager, Cary Wilkinson. Wilkinson had been the overseer of Col. Ludwell's property for many years and he had continued in this capacity after his employer's death. When the settlement had been made, he stayed on in the employ of both William Lee and Paradise. He was an ignorant man, quick to take offense and easy to be antagonized. Although he was uneducated almost to the point of illiteracy, he was shrewd and industrious and he knew the Ludwell estate better than anyone else.

Lee's first experience with him was unfortunate. In the summer of 1769 a bad storm had destroyed practically all the crops on the estate. "Cary Wilkison tells me," Richard Henry Lee informed his brother, "that the gust has prevented him from making a better crop this year than he has for many years last past had a chance of doing."[21] And later: "Cary Wilkinson tells me that he has lost on the whole estate this winter."[22] William had already become dissatisfied with his manager and had let loose a great flood of complaints against him even before he had heard the news of the crop failure: Wilkinson did not write often enough; he had never sent a complete set of details about the estate; not only were his collections poor but those that were made had been badly accounted for or not accounted for at all; such tobacco as had been shipped had arrived in poor condition, owing to the way Wilkinson had packed it.[23]

At the beginning of the next year William received a letter from Virginia which even further confirmed his dissatisfaction. The fact that it was written by

Philip Ludwell Lee, the brother who had withheld his inheritance from him for so many years, could but have increased the bitterness of the dose which it contained: "Y^r head overseer is a poor one & Col. Ludwell just before he went home [*i. e.* to England] tho't so & desired me to look out for one for him . . . y^r houses in W^{ms}b^g are in bad repair always rented to bad tenants always nasty & few rents paid. . ." Philip Ludwell Lee, who obviously took a sardonic pleasure in communicating these bad tidings, ended his letter with insouciance, requesting that William, instead of sending him newspapers, should send "the best minuets, Songs, & Country dances, both music notes & words."[24]

It is obvious that William Lee would have discharged Cary Wilkinson and employed another manager if he had been in a position to do so. However, he was too far away from the scene to act directly and Richard Henry and Francis Lightfoot were inclined to favor Wilkinson and encourage keeping him on. Another difficulty was that Robert Carter Nicholas was Wilkinson's cousin by marriage. William had neglected for months to inform his manager that he intended to continue to employ him and this aroused the fiery Wilkinson's wrath and gave him an excuse for neglecting a number of important matters because of his uncertainty of keeping his position.

On March 20, 1771, William wrote to his manager the first of a series of disagreeable, complaining letters. He reproached him for the few remittances he had sent, for not having written oftener, and especially for his partiality toward Paradise. Wilkinson, he complained, had not asked Paradise for any hoes, but had demanded of *him* as many as last year; he had ordered only one piece of blanket from Paradise and two from himself, although Paradise had as many negroes as he had: "You have already sent an acc^t to Mr Paradise of all these things that are on his estate, and I can't tell why you have not done the same to me."[25] This letter was dispatched by Capt. Gooseley. Two months later, Lee wrote to Wilkinson again. There had not been time for an answer to his former letter, but his impatience would not allow him to wait:

London May 22^d 1771.

M^r/Cary Wilkinson
Green-Spring Virg^a

(By Capt Necks.)

By so good an op^t as Capt Necks I propose to write you a long Letter, & as it will regard y^r general conduct I would have you take care of it & read it over now and then when you are at leisure that the contents may be impressed on y^r memory wch will save me the trouble of repeating them in my future letters. Every year at Christmas I w^d have you settle & ballance all y^r Acc^{ts}, when a list of debts is to be made out; at ye same time take the names, ages, sex & professions of all the Negroes on the several plantations: also then may be taken a list of all the different kinds of stocks; these several lists viz: of ye debts, negroes, & stocks are every year to be sent to me, by ye first Capt that sails after Christmas—who will undertake to deliver them with his own hands, along with y^r annual Acc^{ts} wch are to be made out in the follow^g manner, the wood, & every kind of Provisions, are to be put in Seperate acc^{ts}, unless it be what is sold to the College, wch will always appear in the College Acc^{ts}, the brandy. cyder. & profits of the different tradesmen, are also to be in seperate acc^{ts}; there must also be an annual rent-roll, & acc^t of the different crops on the several plantations: & how they

are disposed of; then a cash Acc^t in wch you sh^d always
mention for what it is you pay money to any one, or for
what it is you receive cash f^{rm} any person, as for Instance whether you have rec^d the money for corn, or
wood &c sold, & whether you have paid it for overseer's wages or smiths work of Taxes &c, & I w^d also
wish every year to have a copy of y^r own private acc^t
with me. When ever any Tob^o is shiped I would have
you send an Invoice of the marks, weights & plantations
where it was made & the warehouse where it was inspected. What you sent me last year in the Liberty
Capt Walker was in general pretty good, tho' too light,
the ᴾ§ᴸ & the ♄ were the best & the ♃ was the worst,
but the ♋ that came to Mr Paradis was [much] finer
than any I had; however mine turn'd out a tolerable
good price. From 1050. to 1100. Nett in the country w^d
be a good weight but as y^r Tob^o seems to be thin to
make it of y^t weight, without being in the least bruised,
wch it must not be by any means, it sh^d be prized as dry
as it can possibly be handled. It would be a great advantage to have each of the heads in a hogshead prized
equally close, wch I suppose might be contrived by turning the hogshead upside down, & prizing ye lower head
a little closer, after the first uppermost head has been
prized full & it always looks better & is more equally
prized when the hh^d is pretty streight without much
bulge. If this method sh^d be tho't two troublesom, I w^d
at least wish you w^d try it next year with two or three
hh^{ds} under your own inspection & see if I can't distinguish ye difference when it comes here. Great care sh^d
be taken in sorting the tob^o, all but what is very good,
sh^d be stem'd of wch there was a very good proportion
last year; Y^e long tob^o sh^d be put in a hh^d by itself, &
the short tob^o sh^d be put by itself; the light color'd tob^o
sh^d be prized by itself, & so sh^d the dark color'd Tob^o
with proper attention to these points, I sh^d not fear
getting as much for y^r tob^o as for any that comes from
Virg^a. It is very proper now & then to change y^r seed,

but always stick to the best kind, some times get seed from Mr Ew^d Digges near York Town, some times from the Hon: William Nelson's estate in Hanover & some times from Chipokes, wch tho' it is the same kind with that at Greenspring, will be some what different as it grows on a different soil; for all seeds in ye world grow worse, if continued too long in the same ground: you say ye land is too poor to make large crops of Tob^o without dung, in this case I must think it w^d be proper to sow a good deal of wheat, wch must always sell well & with the straw you might make a good deal of manure. Let no lambs be killed nor any sheep 'till they have lost their teeth, by wch means in a little time I sh^d hope y^r stock may be so encreased as to yeild wool enough with the assistance of flax and cotton, to cloath all the people, wch is a point y^t I w^d have you pay constant attention to. Let some of the girls & infirm old women be taught to spin flax, & kept constantly at it, as flax grows very well in every part of Virg^a & is much more worth your regard than cotton. I w^d always have a sufficient member of the different tradesmen kept up, by puting Prentices to the old ones whenever it is necessary & I suppose you have no smith, therefore I think you sh^d directly put two of the most ingenious & likely young fellows of 16 or 17 years old prentices for 3 or 4 years to the best Country blacksmith that you have. I w^d wish to have the orchards properly kept up, therefore it may be necessary every spring to make grafts fr^m all the best fruits, so as to have a sufficient stock to replace what may decay or be blown down. I must again remind you how desirous I am that you sh^d not permit any one to hunt on my lands, either for deer or fowl, & if any person sh^d be found trespassing I w^d have you punish them according to Law, without giving Mr Nicholas the trouble of doing any thing in it. I am told the wandering new light preachers fr^m the Northward, have put most of my Negroes crazy with their new

light and their New Jerusalem: These vagabond
preachers I have always observed encourage *in fact,*
more wickedness than any other kind of men, therefore
I w^d have my people discouraged as much as possible,
fr^m going near them: & perhaps the best method of
doing it effectually is to encourage them all to go every
Sunday to their Parish Church, by giving those who
are the most constant attendants at church, a larger
allowance of food, or an additional shirt, more than
the rest, whereby you will Make it their interest to do
their Duty; But above all, let the punishment of those
be very exemplary & solemn who are caught *stealing*
any thing for these vagabond preachers, for I think *that*
is generally the consequence of their preaching. For
fear Capt Gooseley sh^d miscarry, I must again desire
you to send me as soon as possible a plot of all my
several tracts of land, the names of all the plantations
& where they are, a list of all the Negroes, on each
plantation with their ages, sex, & profession; also a list
of all the buildings on them, the Stocks of every kind,
& the utensils; also the country weights of the Tob° y^t
was shiped last year both to Mr Paradise & myself,
specifying the plantations where it was made & the
warehouse where it was inspected; & let me have the
same acc^t of what is shiped this year to both of us. I
hope you are now fix'd to continue on my Estate, & I
will only remind you y^t a good deal of attention will be
requisite to prevent Mr Paradises concerns from being
mixed with mine; & as long as you continue on my Estate,
I will very readily buy for you any thing that you may
want from this place without any commission for so
doing. I shall be glad to know on what terms you have
agreed with Mr Nicholas & hope you will not fail to
write to me by every opportunity y^t I may hear how
things go on with you. We have no news here, at all y^t
is worth writting, but I suppose you are by this time all
full with y^r new governor & new Elections &c. This

Letter as I told you at first, is very long therefore will require more readings y[n] one—I hope you are all well & y[t] y[r] family & the people will enjoy good health this season.

I am y[r] friend &c

W[m] Lee[26]

M[r] Cary Wilkinson.
Green Spring Virginia

Scarcely had this letter started on its way, when Cary Wilkinson dispatched an answer to his employer's first, in which righteous indignation and phonetic spelling combine in illuminating Wilkinson and obscuring the subjects on which he wrote:

Green Spring May 26. 1771—

S[r]

I Rece'd your Letters by Cap[n] Goosely which I now answer. At the Time I made out M[r] Paradise Invoice I intended to give up your Business, was the reason I did not make out yours at the Same Time: if I had I should have left out Hose in yours as well as his for it was just after a new Association & I was directed to have the Hose made in the Country, but finding it difficult to get them made, when I made out your Invoice I sent for them. You take Notice of my sending for but One p[r] of Blankits for M[r] Paradise & two for yourself. I did so for this reason you having more Negroes than he has, and a pese ant nigh a nuf for his. You mention sending Sum Bacon by a Ship to Mr. Henson, but she was Lost & you dont mention any other Ship being sent to him. I saw him in the Cort, but he never mentioned carrying any thing for you. You derect that the Timber blone down by the Storm shou'd be got into Staves the chefest of the Timber you had blone down is Pied Oak and Pine which wont make Staves, What woud make boards is got. Your Goods are not come to hand yet, but when they do I will let you know what order they come in and how they are in quality, you think the

Invoice Very large, if you woud only consider the
Number of Negroes you have you woud not think it is.
that is One reason for [giv]ing up your Business. their
is nothing that I can do semes to give Satisfaction and
without I can, I will sarve no Man. you complain of
the Remittances I doe all I can to rase Money and as
fast as I get it Pay it into Mr Nicholas you likewise
complain of my sending for as many Hoes for your
Part as I did for the hole Estate. I sent but for Eight
Dozen and all ways sent for Twelve, if the Hoes you
sent last year had bin good we might have dun with
fuer this year but the largest Hoes was N° 2 which was
fit for nun but Boys, they wore out before the Crop was
finnished so that we had no Hoes to work this Spring
I sent the Plots of Mr Paradise Lands to him by Col^l
Corbins orders if I had been directed to sent yours, I
should have dun it. your part of Tobacco Twenty five
hhds, but what Ship it will come I cant tell for your
Cap^n hant sent for it & what [?] he intends it or not
I cant tell, their was an ad last year which you had,
their is one this which is to be sent to Mr Paradise all
your Commands shall be complied with as far as in me
lies, you have lost fore Negroes sence my last Letter to
you, One a Young Wench, one of Daphnay's Daughters
by shifting two sune in her lying in, the others ware
Children, they are all well at present, but One Child
which I beleive we shall luse.

Inclosed you have the Plots of your Lands. all but
the Governors and the Thousand Acres that you have in
the Rich Neck Track, which you may see by applying
to Mr Paradise—

from your H^ble Servt
Cary Wilkinson.[27]

Soon after receiving this blast from Cary Wilkinson,
William Lee received another which gave him even
greater cause for unhappiness. Robert Carter Nicholas, offended at Lee's frequent accusations against

Wilkinson, resigned his stewardship.[28] Lee was greatly distressed. Not only was he upset at being on bad terms with so universally liked and so influential a man as the Treasurer of Virginia; but, as he later said, there was absolutely no one else in Williamsburg or anywhere near his estate to whom he could entrust his affairs. He appealed to Richard Henry and Francis Lightfoot, telling them that he was not conscious of having given Nicholas any cause for offense, but showing that he well knew what was the matter by quoting Nicholas's comments on Wilkinson. Wilkinson was, Nicholas had said, a "very faithful steward" and "a man of generous sentiments, as well as great skill and industry in Business and I am sure deserves your utmost confidence." William Lee begged his brothers to comment on this statement and tell him what to do.[29]

The estate had already become so burdensome to Lee and had brought him in so little income that he had some time ago authorized his brothers to sell it, he and Mrs. Lee having decided to remain in London.[30] The best offer the brothers could get was £10,000 currency. This was too little. The estate had been valued at £15,000 currency, which was £12,000 sterling, and Lee would not part from it for less. The next best thing was to rent it for a term of years and this he begged his brothers to do.[31] However, the attempt was unsuccessful.

At the beginning of 1772, when no other course was open to him, Lee wrote penitently to Nicholas, imploring him to keep on with the stewardship. He was obliged to reverse his position regarding Wilkinson and declared in the most emphatic manner that he knew Wilkinson was the best of men and that he hoped he would continue to manage his estate "as long as we both live."[32] To Wilkinson himself he wrote a very pleasant letter indeed, expressing the hope that he would stay on and declaring himself perfectly satisfied with his management.[33] In April he sent another long letter concerning the details of the estate, far milder in tone than those he had formerly written.[34] It was intended to be conciliatory, but it had just the opposite effect on the sensitive Wilkinson who for a long time refused to answer it and when he did answered in "a huffy, insolent manner."[35] It is not difficult to see why he was offended. He had been the manager of the estate for many years before it had fallen into the hands of its new owners. Col. Ludwell, in his ill health and during his absence for so many years in London, had been an easy-going, easily-satisfied employer who allowed things to take their course with very little interference. Wilkinson had been almost completely his own boss, and after so many years of residence at Green Spring had come to look on the place as being in a sense his own. He was an honest and capable man really, but his lack of education and his consciousness of his inferior position had stimulated in him a pride and a sensitiveness that made him difficult to get along with for one who did not understand him. William Lee was far from being the man who could handle such a situation. His eagerness for money was a ruling motive with him always, and he was inclined to ride rough-shod over those who stood in his way. He was shrewd, without being wise, and in his cupidity failed to realize that the longest way round was often the shortest way to gaining his own ends. Being unacquainted with Wilkinson and entirely unfamiliar with the estate of which he had become the master, he was obliged to depend on the information given him by others, and this information was often incorrect and always fragmentary. It was surely mistaken of him to try to direct things in so great detail. If he could have trusted Wilkinson or at least have acted as if he trusted him, the results would have been infinitely better.

William Lee showed his ignorance of farming in Virginia in a variety of ways. In the first place, he made the mistake of trying to economize in the quality of the supplies and implements which he sent from London. Besides being an annoyance to Wilkinson, this really impeded the work of the negroes. Lee was wrongly convinced that his youthful experience at Stratford Hall had equipped him to dictate details about farming to a man who had had years of practical experience. In insisting that Wilkinson try to curb the religious activities of the negroes he was meddling in a most ticklish and difficult matter about which he understood next to nothing. He should certainly have realized, although he evidently did not, that it was next to impossible to ascertain the age of a negro slave, unless a careful record had been kept of the date of his birth. He was as wrong as it was possible to be about the extermination of wild onions, and later experience showed the utter impracticality of cultivating silk in Virginia. The greatest mistake he made in his dealings with Wilkinson was one which he made with almost everyone. He trusted neither his ability nor his honesty and allowed Wilkinson to see this in every letter he wrote. Moreover, he was convinced from the first of the partiality of Wilkinson, as well as that of Nicholas and the rest of the trustees, to Paradise.

In the early part of 1773 William Lee decided with
the advice of his brothers to dismiss Wilkinson, the
relations between them having now become so strained
that it was impossible to do business. "I only regret
that he did not go 4 years ago; he has already done me
more injury than he can ever make amends for."[36] A
long search was necessary before a successor could be
found. At length a man named Fauntleroy was persuaded to undertake the business. William Lee lost
little time in getting on as bad terms with him as he
had been with Wilkinson. The income for the first year
of Fauntleroy's management was not quite £40. Moreover, as William complained to Richard Henry, the
tobacco shipped to England was badly handled and full
of dirt. The demands for supplies were larger than
ever before and the negroes continued to decrease. "All
this surely requires some attention, or else in a little
time the only use of the Estate will be to support M^r F.
like a Gent^n."[37] The only comfort which Richard
Henry could offer was to say that the tobacco complained of had been put up by Wilkinson, who had
insisted on finishing the crop he had begun.[38] Doubtless
the dirt that was mixed with it was Wilkinson's Parth-
ian arrow shot at his detested employer. Fauntleroy
left, or was dismissed, at the end of his first year and a
steward was advertised for in *The Virginia Gazette* "for
the estate of Mr. Alderman Lee at Green Spring."[39]
Fauntleroy could never be made to render his accounts
and as a result of his mismanagement and soon after of
the outbreak of the Revolution, William Lee failed to
receive a penny of income from Virginia for many
years. As for Wilkinson, he continued to be Paradise's

manager until his death, long after the Revolution, and was succeeded by his nephew.

If circumstances had been different, if both Lee and Paradise had, by going to Virginia, taken direct control of their affairs there, the results would have been reversed. Lee would undoubtedly have succeeded and Paradise, with his inexperience and indifference toward affairs, would probably have failed. With things as they were, however, Paradise's brilliant capacity for winning friends stood him in good stead, and he was able to bring others to do for him what he could never have done for himself. Throughout all the trouble and distress that later arose about the Virginia estate, Paradise was never without the friendship and favor of those with whom he dealt concerning it. It was the chain of unhappy circumstances which had their beginning in the Revolution, and never the lack of coöperation from Virginia, that caused Paradise's later difficulties there —these, and his own fatal weaknesses of procrastination, ill-health, and timidity.

CHAPTER III

The Paradise House in London

THE house in which John and Lucy Paradise lived for the first eighteen years of their life together was No. 28 Charles Street, Cavendish Square, and it was here that their only children, Lucy and Philippa, were born.[1]

Some little distance north of Oxford Street the muddy footpath known as Lover's Walk, which led out to Marylebone Gardens, was interrupted by a city square—a "Quadrate of noble buildings," surrounding a central green space which was defended from intrusion by a brick wall, topped with an ornamental railing. Cavendish Square stood there aloof and incongruous, the urban elegance of its neo-classic façade dramatically insisted upon by the rural disorder of its surroundings; for in the mid-eighteenth century St. Marylebone was still a country parish, as empty as Hampstead Heath, with occasional farmhouses set in groves of trees, a number of taverns, several small lakes or ponds, the Rev. George Whitefield's Methodist tabernacle, and little else. Amidst all this, the Square had been hopefully constructed by Lord Harley just a year before the bursting of the South Sea Bubble, and for more than a quarter of a century it had stood lonely in the fields, its fine houses with their fashionable inhabitants a glittering but vain decoy for a city which had refused to move in any direction after the disaster of 1720.[2] By the middle of the century, however, prosperity had been restored and London, until then a city

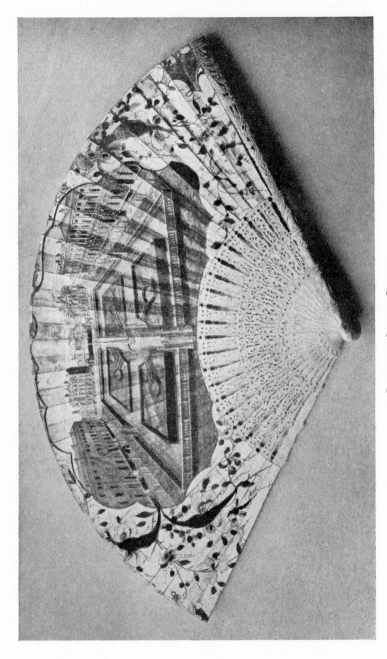

CAVENDISH SQUARE, LONDON.

The neighborhood of the Paradise house at No. 28 Charles Street.

Photograph of fan attributed to Canaletto.

of no more than five or six hundred thousand, began the stupendous period of growth which has never since been checked. "London is literally new to me; new in its streets, houses, and even in its situation," Smollett made Matthew Bramble write in 1771. ". . . What I left open fields, producing hay and corn, I now find covered with streets and squares, and palaces and churches. I am credibly informed, that, in the space of seven years, eleven thousand new houses have been built in one quarter of Westminster, exclusive of what is daily added to other parts of this unwieldly metropolis. Pimlico and Knightsbridge are almost joined to Chelsea and Kensington; and, if this infatuation continues for half a century, I suppose the whole county of Middlesex will be covered with brick."[3]

Between 1750 and 1800 there was no section of London which grew more rapidly or substantially than that surrounding Cavendish Square, and there was none which better epitomized the changing social conditions which marked the rise of England's middle class. The reflected glory of the Square itself shone on the entire neighborhood and made it easily the most desirable, as well as the most expensive, of the newer parts of London. The newly-rich City merchants came here to satisfy their old ambition of belonging to society, and for much the same reason came the Indian nabobs and the wealthy colonials from America and the West Indies. Old, established county families, able for the first time to afford a London residence, took houses in Mortimer and Harley and Charlotte and Wimpole and Margaret Streets alongside of foreign diplomats and refugees and other international gadabouts. Successful authors, sculptors, painters, engravers, and musicians

also flocked here in this period before Bohemianism
had become the conventional life for artists. Scholarly
men of means, who like John Paradise were not bound
by traditional ties to any particular spot in London,
found in the varied, though highly respectable, society
of this new suburb the most suitable possible background. At No. 7 Bentinck Street, Gibbon wrote the
first volumes of his great history. At No. 23 Foley
Place, Edmund Malone helped Boswell revise his *Life
of Johnson* and Boswell himself, on Malone's recommending it as "quite a genteel neighborhood," took a
"neat, pretty, small house" in Queen Anne Street West,
and afterwards another at 122 Great Portland Street,
in which he died.[4] It was a section much favored by
painters. George Romney, in his prosperous years,
lived at No. 24 Cavendish Square and here painted
some dozens of his portraits of Lady Hamilton; it was
Sir Joshua Reynolds who contemptuously dubbed him
"the man of Cavendish Square."[5] Another painter who
was the object of Sir Joshua's enmity was James Barry,
notorious for bad manners and personal untidiness. For
a time he kept bachelor's lodgings in Castle Street, just
around the corner from the Paradises. Here the great
Burke, who lived not far away, would come bearing a
steak to take an evening meal with him. On these occasions Barry would hasten off to the Oxford Market
to fetch a pot of porter and returning would pass in
front of the Paradise residence, his face set with annoyance because the porter had lost its foam at the windy
corner of Great Titchfield Street. No farther away
from the Paradises in the opposite direction, lived the
great landscape painter Richard Wilson who would
often "throw open his window and invite his friends to

enjoy with him the glowing sunset behind Hampstead
and Highgate hills," a view shared by the Paradises
and at that time uninterrupted by streets and houses.
Wilson and the pestiferous Baretti, Mrs. Paradise's
bête noir, could often be seen by her from her windows,
walking together in the shade of the two magnificent
rows of elms which adorned the Middlesex Hospital
across the street.[6]

This locality was celebrated in the eighteenth century for the salubrity of its air. It was high and consequently free from much of the smoke and dust of
London, and it was for this reason that Charles Street
had been selected for the site of the great Hospital.
The main building, "neat, plain, and not inelegant,"
with a Wren-like cupola, was constructed in 1775 in
what was still known as Marylebone Fields. In the
succeeding twenty years the city had grown out to meet
it, and it now occupied, with its extensive grounds,
almost half the north side of the street. The high
situation, the pure air, the spaciousness and view
afforded by the Hospital grounds, and the fact that it
was only a few minute's walk from the residence of
Peter Paradise in Rathbone Place, made Charles Street
one of the most desirable locations the Paradises could
have found.

The early years of their marriage were by far the
happiest which they spent together, but even then there
were differences in their interests and in their respec-
tive backgrounds which produced a lack of harmony.
Even so, all might have been well if only Lucy had in
the least resembled her husband in her tastes and aspi-
rations. So far from resembling him she was in all

respects his opposite. He was intellectual, she social in
her tastes. He cared little for the formalities and func-
tions which she adored; on the contrary he shrank from
them, finding his principal enjoyment in the easy, un-
pretentious society of his scholar friends, a society of
which he was "passionately" fond. Lucy was entirely
out of her element where any mental exertion was required; her pleasures were cards and dancing, evening
parties at Vauxhall or the Pantheon, and musicals at
private homes, where the music served only as an ac-
companiment for social chatter. Perhaps she might
have become contented with what she had, or at least
with what she could gracefully acquire, had it not been
for her recollection of her family's Virginia glory,
which had made so strong an impression upon her
childish mind. The realization at which she was never
able to arrive was that being a Ludwell in Virginia,
with Green Spring and her ancestors' reputation supporting her, was a very different thing from being a
Ludwell in London, married to the son of a retired
merchant. It was not in her stormy nature ever to become reconciled to the inevitable. The advantages
which her husband's intellectual connections brought
her were unparalleled from every point of view except
that of "society," and yet to her proud, ambitious spirit
they gave but little satisfaction. She chose to struggle
to the end for that which she was never able to obtain,
and the scars of her struggle were left upon her and
upon every member of her family.

The world in which John Paradise's attainments
enabled him to take a secure position was one with the
widest activities and associations. It was a world of
scholars, professional men, artists, one to which the

SIR JOSEPH BANKS.
President of the Royal Society of London.
From a picture by T. Phillips in the possession of the Royal Society of London.

passports were intellect and talent, and to which respectability, rather than gentle birth, was a prerequi-
site to admittance. It was bounded by the meetings of
the Royal Society and by the free intercourse of literary
scholars, by the "conversations" of the Blue-stockings,
the musical evenings of Dr. Burney, and by dinner
parties where talk took precedence over food. Its fixed
stars were Dr. Parr, Sir William Jones, Mrs. Thrale,
Sir Joseph Banks, Gibbon, Burke, Goldsmith, Garrick,
and Sir Joshua Reynolds. Its transcendent sun was Dr.
Johnson, the bright beams of whose colossal reputation
warmed and lighted all. Often it was visited by personages from the superior realm of fashion—pearl-divers
for wisdom like Topham Beauclerk, Horace Walpole,
William Windham, and Georgiana, Duchess of Devonshire. Like its Tory master, Dr. Johnson, it was shot
through with the prejudices and conventions of late
eighteenth-century England; but it was, nevertheless,
surprisingly democratic and could accommodate with
equanimity a prude like Fanny Burney, a coxcomb like
James Boswell, a scapegrace Italian count, an exiled
Corsican general, a visiting savage from Tahiti, occasional Americans, and at least once the demagogic
rake, "Liberty" John Wilkes. It was a decent, though
not a squeamish world, with great contrasts and inconsistencies, teeming with men and women of talent who
on the whole respected its conventions and obeyed its
laws. Its contributions to the culture of the English
race were very great, even when compared with those
of Shakespeare's age. Within the immediate circle of
Dr. Johnson were the greatest actor, the greatest painter, the greatest historian, and one of the most versatile
writers that England has ever produced and there were

many more both within his circle and on the edges of it who bear testimony to its brilliance. Interestingly enough, the informing genius, the true spirit of the age was not literary, or artistic, or even political, but rather than any of these, humanistic. Great in hospitality and conviviality, it set upon the broader social virtues a value that has since been lost, and produced within the circle of which we speak the most glorious conversation that has ever been recorded in the English-speaking world.

Among the Paradises' nearest neighbors, who were also friends, were the sculptor Joseph Nollekens and his wife, the former Mary Welch. The acquaintance-ship came about through Paradise's intimacy with Saunders Welch, Mrs. Nollekens' father, and with Anne Welch, her sister. Saunders Welch was a wealthy man of literary tastes and a lifelong friend of Dr. Johnson and Henry Fielding, whom he accompanied as far as Gravesend on Fielding's final journey to Lisbon, and whom he succeeded as Justice of the Peace for Westminster. His house became during the middle of the century "a resort of persons distinguished in the arts and belles lettres," partly through his own in-fluence and partly through that of his younger daughter Anne, whom Boswell described as "a young lady of uncommon talents and literature." It was she who was the particular friend of the Paradises. According to Laetitia Hawkins, "She fell into the literary societies of her father's house, and while her sister addressed herself to the ladies of those who were family-men, 'little Nanny' cultivated the friendship, and enjoyed the conversation of Johnson, and his friends, Charlotte Lennox, Baretti, Paradise, Sir Joshua Reynolds, the family of Mr. Wilton, and many others of the first colloquial talents of the time."[7]

Mary Welch, the elder and more domestic daughter who is said to have been the original of Dr. Johnson's Peknah in *Rasselas*, became the wife of Joseph Nollekens. His distinction as a sculptor must have weighed very heavily indeed in the scales of her decision. Very short, with a huge head and almost no neck, bowlegged, and slovenly in his dress, "Little Nolly," as Dr. Johnson dubbed him, was noted for his boorish manners, his illiterate speech, and his stinginess. On her marriage, Miss Welch was described as a beauty—with an "elegant figure and auburn ringlets";[8] but she more than matched her husband in parsimony and possessed a temper which he himself described as "scorney."

Nollekens brought his wife to live in a house at the corner of Mortimer and Great Titchfield Streets, a block away from 28 Charles Street. He soon became a familiar figure to Mr. and Mrs. Paradise on their passings to and fro, for it was his habit to stand at his gate, his arms behind him, when his day's work was done, accompanied by his great dog Cerberus. If he did not like the people who passed or became otherwise displeased, he would bar the gate securely and retire into the house, murmuring, "Come in, my Cerberus, come in."[9] Often Sir Joshua Reynolds, accompanied by Dr. Johnson, would call for him in his carriage to take him out to Richmond, where Sir Joshua had a villa. Once he kept them waiting unreasonably long and Dr. Johnson, in a great pet, called out loud for the whole street to hear him, "Come, Nolly! Nolly!"[10] The street was delighted, for as usual a crowd had gathered to feast their eyes upon the two celebrities.

John Thomas Smith, the offended friend and candid biographer of Nollekens who was spiteful enough to tell all that he remembered—and a great deal more— has told of a Nollekens dinner-party at which the Paradises were present. About the time the invited guests were expected, the entire family of Sir John Hawkins appeared to pay a call, causing the greatest consternation to Nollekens and his lady, who realized that the dinner was scanty enough as it was. The Hawkinses, overhearing their whispered conference in the next room, silently took their departure.

Smith, who was then a young boy, was caught stark naked behind a screen, where he had been posing for a statue of Mercury. Curiosity impelled him to remain in the studio and there he was able to obtain a keyhole view of the dinner. Although it was described by him as being a very poor repast indeed, it consisted of a roasted leg of pork, a celery salad, lobster, and mashed turnips, with side dishes of chicken, reindeer's tongue, watercresses, and cheese. The conversation was often interrupted by the little sculptor's vulgar remarks to the serving-maid, whose name was Bronze and who had her sore throat wrapped up in flannel. He insisted on sending her out of the room to find his back-scratcher and on making all the ladies test its merits. In an effort to elevate the tone of the occasion, the learned Miss Welch introduced a quotation from Cowper, and Mrs. Nollekens, as a diversion, passed a bottle of claret to her most elegant guest:

"'My dear Mrs. Paradice, you may safely take a

glass of it; for it is the last of twelve which Mr. Caleb
Whitefoord sent us as a present; and everybody who
talks about wine, should know his house has ever been
famous for claret.'

"Mr. Nollekens: 'Don't crack the nuts with your
teeth, Miss Moser; you'll spoil them.'

" 'Ay, and what would Mr. Fuseli say to that?' asked
Mr. Saunders Welch, who now spake for the first
time.''[11]

The social world in which the Paradises moved has
nowhere been better reflected than in Fanny Burney's
novel *Evelina*. The young heroine, whose well-born
father had married beneath him, is, on her entrance
into the world of London, ground between the upper
and nether millstones of her father's fashionable connections and her mother's common ones. On the one
hand were her Branghton relations whose manners, like
those of the Nollekens, were frankly rough and vulgar;
on the other was the fashionable set in which Lord
Orville, the most resplendent of her suitors, moved. In
the actual world of Fanny Burney herself, which was
also the world of John and Lucy Paradise, the conflicting social elements were just as evident; but in this
real world the social gulf was bridged by intellect and
talent. Here we find tradesmen, artisans, and their sons
and daughters in frequent intercourse with bishops,
duchesses and noble lords. The well-known intimacy
between a fashionable descendant of Charles II and
the son of a Lichfield bookseller is a fair indication of
how social extremes could meet in this democracy of
the intellect. It is true that friction occurred when

fashionable manners met middle-class simplicity, but usually, as Fanny Burney showed in town and Jane Austen in the country, the result was comedy.

No better vantage point for the observation of contemporary manners could be conceived than Dr. Burney's house in St. Martin's Street. Here Fanny and her sisters met and observed the great musicians, painters, writers, philosophers, and scientists as well as those who came to meet them. Charlotte and Susanna Burney, as well as Fanny, were talented diarists and letter-writers, and nothing gave them more pleasure than the writing down for their own and their friends' delight the peculiarities of appearance and manner, the witty sallies, the amusing incidents, the affectations, and the conversations of their father's guests. The Burney sisters were all "character mongers," and since Mrs. Paradise, even in her youth, was one of the most colorful of the "characters" who visited their house, she was included in the gallery of each of them.

Susanna first mentions the Paradises in her account of a performance of Sacchini's opera *Rinaldo* at the great theatre in the Haymarket. The occasion was important both socially and musically, for the leading tenor was no less person than the great Pacchierotti, newly arrived in England, but already the favorite singer there. "We arrived just as the overture began. Our Box was next to the Duke of Dorset's . . . . Lady Hales was on the stage of our side, Mrs. Castle and the Ogles in an upper Stage Box, Lady Clarges and Miss Clarges in the former's own Box; Lady Edgecumbe in the Pitt, Miss Bull, Miss Streatfield, Mr. and Mrs. Locke, the Duchess of Devonshire in her Box, Mrs. Crewe likewise. . . . Rauzzini sat close to the Orchestra,

then Mr. Brudenell, and Mr. Harris, behind them my
Father, Mr. Mason, Sir Joshua Reynolds, Miss Palmers, Miss Basil, Mrs. Hayes, Lord Ailsbury in his Box
with Lord Ashburnham, . . . Marchetti with her husband; Tenducci, and Mota in the front Boxes, in the
1st Gallery Mrs. and Miss Kirwans with Mr. and Mrs.
Paradise—in short we had the satisfaction of seeing
faces we knew everywhere—and indeed a most brilliant
House.

"The Opera went off extremely well . . . . P[i]ozzi
did not sing so well as usual—but Pacchierotti—oh,
Pacchierotti—how divine he was!"[12]

Gasparo Pacchierotti, one of the many Italian singers
in the eighteenth century who lost manhood and put
tenorhood on, soon became a valued and beloved intimate of the Burney household. He was a sweet, loveable man with a voice which the Burneys were not
alone in considering one of the greatest of their day.
Not long after the performance of the opera described
by Susanna, Mrs. Paradise engaged him to entertain
her guests at one of her routs. The occasion is described
by Fanny Burney, in her usually lively but self-centered
manner, in a letter to one of her sisters.[13]

Fanny, Charlotte, and their father arrived late, after
Pacchierotti had sung his opening number, which was
an aria from "Artaxerxes." Many of Fanny's acquaintances were present: Queeney Thrale, the eldest daughter of Dr. Johnson's friend; the Miss Kirwans; Dr.
Solander, the Swedish botanist; Sir Sampson and Lady
Gideon, city folk whom she had met at the Thrales'
house in Streatham; the Rev. William Coxe, the
traveler; and Signor Sastres and Count Zenobio, both
of them scholars and political liberals who were friends

of Mr. Paradise. After Pacchierotti had sung "Dolce speme," set by Bertoni—"less elegantly than by Sacchini, but more expressively for the words"—Fanny was accosted by Mrs. Paradise who told her that Lady Say and Sele desired the honor of being introduced to her. Her ladyship seemed to be "pretty near fifty—at least turned forty; her head was full of feathers, flowers, jewels, and gew-gaws, and as high as Lady Archer's; her dress was trimmed with beads, silver, persian sashes, and all sort of fine fancies; her face is thin and fiery, and her whole manner spoke a lady all alive." Lady Say and Sele went into raptures over *Evelina,* declaring it to be the most elegant novel she had ever read in her life. She then quickly turned to introduce her sister, Lady Hawke, but Mrs. Paradise was ahead of her: "Miss Burney, ma'am, authoress of 'Evelina.'"

Lady Hawke, herself the authoress of an unpublished novel called *The Mausoleum of Julia,* rose and curtsied. "She is much younger than her sister, and rather pretty; extremely languishing, delicate, and pathetic; apparently accustomed to be reckoned the genius of her family, and well contented to be looked upon as a creature dropped from the clouds." The three ladies discussed, first *Evelina* and then *The Mausoleum of Julia,* from which Lady Say and Sele was easily persuaded to quote a passage. Just then Mrs. Paradise came up again, this time with Lord Say and Sele, "a square man, middle-aged, and hum-drum." "Miss Burney," she said, "authoress of 'Evelina.'"

Lord Say and Sele had never heard of *Evelina,* and conversation was beginning to languish when Mrs. Paradise came forward with "another gentleman, younger, slimmer, and smarter," saying,

"Sir Gregory Page Turner—Miss Burney, authoress of 'Evelina.'"

After Fanny had heard all that her new acquaintances could say in favor of her novel, she went to seek for Pacchierotti. But Mrs. Paradise interrupted her once more:

"Miss Burney, Lady Say and Sele wishes vastly to cultivate your acquaintance, and begs to know if she may have the honour of your company to an assembly at her house next Friday?—and I will do myself the pleasure to call for you, if you will give me leave."

"Her ladyship does me much honour, but I am unfortunately engaged."

Fanny Burney was a strange mixture of vanity and shyness. She was as pleased as any other normal human being at the success of her book and as keenly alive to the praise of her friends, which she never failed to set down carefully in her letters and diary. On the other hand, she shrank from notice even while she enjoyed it. Those who knew her well, like Mrs. Thrale and Dr. Johnson, would contrive to wring from her admirers the last sweet drop of commendation while at the same time shielding her from undue attention. This was the sort of treatment which her nature, at the same time inordinately sensitive and inordinately vain, required. The fussy attention of Mrs. Paradise, however well meant, was really torture to her. "Poor Fan's *such* a prude!" her father once remarked. Mrs. Paradise, with her fine clothes and her fine manners and her incorruptibly social nature geared to the lightest of conversational paces, was always the object of Fanny Burney's jealous contempt. She despised her for her follies and yet stood a little in awe of her superior social position.

"As I had the coach," she once wrote in her diary, "I then *spit* cards at Mrs. Chapone's, who has sent me an invitation. I declined; for so I do by at least half I receive, much as I go out;—and at Mrs. Hatsell's, and Mrs. Paradise's, and Lady Gideon's."[14]

The social aggressiveness in Mrs. Paradise to which Fanny Burney objected was after all a rather harmless trait which arose more from a desire to be pleasant than anything else. Unfortunately, though, as time went on this aggressiveness often turned to violence. Lucy's Ludwell temper, fortified by ignorance, by over-developed pride and a ruthless determination to have her own way, came more and more to the surface and occasionally gave rise to incidents which were disgraceful indeed. John Paradise unluckily possessed a superlative sensitiveness of nature—the "sensibility" of his contemporaries—which made him tender of feeling himself, painfully perceptive of the feelings of others, and consequently susceptible beyond reason to his wife's ungovernable outbursts. These were by no means restricted to their private differences. Her temper was as quick as it was violent and when the fit was upon her she gave it full play, no matter what the place or who the company.

"Nothing," said Laetitia Hawkins, "could be more elegant or refined than Mrs. Paradise's whole exterior; her countenance was indeed unquiet, but her voice was gentle and her manner deliberate. At the head of her table, with a large dinner party, perceiving that a plate before her was not quite clean, she beckoned the servant and said to him in an audible whisper:—'If you bring me a dirty plate again I will break your head with it.'"[15] If the servant had again offended, she would assuredly have carried out her threat. The Italian, Giuseppe Baretti, tutor to the Misses Thrale, was hated and feared by most women for his overbearing ways; but in Lucy Paradise he more than met his match. At one of her evening parties he goaded her by his importunities into a passion beyond speech, and without any warning such as she had given the servant she seized the scalding tea-urn beside her and poured its contents over him.[16] At the rehearsal of a dance in which her two young daughters had a part she arose, and with a look of unruffled composure upon her face sailed across the ball-room floor and gave one of them a resounding slap upon the cheek for having made an awkward step.[17]

Fanny Burney and her sisters, with their gift for burlesque exaggeration, found Mrs. Paradise an easy target for satire. "I suppose Bessy K[irwan] either has, or will, write you a *succinct* account of Mrs. P[aradise]'s ball on Twelfth Night, so I shall only give a few *nanny goats* of it," wrote Charlotte Ann Burney to her sister Susanna. "It was a very pleasant evening— There were eight couple, and more gentlemen than ladies, which I think was very *proper*, as it made the ladies of more consequence. There were but two good dancers among the gentlemen, Mr. Smith, and Mr. Frieri, a Portuguese, whom you have seen at the K[irwans]. He is a scholar of Le Picq's. They mixed the fans together, and drew for partners with them, the first dance or two, and then changed partners every dance or two. I say *they*, for *I* was destined, some how or other, to dance with Mr. Smith the whole evening, for he ask'd me to dance with him as soon as I went in, and took it in his head to contrive for me to dance with him every dance. I don't know how he managed it, but

he and Mrs. P[aradise] caballed together about it, and
so it was.—I didn't much care, for unless I had danced
with Mr. Frieri, I had as lieve have danced with him
as any of the others. Mr. Planta of the Museum was
one of the dancers, and Dick, and some more whom I
didn't take the trouble to enquire the names of. Miss
Kirwans and Miss Planta, Mrs. Northy, painted like
Agujari, in a balloon hat, and Mrs. P[aradise] and her
two daughters, were all the fair females that danced.
But the behavior of the lady, who had one of her tea-
cups broke by the all-knowing P[lanta?] was really
too rediculous!—She took a great fancy to dance with
Mr. Frieri, who is acquainted with our friends in
Newman St. [the Miss Kirwans] and after the first
two dances, engaged the eldest of them for his partner.
As soon as he had gone down one dance with her, he
engaged her for the next, and immediately after, up
came Mrs. Teacup and *asked* him to dance the next
dance with *her*! He looked rather confused, and said
he was *engaged* to Miss Kirwan. 'Oh, never mind, replied she, you can go down this one dance with *me.*'
He excused himself as politely as he could, but [she]
told him she had got another partner for Miss Kirwan,
and that he *must* go down that dance with her; so he
submitted,—but as soon as it was over, he went and
secured Miss Kirwan for the *next*, which he had no
sooner done, than Mrs. Teacup flew up to him a second
time, with a request that he would go down that *next*
dance with her eldest daughter!—He again pleaded a
pre-engagement, but all in vain, for she stuck to her
request, altho' he repeatedly told her he was engaged!
—being a *foreigner*, she thought to impose upon him
I suppose, for she said he must go down *that* dance with

Miss P[aradise] for it was *customary!* so he again
submitted to be *led a dance* against his will!—He then
secured Miss Kirwan for the next, and as soon as that
was over, for the next, but he might have spared
himself the trouble, for before he began the second,
Mrs P[aradise] came up to him again with 'Mr.
Frieri, who do you dance this dance with?'—'With
Miss Kirwan, Ma'am.'—'No, but you must dance
this dance with me.'—'Why, really, Ma'am,' replied
he in great confusion, 'I am engaged to Miss Kirwan;
she has promised to dance this dance with me.' 'Oh,
never mind that,' answered she with the most noble
perseverance, 'I have got another partner for Miss
Kirwan, and I insist upon your dancing this one
dance with me.—I say I insist upon it—I'll never
forgive you *if* you don't!'—So she again carried her
point. The partner she gave Miss Kirwan as a substitute for Mr. Frieri who was the best dancer in
the room, was a German doctor, a thick, squob, square
man of fifty, with a club [of hair] as thick as my
two hands, and two squinney curls, and a broad grin
on his face, that set every one a grinning that looked
at him, and so bad a dancer that he only ran about
among them all, and took his chance whether he was
right or wrong! Poor Miss Kirwan was monstrously
provoked, as well as she might!—About one o'clock
Mr. Friarey was missing. 'Now' says Mrs. P[aradise]
'I'll be crucified if Mr. Frieri hasn't made his escape!
Miss P[aradise] go down and see if he is in the
parlour with Mr. P[aradise], and bring him up
again.' Miss P[aradise] would fain have avoided the
task, but Mrs. P[aradise] said she insisted upon it, so
away the poor girl went, and presently returned, fol-

lowed by Mr. Frieri, who had got on his great coat to
go, but that was a trifle, Mrs. P[aradise] insisted on
his taking another dance, which she did him the favour
to make him go down with Mrs. Den, an old harridan
—so that the poor man was absolutely persecuted! The
lookers on were General Paoli, to whom I was introduced for the second time, Dr. Blagden, who was too
elegant to undergo the fatigue of dancing, the Venetian
Resident [Count Soderini], and two or three more; to
my great joy Mr. Seward was not one, tho' he was
invited. We drew Twelfth Cake, but the names were
very dull—we got home about two in the morning."[18]

That which was meat for the gossips and memoir-
writers was poison for John Paradise. No more ex-
quisite torture could have been devised for one of his
nature than to have his wife suggest, by her outrageous
conduct before the world, the unloveliness of their
domestic relationship. As for her, she seems to have
been almost oblivious of the disgrace her conduct
brought upon them and too lacking in self-control to
quit it under any circumstances. Certainly her husband
could not control her. Quiet, peace-loving scholar that
he was, what force could he oppose against her stormy
Ludwell will? Although the merciful modern provision of divorce was for their time and circumstances
all but out of the question, he might indeed have left
her. To this there was one insuperable obstacle. Incredible though it seems, there is not the slightest doubt
that he was still in love with her and continued to be in
love with her until so much time had passed and such
events occurred as would have made the act of separation a futile anticlimax. Fate, it seemed, had destined
him to remain the victim of both irresolution and love,

and, more than either, of a foolish though attractive woman—electrified with misdirected energy.

Mrs. Paradise was never popular with her husband's friends or in the social set in which his position obliged her to move; the circle of Dr. Samuel Johnson provided but slight accommodation for the socially frivolous. With all her beauty and graces, her wealth and her unbending determination, she seldom won social victories there. The outbreak of the Revolution also caused social gaps; but for these she cannot be held responsible. Such success as she finally did achieve was that of an American hostess to other Americans and to such of the English and other foreigners as were sympathetic to the American cause. Here indeed, her social talents served a highly useful purpose, and in the later days of the Revolution and the years immediately following, the Paradise house in Charles Street, Cavendish Square, was a social center for Americans not second even to that of the American minister. Here was the one point on which Lucy Paradise and her husband agreed—their loyalty to America—and here their one joint success was to be achieved.

CHAPTER IV

Scholarship for Delight

JOHN PARADISE'S lack of ability in business had aroused the contemptuous dislike of William Lee; but this was offset by his accomplishments in another direction, accomplishments which won him the respect of men whose opinions he valued far more. His good fortune in being the son of a well-to-do father and the husband of a rich wife made it feasible for him to indulge his interest and develop his talents in scholarship. To him this was a pleasanter way of life by far than that which led to wealth. The decade in which he reached maturity—that which preceded the American Revolution—marked the close of what was perhaps the last age in which scholarship was generally recognized as being in itself a worthy and commendable aim. The industrial era with its demand for material results in every field of endeavor—even the ideal—had not yet imposed its standards upon the judging part of mankind, and fame and distinction were still rewards for those who embodied the results of their learning in themselves. Books and experiments and practicable inventions, which today are demanded as a proof of learning—often indeed as an excuse or apology for it—were then considered more as the happy incidental results of scholarly pursuit, which pursuit was in itself of sufficient value to justify the occupation of a lifetime.

Like many of his contemporaries, Paradise won his honors merely on the reputation of being a learned man; the proof lying in his ability to converse and otherwise conduct himself as such, and the rewards in the personal satisfaction which he himself derived and in the esteem which was accorded him by those with similar interests. The fact that he read and spoke Italian, French, English, Turkish, Latin, and both ancient and modern Greek with fluency and inconspicuous ease gave him access to almost every field of knowledge then known to European scholars and enabled him to hold his own among the veritable Titans of erudition. These and his other accomplishments were a part of the man himself, not flaunted as an adornment, but organic to his personality and adding to his value as a human being.

The recognition accorded his abilities was early. On May 2, 1771, only two years after he received his M. A. from the University of Oxford, he was elected to the Royal Society, "for his skill in geometry, philosophy & ancient literature," and at the next weekly meeting, on the payment of thirty-one guineas, he was admitted as a Fellow.[1] Five years after this his remarkable abilities as a linguist were still further recognized by Oxford in an honorary award of the degree of Doctor of Civil Laws.[2]

The five men who sponsored his election to the Royal Society reflect, naturally enough, the background and associations which had up to this time formed his life. The most prominent of them was Sir James Porter,[3] who had recently been offered but had declined the presidency of the Society. Generally considered the ablest Ambassador to Turkey which England had had up to that time, Sir James was a self-made man, a City merchant, and a self-taught linguist. His retirement in 1762 allowed him the leisure to pursue his studies of

languages and science at his newly-acquired country
estate near London. Here he became well known as a
kindly, hospitable patron of men of learning. Sir
James' acquaintance with Peter and John Paradise
had begun during his eighteen years' residence in the
Near East, as had also that of the second of the sponsors, Dr. Anthony Askew.[4] Although he was a prac-
ticing physician, Dr. Askew was far better known as a
classical scholar and as a linguist. After a year at the
University of Leyden, he had traveled in Italy and
Hungary and had also made protracted stays at Athens
and Constantinople. His reputation as a linguist was
so great that he was popularly reputed to know every
language—a claim, not his own, which was proved
untrue when he was once confronted with a Chinese:
neither could understand the other. It was Dr. Askew's
ambition to possess "every edition of a Greek author,"
and he actually did collect one of the greatest classical
libraries of his time. Dr. Swithin Adee,[5] another spon-
sor who was also a physician and a classical scholar,
was a noted archæologist as well. All three of these
were much older men than John Paradise; the remaining two sponsors were nearer his own age. Isaac
Hawkins Browne the Younger,[6] who remained a lifelong friend, was the son of a father of great attainments,
according to Dr. Johnson, but one who had "drank
freely for thirty years,"—a remark which Boswell
found "encouraging." The son as well as the father
was a friend of Dr. Johnson. A classical scholar and a
philosopher, Browne was reputedly one of the wittiest
men in England; but in Parliament, of which he was a
member for many years, he was never heard to open
his mouth. The fifth and last of Paradise's sponsors

was his wife's Virginia cousin, Dr. Arthur Lee. Lee was one of the two American members of the Royal Society at this time. On May 29, 1756, Benjamin Franklin, who "had not the least expectation of ever arriving at that honour,"[7] had been elected for his theories and experiments in electricity. At the time of Paradise's election Franklin was in London and was one of the most active members of the Society; it was probably then that Paradise became acquainted with him.

Paradise's election as an F.R.S. under the sponsorship of men so well qualified to vouch for him was proved by its results to be one of the happiest events of his life. The meetings of the Society, which he attended very regularly, the dinners which invariably preceded them, and the informal talk among groups of friends both before and after the meetings—these were the advantages that most appealed to him. Although on his election he submitted the customary treatise and later on translated and read before the Society several scientific papers of the Abbé Fontana, Secretary to the Grand Duke of Tuscany,[8] he was never a productive scholar; his genius, like that of the age in which he lived, was social. "He is distinguished not only by his learning and talents," Boswell wrote of him, "but by an amiable disposition, gentleness of manners, and a very general acquaintance with well-informed and accomplished persons of almost all nations."[9] It was his fondness for the society of scholars that made the Royal Society with all its rich and varied contacts the "happy valley" of an otherwise chaotic life.

At the time of his election, the meetings were held at a house in Crane Court, Fleet Street; but by 1780, the rooms there having become too small, space was granted by the Government at Somerset House in the Strand. Here in a spacious, oblong, high-ceilinged room, its walls adorned by the portraits of distinguished members and its rostrum with a bust of Charles II, the society convened every Thursday, its members ranged on two rows of high-backed, uncomfortable benches divided by a middle aisle. Here the learned papers were read and discussed, and here transpired the "philosophical" transactions so copiously recorded in whole shelves of folio volumes. However, not all the transactions were of this nature, as Paradise was soon to discover. On occasions the members of this august body could be stirred by passions and prejudices that were far removed from higher reaches of philosophic thought.

One such occasion occurred soon after he became a member and since it gave rise to a controversy which very seriously affected his friend Sir John Pringle, the President, and in other ways involved interests that were close to his heart, he must have followed its developments and ramifications with much concern.[10] In 1772 the British Government determined to protect its magazines at Purfleet with the lightning conductors which had been invented not long since by Benjamin Franklin. It requested the advice of the Royal Society as to the best type of conductors to be used. A committee of five members, including Franklin, was appointed to inspect the buildings. With one dissenting vote they advised the use of pointed conductors, the type which Franklin had found most efficacious in his experiments and which as a member of another committee he had three years previously recommended for St. Paul's Cathedral. The dissenting member, Benjamin Wilson, was not content with submitting a minority report in which he protested against the decision, but soon afterwards read before the Society a very long paper setting forth in detail his preference for blunt conductors, as being less apt to attract lightning from a distance. Many meetings of the Society were then occupied by discussions of the subject and many pages of the *Transactions* filled with papers about it, all in a proper scientific spirit. The Government meanwhile had acted on the committee's report and installed pointed conductors.

A few years later, much to the triumph of Benjamin Wilson and his party, one of the magazines was struck by lightning and slightly damaged. The Board of Ordnance at once appealed to the Royal Society to reconsider its decision. Another committee was appointed, but this time Franklin was not a member; he had gone to America at the outbreak of the Revolution. On the new committee's reporting again in favor of pointed conductors, Wilson began a series of experiments in which he proved to his own satisfaction that blunt conductors were preferable. He submitted his findings in an even longer paper to the Board of Ordnance, who promptly referred it to the Royal Society for their further consideration. After the several meetings required for the mere reading of Wilson's paper, a third and larger committee was appointed which again declared in favor of pointed conductors. Wilson was infuriated; he managed to persuade the Government that the committee was a prejudiced one and that the majority of the Royal Society were on his side. The Board of Ordnance therefore demanded that the question be submitted to the Society as a whole and decided by a majority vote. A conscientious attempt was made to carry out this request, but the strong feeling and prejudice among the members had now reached so high a pitch that all attempt at orderly discussion proved impossible and the discussion was ignominiously abandoned. The report of the committee consequently stood.

The issue had by now become public and was no longer conducted on scientific but on political grounds. The fact that pointed conductors had been recommended by the American leader, Benjamin Franklin, was reason enough in 1777 for many patriotic Englishmen to support the other side. The Whigs and most disinterested scientists were for the pointed, while the Tories presented a solid front in favor of the blunt conductors. Franklin, who was by now in Paris, was appealed to by Dr. Ingenhousz but he sagely replied that he always allowed his philosophical opinions to take their own chances in the world. "If they are *right,* truth and experience will support them; if *wrong*, they ought to be refuted and rejected." George III was affected by no such scruples; it was clear to him that if pointed conductors had been recommended by one of his rebellious subjects, then blunt conductors ought to be and *must* be installed. To show how he stood he ordered his palace to be equipped with blunt conductors and then awaited developments. When it became clear that there would be no developments and that the Royal Society was stubbornly holding to its original position, Sir John Pringle was summoned into the

Royal presence. The extraordinary monarch demanded that the opinion of the Society should be reversed.

"Sire," was the reply, "I cannot reverse the laws and operations of nature."

"Perhaps, Sir John, you had better resign."

And Sir John did resign, much to the expressed regret of the majority of the Royal Society and even more to his own, for, as he declared, he considered that being its President was the highest honor he ever received. Soon after this a friend of Franklin's wrote:

> While you, great George, for knowledge hunt,
> And sharp conductors change for blunt,
> The nation's out of joint;
> Franklin a wiser course pursues,
> And all your thunder useless views,
> By keeping to the *point*.

The illiberality and foolish prejudice manifested by George III and by some members of the Royal Society on this occasion contrasts strongly with an action of Franklin's some two years later. In March, 1779, John Paradise was on a visit to him in Paris. At this time Captain Cook the navigator, with whom Franklin had been personally acquainted in London, was thought to be returning to England from his third voyage. Franklin, in one of his first acts as Minister from the United States to France, wrote a safeguard for him addressed to "all Captains and Commanders of armed ships acting by Commission from the Congress of the United States."[11] This safeguard, a copy of which was confided to Paradise for delivery in England, recommended that if Cook's ship fell into the hands of the Americans they should not plunder or obstruct or detain it but "treat the said Captain Cook and his people with all civility and kindness, affording them, as common friends to mankind, all the assistance in your power, which they may happen to stand in need of." This safeguard was dated March 10, 1779; but the as yet unknown fact that Cook himself had been killed in the Hawaiian Islands on February 14 did not destroy its potential value for his ship and his fellow-voyagers. Paradise presented the copy which Franklin had confided to him to Sir Joseph Banks, the successor of Pringle as President of the Royal Society, who duly acknowledged it.

This was not the end of the incident, however. In 1784, when the account of Cook's third voyage was published, Franklin was given a copy of it by the King's permission, obtained, as Banks rather tactlessly wrote Franklin, "with a little difficulty."[12] Franklin also received one of the gold medals which the Royal Society had struck in Cook's honor. Several years later Dr. Andrew Kippis in his life of Cook made the unfortunate and untruthful statement that Franklin's safeguard had been immediately withdrawn by the American Congress. A number of Americans immediately protested, whereupon Kippis handsomely retracted his statement.[13]

The meetings of the Society were held at eight o'clock in the evening. Dinner was usually at five, but the three-hour allowance of time was none too liberal for the many courses of food and wine and talk of which this meal consisted. It was a widespread habit among the members to invite their friends to dinner before the Thursday meetings, together with any strangers of distinction who happened to be in London. Not long before the middle of the eighteenth century some forty of the members had banded together into the Royal Society Club,[14] which gave a dinner preceding every meeting, first at the Mitre Tavern and after 1780 at the Crown and Anchor in the Strand. Although not a member of this Club, Paradise was perhaps more frequently invited to dine there than any other outsider. The first of these occasions was on January 25, 1772, when he and his friend Sir William Jones were present as the guests of Dr. Charles Morton, physician to the Middlesex Hospital, member of the Society of Antiquaries, and later Librarian of the British Museum. The menu for Paradise's first dinner there is a typical one: "Fresh Sturgeon broiled, Rump of beef roast, beans & bacon, Collyflower, 2 Chicken Roast, 2 Gooseberry Pyes, Veal Ragoust, boiled Salmon, Lambs Head, Knuckle of Veal, Cold Neck of Lamb, 2 dishes pease, 2 Lobsters, Butter & Cheese."[15] A fellow guest at this time was Dr. Daniel Solander, the distinguished Swedish botanist who had accompanied Capt. Cook on his first voyage in the *Endeavor*. Solander afterwards became a member of the Club and some time later Paradise and Bennet Langton dined together at the Club as his guests.

Among Paradise's other hosts at the dinners of the Royal Society Club were Sir John Pringle and Sir Joseph Banks, both of them his intimate friends. He was twice invited by Dr. Patrick Russell, who was for many years a resident of Aleppo, where he was physician to the English factory. A bond which he had in common with Paradise was his ability to converse fluently in Arabic. On January 13, 1780, Paradise was

the guest of the Rev. Nevil Maskelyne. One of the
most active members of the Royal Society, this clergyman, who was also an astronomer, was appointed in
1760 by the Council of the Society to head an expedition to St. Helena to observe the transit of Venus.
Although the expedition was unsuccessful in its main
object, owing to cloudy weather, it could hardly have
been considered a dismal failure since approximately
half of the two hundred and ninety pounds expended
by Maskelyne, according to his expense account, went
for "Liquors."[16] Shortly afterwards, this reverend
scientist was appointed Astronomer Royal and placed
in charge of the Observatory at Greenwich, where
Paradise took Thomas Jefferson to visit him. The Hon.
Henry Cavendish, the discoverer of nitrogen and the
first scientist to determine the consistency of water and
of the atmosphere, was another of Paradise's hosts.
Although he was extremely rich, Cavendish lived the
life of a recluse, being so morbidly shy that, rather than
encounter the maid servants in his own house, he would
leave a note on the hall table containing the menus for
the day and other household instructions. His only
interest was in science and his only social life the meetings of the Royal Society and the dinners of the Royal
Society Club. Sir William Watson, the Vice-President
of the Royal Society and the first publisher of Franklin's discoveries in electricity, was a physician and a
botanist, being known because of his remarkable memory as "the living lexicon of botany." He and his son,
William Watson, Jr., were both friends of Paradise
and both were his hosts at the Royal Society Club.

A full description of one of the Club's dinners, written by the French traveler and geologist, B. Faujas de

Saint Fond,[17] shows that the men who liked to style themselves "Royal Philosophers" were accustomed to demand both royal food and drink. Saint Fond was amazed to discover that guests, even foreigners like himself, were, according to the frugal English custom of the day, expected to pay for their meal. The cost to guests, as to members, was six shillings. The menu on the occasion of his visit consisted of "Soals, Chickens Boild, Pye, Bacon and Greens, Cold Ribs of Lamb, Veal cutlets, Potatoes, Rabbits and Onions, fruit Pye, Sallad, A Lambs head and minced, Collyflower, Chine of Mutton R^t [roasted], Pye, Soals." In the Frenchman's somewhat spiteful account, it is recorded that no napkins were supplied, the dinner being "truly in the English style." After the company and the food had been blessed by a clergyman present, the first course, consisting of the dishes mentioned above, was served. The meat, seasoned to taste by each individual from the sauces and other condiments placed in bottles upon the table, was washed down with bumpers of porter, "drunk out of cylindrical pewter pots, which are much preferred to glasses, because one can swallow a whole pint at a draft." After this the cloth was removed and the table covered "as if it were by magic, with a number of fine crystal decanters" containing the best port, madeira, and claret. Each guest being provided with several glasses, "the libations began on a grand scale, in the midst of different kinds of cheese, which, rolling in mahogany boxes from one end of the table to the other, provoked the thirst of the drinkers." A health was drunk to the Prince of Wales because it was his birthday; to the Elector Palatine because he was being admitted to the Royal Society; to each of the five

foreigners present because they were foreigners; and
then to each member present because it was the custom.
Champagne followed; then tea; then coffee, of which
each Englishman drank several cups. After this, brandy, rum, and several other liqueurs, and the dinner
was over at half-past seven. "I repaired to the Society
along with Messrs. Banks, Cavendish, Maskelyne [the
clergyman], Aubert, and Sir Henry Englefield; we
were all pretty much enlivened, but our gaiety was
decorous."

Whenever any distinguished foreigner appeared in
London, or when anyone, foreigner or native, came
suddenly into prominence, he was immediately invited
to partake of one of these remarkable dinners—at his
own expense. The enthusiastic President of the Society,
who was *ex officio* the host of the Club, won the applause of his fellow-members by the "rapidity and
energy" with which he could catch a celebrity with his
honors fresh upon him. Bougainville, the French
traveler; Captain Cook, immediately on his return
from his first voyage around the world; the King of
Poland's brother, Michael Poniatowski; Marie Antoinette's Swedish friend, Count Fersen; Omai, the
Otaheitan savage chieftain; and Rudolf Eric Raspe,
the author of *Baron Munchausen*, were all guests
during the seventeen-seventies—the period at which
Paradise was most frequently a visitor. The Italian
Lunardi, the first man to make a balloon ascent in
England, (who immediately became so fashionable that
his name like Tristram Shandy's was given to wigs,
coats, hats, bonnets, etc.), was soon after his flight a
guest of the Club. Perhaps the most rapid capture of
all was that of "Breadfruit" Bligh of the *Bounty*, who

four days after his return to England from his epochal
voyage was brought to a Club dinner by the triumphant
Sir Joseph Banks.[18]

Paradise often gave dinners preceding the meetings
of the Society at his own home. His wide acquaintance
with foreign scholars and diplomats gave him the
opportunity of bringing many distinguished strangers
to the meetings: a whole bevy of Italian counts—
Andriani, Zenobio, Luni, Alfieri the poet, Soderini the
Venetian minister—and Count Woronzow, the Russian
Ambassador. On December 14, 1785, he entertained an
American party, whom he afterwards conducted to the
meeting of the Royal Society. It consisted of two young
secretaries, Cols. David Humphreys and William
Stephens Smith, and the first American Minister to
England, His Excellency John Adams.[19]

The personnel of the Royal Society was a far more
varied one in the eighteenth century than it is today
when its membership is limited strictly to men of
science. Such a restriction would then have been impossible, for the scientist of the day was generally a
philosopher, and more often than not, a man of literature as well. The group of men of whom Paradise
became the associate consisted therefore of the leading
intellectuals, whose interests covered almost every field
of thought. Sir John Pringle was physician in ordinary
to Her Majesty Queen Charlotte; Sir Joseph Banks
was an explorer and a botanist who, with the "philosophical gossip," Solander, had accompanied Captain
Cook around the world in the *Endeavor* on his first
voyage in 1768-71. The collection of exotic plants and
other scientific curiosities which the two men had
brought back with them aroused the interest of the

whole world. Even *The Virginia Gazette* in faraway
Williamsburg published several enthusiastic accounts
of their expedition, interest in botany in the colonies
being at this time very much alive. There were many
physicians in the Society, several of whom were among
Paradise's more intimate friends. There was Dr.
Blagden, later Sir Charles Blagden, who had a high
reputation as a doctor and as a cheerful companion:
"Blagden, Sir, is a delightful fellow," said Dr. Johnson.
He was frequently among Paradise's guests and was
invited to his house in Charles Street to meet Franklin's
grandson, William Temple Franklin, to whom the
Paradises gave a dinner before one of the meetings of
the Society.[20] In Paris a few years later Paradise introduced Blagden to Thomas Jefferson. When he was
made Secretary of the Royal Society with the responsibility of preparing for publication the voluminous
Philosophical Transactions, Blagden was lampooned
by the sarcastic T. J. Matthias:

> While o'er the bulk of these transacted deeds
> Prim Blagden pants, and damns them as he reads.[21]

Another physician in the Society who was an even
closer friend of Paradise's was Dr. Richard Warren.
Among his other manifold duties he held a post in the
Middlesex Hospital, just opposite the Paradise house
on Charles Street. He was Paradise's physician and
one of the lifelong friends who aided him financially
and whom Paradise remembered in his will. "Warren
is a coxcomb," said Boswell's witty friend Hamilton,
"but a satisfactory coxcomb." Certainly he must have
been satisfactory, for besides being physician to George
III he earned the largest income from the private

practice of his profession that had ever been earned in
England up to that time. He attended Dr. Johnson on
his death-bed and received a copy of the *Lives of the
Poets* for his fee; he was also Boswell's physician. Mrs.
Inchbald, the novelist and actress, when suffering with
the face-ache, went to his office where he "behaved
sweetly." She fell in love with him, and sentimentally
used to tell her friends how she would walk up and
down before his house in Sackville Street watching to
see if there were lights in his apartments, and follow
his carriage about London in the hope of catching a
glimpse of him.[22] Dr. Warren was a member of the
Royal Society Club and Paradise often dined there on
his invitation.

While the Royal Society was in no sense a political
organization, it was not, as the episode of the lightning
conductors shows, entirely free from political influences.
It is likely that if a canvass of the opinions of its members during the seventeen-seventies and eighties could
be taken, it would show that the great majority were
Whigs, many of them in the liberal wing of the party
which so actively opposed the war with America and
defended the right of the Americans to resist taxation
by the English Parliament. Among this group the outstanding men were the two clergymen, Dr. Richard
Price and Dr. Joseph Priestley, famous in America and
both famous and notorious in England for their extremely liberal views in politics and religion. Dr.
Price's writings on morals and philosophy had won him
widespread fame, as had his sermons also. The family
of John Adams during their residence in London frequently attended his church at the suburban village of
Hackney, and Mrs. John Adams considered him the

finest preacher she had ever heard. At the outbreak of
the Revolution, Price, who had not long before joined
with Franklin in an unsuccessful scheme for a peaceable solution to the quarrel, was invited in a letter from
Congress to become an American citizen. Although he
declined the honor on the grounds of domestic affili-
ations, he ever remained a true friend to America and
political freedom.[23]

Priestley, who was described by Mrs. Adams as "a
gentleman of a pale complexion, spare habit, placid,
thoughtful countenance, and very few words,"[24] was
even more outstanding for his liberalism, which finally,
at the time of the French Revolution, aroused such
hostility against him in England as to force him to
leave the country and take refuge in Pennsylvania.
Thus is America able to claim as a citizen one of the
greatest scientists of the eighteenth century, the man
whose brilliant experiments on air had led him to the
discovery of oxygen.

Sharing as he did the political opinions of these two
men as well as their interest in science and philosophy,
John Paradise was intimately thrown with them both
in the Royal Society and elsewhere. For some years
before the Revolution, while Franklin was still in
London, a certain supper club existed which met at
irregular intervals at the London Coffee House on
Ludgate Hill. There the members met in the evening
and talked "pretty formally, sometimes sensibly, and
sometimes furiously," with the convivial concomitants
of tobacco and wine and a supper at nine o'clock. The
name of the club was the "Honest Whigs" and until
Franklin left England in 1775 he was its presiding
genius.[25] It continued, however, for more than a decade

thereafter and soon after the beginning of the Revolution Paradise became a member of it. It had been
Franklin's favorite club and it remained one of his
happiest memories of his life in England. "I love all
the honest souls that meet at the London Coffee-house,"
he wrote Priestley from Paris during the War. "I only
wonder how it happened that they and my other friends
in England came to be such good creatures in the midst
of so perverse a generation."[26] Not long before he was
to leave Europe forever he wrote Price that he often
thought of the happy evenings he had spent with the
Honest Whigs; if he were able to visit London on his
way home from Paris, perhaps he might "pop in" on
them some evening when they least expected it.[27]

Nearly all of those who belonged to the Club of
Honest Whigs were members of the Royal Society as
well, and thus Paradise, when he joined it, found himself in a society doubly congenial. There were the
electricians John Canton and Dr. William Matthew
Maty, for many years Secretary of the Royal Society,
and Dr. John Fothergill, the Quaker physician and
botanist. Another "Honest Whig" and a man well-
beloved by all who knew him was Peter Collinson.
"Our Collinson taught me to love flowers," wrote
Fothergill to Linnaeus; ". . . what manner of man he
was I need not say to thee." Collinson also was one of
the recipients of Bartram's boxes of American plants.
These he planted in his garden at Mill Hill. From
there he wrote to Bartram in his old age: "I am here
retired all alone. The old Christmas log is burning,
and the fire of friendship is blazing. Franklin has been
staying here with me. . ."[28]

But not all of Paradise's acquaintances in the club were so peaceable and mild. William Hodgson, (who was a member of the Royal Society as well,) remained throughout the Revolution an active friend of America and kept Franklin informed by correspondence of much that the American commissioners in Paris desired to know. Hodgson was a fire-eating radical who was later so sympathetic with the French Revolution that he was imprisoned for two years in Newgate for having proposed the toast, "The French Republic," at the same time referring to His Majesty George III as a "German hog-butcher."[29] In the company of such men as these and in his particular association with Price and Priestley, it is no wonder that Paradise's liberal principles grew in intensity until he was led, with Franklin's assistance in Paris, to take the step that placed him irretrievably among the sons of liberty.

Paradise's interest in the Royal Society continued until his death, and never, except when he was absent from London, did he fail to attend its meetings regularly. There is no doubt that he agreed with his contemporary who wrote of it as "the premier scientific society of the English world, a society whose fellowship was a cachet no other approaches—for it is the hallmark of the scientist who has been accepted by his peers." That Paradise was not merely accepted by his peers, but highly respected by them as well, is proved by his election, not many years before his death, to the Counsel of the Royal Society.[30] This honor was given to him at a time when adverse circumstances and wretched health had greatly impaired his usefulness, and was evidently a gesture of encouragement and appreciation from the group of distinguished men. They had known him at his best and at his worst and still valued him for his personal attributes of charm and intelligent sympathy and for his unquenchable interest in the ideas and ideals for which their great organization stood.

CHAPTER V

The Vast Presence of Dr. Johnson

THE earliest recorded incident in Dr. Samuel Johnson's friendship with John Paradise occurred on Monday, April 3, 1773, when he dined with him at his home.[1] Although it is impossible to say when and under what circumstances the acquaintanceship began, it seems likely that it was already well advanced, for at this time he spoke of Paradise to Mrs. Thrale without amplification as if he were a person known to them both. Of the half a dozen men who might have introduced them the most likely is Bennet Langton. He was one of Dr. Johnson's oldest and closest friends, and he and Paradise were at this time well known to one another, having been drawn together as planets in the firmament of Dr. Samuel Parr. Whether or not Langton actually performed the introduction, he was the man who was oftenest present when Paradise was in Dr. Johnson's company.

Dr. Johnson's respect and liking for Paradise increased with the years. In another letter to Mrs. Thrale he gives her a circumstantial account of an attack of asthma, from which he was beginning to suffer more and more, of his "labour of respiration," and of how he has been bled for it a number of times, but remarks at the end: "When I have bled to-morrow, I will not give up Langton, nor Paradise."[2] In the last few years of his life, as is shown by Boswell's accounts and by his own, it became an almost weekly habit of his to dine at the Paradise house in Charles Street, Cavendish

Square. It was one of the houses whose standing hospitality provided some palliation for the loss of Streatham Park, and he informed Mrs. Thrale of his Monday dinners with Paradise, as well as his other social activities, with a pathetic air of assuring her that though old and ill he was as much sought after as ever. When his quarrel with her over her marriage to Piozzi had lost him her friendship as well as her hospitality, he grew more dependent than ever on friends like Paradise, who kindly and generously cheered his lonely hours.

"I am willing to love all mankind," said Dr. Johnson, *"except an American."* This pronouncement, although made in the heat of argument, reflected a prejudice that was much deeper-seated than that against the Scotch. He could make jokes about Scotland in which he frequently gave away the fact that his dislike was more than half put on for his own amusement, really a peg on which to hang a Johnsonian witticism. He could joke about Scotland even with an American. When Alderman William Lee, Paradise's Virginia-born brother-in-law, remarked with patriotic groans that Old England was lost, he had quickly parried with "Sir, it is not so much to be lamented that Old England is lost, as that the Scotch have found it." But on that same memorable occasion—the dinner with Wilkes— when Dilly informed him that one of the strangers in the company was Dr. Arthur Lee, celebrated at the time for his letters signed "Junius Americanus," Johnson had most ominously muttered "Too, too, too," and for a moment Boswell must have trembled for the success of his well-laid plan.[3] Johnson's Jacobite loyalty to his Hanoverian monarch is nowhere more stoutly

manifested than in his hatred of the rebellious colonies
and of all, or nearly all, who were sympathetic to them.
And yet Paradise's Americanism, even before he became a citizen in 1780, was known to all his friends.
How then, did Dr. Johnson come to make him the one
exception? He might very conceivably have let down
the bars of friendship to one who had had the misfortune to be born an American and then, repentant,
shifted his loyalty to England; but Paradise had done
the opposite. He had been born a British subject and
deliberately, because of conviction, had himself made
into an American. Notwithstanding this, Johnson's
friendship for him did not diminish, but increased. It
was partly no doubt respect for the sincerity of his
friend's convictions and for his courage in backing
them up with action. Paradise possessed sufficient tact
to avoid an occasion for quarreling over politics and
Dr. Johnson's fairmindedness, of which when calm he
had a normal amount, had been allowed to be brought
into play. Most of all, however, it had been his real
affection for the generous, sympathtic gentleman whose
intelligence, high learning and hospitality so alleviated
the misery of his lonely later years. American or not,
Paradise was and continued to be the valued friend of
Dr. Johnson.

As friends of Dr. Samuel Parr also, Paradise and
Langton often acted as liaison agents between him and
Dr. Johnson. Dr. Parr was as vigorous a Whig as
Johnson was a Tory; moreover, there was more than a
suggestion of rivalry between them, for although there
could be no real question as to Dr. Johnson's pre-
eminence in intellectual force and conversational
ability yet Parr was generally recognized as coming

closer to him in these respects than anyone else. It was at Langton's that these two intellectual giants spent one of their first evenings together. Boswell was not present, but he gives the record of it from Langton's lips.[4] He reported Johnson as being much pleased; after Parr had left he said, "Sir, I am obliged to you for having asked me this evening. Parr is a fair man. I do not know when I have had an occasion of such free controversy. It is remarkable how much of a man's life may pass without meeting with any instance of this kind of open discussion." Parr was equally delighted with the meeting, and said years later: "I remember that evening well. I gave him no quarter. The subject of our dispute was the liberty of the press. Dr. Johnson was very great. Whilst he was arguing, I observed that he stamped. Upon this, I stamped. Dr. Johnson said, Why do you stamp, Dr. Parr?—I replied, Because you stamped; and I was resolved not to give you the advantage even of a *stamp* in the argument."[5] Dr. Parr spoke in reminiscent vein of still another evening with Dr. Johnson: "Once, Sir, Sam and I had a vehement dispute upon that most difficult of all subjects, the origin of evil. It called forth all the powers of our minds. No two tigers ever grappled with more fury; but we never lost sight of good manners. There was no Boswell present to detail our conversation: Sir, he would not have understood it. And then, Sir, who do you think was the umpire between us? That fiend Horsley."[6]

When Parr decided to become a candidate for the headmastership of the school at Colchester, he enlisted the services of Paradise and Langton to secure for him a letter of recommendation from Johnson. The happy result was reported by Langton: "Yesterday morning

Mr. Paradise and I went to his house. . . It is, I assure you, dear Sir, but doing justice to his expressions, or our application to say, that nothing could be more friendly than they were. He said he knew of few, if of any, that were so well entitled to success as yourself in an application for presiding over a seminary of education; and expressed the opinion of your possessing all the kinds of learning requisite for that purpose, in very high terms of praise."[7]

Dr. Parr's liberalism and his friendliness toward the American colonies was well known, but he was by no means so outstanding in these respects as another friend of Paradise's—the Reverend Dr. Joseph Priestley, whose radical views in both politics and religion eventually drove him from England to the refuge of American citizenship. If there was one thing which Dr. Johnson detested more than a Whig it was a latitudinarian; Priestley was both. "Why do we hear so much of Dr. Priestley?" he once sternly and impatiently inquired. The ready answer was that it was probably because of his great scientific discoveries, and even Johnson was obliged to admit the justice of this.[8] But that did not necessarily imply a willingness to allow himself to be introduced to Priestley and to behave politely to him, rather the reverse; and Boswell, who did not like Dr. Priestley either, rashly conjectured not only that Johnson never would but actually never did allow himself to be brought into his company: "The Reverend Dr. Parr," reads a footnote to the second edition of the third volume of his *Life*, "in a late tract, appears to suppose that *Dr. Johnson not only endured, but almost solicited, an interview with Dr. Priestley.* In justice to Dr. Johnson, I declare my firm belief that he never did. My illustrious friend was particularly resolute in not giving countenance to men whose writings he considered as pernicious to society. I was present at Oxford when Dr. Price, even before he had rendered himself so generally obnoxious by his zeal for the French Revolution, came into a company where Dr. Johnson was, who instantly left the room. Much more would he have reprobated Dr. Priestley."

Dr. Parr, who dearly loved a controversy, was immediately aroused to action by Boswell's denial, Priestley being already in Pennsylvania and unable to defend himself. He wrote letters to Dr. Johnstone of Birmingham, to a Mr. Bearcroft of Francis Street, and to Samuel Rogers the poet, requesting all of them to reaffirm what he had heard them state: that they had heard Priestley himself refer to such a meeting. The replies were unanimously in favor of Priestley; all three men remembered hearing him speak of having dined with Dr. Johnson, and all three of them were under the impression, although none of them could be sure of this, that the interview had been solicited by Dr. Johnson! The dinner was at the house of Paradise, and Bearcroft in his letter recalled hearing Priestley remind Mr. Paradise of the particular civility with which Dr. Johnson had behaved toward him. Bearcroft, moreover, had taken the trouble to call on Paradise the very afternoon he wrote his letter and Paradise had said that although he did not recall the exact circumstances, he very well remembered that Johnson was previously informed that Priestley would be present and that he manifested great civility to him. Dr. Parr set all this forth in an indignant letter to the *Gentleman's Magazine*.[9] All the deponents, including

Boswell and Parr themselves, seem to have overlooked
a passage written by Priestley three years before in the
second part of his *Appeal to the Public*, in which he
had clearly stated the same facts, adding that Dr.
Johnson was not only "particularly civil to me" but
that he "promised to call upon me the next time he
should go through Birmingham."[10]

The praise that is due to Paradise for having brought
about this amicable meeting between two such foes
must be somewhat clouded when it is recalled that he,
with Sir Joshua Reynolds, was indirectly responsible
for preventing a sequel to Dr. Johnson's famous dinner
with Wilkes. It was in May, 1783, that Boswell, inspired by his former achievement, set to work to
negotiate another meeting; this time Dr. Johnson was
to dine not only in the company of Wilkes, but in his
house. The consent of Johnson having been gained,
Boswell dispatched a note to Wilkes on Wednesday,
May 21st, informing him of that fact and adding that
the invitation should be given for Monday, Tuesday,
or Wednesday of the next week. "The thing would be
so *curiously benignant*," said Boswell plaintively, "it
were a pity it should not take place." The invitation
was given for Tuesday or Wednesday, but the dinner
did not occur. Dr. Johnson, perhaps not unwillingly,
was obliged to decline:

24th May, 1783.

Dr. Johnson returns thanks to Mr. and Miss Wilkes
for their kind invitation; but he is engaged for Tuesday
to Sir Joshua Reynolds, and for Wednesday to Mr.
Paradise.[11]

Besides the many occasions on which Dr. Johnson
was a guest at Paradise's house, he was often in his

company elsewhere. On Saturday, April 24, 1779, the company at dinner at Topham Beauclerk's house in Great Russell Street, Bloomsbury, were Dr. Johnson, Boswell, Sir Joshua Reynolds, Bennett Langton, Steevens, Dr. Higgins, Paradise, and William Jones. The conversation was lively and Boswell's recording of it is in his best vein. He encouraged Dr. Johnson to talk about Garrick, who had been dead only a short time, and about the effects of drinking. Beauclerk, according to Boswell himself, was unusually entertaining and "told us a number of short stories in a lively elegant manner, and with that air of *the world* which has I know not what impressive effect, as if there were something more than is expressed, or than perhaps we could perfectly understand." Beauclerk put Dr. Johnson in a good humor by reminding him of his witticism on Taylor, the quack physician: "I remember, Sir, you said that Taylor was an instance of how far impudence could carry ignorance." But Johnson remarked as he and Boswell drove away in Sir Joshua Reynolds's coach, "There is in Beauclerk a predominance over his company, that one does not like."[12] Perhaps that was why, as Boswell recorded in his journal (although not in his *Life of Johnson*), Paradise said not a word during the evening, and Jones, usually talkative enough, little more than to ascertain what Johnson said about Wilkes having a cheerful countenance and a gay voice.[13]

Both Mr. and Mrs. Paradise were with him one evening in July, 1780, at Dr. Burney's when he was again in unusually good form. The intellectual and unimpeachable Mrs. Ord, encourager of conversation and enemy to card-playing, was there, of whom Dr.

Burney once remarked that in putting together the ingredients of society she was "an excellent cook." There was John Hoole, nephew of Dr. Johnson's "metaphysical tailor" and a learned clerk in the East India Company who wrote tragedies for the stage in heroic couplets, one of the least successful of which was "corrected" by Dr. Johnson. Hoole and Paradise had become friendly through their common interest in Italian, of which Hoole had become a sufficient master in his maturity to translate Tasso and Ariosto to Dr. Johnson's satisfaction. There was also Dr. Dunbar of Aberdeen—"acute frosty-faced little Dunbar, a man of much erudition and great good-nature"—who was a staunch defender of American rights. And there were Miss Frances Reynolds, Sir Joshua's sister; and the Castles; and Baretti; and Sir Lucas Pepys, the physician with a "firm, dictatorial manner" who was such a great friend of the Burneys. In her account of the evening Fanny Burney says that Dr. Johnson was "in high spirits and good humour, talked all the talk, affronted nobody, and delighted everybody. I never saw him more sweet, nor better attended to by his audience."[14] Dr. Johnson's own account to Mrs. Thrale is more succinct: "Pepys and I had all the talk."[15]

Besides another evening at the Burney's when Dr. Johnson and Parr were both there, an evening which also passed off pleasantly, Paradise, accompanied by his wife, had in 1780 been present by invitation at an evening party there which had turned out quite otherwise.[16] In the first place Dr. Johnson, as Susanna Burney said, had not been "in extraordinary good cue," and that of course had cast a damper over everything. It was Mrs. Paradise who provided the unfortunate

DOCTOR JOHNSON.
Portrait by Sir Joshua Reynolds.

diversion on this occasion by appearing in the splendour of full evening apparel—"dressed enough for the Pantheon," as Susanna expressed it. Although she was perhaps slightly over-dressed for the occasion, this might ordinarily have been passed off as another instance of Mrs. Paradise's eccentricity, except that, unfortunately, the other principal female guest was Miss Reynolds, who, with her "habitual perplexity of mind and irresolution of conduct," had come in *"déshabille."* This sensitive, difficult lady, who cared even less for Mrs. Paradise than Fanny Burney did, was "shocked to death" at the discrepancy, with the result that all the ladies spent a thoroughly uncomfortable evening; that is, all except Mrs. Paradise, whose unruffled elegance of manner maddeningly asserted her ignorance that anything was amiss.

All present must have been reminded of another occasion at Dr. Burney's, an evening party at which there was dancing, when Mrs. Paradise was again in one of her irresistible, imperious moods. To the utter amazement of the assembly she persuaded the crochety painter, James Barry, who was never known to dance and whose politeness was "as rare as a bit of Peg Woffington's writing," to lead her through a minuet in the "vast presence" of Dr. Johnson.[17] It was such triumphs as these that Lucy Paradise's women acquaintances found it hard to forgive or forget.

In no sense a woman's woman, Mrs. Paradise was far from popular among the bluestocking ladies who formed so large a part of the coterie of Dr. Johnson. She for her part was bored with their intellectuality, which she could not share, and they on theirs were offended with her superior airs of elegance and fashion. The fact that she could dress better, dance better, and when not victimized by her atrocious temper grace a social occasion far better than they themselves aroused their jealousy and dislike. Never were the claws of the speciously gentle Miss Burney so far extended as when Mrs. Paradise became the object of satire in her diary and letters. Laetitia Matilda Hawkins was less re-criminative, but even so all her anecdotes of Mrs. Paradise show her in a disadvantageous light. Mrs. Thrale mentioned her only once and since the occasion on which she did is narrated in a letter of Fanny Burney's, allowance must be made for the talent possessed by the author of *Evelina* in dressing up an incident, as well as for the license she always permitted herself when the faults of Mrs. Paradise were her theme.

On the afternoon in question Mr. and Mrs. Paradise had taken tea at the Burney's home. Dr. Johnson and Mrs. Thrale were also present. When the Paradises had gone, according to Miss Burney's story, Mrs. Thrale turned to Dr. Johnson and complained that she "was quite worn out with that tiresome silly woman, who had talked of her family and affairs till she was sick to death of hearing her."

"'Madam,' said he, 'why do you blame the woman for the only sensible thing she could do—talking of her family and her affairs? For how should a woman who is as empty as a drum, talk upon any other subject? —If you speak to her of the sun, she does not know it rises in the east;—if you speak to her of the moon, she does not know it changes at the full;—if you speak to her of the queen, she does not know she is the king's wife;—how, then, can you blame her for talking of her family and affairs?'"[18]

Unqualified, this appears to be a pretty sweeping condemnation of Mrs. Paradise to come from one who so frequently enjoyed the hospitality of her home, and it reflects as much discourtesy on the part of Dr. Johnson as did the distorted anecdotes of Mrs. Thrale herself, until they were brought into focus by Boswell. Unhappily Boswell never had the opportunity to qualify into accuracy the statements of Fanny Burney; she guarded them too jealously. Placed in a different light, Dr. Johnson's diatribe might actually be read as a defense of Mrs. Paradise and a rebuke to Mrs. Thrale. It is true that Mrs. Paradise was ignorant, with an ignorance that was as amazing as it was common among the women of her day; but she was pretty and vivacious, while Mrs. Thrale was merely vivacious. Knowing herself to be no match for the intellectual ladies by whom she found herself surrounded, she had doubtless assumed her most unassailable air and swept the conversation into a channel that was not out of her depth, meanwhile drawing on her reserves of beauty and high spirits to attract and hold the attention of Dr. Johnson. He, ever a willing victim to the devices of a pretty woman, had allowed himself to be seduced into a discussion of trivialities in which Mrs. Thrale and Miss Burney either could not or would not join. Mrs. Thrale's attack, delivered after the enemy had retired victorious, was hardly fair and certainly not subtle. But Dr. Johnson was willing to mollify his "mistress" with an acknowledgment of the fair one's shallowness, at the same time commending her sagacity in choosing to fight with the only weapons of which she had command.

That Dr. Johnson could regard Mrs. Paradise's eccentricities with good-natured tolerance is shown by an incident which took place at the dinner-table of Nollekens, the sculptor. Among the company was Miss Mary Moser, a distinguished painter of miniatures, who was, nevertheless, so near-sighted that she was obliged to hold her nose within an inch of the canvas. Although she did not like Mrs. Paradise, she was inspired by the general amiability of the occasion to pay her a compliment on her small, elegant figure. This was indeed a subject of much admiration. Miss Moser compared her to a sylph. Poor Mrs. Paradise, in her ignorance, supposed that "sylph" was an insulting word.

"Better to be so," she blazed out, "than to be as dull-looking and blind as a mole."

"Mole as I am," was the retort, "I never added to the weight of Paul Jodrell's phæton."

It was time for somebody to interpose, and with lumbering playfulness Dr. Johnson did so.

"Fie! fie! my dears, no sparring; off with your mufflers, and fight it fairly out!"[19]

It is only fair to Mrs. Paradise to add that this one strongly-provoked insinuation is the only shadow that contemporary records cast upon the propriety of her conduct with the opposite sex. In other respects, however, as Dr. Johnson and all their friends were well aware, she led her husband a most unhappy life. Her incredible temper, her folly in the management of her children, and her extravagance had more than once reduced the gentle Paradise to despair and actually to illness. He called it hypochondria, that being the term adopted by the age for any kind of nervous debility for which no definite physical cause was apparent. There can be little question that he confided his trouble to Dr. Johnson, who referred to it delicately in a letter and who permitted himself the satisfaction of confiding to Paradise some of the symptoms of his own peculiar form of the same complaint—that "morbid melancholy" which had been the bane of his existence ever since his early days at Lichfield.

When financial troubles were added to physical and domestic ones, Paradise again made Dr. Johnson his confidant. By the early spring of 1782, it became apparent that even the powerful aid of Benjamin Franklin had not been enough to win back the Virginia estate from confiscation. He despaired of ever regaining it, and driving in a coach with Dr. Johnson to visit the Thrales at Streatham, on the afternoon of March 21, he told him the unhappy story. Dr. Johnson was impressed, and before retiring that evening set it down in the remarkable record called his "Prayers and Meditations" in the form of a lugubrious pun: "Paradise's loss."[20]

During the early morning hours of June 17, 1783, Dr. Johnson, having retired in unusually good health and spirits, suddenly awakened and sat up in bed, feeling a "confusion and indistinctness" in his head which lasted about two minutes. "I was alarmed," he wrote Mrs. Thrale, "and prayed God, that however he might afflict my body, he would spare my understanding. This prayer, that I might try the integrity of my faculties, I made in Latin verse. The lines were not very good, but I knew them not to be very good: I made them easily, and concluded myself to be unimpaired in my faculties. Soon after I perceived that I had suffered a paralytick stroke, and that my speech was taken from me. . ."[21] He was then in his seventy-fifth year.

At daylight, still unable to speak, he wrote letters summoning assistance, (for it had "pleased God" to spare his hand,) and dispatched his Negro servant Francis Barber for Dr. Brocklesby. For two days after this attack, borne with such fortitude, he lay practically speechless; only one or two friends, he wrote, were admitted to see him. Among them was Paradise. At the end of two days he had sufficiently recovered his speech to be able to repeat the Lord's Prayer and henceforward his recovery continued to be rapid. "Nobody," he wrote Mrs. Thrale on the 21st, "has shown more affection than Paradise. Langton and he were with me a long time today."[22]

"Such was the general vigour of his constitution," says Boswell, "that he recovered from this alarming and severe attack with wonderful quickness." Two weeks after it he was able to take an airing in Hampstead and dine with the Club on the same day, and in a short time he made a visit of a fortnight to Bennet Langton at Rochester. He returned to London on the 23rd of July, but the weather being unusually hot he remained quieter than was his wont: "Since I came home I have only been to church, once to Burney's, once to Paradise's, and once to Reynolds's.[23]

There was scarcely any house in London at which Dr. Johnson was a more frequent visitor during the closing years of his life than that of John Paradise. Here he was almost always sure of meeting an agreeable company of men, most of them scholars of deep and curious learning, with a sprinkling of scientists, artists, and foreign diplomatists. The "Erse man," William Shaw, from the island of Arran and author of the first Gaelic dictionary, was sometimes there and was pronounced by Dr. Johnson to be a "modest and decent" man. There was also the erudite Jacob Bryant, librarian at Blenheim, of whom Johnson said, quoting a friend, "Bryant is a very good scholar, and knows all things whatever up to Noah, but not a single thing in the world beyond the Deluge." A lifelong friend and benefactor of Paradise's with whom he dined there was William Seward who, as Mrs. Thrale said, was always "doing good to everybody, but speaking well of nobody." It was he who, although himself a member of the Royal Society, said that the letters F. R. S. stood for Fellow Remarkably Stupid. Seward, like Johnson and Paradise and Boswell, was a confirmed hypochondriac and was accustomed to consult physicians everywhere he went on the subject of his disease; their instructions, however, he generally disregarded, preferring his own favorite remedy of strong drink. Richard Paul Joddrell and his brother Sir Paul Joddrell, M. D. (with whom he has not unnaturally been often confused), were both intimate friends of Paradise. It is the former who was Dr. Johnson's friend in whose company he often dined, both at Joddrell's own home and at Paradise's. The Joddrells were a distinguished Oxfordshire family with a country home at Lewknor. Richard Paul Joddrell was a classical scholar, a playwright, and a student of Persian. Like Paradise, he was a Fellow of the Royal Society and a D.C.L. of Oxford. His play *The Persian Heroine,* rejected for production at Covent Garden, was later acted at Drury Lane under the patronage of the Persian Ambassador. It was probably through Paradise that Dr. Johnson became acquainted with the Venetian, Count Zenobio, a liberal who was a political fugitive from almost every country in Europe except England, and one of Paradise's most intimate friends. Another visitor at the Paradise house, when he was in London, was the Italian poet, Count Alfieri; but it is doubtful if Paradise ever invited Dr. Johnson to meet the man who ran away with the Young Pretender's wife!

A year before his death Dr. Johnson founded a club which from the place of its meetings came to be known as the Essex-Head Club. Paradise was one of its twenty-four members, all of whom were chosen by Johnson himself. Sir John Hawkins, whom Johnson had deemed "a very *unclubable* man," was not invited to join, and spoke very spitefully of it indeed in his *Life of Johnson.* It was a great mortification to some of Dr. Johnson's friends, he said, to be obliged to "associate in idea the clink of the tankard, with moral disquisition and literary investigation."[24] Sir Joshua Reynolds was invited, but Dr. Johnson took pains in his letter of invitation to tell him that Barry, with whom he had had a violent quarrel, was also to be a member and Sir Joshua declined, afterwards terming the club "a strange mixture of very learned and very ingenious odd people."[25] The "learned" members he mentioned by name: Dr. Heberden, William Windham, Boswell, Steevens, and Paradise; but he said that he did not think it proper to enumerate the others. If he had, doubtless Barry's name would have led.

Boswell, among others, protested with some violence

and perfect justice against Hawkins's misrepresentation of the Essex-Head Club, mentioning Paradise as one of those whose membership gave testimony of its respectability. "I believe there are few societies where there is better conversation and more decorum." Laetitia Hawkins was afterwards obliged to acknowledge that he was right: "Boswell was well justified in his resentment of my father's designation of this same Essex-Head Club, as a sixpenny-club, meeting at an ale-house. . . I am sorry my father suffered himself to seem pettish on the subject. . . Honestly speaking, I dare say he did not like being passed over. . ."[26]

The club met, as a matter of fact, at a tavern in Essex-street which was kept by Samuel Greaves, an old servant of the Thrales. Dr. Johnson not only chose the members but laid down an elaborate set of rules, with forfeits for absence, etc. The meetings were held on Monday, Thursday, and Saturday evenings on every week in the year excepting that before Easter. The club was altogether his, and when he was ill or out of Town, attendance languished. By the kindly coöperation of its members, who found ample reward the honor of being associated with him, many of the evenings of his last year of life were eased of the dread he ever continued to feel of being left alone.

John Paradise was one of the many friends who attended Dr. Johnson on his death-bed; in the company of Langton and Count Zenobio he was with him on the second day before his death. He was also one of the select group who received an invitation to attend his funeral in Westminster Abbey:

Sir,—The Executors of the late Dr. Samuel Johnson request the favor of your attendance on Monday next,

the 20th of December inst., at 10 o'clock in the fore-
noon, at the Doctor's late Dwelling-house in Bolt
Court, Fleet Street, to accompany the corpse from
thence to Westminster Abbey.

18th December, 1784.[27]

Three mementoes of Paradise's friendship with Dr.
Johnson survive. The chief one of them is a letter
written from Lichfield, his birthplace, on his last visit
there shortly before his death. The original copy was
relinquished to Boswell for use in his biography and
was preserved among Boswell's papers at Fettercairn
Castle. No other words than those which Dr. Johnson
wrote to Paradise can so well epitomize their affectionate relationship:

Dear Sir,—Though in all my summer's excursion I
have given you no account of myself, I hope you think
better of me than to imagine it possible for me to forget
you, whose kindness to me has been too great and too
constant not to have made its impression on a harder
breast than mine. Silence is not very culpable when
nothing pleasing is suppressed. It would have alleviated none of your complaints to have read my vicissi-
tudes of evil. I have struggled hard with very formidable and obstinate maladies; and though I cannot talk
of health, think all praise due to my Creator and
Preserver for the continuance of my life. The dropsy
has made two attacks, and has given way to medicine;
the asthma is very oppressive, but that has likewise once
remitted. I am very weak, and very sleepless; but it is
time to conclude the tale of misery. I hope, dear Sir,
that you grow better, for you have likewise your share
of human evil, and that your lady and the young
charmers are well. I am, dear Sir, &c.

                                        Sam. Johnson.[28]

Lichfield, Oct. 20, 1784.

The second memento is a two-volume folio edition of his *Dictionary*, the last to be revised by its author, which is now in the Library of the College of William and Mary, having been placed there by one of the American descendants of John and Lucy Paradise. Brought to Virginia by Mrs. Paradise when she came there in 1805, it was for many years after her death, as certain marginal markings indicate, put to its intended use of instruction in the English language. The flyleaf of the first volume is unfortunately missing, but on the inside of the front covers of each volume is written in a bold and unmistakable hand: "This Book belongs to Mrs. Paradise."

The third is a rectangular table of the finest mahogany, undecorated, but gracefully designed. It, too, came with Mrs. Paradise on her summer voyage to Virginia in 1805. For more than a century it remained in Williamsburg, and although privately owned there, it was one of the proudest possessions of a locality rich in historic treasures. Lately it has emigrated to the western frontier of the State, but it still bears its rich load of association. Many of America's greatest patriots have feasted from it on the good food, good wine, and good talk provided by its host and hostess. John Adams and John Jay and Thomas Jefferson have all sat around it. But perhaps its most remarkable distinction is that between the years of 1776 and 1781 Samuel Johnson, the greatest Tory in England except the King, sat there many times, his host a naturalized American and his hostess the Virginia-born Lucy Ludwell, who never allowed her English friends to forget that her sympathies lay with her own people. No, that distinction is unique: it is the only American table at which the Great Lexicographer ever broke bread.

CHAPTER VI

Accomplished Jones

OF Paradise's many friendships with the great and near-great perhaps none was more satisfactory while it lasted than that with Sir William Jones, the Indian judge and distinguished Orientalist.[1] The two men had much in common. Contemporaries at Oxford, although Paradise was three years the senior, they were also fellow-members of the Royal Society, Jones having been elected in 1772, just a year after Paradise. Not long after, being politically in accord in their detestation of the American war and in their enthusiasm for individual liberty, they together became members of Franklin's Club of Honest Whigs.[2] Their greatest bond, however, was in scholarship. Their passionate love of learning—with Jones it was almost a sensual love—and their profound knowledge of ancient and modern languages drew and held them the closer because there were so few to share it with them.

In languages Jones was eventually to outstrip all scholars of his own or any former time. Shortly before his untimely death, he was able to state with his customary preciseness in such matters that he had studied "critically" English, Latin, French, Italian, Greek, Arabic, Persian, and Sanskrit; "less perfectly, but all intelligible with a dictionary" Spanish, Portuguese, German, Runick, Hebrew, Bengali, Hindi, Turkish; and "least perfectly, but all attainable" Tibetian, Pali, Phalavi, Deri, Russian, Syriac, Ethiopic, Coptic,

SIR WILLIAM JONES.
Oriental scholar.
From the picture in the Hall of University College, Oxford.

Welsh, Swedish, Dutch, and Chinese.[3] He was the first
Englishman ever to know Sanskrit and was the first
scholar to discover the similarities that exist among
what is since his day recognized as the Indo-European
group of languages.[4] Clearly without a rival in Europe,
he was in England almost without a companion with
whom he could converse on anything like equal terms.
Of the few who shared his knowledge to any appreci-
able extent, John Paradise, who spoke and wrote
fluently in seven languages, was the most outstanding.
Actually, since during the intimacy of the two men
Jones was still without the linguistic knowledge he
later acquired in India, Paradise then was almost his
equal. Certainly the companionship was highly valuable to Jones, for Paradise possessed an idiomatic
knowledge of modern Greek, Turkish, and Italian such
as can be gained only by early association, and could
strengthen his friend's theoretical knowledge by the
practical aid of conversation and by criticism and
correction based on experience. Jones was not a man
to fail to profit by such an opportunity.

As is so often the case with friends, the two men were
totally dissimilar in nature. Paradise was a naturally
silent, Jones a naturally fluent man. Paradise was without ambition; Jones burned with it. With Paradise
scholarship was a pleasure and a recreation; with Jones
it was a profession. Paradise was inept and inactive in
business affairs and possessed little practical knowledge
of the world; Jones, with all his scholarship, was an
adroit, experienced politician who knew how to give
and to withhold, with the utmost delicacy of touch,
just so much of his friendship and opinions as would
bring the greatest return for what he had expended.

Paradise was emotional, impulsive, and without reserve. Jones, a typical product of the age of reason, was ever guided by his mind and never once leaped, not even into matrimony, without having measured the distance and tested the ground on which he was to land. It is seldom indeed that such clarity of mind, such an uncanny ability to calculate values both material and immaterial, and such relentless force of will to carry out a preconceived design are found in a human being. And yet to judge by the opinions of almost all of his contemporaries, Sir William Jones possessed these qualities, and others, in a superlative degree.

In an age famous for its eulogies on the great, Jones received such adulation both in his lifetime and at his death as makes the eulogies on Dr. Johnson, Burke, Gibbon, Garrick, or anyone that can be named, seem paltry in comparison. "I could dwell with rapture," wrote Lord Teignmouth, "on the affability of his conversation and manners, on his modest, unassuming deportment . . . his presence was the delight of every society, which his conversation exhilarated and improved."[5] Dr. Johnson called him "one of the most enlightened of the sons of men."[6] Dr. John Johnstone said of him that he possessed "a mind whose irradiations illuminated both hemispheres of the globe, and whose intellectual powers have founded a new dynasty of learning in the colleges of Brahmah, and by a surer though slower method than that of a conquest, will finally overturn the superstition of Islam, and idolatries of the Vedas."[7] John Courtenay digressed in his poem on Dr. Johnson to chant:

Here early parts accomplished Jones sublimes,
And science blends with Asia's lofty rhimes:

Harmonious Jones! who in his splendid strains
Sings Camdeo's sports, on Agra's flowery plains;
In Hindu fictions while we fondly trace
Love and the Muses, decked with Attic grace.[8]

Dr. William Bennet, Bishop of Cloyne, and Jones's
former school-fellow at Harrow, closed his eulogy thus:
"In a word, I can only say of this amiable and wonderful man, that he had more virtues, and less faults, than
I ever yet saw in any human being; and that the goodness of his head, admirable as it was, was exceeded by
that of his heart. I have never ceased to admire him
from the moment I first saw him; and my esteem for
his great qualities, and regret for his loss, will only end
with my life."[9] George Dyer in *The Poet's Fate* celebrated a quality of Jones which most of his eulogists
neglected to mention. Recalling that after years of
solicitation from his influential friends he had been
appointed a judge in India with a salary of £8,000 per
annum, and that, though born penniless, he had died
worth £70,000, Dyer alluded to him thus:

Yet *Jones* was blest with learning and with pelf;
Courted the Muse, without forgetting self;
.   .   .   .

But whence [his] wealth? Was *Jones* the Muses'
    grudge?
Jones shone in India,—was an ermin'd Judge;
Mid circling nabobs liv'd at small expense,
And, though a poet, had some common sense.[10]

The most famous of all the tributes was made by
Dr. Thackeray, the headmaster of Harrow, while Jones
was still his pupil and a lad in his early teens. Un-
cannily penetrating, perhaps unwittingly so, was his

recognition at this early age of Jones's resourcefulness
and common sense: "If he were left naked and friend-
less on Salisbury plain, he would nevertheless find the
road to fame and riches."[11]

At Harrow, where Jones as a boy of twelve is said
to have kept himself awake with tea and coffee in order
to study longer, he was associated with Samuel Parr
and William Bennet, who were second only to him in
scholarship. It was for relaxation that these three
paragons would divide the neighboring fields into the
states and kingdoms of ancient Greece, each assuming
the name of some Homeric chieftain and defending
their domains from the rest of the boys, who were
willing enough to act the part of "barbarians."[12] Into
the companionship of this trio John Paradise was introduced in later years by Jones. At Stanmore, where Dr.
Parr maintained a school, at Paradise's house in Charles
Street, or at some convenient tavern, they would meet
to smoke, drink, and talk a night away. Conversing
frequently in Greek or in Latin, they would pounce
with avidity upon each other's lightest errors and criti-
cize each other's criticisms of other people's commentaries on ancient authors, sniffing a plagiarism or a false
quantity from afar and giving chase like a pack of
delighted hounds, with Dr. Parr in the lead. The letters which passed among this group of savants, which
also included Richard Warburton Lytton, Bennet
Langton, Dr. William Scott, and William Windham,
are as frequently in Greek, or Latin, or French, as in
English. The following letter from Jones to Parr (in
English, owing doubtless to Jones's "lippitude") gives
some reflection of the activities and political views of
the group. Parr had just published "A Discourse on

the late Fast, by Phileleutherus Norfolciensis," containing a defense of the American people and a condemnation of the war. This work, published by Dodsley, was characterized at the time as "a treatise of the highest value, abounding with acute and important observations, striking and energetic language, sublime and pathetic eloquence, seldom equalled in wisdom, piety, and animation."

Lamb Buildings, Temple, London
29th Nov. 1781

My dear Parr,

Your eloquent figures would give eyes to Tiresias himself, or compel him at least to use his tongue. The cause of my silence has been a weakness in my eyes, the remains of an inflammation in the summer, which makes it imprudent for me to read or write by the light of a candle, however shaded. In the day-time I am obliged to write and read immoderately, especially at present; and Arthur, to whom I could dictate, is in the country for his health. Of the Alcaic Ode to Liberty I have not one copy; but Paradise has engaged to reprint it, with notes, historical and explanatory. I was forced to transcribe it myself for Bennet, but I cannot *now* find leisure to copy it. I send you instead of it, a Pindaric ode, written almost extempore, on Lord Althorpe's marriage. It is incorrect and careless, but full of fire. The translation of the Ode to Pyrrha was merely a whimsical contest with Milton, who professes to have rendered it "as near the Latin measure *as may be.*" No, say I, you may approach nearer to the original measure; and I give a proof. I did not send the law tract to any but professional men; and this rule made me forget Halifax, who was entitled to a copy; but the Civilian was *merged*, as we say, in the Divine. My lippitude, which prevented me from writing, prevented me also from reading Phileleutherus; but Paradise speaks highly of it, and has promised to read it to me. The style seems very masterly, and the sentiments just. I smiled at your exhortation to *forgive* the Americans; but they will *forgive you*, and *if possible, your* Country. I have been fighting your battles in many companies, and bearing ample testimony to your *integrity*. I find more difficulty in supporting your *reasons*, especially your sheet-anchor—"that we should unite in upholding the Government, because our enemies are so numerous and virulent." What! must we, because we have many misfortunes already, add to them the last and worst of human misfortunes, a despotism in substance, with freedom in shadow? This I cannot comprehend; but I think that wise men ought to diminish, instead of increasing, the number and magnitude of their calamities. I will not exult on account of the late masterly stroke of Washington; but I confess, that I rejoice with an *exceeding great joy.* I heard much of your theses, [for Parr's LL. D. degree] and hope you will print them. I am ever happy to receive your letters, but cannot write again till Christmas. Farewell!¹³

Jones's translation of the *Ode to Pyrrha,* written "in whimsical contest with Milton," is typical of his verse, which was received by his contemporaries with solemn approbation. Milton's "dropping weeds" is improved by him into "watery vestments"; for "flattering gales unmindful" Jones prefers "unmindful of breezes fallacious"; for "plain in thy neatness" Jones substitutes "plainness elegant"; and for "vow'd picture" he gives "votive monument." The unhappy addiction of the later eighteenth-century English poets to elegant epithets and other "poetic" diction is nowhere more apparent than in Sir William Jones's poetry, which slumbers undisturbed in the six large volumes of his works which his widow issued shortly after he died.

DR. SAMUEL PARR.
Classical scholar and divine.
Photograph from the *European Magazine*, 1809, Part II.

"Careless and incorrect" his poems may or may not be; they are certainly not "full of fire."

If Jones was the brightest star in this galaxy of scholars in which Paradise moved, its shining sun was the Reverend Dr. Samuel Parr. As schoolmaster at Harrow, Stanmore, and Colchester, and later as parson at Hatton, he whirled in his fiery orbit, outshining his satellites not so much by his knowledge, which was very great and very useless, as by his robust, splenetic, independent spirit. He was often in his day compared to Dr. Johnson and fairly so, for he had a vigorous, forthright personality, great courage, and much wisdom and goodness; but he lacked his great contemporary's depth of humanity. His interests were narrower and his spirit was too contentious and recriminative. "Doctor," said a friend to him in his later years, "the public are aware of the depth and extent of your erudition, and many of us have wondered that you were never made a Bishop." The frank, animated reply was characteristic: "Aye, Sir, I think I have the stuff in me to make a Bishop of. But, Sir, I have barred my promotion by my independent spirit. Sir, I would always speak my mind. I burnt my quarters with the old gentleman [George III] by loudly protesting against that wicked American war, and with the young gentleman [George IV] I have ruined myself by taking part with his much-injured wife. . ."[14] The most honest and uncompromising of men, he was a champion of lost causes, some of them worthy of his powers but too many of them mere scholars' squabbles over which he wasted infinite ink and energy.

His ponderous frame and his wrinkled, almost ridiculously ugly countenance gave him at less than forty the appearance of an old man, but he was always hearty in conversation and up to his death a convivial companion who loved his bottle of port and pipe of tobacco. He early became a well-known figure about London, celebrated as a polemical reformist and as one of the first Greek scholars of the age. When the balloon ascensions were first in vogue he once ventured shamefaced to a field where a flight was to take place. Evidently feeling that his presence there was a little beneath the dignity of a parson and a scholar, he lingered on the outskirts of the crowd. But he was recognized, and soon a delighted London was telling the story that Dr. Parr had taken a flight in a balloon. A squib was published in the newspapers:

> What's that? what is it flying yonder?
> 'Tis Doctor Parr outflying Pindar.[15]

He was justly proud of his ability as a Greek scholar, and when Paradise introduced to him his visiting Greek friend Nicholaides, who had but little English, Dr. Parr told afterwards how they were obliged at times to converse in Greek, adding pompously, "and I endeavoured as well as I could to pronounce my accents."[16] He was actually once at a social gathering heard to quote Sophocles on the subject of a sofa.[17] The occasion of his meeting with Nicholaides was a performance by his pupils of Sophocles' *Œdipus Tyrannus* in the original language. The costumes were borrowed from Garrick by Bennet Langton and the scenery was supplied by Samuel Foote. Paradise,

Thomas Plumer, Jones, Langton and other scholarly friends were invited and the occasion was considered a success.[18]

The loveable and agreeable Bennet Langton, with whom Paradise at this time formed an enduring friendship, belonged to an ancient county family who lived at Langton near Spilsby in Lincolnshire, where Paradise frequently visited him. He was "a very tall, meagre, long-visaged man, much resembling, according to Richard Paget, a stork standing on one leg near the shore, in Raphael's cartoon of the miraculous draft of fishes."[19] He was well esteemed for his polished manners, his mild but pleasing conversation, and his learning, especially in Greek. It was he who with Topham Beauclerk, in their younger days, had "knocked up" Dr. Johnson at three o'clock in the morning, causing him to appear at the window in his shirt "with his little black wig on the top of his head, instead of a nightcap, and a poker in his hand, imagining, probably, that some ruffians were coming to attack him." When he saw who it was, he fell with great good humor into the spirit of the occasion exclaiming, "What, is it you, you dogs! I'll have a frisk with you."[20]

A conservative in politics, Langton did not care for Edmund Burke, whom he protested was rude and violent in conversation, and that "if anyone asserted that the United States were wrong in their quarrel with the mother country, or that England had a right to tax America, Burke, instead of answering his arguments, would, if seated next to him, turn away in such a manner as to throw the end of his own tail into the face of the arguer."[21] In spite of his Toryism Langton was well liked by the contentious Dr. Parr and most of the

members of his circle, who, like Paradise, his closest
friend there, were extremist Whigs. William Jones
was the one member of the group who was not friendly
to him. "Captain [Langton]," he remarked malicious-
ly, "is one of the worthiest, as well as tallest men in the
kingdom; but he, and his Socrates, Dr. Johnson, have
such prejudices in politics, that one must be upon one's
guard in their company, if one wishes to preserve their
good opinion."[22]

In 1778 England was at war with France and Spain
as well as with America and some fear arose of an
invasion from the combined French and Spanish forces.
The militia was called out and during the spring and
summer the country became dotted with camps. "The
King's behavior," jeered Horace Walpole, "was childish and absurd. He ordered the camp equipage, and
said he would command the army himself."[23] The
camps immediately became the fashion, and everybody
who could paid a visit to one of them. That on Warley
Common, because of its close proximity to London, was
the most popular. Bennet Langton was stationed here
first as a captain and later as a major of the Lincolnshire Militia, where he was visited by General Paoli,
Sir Joshua Reynolds, and Dr. Johnson. Dr. Johnson
was enormously impressed. During his week's stay he
sat patiently through a regimental court-martial, made
the rounds of the guard at eleven o'clock at night, and
conversed expansively with the officers on gun-powder
and other military topics. During a drill, he walked
close up to the men and peered at them attentively,
remarking, "The men indeed do load their musquets
and fire with wonderful celerity."[24] To Mrs. Thrale he
afterwards wrote: "A camp, however familiarly we

may speak of it, is one of the great scenes of human
life."[25] Very early on the morning of August 27, Mr.
and Mrs. Paradise drove in their carriage out to Warley with their Greek friend Nicholaides. Langton was
"very agreeably surprised" to see them and invited
them to breakfast in his tent and afterwards showed
them all the sights.[26] Soon after this Dr. Parr visited
Langton at the camp and passed a convivial evening
with him and his fellow officers. A friend of Parr's
once said of him that he could drink more wine than
any man he ever saw for one "who did not mean to get
drunk." After Parr's return, Jones wrote accusingly to
him: "I have heard of the evening which you passed
at Warley in Langton's tent."[27]

The friendship of Jones and Paradise, founded and
long continued on their common interests in scholarship
and politics, was destined to have still another basis.
Early in life Jones had considered entering the profession of law. He had even begun to read for it while he
was a student at Oxford and had found much interest
in the subject. Soon, however, he gave it up. The bad
Latin in which most of the old law books were written
was, he declared, too offensive to his scholar's ear. In
1765 he accepted a post as tutor to the son of Lord
Spencer. He lived and traveled luxuriously in the
Spencer household for almost ten years, perfecting
himself in Persian and Arabic and acquiring the accomplishments of dancing and performing on the
Welsh harp. There then occurred a misunderstanding
between him and Lady Spencer about the educational
method he was pursuing for her son. Soon afterwards

Jones published his "Commentaries on Asiatick Poetry." This closed with "an elegant address to the Muse" announcing that he would thenceforth abandon polite literature and devote himself entirely to the pursuit of the law. He took up residence at the Middle Temple, nobly overcame his aversion to bad Latin, and was called to the bar in 1774.[28] This was fortunate for Paradise, who now for the first time began to have need of legal advice.

On the outbreak of the American Revolution, Paradise's income from his wife's estate in Virginia was at once cut off. All trade between Great Britain and the newly-formed "Commonwealth of Virginia" immediately ceased. The Virginia Assembly, by its resolution of June 15, 1776, caused the property of the Royal Governor, Lord Dunmore, to be seized and placed in the hands of commissioners.[29] Although no law was passed on the subject until later, this action determined Virginia's policy toward all British property holders. Henceforth for many years Paradise, who was presumably a British subject, did not receive a single penny of income from the Virginia estate.

At first the situation was not particularly alarming. The war would not last forever and there were few people in England who in the first years of it ever imagined that the Colonies would win complete independence. Moreover, Paradise possessed a small income of his own from the English funds; Peter Paradise too was still alive and might reasonably be expected to make up the temporary shortage in his son's income. He was seventy years of age and of more than ample means. The prospects of John and Lucy Paradise could not have seemed completely discouraging, even if they should be permanently deprived of their Virginia income, an eventuality which seemed unlikely enough in 1776.

It was at this most unfortunate of all times that there occurred a serious quarrel between John Paradise and his father. Peter Paradise was as warm a Tory as his son was a Whig. His life had been spent in the Levant Company, an organization dominated by the family of Lord North who was the willing instrument of the King's unyielding policy toward the Colonies. Of this policy Peter Paradise was a staunch defender. He approved the war as much as John Paradise deplored it. At seventy he was not too old to defend his views with vigor against a son who was, in the words of Thomas Jefferson, "from principle a pure republican." According to Jefferson, John Paradise's "attachment to the American cause and his candid warmth brought him sometimes into altercations on the subject with his father, and some persons interested in their variance artfully brought up this subject of conversation whenever they met. It produced a neglect in the father. He had already settled on him a sum of money in the funds, but would do no more and probably would have undone that if he could. When remittances from Virginia were forbidden the profits of the Virginia estate were carried into our loan office. Paradise was then obliged to begin to eat his capital in England; from that to part with conveniences and to run in debt."[30]

Meanwhile further difficulties arose in Virginia. In October, 1777, there was introduced into the House of Delegates "An Act for Sequestering British Property."[31] By the passing of this act the earlier policy became the law. It meant that the Paradises' Virginia

property, real and personal, was to be temporarily
taken over by the Commonwealth of Virginia. The
profits from the estate, as well as any money already
owing to Paradise by citizens of Virginia, would be
converted into Virginia bonds and held for the owner,
presumably until the end of the war. The Governor
and the Council were delegated to appoint both a
commissioner and an agent for the property. It was
naturally of the greatest importance to Paradise that
the men appointed to these positions should be friendly
to his interests. However, long before he could have
taken any action in the matter, probably before the
news of the Act's passing had reached him in England,
his wife's cousins the Lees had begun to take a hand.
On January 25, 1778, Richard Henry Lee wrote a
letter to Governor Patrick Henry requesting that Mr.
Ellis, William Lee's manager at Green Spring, should
under the new law be appointed agent for Paradise's
property. He also requested that his cousin, Henry
Lee, be appointed commissioner for it. In regard to
the appointment of Ellis, he urged that the two estates
could be made to pay better under single management;
and in regard to Henry Lee, that he was Mrs. Paradise's uncle (actually he was her uncle-in-law) and
consequently might be supposed friendly to her interests.[32] There was one advantage, from his own and his
brother's point of view, that Lee did not see fit to point
out. This was that the entire Ludwell property would
be, for the time being at least, under the control of the
Lee family, whose motto, "Non Incautus Futuri," may
be appropriately quoted here.

Richard Henry Lee was at this time one of the most
powerful men in Virginia and he was also a close friend

of Governor Henry. It therefore seems surprising that
his request should have been disregarded, and yet such
was the case. Shortly after it was received, the following order appeared in the Journal of the House of
Delegates:

> Cary Wilkerson esquire is appointed, by the Gover-
> nor & Council, Commissioner for the Estate of . . .
> Paradise in the Counties of York James City &
> Surry . . .[33]

It was one of Paradise's few pieces of good fortune in
the whole affair that the friendly, if not very efficient
Cary Wilkinson should have been put in charge of
his estate.

Owing to the general confusion William Lee had
also been deprived, quite unfairly, of his income from
Virginia. Worse than this, he had still not received by
the end of 1778 a single cent from Congress for his
services as commercial agent. As a final blow the news
reached him in Frankfurt-on-the-Main that his houses
in Williamsburg had been used as a barracks for
American troops and "very greatly damaged thereby."[34] In his despair he decided again to sell the entire
estate. On October 15, 1778, he sat down and wrote
four frantic letters on the subject.[35] One was to Richard
Henry Lee; one was to Francis Lightfoot; one was
addressed jointly to "Squire" Richard Lee, Robert
Carter Nicholas, Richard Henry Lee, and Francis
Lightfoot Lee; the fourth and last was addressed to
Richard Henry and Francis Lightfoot Lee jointly. It
is easy to read between the feverish, repetitious lines of
these letters that the cautious merchant was in the
throes of desperation at being obliged to entrust his

affairs to anyone else. In the extremity of his caution, he endeavored to make each of his brothers feel that that brother alone was the real recipient of his confidence. In the most impassioned language, he assured each of them, separately and collectively, that the fate of himself, his wife, and his helpless little ones was in their hands. They must sell the estate as a whole or not at all. He said that he and Hannah Philippa wished their children to have a landed inheritance in America and thought of investing the money in the new lands on the Ohio River. However, if it did not seem advantageous to sell at this time, they must not do so. With the air of one who was staking the last remnant of his fortune upon a wheel of chance, he enclosed a Power of Attorney signed by himself and his wife. Poor William Lee! It is more than probable that none of his letters reached Virginia for more than a year. At any rate nothing was done about selling the estate, and the next news he had of it was that a battle had been fought upon his very land, only a few miles from Green Spring itself, between Lafayette and Cornwallis, that he had been robbed by the English of sixty or seventy slaves, and that the mansion at Green Spring was in a "ruinous" condition! It may or may not have been some mitigation to his distress to learn that at the same time Paradise had lost all his slaves but one.[36]

By June of 1778 the news of the Sequestration Act had thrown Paradise into a profound state of dejection. For the first time he realized the very real danger of losing his property altogether. Moreover, his annual income had for the past three years been reduced by five or six hundred pounds, owing to the quarrel with his father. The expensive scale on which he and Lucy

continued to live made it necessary for him to delve
more into the English principal and to run more and
more into debt. It was now that he turned for help to
William Jones, whom he made not only his legal ad-
visor but the guardian of his two daughters as well.
Jones seemed in all respects an excellent choice, possessing, besides his other qualities, more knowledge of
the world and of the conduct of affairs than Paradise
ever was to have. Jones urged that Paradise should go
at once to Virginia, and offered many plausible reasons
for his doing so. Married to a Virginia woman whose
family had for generations played a conspicuous part
in affairs of the State and himself a known advocate of
American independence, he would have been welcomed
as a friend. The complications over his wife's property
would have immediately been resolved. "But you
know," wrote Jones to Arthur Lee at this time, "how
incapable he is, with all his good qualities, of stirring
for himself in active life."[37]

There was more reason in Paradise's refusal to go to
Virginia at this stage than there was to be later. The
wording of the act for sequestration was by no means
unfriendly to the property owners and their money was
to be, so to speak, only "borrowed" by the Commonwealth and returned with interest when the hostilities
were over—if the Colonies were victorious. If they
were not, then Paradise as an English resident would
certainly receive indemnity, a chance which he would
lose if he definitely established himself as an American
by going to Virginia. Moreover, there was still the
hope of a reconciliation with his father, now in his
seventy-fifth year. Whatever his reasons, Paradise per-
sistently refused to act.

Meanwhile his inaction, well or ill-advised, was brought to an end by the death of Peter Paradise on February 1, 1778.[38] Definitely excluded from his father's will, his only resource, except for what was left of the money in the funds, was Lucy's Virginia estate. Thus his financial interests were now where his political interests had always been—in America. This and the added fact that his losses in England were owing to his friendship for the Colonies naturally caused him to turn to America and to the friends of America for help.

It is not possible to say who suggested that he should solicit the aid of Benjamin Franklin. There was every reason for him to do so. He was assured of a friendly reception not only from their association in the Royal Society but also through Franklin's former friendship with his father-in-law, Philip Ludwell. Later circumstances indicate that it was probably Jones, as Paradise's counsel, who proposed the step. If so he had the important backing of two of Franklin's closest friends, Dr. Price and Dr. Priestley. In any case on May 20, 1779, a little more than three months after the death of Peter Paradise, John Paradise and William Jones arrived at Paris and took lodgings at the Hotel du Port Mahon in the Rue Jacob. Immediately they dispatched a note to Franklin at Passy:

Mr. Paradise and Mr. Jones present their best respects to Dr. Franklin. They are just arrived at Paris; and, as they were desired by their worthy friends, Dr. Price and Dr. Priestley, to deliver to him their publications, they have left the books and letters at Passy, where they propose to have the honor of waiting upon the most respectable of patriots and philosophers, on any morning when they hear that he is likely to be at leisure.[39]

CHAPTER VII

Citizen Paradise

SOON after receiving their polite note, Franklin sent Paradise and Jones an invitation to dine with him. In May, 1779, he was still living in one of the outer buildings of Donatien Le Ray de Chaumont's handsome chateau at Passy.[1] His household consisted of himself and his grandson—William Temple Franklin—a French clerk, and three servants. Ordinarily he took his meals at the table of M. de Chaumont, but on occasions like the present one when he desired private conversation it was his custom to have his meals served in his own apartments by his own servants from de Chaumont's pantry. Passy was then a suburban village, with villas, several chateaux like the Hotel de Valentinoir at which he lived, a parish church, and shops. It was on a hill-top overlooking the Seine, and only a few minute's pleasant drive along a paved road from Paris.

Franklin's appearance, though familiar, must have struck the two visitors from London with new force. He was seventy-four years of age, stout, and so crippled with the gout that he was obliged to use a cane as he walked, according to his custom, across the lawn to greet his guests. His straight hair, grown thin, was brushed back from his high, benignant forehead, beneath which his eyes, gleaming with awareness of the world around him, at once corrected a first impression of passivity and complacence. Age and experience had lined his face with many wrinkles, but his whole ex-

pression was one of calm, unboastful triumph over life.
As always he wore glasses, contrary to the custom
though it was. His clothes were of plain brown cloth,
unrelieved by embroidery. Sage, philosophic, vener-
able—none of these words so often applied to him
seemed sufficient for a man whose appearance reflected
intelligence that was cosmic, and knowledge as varied
and complex as life itself.

Paradise and Jones could not have selected a more
favorable time to visit Franklin in Paris. He was easily
the greatest celebrity there. Several years of residence
among the French people had won for him their enthusiastic affection and respect, and he in turn was completely sympathetic with them. He avowed that unlike
other peoples they had no national fault; even their
frivolity was "harmless." Throughout his stay he wisely
maintained an aloofness, aided by his residence at Passy,
that was calculated to perpetuate his popularity. This
popularity he enjoyed, but he accepted it gracefully
and with dignity. His calm, unruffled manner, his wit,
his cleverly maintained semblance of naïveté, and above
all his unique, though distinguished, personal appearance appealed tremendously to French taste. "Figure
to yourself," he wrote, "an Old Man, with grey Hair
appearing under a Martin Fur Cap, among the Powder'd Heads of Paris." The vogue for the "natural"
man was then so great among the French and in their
view Franklin so completely fitted the rôle that nothing
he could do but added to the delightful picture. Even
his fur cap was regarded as some special trans-Atlantic
badge of honor. The adroitness with which he played
the part that came to be expected of him and the innate

good sense that prevented him from ever overdoing it
had been important factors in winning for the Colonies
the badly needed aid of the French.

Shortly before the arrival of his English guests,
Franklin had received from Congress his credentials as
Minister Plenipotentiary, delivered to him by young
Lafayette. On March 23, he had been graciously received at Court in his new capacity. For more than a
year now, he was to enjoy some respite from the strenuous life he had been obliged to lead and was to lead
again during the negotiations for peace. The appointment from Congress had freed him from the quarrel-
some importunities of Arthur and William Lee, with
their endless allegations of dishonesty against himself,
his nephew, and his friend, Silas Deane. These had
proved very upsetting indeed. Less upsetting, but difficult enough, had been the necessity to work with a man
like John Adams, who also disliked him and who half
believed the accusations of the Lees. Now all that was
over and for a time he was to be comparatively undisturbed in carrying on the work of America's unrivalled,
in fact almost her only representative abroad. The
comparative peace and leisure of his present life
enabled him to welcome his visitors with unalloyed
cheerfulness.

Ordinarily Franklin was cold and reserved to
strangers, but according to Priestley, "where he was
intimate, no man indulged in more pleasantry and good
humour."[2] To Jones and Paradise he was friendly from
the beginning, favoring them with his "kind notice"
during their entire stay in Paris. "We dined with him
twice and conversed with him frequently," said Jones.[3]
They had other interests in common besides their

friends. With Paradise Franklin could discuss the
activities of the Royal Society: the newest theories
about "inflammable air" about which Paradise had
read a paper a few weeks before, the reports on experiments in electricity which Franklin's own discoveries
had stimulated, the quarrel about the blunt and pointed
conductors which had not long ago resulted in Pringle's
resignation as President. Politically the three men were
in almost perfect agreement. The two visitors conveyed
the latest news from England, news which they had
canvassed with Franklin's oldest group of friends, the
Club of Honest Whigs. And Franklin doubtless told
them as much as he wished them to know about developments in America and France.

Such conversations between Englishmen and Americans during the Revolution, although at first thought
they may seem surprising, were actually far from
uncommon. The radical wing of the Whig party, to
which Paradise and Jones belonged, differed little in
political opinion from the Americans themselves. Few
of them, it is true, were advocates of complete independence for America and yet in all but that they were
eager for her success. They looked on George III and
his Tory ministers as tyrants who in violating the rights
of the Colonies were endangering the liberty of all his
other subjects. As Jones wrote Franklin from England,
on the very eve of the battle of Yorktown, "All virtue
and public spirit are dead in this country: we have the
shadow merely of a free constitution but live in truth
under the *substance* of despotism."[4] Such words, coming at this time from an Englishman who not many
months before had sought a seat in Parliament and
who was to accept a lucrative appointment under the

JOSEPH PRIESTLEY.

Scientist and Liberal.

An engraving from the statue by Williamson.

Government in less than a year, seem almost treasonable until we reflect that they represent the expressed opinion of a considerable group. In fact the interests and point of view of the English Whigs and the Americans, many of whom had been born in England, must have created some confusion at the time as to where the Englishman ended and the American began. There were many instances where individuals failed to make the distinction for themselves, a situation which led to some harsher judgments of so-called traitors than were perhaps deserved. It was not until 1783, when the independence which America had long since won was finally acknowledged by England, that one could point to certain individuals and say with finality, "That man is an English Whig," or "That man is an American." Franklin and other Americans in Paris received during the War many visits from friends in England, such as was now being paid by Paradise and Jones.

Jones found enough time to spare from his activities on Paradise's behalf to perform an action entirely characteristic of him and one which was to have startling repercussions later on. During some idle hours in his room at the Hotel du Port Mahon, he "amused himself" by writing an allegorical essay which he delivered to Dr. Franklin, who easily read between the lines. Under the pretense of being a "Fragment of Polybius" it presented the situation as it then existed between the United States (the Islands) and England (Athens). Louis XVI figured as Mausolus and France as Caria, the ally of the Islands. Franklin was represented as Eleutherion, a philosopher sent to Caria, "eminent for the deepest knowledge of nature, the most solid judgment, most approved virtue, and most ardent zeal for the cause of general liberty." The purport of it all was to persuade Franklin that England would never consent to give up the Colonies and that there was "a *natural* union between her and the islands, which the gods have made, and which the powers of hell cannot dissolve." The only course for America was to give up her dream of being a separate nation and sue for peace on terms of "independence" but not "disunion." The "Athenian," *alias* Jones, said that the idea of such a peace "fills and expands my soul and *if* it cannot be realized, I shall not think it less glorious, but shall only grieve more and more at the perverseness of mankind." Jones sent this effusion to Franklin in a letter on the 28th of May, in the hope that it might possibly afford him "some little amusement."[5] Doubtless Franklin, a realist if there ever was one, was "amused" in a way that Jones did not intend.

Franklin found an opportunity to take Paradise to call on his friend Madame Helvétius.[6] This lady was now well on in middle age, but she still possessed her ability to charm men and inspire other women with envy. She lived in a small villa at Auteuil, the next village to Passy, on the edge of the Bois de Boulogne. Here she kept her lively salon, of which Franklin was a most intimate and beloved frequenter. Nothing could have been more French than it was. A large room, furnished with chairs and settees, it contained the usual superfluity of pictures and small ornaments. In the center was a marble table on which was a set of china, a number of small figurines, and a circle of earth in which was planted a miniature forest. The room was alive with pets: the inevitable lapdog, an English bull-dog presented by Franklin, and innumerable birds,

domestic and wild. Mrs. John Adams and her daughter
Abigail, fresh from Boston in 1784, found the manners
of Madame Helvétius to be extremely free and easy.
When one of her pets had soiled the floor, she did not
turn away and pretend not to notice it, but ordered a servant to come and clean the mess up. And then she called
Dr. Franklin merely "Franklin" and held his hand in
public and put her arm around his neck. Mrs. Adams
found it hard to believe Franklin's assurance that she
really was one of the best women in the world. "For
this I must take the Doctor's word," she said; "but I
should have set her down for a very bad one."[7] The
younger Abigail was even more severe: "Odious indeed do our sex appear when divested of those ornaments, with which modesty and delicacy adorn them."[8]
Although Mme. Helvétius must have been a beautiful
woman when she was young, Miss Adams thought that
she had now been well compared to the "ruins of
Palmyra." Ruin or not, she continued to charm the
men. From Paradise she secured the promise to bring
her some of the exotic red birds, (so much desired by
every fashionable woman in Europe at this time,) when
he should go to Virginia. Eight years later he had not
forgotten.

Franklin was able to give Paradise considerable help
in his affairs. Besides writing several letters to persons
of influence in Virginia, including one to Thomas
Jefferson,[9] he advised Paradise in the writing of letters
of his own and allowed these to be sent under his own
cover, one of the few safe means of conveyance at this
hazardous time.

On one of the very days when Paradise was advising with Franklin in Paris about his estate in Virginia, an event of very far-reaching consequences to that very affair was transpiring in the Virginia Assembly in Williamsburg. Thomas Jefferson, who was later to give Paradise more help than he ever received from anyone else, was appointed to draw up a bill "Concerning Escheats and Forfeitures from British Subjects."[10] This was ordered on May 27, 1778, and Jefferson drew it up and presented it on the same day, just four days before he was elected Governor of Virginia. After being read before the Assembly the customary number of times, the bill became a law on June 11. This new law, of which Franklin and Paradise were to remain in ignorance for weeks, in effect cancelled the former act of sequestration and declared that all real property of British subjects should be escheated and all personal property forfeited, and "shall be deemed to be vested in the commonwealth." A British subject was defined in part as any subject "of his Britannick majesty" who had been absent from the United States on April 19, 1775—the date of the battle of Lexington—and had not since returned and adhered to the United States by some overt act. To John Paradise, who had never been in the United States, and to Lucy, who had not returned there since she left in 1760, this meant that their property was to be confiscated by the State of Virginia. Even if Franklin had known about this new law, it is unlikely that he could have been more helpful to Paradise than he actually was, by giving him, through the letters referred to, the powerful support of his friendship.

Encouraged by Dr. Franklin's help and delighted at the cordial reception he had been accorded, Paradise made his arrangements to leave for England with Jones early in June. Owing to a complication about their passport, they appealed to Franklin again and he readily gave them one signed by himself, a document which they proposed to keep "as a valuable testimony of his friendship." Jones requested Franklin to prevaricate to the extent of describing Paradise as "an American gentleman, *born in Greece*."[11] The facts that he had never been in America and had as yet taken no steps to become a naturalized citizen were to be swept aside in the consideration that he owned property there and was politically sympathetic. Besides, who was to say at this time just what constituted being an "American?" Jones summed up the results of the journey concisely in writing to Parr: "We had more success than I expected; our friend has some chance of receiving the profits of his Virginian estate."[12]

Not long after returning to London Paradise received news from Virginia of the new law concerning escheats. This required prompt action, and for once he gave it. Acting no doubt on advice from Franklin and Jones he instructed his manager, Cary Wilkinson, to present a petition to the autumn session of the General Assembly of Virginia. This Wilkinson did on October 26, 1779, setting forth "that a considerable estate of . . . John Paradise which he held in right of his wife, who is a native of this country, hath been found, by inquisitions lately had thereon, to be forfeited. . ."[13] This was only too true. No time had been lost in forming courts of inquisition in the various counties and in York, James

City, and Surry, piece after piece of the Paradise
property had been formally confiscated by the Commonwealth.[14] Paradise petitioned on the ground that
he was not a British subject but "a native of Thessalonica in Greece, and only resident in England from
commercial views having never been a naturalized
subject thereof, has been uniformly attached to the
American cause."

Even before Paradise's petition was presented, action
favorable to his case had been begun. The definition of
British subjects in the Act of the preceding spring was
manifestly unfair. It meant that many loyal American
citizens were condemned to lose their property from
the mere accident of having been absent from the
country at the stated time, citizens who, owing to circumstances beyond their control, had been prevented
from returning since. From the beginning of October,
petitions poured in from such injured property-owners.
A committee, with General Thomas Nelson as chair-
man and George Mason as one of its fifteen members,
was promptly appointed to draw up an amendment to
the Act. It was to this committee that Paradise's petition was referred. At length, on November 16, the
committee recommended certain changes which were
adopted by the General Assembly.[15]

In a letter to Franklin, referring to this amendment,
William Jones stated that Paradise was "certainly
described particularly and by design in a special
clause" and that the clause was "inserted through
indulgence in consequence of his letter sent in your
dispatches."[16] This seems to be an exaggeration, for it
is impossible to detect in the general wording of the

amendment any particular description of Paradise's case. However, there is no doubt that in some round-about way Franklin's influence was definitely helpful, for the courts of inquisition, which continued to be held over other people's property, were discontinued on Paradise's by the middle of November.

It was almost a year before he acted again in the matter. The cessation of the courts of inquisition had set his mind at ease for the present and better than that the new amendment allowed him two full years of grace. Perhaps by that time the war would be over, (as it very nearly was,) and then if the voyage to Virginia were still necessary it could be made with far less risk. Meanwhile, with the advice of Jones and Dr. Franklin, he resolved on taking an important and almost unprecedented step. This resolution involved another visit to Franklin in Paris and on September 18, 1780, Paradise and Jones again embarked from Dover. Jones was vastly excited and a little awed at himself for the assistance he was about to give his friend in acting so boldly. Before leaving, he dashed off a mysterious note to Dr. Parr:

September 17, 1780

My dear Parr,

To-morrow I set out for Paris, in dangerous times, and at a dangerous season. I hope to return in a month; but if it should please the Author of my being to put an end to my existence on earth, I request you and Bennet, my oldest friends, to examine all my papers and letters, which you will find in my chamber, and to compose an account of my life, studies, and opinions (as far as you know them); but to take care that no unfinished work of mine shall see the light, much less any idle thing that you may meet with in my drawers.

I hope you are restored to health and strength. I would write more, but am very much engaged. Farewell, and believe me wholly yours,

W. Jones[17]

In spite of Jones's forebodings, the two travelers arrived safely at Paris. This time they put up at the Hotel de Dannemare, also in the Rue Jacob. They were received with great cordiality by Dr. Franklin as his "valuable friends." The seeming enthusiasm of Jones for the American cause and that of Paradise, which was about to be proved sincere in an unmistakable way, had completely won him. The successful object of the journey is disclosed in a letter from Paradise to Franklin:

Dear Sir,

Since I shall have the happiness (and I shall ever esteem it a great one) of seeing you at Passy tomorrow morning I would not at this time trouble you with a letter if I were not extremely anxious to be honoured with your company at dinner, and consequently fearful lest you should be previously engaged on the day when I shall have the happiness of becoming a complete member of an American republick, a day, on which I shall through life reflect with pleasure, and which I therefore am desirous of celebrating with the ambassadour. What higher pleasure, indeed, can be felt by a man, who may without vanity profess himself a lover of liberty and virtue, than to be admitted as an affectionate and zealous citizen by one of those illustrious states, who by the noblest exertions of unexampled virtue, have established their liberty on the surest basis. Mr Searle and such American gentlemen as I have the honour of knowing at Paris, will favour me with their company at half an hour after two o'clock and, if din-

ing in town be not contrary to any rule that you may
have made, I cannot express how much I should think
myself honoured and flattered if the excellent ambassadour of those States and his amiable grandson will
partake a republican dinner with, dear Sir,

Your much obliged
and ever grateful servant

John Paradise.[18]

Hotel de Dannemare
Rue Jacob
2 Octr 1780.

The note of sincere enthusiasm which sounds through
the formal phrases of this letter is not the only proof
we have that Paradise, in becoming one of the first
naturalized Americans, was motivated by deeper causes
than self-interest. He well knew that the step he was
taking would be of much discomfort to him in his life
in England and of misunderstanding by people who
did not know him well. There were some, like Dr.
Johnson, who not only continued to give him their
friendship but gave it in fuller measure and this, at a
time when feelings were aroused to such a pitch, was
no small tribute to him. There were others, however,
to whom his becoming an American made a difference
that was great and important to him; but never once
did either he or Mrs. Paradise express a word of regret
at his action—even when his American citizenship not
only failed to win him justice but heavily added to his
burdens. Throughout all their vagaries, neither of them
ever wavered in their loyalty to America.

Paradise and Jones remained in Paris until mid-
October and then set out for England laden as before
with messages and letters from Franklin to his friends,

in which he spoke with emphasis of the pleasure he had received from their company.[19] As for Paradise, in his patriotic fervor for his adopted country he had decided to set sail for it almost at once. He would not only go to Virginia and settle his affairs but he would become a citizen there in deed as well as in name. His family must remain behind for the present until he could prepare a place for them to live. The war over, they would settle at Rich Neck or Chippokes or perhaps at one of the houses in Williamsburg, where he would lead the life of a scholarly gentleman farmer. But after his arrival in London the enthusiasm somehow began to die away. His wife was not as keen for the proposal as he had anticipated, and besides the winter was about to begin and that was hardly the time for a sea voyage that could be postponed. He would go in the spring. But in the spring he was obliged to write to Franklin that "affairs" would for a time detain him in England. Franklin, in writing again to Jefferson on the Paradises' behalf, made out the best case he could for them. They were unable to leave England for the present, he wrote, but it was "their Intention . . . to go to Virginia as soon as possible; and as they have ever been firm in the Sentiments of good Americans, I hope their Absence will not be prejudicial to them. . ."[20]

This was in May, 1781, but by September Paradise had still made no move, although his business affairs were drifting into a worse and worse condition and the time limit set for his appearing in Virginia was within a few months of expiring. He was in one of those lamentable and pitiable states of indecision of which he was to become more and more the victim. "Poor Paradise is very unhappy about his affairs in Virginia," wrote Jones to Franklin, "since the term limited for his appearance there is nearly expired. Have the kindness to send your advice and mandate, *Qu'il aille*, or *qu'il reste*: if the former be your direction, will a French frigate be his best conveyance, or could he, without offending his countrymen, go to New York, [New York was at this time in the hands of the British] and thence, with a flag and proper certificates, to his estate? he ought to be on it before next January."[21] It would have been "poor Paradise" indeed, if he had arrived in Virginia at this time, whether by land or sea. The Battle of Green Spring, fought partly on his land, and the Battle of Yorktown, fought at the port where he most likely would have landed, would have provided a lively welcome for him to a land where liberty was in the act of being born.

Soon after this, a respite arrived for him in the form of a remittance from Virginia. This and the news of Yorktown encouraged him to delay his journey still longer. Although the money was the first he had received for years, the ever-watchful William Lee got wind of it as far away as Brussels, where he was now residing with his family. He was furious. He wrote at once to his brother Arthur, who was now in Virginia. Paradise, he said reproachfully, has received "a remittance of between 3 & 400 £ st^r in bills, from his steward, which is double of what I have received. Pray explain this to me."[22]

The good will between the families of Paradise and Lee which this stroke of good fortune interrupted had dated at least from the beginning of 1780, at which

time the two sisters were in regular correspondence. In
March of that year, when the Lees' second daughter
was born, Paradise had received a letter in William's
most jocose and friendly style, which incidentally gives
the perfect description of a new-born baby: "The
Infant is as compleat in form as a fond Parent can
wish. . ." Little Cornelia had already been christened
and her father went on to say in the most tentative way
that he had ventured to make Paradise's daughter Lucy
her godmother. But if there were the slightest objection on the part of Mr. and Mrs. Paradise or his niece,
he himself would take on "ye serious obligation of y^e
solemn contract entered into." Belgium, he declared
was a country where "Nature seems to have poured out
with a liberal hand her choicest gifts on a stubborn,
heavy, & ungrateful race," a remark perhaps colored
by the lack of success of his diplomatic and business
ventures there. Friendly as he meant his letter to be,
William Lee could not resist one jealous dig at the
Paradises for their pretensions to fine living and high
society. He said that if they should ever come to
Belgium he and his wife would be happy to see them in
their "little peaceful tenement where no gaudy Grandeur shews its face, but where more quiet & contentment
reigns y^n is to be found in all the Pallaces in Europe."[23]

It was not until late in the spring of 1782 that Paradise finally made his decision to go to Virginia. All
along his hesitation had been due in part to his dread
of going alone, and about this time he was overjoyed to
learn that his friend William Jones might for reasons
best known to himself be persuaded to go with him.

"My friend of Virginia must very soon set out for
his State," Jones wrote Franklin in March, "of which

he will be an excellent citizen. Should I accompany
him, I shall again have the happiness of enjoying your
conversation at Passy. I have no wish to grow old in
England; for, believe me, I would rather be a peasant
with freedom than a prince in an enslaved country."[24]
This remark about "prince" and "peasant" may or may
not have sounded well to Franklin's ears, it being the
sort of cant that was on the lips of all the liberals of
the time. The truth was that Jones, his eye ever fixed
on the main chance, was beginning to suspect that the
main chance for him was no longer in England but
America. Pennsylvania was the state he had in mind.
There, with Franklin's backing, he saw excellent prospects for a learned young lawyer who could instruct the
crude but liberty-loving Americans in the ways of the
British constitution. The British constitution was also
very much his concern these days and he had recently
become active in a club whose object was to preserve it.
The purposes of that club may have supplied him with
another motive for going to America. Still another, a
negative one, was the lack of success he had met with
in his efforts to obtain an Indian judgeship. Owing to
the enmity of the conservative Lord Thurlow, in whom
the appointment rested, his chances had begun to seem
very slight indeed.

To Paradise, Jones's only avowed motive was simple
kindness—kindness that was of course to be compensated for out of the proceeds from the Virginia estate.
Eager to have him, Paradise urged him to go with
every argument he could summon, and at length Jones
allowed himself to be "persuaded." In an angry but
scholarly letter to Edmund Burke, he complained in
Greek, Latin and English of the minister who had

thwarted his efforts to obtain the Indian judgeship and then he announced his decision: "My situation for the past four years having ruined me at Westminster Hall, where I was certain of brilliant success, I have accepted the management of Mr. Paradise's cause in Virginia; and shall set out, I believe, in the course of the next month, having an opportunity of sailing from a foreign port, with as much convenience and safety as can reasonably be expected. As his friend, and the guardian of his two children, I have an interest in preventing, and think it my duty to prevent if possible, the confiscation of his large and fine estate; and in the progress of his cause I cannot but know, that my advice and my assistance will be useful, if not absolutely necessary. His liberal offers of professional compensation are the least part of my inducement to undertake his cause. I shall probably return to England in six or eight months; but as it is possible, though improbable, that various motives may induce me to change my country, I shall decline the painful ceremony of taking leave of my friends. . . Of my personal safety during my voyage, I am neither weakly solicitous, nor madly regardless; and if I could, without impropriety, ask Lord Keppel, through some common friend, for a pass to be used in case of capture, directing all commanders of British vessels to give no molestation to my friend, myself, and my servant, but to let us proceed in our course, I should be glad to have such a security from delay. . . Were I to sail in an English ship to New York, the journey thence to Virginia would be extremely inconvenient in the summer. I shall, therefore, prefer a foreign vessel; and, above all, a strong swift-sailing frigate. . ."[25]

On June 19, a little more than a month after this letter was written, Paradise and Jones set sail from Dover for the third and last time. Another visit to Franklin in Paris for his instructions and final blessing and they would leave for L'Orient or Nantes, where they would board some "strong swift-sailing frigate" for America. Which one of the half-a-dozen avowed motives was now uppermost in the active mind of Jones? Was it love for America and liberty? Was it hatred for his "enslaved" country which had refused him the sinecure he felt he so richly deserved? Was it the liberal compensation offered him by Paradise? Or was it simply friendship and a sense of duty? Perhaps it was all of these; perhaps it was none of them. Paradise would learn, soon enough.

CHAPTER VIII

An International Accident

IT is impossible even now, with a fuller knowledge of the facts than anyone could have possessed at the time, to gauge the full consequences of the visit of Jones and Paradise to France in the summer of 1782. The personal consequences are clear enough: for Jones they led to brilliant success, for Paradise to failure and years of unhappiness. It is the political consequences, which under ordinary circumstances would not have existed at all, that give to their visit a significance far greater than any mere private action would normally have done.

When the two men arrived in Paris on the 21st of June, 1782,[1] the peace negotiations between the United States and Great Britain had been unofficially in progress for a little more than two months. There had been much unnecessary delay. George III was unconvinced by the decisive victory at Yorktown in the preceding October and still wished to continue the war with America. It was not until February 28, 1782, that the House of Commons passed without division an address declaring that whoever should advise the king to continue offensive war against the Americans, or attempt their reduction by force, would be highly criminal and an enemy to his country.[2] About a month after that the die-hard North ministry was forced to resign, but the inexorable monarch was still unreconciled. Although the war might be ended against his will, nothing, he resolved, would ever induce him to

grant independence to the American colonies. Rather
than that, he would abdicate. He drew up an instrument of abdication, complete except for his signature,[3]
and then sent for Lord Shelburne, the new Prime
Minister: "I will be plain with you," he told him;
"the point next my heart, and which I am determined,
be the consequence what it may, never to relinquish,
but with my crown and life, is to prevent a total un-
equivocal recognition of the independence of America.
Promise to support me on this ground, and I will leave
you unmolested on every other, and with full power
as the prime minister of this kingdom." Shelburne
agreed.[4] It was thus that the guiding policy of the
English during the first six months of the negotiations
in Paris was: Peace without disunion. This, incidentally, was precisely the policy urged in the *Fragment of
Polybius* which Jones had presented to Franklin on his
first visit to Paris. There were several difficulties in
the way of it. In the first place, it was opposed to
English public opinion and to that of the majority of
the ministry. Disgusted with the war from the beginning, they were now willing to end it on almost any
terms. In the second, the American peace commissioners, who had been ordered by Congress to act under
the advice of France on all other points, were instructed
to demand independence as the *sine qua non* of peace.[5]
Lastly, as Franklin smilingly expressed it, the Americans had already won their independence at Yorktown.

Shelburne selected for his agent a Scottish merchant
named Richard Oswald, an elderly man who had spent
some years of his youth in Virginia. "He was of a
philosophic disposition, calculated to soften the tamer
of lightnings."[6] The several conferences which he and

Franklin held during April and May were informal
and inconclusive for the reasons that Oswald was not
accredited—the English would accredit no one to the
"United States"—and that Franklin had no power to
act without the rest of the American commissioners.
Of these, John Adams was in Holland; Henry Laurens,
a prisoner in the Tower of London; Thomas Jefferson,
in Virginia, where he remained until after the Peace
was signed; and John Jay, in Madrid as America's
unrecognized diplomatic representative. The most important matter broached by Franklin and Oswald in
their unofficial, though significant, conversations was
the cession of Canada to the United States—a proposal
of Franklin's which by June Oswald had been brought
to favor. When Franklin felt that these preliminary
interviews had reached a point to justify it, he summoned the rest of the commissioners to Paris. The only
one who was able to answer the summons immediately
was John Jay, who reached Paris just two days after
the arrival of Jones and Paradise.[7]

Meanwhile the English had been active in another
direction. If by some means America could be divided
from her allies, France and Spain, and induced to
make a separate peace, then the terms of this peace
would be much more favorable to England. Shelburne's hope was to induce America to accept "union
without independence," with separate parliaments,
according to the pattern of the recent Irish settlement.
In order to accomplish the separation which would
lead to this desired arrangement, Admiral Digby and
General Sir Guy Carleton, both of them being in
America at the time, were instructed to negotiate with
Congress and with General Washington over the heads

of the commissioners and without the knowledge of France and Spain. To insure success, British agents under various guises were to be sent to America to stir up feeling among the citizens and the members of Congress favorable to a separate peace and especially to the idea of peace on terms of continued union with England. Naturally the men selected for this mission were to be Englishmen who were to a certain degree sympathetic with America but who opposed granting her absolute independence. It so happened that Jay, within a day or two of his arrival in Paris, received "letters and instructions" from America which gave him full information concerning this matter.[8] His naturally suspicious nature was aroused to the highest pitch. Every Englishman in Paris who was on his way to America was in his eyes one of Carleton's agents.

Jay's diary records that on the afternoon of June 27th, four days after his arrival in Paris, he went to Dr. Franklin's at Passy and "found Mr Jones and Mr Paradize there."[9] He learned that they had arrived from London and were on their way to America. In his present state of mind this was enough to make him suspect that they were British agents, and the next morning he indited an official letter to Robert R. Livingston, the Secretary of Congress for Foreign Affairs: "If one may judge from appearances, the [English] Ministry are very desirous of getting some of their emissaries into our country, either in an avowed or in a private character, and, all things considered, I should think it most safe not to admit any Englishman in either character within our lines at this very critical juncture." He did not believe that there was any danger that such agents would "deceive or divide us" and yet the knowledge that they were being admitted might easily alarm the French. The French, he continued, were already of the opinion "that in the mass of our people there is a considerable number who, though resolved on independence, would nevertheless prefer an alliance with England to one with France. . . This circumstance renders much circumspection necessary."[10]

Circumspection was one of John Jay's most conspicuous talents. It was reflected in his keen, deep-set eyes that never wavered but were never in repose. He was an upright man, proud and honest, but watchful—for experience had taught him that he could seldom expect to find in others the rectitude of which he was almost painfully conscious in himself. He knew that this was especially true of Europeans, whose subtle, devious diplomacy was already proverbial among Americans. He was only too eager to show them that here was no mere backwoods politician, but an alert, intelligent guardian of his country's interests. Although the useful phrase had not then been created, Jay was determined that no one in Paris, not even the great Dr. Franklin, should "put over anything" on him.

Jones and Paradise at once became the objects of his closest scrutiny. He made opportunities to see them and converse with them. Almost certainly he read the two items that appeared about them in a London newspaper:

The destination of Mr. Jones is not Asia, as from his skill in Asiatic Languages might have been inferred, but *America*; and not having any private Concerns in any Part of America, it is supposed that the Object of his Departure is Business of a Public Kind.

When we call to Mind some other Circumstances

connected with the above mentioned Mr. Jones, such as his very confidential Intimacy with all the Spencer Family, his peculiar Enthusiasm for Liberty of every Kind and in every Place, and above all, his Fame not only for Literature, but the Business of Politics, it seems to the highest Degree probable that Mr. Jones is now appointed, and surely with the best possible Reason appointed, to assist in the Pacific Negociation with America.

Mr. Paradise, the Gentleman who is a Native of Greece, and so well known for his Proficience in Grecian Literature, has also just left England, on a Voyage to America.[11]

Such suggestion from an English source was calculated to confirm his worst suspicions. It was not until after the terms of the Treaty had been arranged, however, that he revealed in a self-justifying letter to Congress the full extent of these suspicions. It can be judged from his own account how far they must have affected his attitude:

"About this time, that is, in June last, there came to Paris a Mr. Jones and a Mr. Paradise, both of them Englishmen, the former a learned and active constitutionalist. They were introduced to me by Dr. Franklin, from whom they solicited recommendations for America. The story they told him was, that Mr. Paradise had an estate in the right of his wife in Virginia, and that his presence there had been rendered necessary to save it from the penalty of a law of that State respecting the property of absentees. Mr. Jones said he despaired of seeing constitutional liberty re-established in England, that he had determined to visit America, and in that happy and glorious country to seek and enjoy that freedom which was not to be found in Britain. He

spoke in raptures of our patriotism, wisdom, etc., etc.
On speaking to me some days afterwards of his intended voyage, he assigned an additional reason for
undertaking it, viz., that his long and great friendship
for Mr. Paradise had induced him to accompany that
gentleman on an occasion which, both as a witness and
a friend, he could render him essential services in
Virginia.

"I exchanged three or four visits with these gentlemen, and, in the meantime, was informed that Mr.
Jones was a rising character in England, that he had
refused a very lucrative appointment in the Indies,
[Jay was slightly misinformed; the appointment was
to India, and Jones had not *yet* received the offer of it],
and had, by his talents, excited the notice of men of
power.

"In conversing one morning with this gentleman on
English affairs, he took occasion to mention the part
he had taken in them, and, at parting, gave me two
pamphlets he had published. . .

"As it appeared to me a little extraordinary that a
gentleman of Mr. Jones' rising reputation and expectations should be so smitten with the charms of American
liberty as 'to leave all and follow her,' I began, on
returning to my lodgings, to read these pamphlets
with a more than common degree of curiosity, and
I was not a little surprised to find the following para-
graphs in them."

Among the many statements that Jay found incrimi-
nating was one made by Jones only a few weeks before
his departure for Paris, declaring that his future life
should certainly be devoted to the support of the British
constitution and that from this object "no prospects, no

connections, no station here or abroad, no fear of danger or hope of advantage to myself, shall ever deter or allure me." In another speech, Jones in his modest way had suggested a comparison between himself and the Roman patriot Ligarius who rose up from his bed of illness when Roman liberty was at stake and, grasping the hand of a fellow citizen, said, "If you have *any business worthy of yourselves, I am well.*" The business which Jones considered worthy of his powers was mysteriously referred to as *"a very particular and urgent occasion, which calls me some months from England."* [The italics are Jay's.]

"To make comments on these extracts," Jay continued in his letter to Congress, "would be to waste time and paper. On reading them I became persuaded that Mr. Paradise and American liberty were mere pretences to cover a more important errand to America, and I was surprised that Mr. Jones' vanity should so far get the better of his prudence as to put such pamphlets into my hands at such a time.

"I pointed out these extracts to Dr. Franklin; but they did not strike him so forcibly as they had done me. I mentioned my apprehensions to the Marquis de Lafayette, and I declined giving any letters either to Mr. Paradise or to Mr. Jones."[12]

On July 15, the two gentlemen in question left Paris for the seaport of Nantes.[13] Presumably they had sailed for America. Then, one day in August, Jay encountered John Paradise in Franklin's house at Passy. The answers which he received to the questions he immediately began to ask were far from satisfactory. "He told me," Jay wrote to Congress, "Mr. Jones and himself had parted at Nantes, and that Jones had returned directly to England. How this happened I never could learn. It was a subject on which Mr. Paradise was very reserved."[14]

This unaccountable conduct made Jay more suspicious than ever. He became skittish, untrustful of everybody, and inclined to be technical about inconsequentialities. When Oswald's commission arrived, it accredited him to treat not with the "United States" but with the "Colonies and Plantations." Convinced, and rightly convinced, that England was thus withholding her acknowledgment of our independence, Jay flatly refused to deal with anyone who was not accredited to the "United States of America." The episode with Jones and Paradise, added to what he already knew, had convinced him that England was willing to use any means whatsoever to avoid the recognition that he was demanding as a preliminary to formal negotiation. Both Franklin and Vergennes, the French Foreign Secretary, implored him to yield—the term "Colonies and Plantations" could easily be altered later and meanwhile valuable time was being lost. But Jay was firm, and although he finally won his point, it was a belated and a costly victory. Weeks of delay were required for the drafting of the new commission and meanwhile the English, on September 30th, won a naval battle over the Spanish at Gibraltar which placed them in a far better bargaining position than they had been before.[15] Up to then, thanks to Franklin's clever dealing with Oswald the spring before, it had been reasonably sure that England would cede Canada to the United States as a part of the terms of the peace; afterwards, that hope was abandoned forever.[16]

The effect of Jay's overweening cautiousness upon

the terms of our treaty with Great Britain is still a
disputed question among historians, and probably always will be. But whether its consequences were good
or ill, there is no doubt that this attitude was very
greatly influenced by his suspicions of the specious and
bombastic, but completely innocuous, Jones and his
guileless friend, John Paradise.

When Paradise and Jones left Paris late in the afternoon of July 15, their immediate plans were still uncertain. They were going to Nantes, that much was
sure, and from thence they would set sail for America.
What vessel they would board, and what American
port that vessel would be bound for were questions
which the haphazard sailing schedules of the day
obliged them to defer until they reached the port.
Even here it must be largely a matter of good or bad
fortune. It might be weeks before a ship with even
tolerable accommodations would sail for a suitable
port. New York, which at the time was still in British
hands and consequently safer for an Englishman, was
Jones's choice. But if there were no vessel sailing for
New York, they would probably take one for York
Town in Virginia or, failing that, for Boston.

There could have been no question in Paradise's
mind as to the sincerity of his friend's intention of
sailing with him. In Paris, Jones had allowed all the
final preparations to be made without a word. All their
baggage was packed and dispatched; their intentions
were made known to all their friends; their farewells
were said. Their final leave was taken of their "inesti-

mable friend," Dr. Franklin, who on the day of their departure wrote letters in which he recommended them jointly as fellow voyagers to various of his friends. Two of these letters have been preserved. One was to Thomas Jefferson in Virginia:

Passy
July 15, 1782

Dear Sir,—I was in great Hopes when I saw your Name in the Commission for treating of Peace, that I should have had the Happiness of seeing you here, and of enjoying again in this World, your pleasing Society and Conversation. But I begin now to fear that I shall be disappointed, as I was in my expectation of your Company, when I first undertook the voyage hither.—

Mr. Jones, who possibly may have the honour of delivering this into your hands, is a particular Friend of mine, and a zealous one of our Cause and Country. I am sure you will be pleas'd with his Conversation, and therefore I make no apology for recommending him to your Civilities. His Fellow Traveller too, Mr. Paradise, an amiable and worthy Character, will merit, your Regards. He has affairs in Virginia, in which affairs possibly your Counsels and Countenance may be of use to him, & which I therefore beg you would afford him. If in anything I can render you or your Friends any service here, you will do me a Pleasure in commanding freely."[17]

The other letter was to Governor James Bowdoin of Massachusetts, evidently written on the chance that circumstances would oblige them to sail for Boston:

Passy
July 15, 1782

Dear Sir,—I take the liberty of introducing to your acquaintance, two of my particular friends, members of the Royal Society of London, Mr. Jones and Mr. Paradise. You will find them men of learning and ingenuity, and have great pleasure in conversing with them. I recommend them warmly to your civilities; and to your counsels respecting their intended journey to the Southward. They are staunch friends of our cause and country. Be pleased to make my respectful compliments acceptable to Mrs. Bowdoin, and, believe me to be, with great and sincere esteem, dear Sir, &c.[18]

With these letters in his possession and all their preparations for departure made, Jones took one final precaution which he was careful to keep secret from Paradise. He dispatched a letter to his powerful friend Lord Shelburne giving him to understand that although he had been disgusted about the delay regarding the Indian judgeship, he could still be prevailed on to accept it if it were offered to him. He also gave Shelburne an address at which a letter would reach him in Nantes.[19]

Nantes, a city of bridges and crooked, narrow streets, was the principal naval and shipping base for the American colonies during the war with England. It was here that Commodore John Paul Jones many times found haven after engagements with the British and here at least once he was accorded a triumphal welcome after a victory. The city's booming prosperity, later so suddenly checked by the French Revolution, was owing chiefly to the traffic in slaves that was carried on between the French traders and the Turkish and Saracenic corsairs. The latter brought in their shiploads of miserable Negro captives to be disembarked at this half-way station between the Guinea Coast and the West Indies. Here, still in chains, they were kept in prisons or in areas of the city restricted for the purpose until they were ready to be herded into the hold of an out-going vessel. This was the commerce that won for Nantes its name for filth and lawlessness and its soubri-quet—*"La ville des négriers."* Even the phlegmatic William Lee was moved to exclaim in a letter to his brother Arthur, "What a horrible place this is—I tremble at the thoughts of what a friend of ours will feel on being here."[20]

Paradise and Jones spent their first few days among the teeming docks and wharves searching for an Ameri-can-bound vessel with decent accommodations for passengers. Even with the friendly aid of Franklin's nephew Jonathan Williams, long a resident of Nantes, they found it a difficult task. At length Jones, with the assent of Paradise, declared his preference for a French frigate—the "Annette."[21] Whether its accommodations were superior or not, it had one distinct advantage in Jones's eyes. It would not sail for five weeks. There would be plenty of time to receive a letter from England.

Without doubt both Jones and Paradise dreaded and feared the voyage across the Atlantic. It affected them in different ways. Paradise frankly declared his trepi-dations and from the first had sworn that no power could make him undertake so difficult and dangerous a journey alone. Jones was all bravado. Every letter he wrote spoke of the risks and dangers they were about to run, but each contained the elaborate assurance that he was able to rise above them. He protested far too much to be believed. "To me who had so long been thinking of a voyage to India," he wrote to Edmund Burke, "the

passage to America would have been easy."[22] Just why
the prospect of a voyage to India should have alleviated
the hardships of an actual voyage to America, he does
not make very clear. A trans-Atlantic crossing in the
eighteenth century even under the most favorable circumstances was arduous enough. Four or five weeks
were required at the least, and as the small sailing-
vessels of the day were almost completely at the mercy
of the wind and waves, five weeks might easily be
stretched out to eight or even more. The practical
certainty of sea-sickness was the least of the discomforts
to be faced. Passengers as well as crew were subjected
to the cramped, close confinement of miserably inadequate quarters, (since few vessels were especially
equipped for carrying passengers,) in a ship that was
invariably filthy and often disease-ridden. The only
alternative to a steady fare of salted meat, dried fruit,
and hard tack was to carry one's own provisions and
have them specially prepared, and this was an expense
that few could afford. More than that, the coarseness
and brutality of the sailors and even the captains and
other officers was proverbial. "A ship is worse than a
gaol," said Dr. Johnson after his tour to the Hebrides.
"There is, in a gaol, better air, better company, better
conveniency of every kind; and a ship has the additional disadvantage of being in danger."[23]

But leaving the voyage itself out of account, there
were for an imaginative European like Paradise perils
and lurking dangers in America itself which no amount
of reassurance could reason away. With but slight
allowance for poetic license, Goldsmith's description of
Georgia in the *Deserted Village* reflected the average

Englishman's conception of what southern America was like. The piteous exiles from England's pleasant land are pictured as inhabiting

>   . . . a dreary scene,
> Where half the convex world intrudes between,
> Through torrid tracts with fainting steps they go,
> Where wild Altama murmurs to their woe.
> Far different there from all that charm'd before,
> The various terrors of that horrid shore;
> Those blazing suns that dart a downward ray,
> And fiercely shed intolerable day;
> Those matted woods where birds forget to sing,
> But silent bats in drowsy clusters cling;
> Those pois'nous fields with rank luxuriance crown'd,
> Where the dark scorpion gathers death around;
> Where at each step the stranger fears to wake
> The rattling terrors of the vengeful snake;
> Where crouching tigers wait their hapless prey,
> And savage men more murd'rous still than they;
> While oft in whirls the mad tornado flies,
> Mingling the ravag'd landscape with the skies. . .

Virginia, Paradise knew, was not so far from Georgia but that some of these dangers might be found there too. And there was one that Goldsmith had left out of his terrifying catalogue, but which every educated European of the day was particularly alive to. This was lightning. The discoveries of Franklin and Watson had made the whole world lightning-conscious. It was the most popular subject of investigation by learned organizations like the Royal Society, and for a time papers were read on it at almost every meeting, with reports of investigations and observations which were sent in not only from all parts of England but from abroad. The subject was taken up by the newspapers

of the day. These were filled with the most lurid and
unlikely accounts of death and destruction by storms
and other electrical phenomena. So little was known
that almost anything could be believed. Paradise's
conversations on the subject with Franklin, the very
source of such knowledge, had fixed in his mind an
ineradicable dread of lightning. He knew from his
wife and other Virginians of the severity of thunderstorms in eastern Virginia and, strange though it may
seem to us today, his fear of them had a large part in
his reluctance to set out for America. He later confided
this fear to Thomas Jefferson, who heard him sym-
pathetically.

One day in the early part of August, a little more
than a fortnight after they arrived in Nantes, Jones
received his letter from Lord Shelburne. He learned
from it that the chances of his appointment in India
had very much improved. There was no definite
promise, but Shelburne said emphatically that he had
"nothing more at heart than to procure a desirable
situation" for him in Bengali.[24] And Shelburne was
Prime Minister. Jones carefully weighed his chances.
If he continued his journey to America with Paradise,
he had the certainty of a generous remuneration for his
legal services and, with the backing of Dr. Franklin, a
very fair prospect for a career as a lawyer in Pennsylvania. On the other hand, if he returned to England,
there was the strong probability of his receiving the
Indian judgeship. This would mean not only a salary
of £8,000 a year but the leisure and the opportunity to
pursue his favorite study of Oriental languages. There
was another consideration; this was a young lady whom
he admired, the daughter of Bishop Shipley, Franklin's

great friend. Her name was Anna Maria, and although it was hardly in Jones's nature to be passionately in love, he certainly admired and respected her and was convinced that under prudent circumstances she could be induced to reciprocate his feelings and marry him. On the whole, Jones decided, the glittering bird in the nearby bush was to be preferred to the soberer one he held in hand. He would return to England and hope for the best.

This was a perfectly natural decision for an ambitious man like Jones, and although it would be a terrific blow to his unsuspecting and singularly helpless friend, who can blame him for being unwilling to sacrifice his future career merely to perform a benevolent action? It was true that he would be obliged to eat a good many of his words about duty and friendship, about his love of American liberty and his detestation of English tyranny, but words, in a sense, were Jones's profession and he could manipulate them almost as adroitly as he could ideas. Already England had begun to seem less tyrannical and America less free in the light of the new day that was dawning for him in the East.

Like so many kind-hearted persons, Jones was constitutionally incapable of speaking the truth when the truth was disagreeable. He told Paradise that he must return to England, but that if he possibly could, he would come back in two or three weeks and sail with him as he had planned. There are two reasons for knowing that he had no intention whatever of doing so. One is, that he spent three or four weeks travelling in Belgium and Holland before he even proceeded to England. The other is that he had been told in Lord Shelburne's letter that nothing could be done about the appointment until the first of the year. This deception, however well intended, was unsuccessful. Paradise was thoroughly aroused by the shock of Jones's announcement and he saw the whole truth in a flash. Whatever Jones might say, it was clear that he no longer intended going with him to America and was, in fact, deserting him on the very threshold of their adventure.[25]

The fit of nervous depression that now seized on Paradise was the most severe that he had ever experienced. The atmosphere of Nantes with its wretched Negro slaves, its dives, its corsairs and drunken sailors, its filth and disease, had already tortured his sensitive nature almost beyond endurance. The unexpected blow of Jones's desertion meant that he must remain in this hell-hole for another three weeks — alone; that he would have to make the voyage alone; and that he would be obliged to travel alone in an unfamiliar country which was still at war. The entire arrangements for the journey had from the first been planned for the two of them. The accommodations in the ship, the letters of introduction for America, all the legal and business transactions had involved the presence of Jones. Paradise became physically as well as mentally ill. Taking to his bed, he turned his face to the wall and refused to be comforted; one more week in Nantes, he declared, would cost him either his sanity or his life. Jones used every argument and means of persuasion at his command—a no mean assortment for one with his gift for rounded phrases; but Paradise was now in one of his moods of unreasoning stubbornness and swore by all the gods that nothing would induce him to go. Jones cajoled, threatened, abused, and shamed him by turns.

He really wanted Paradise to go, partly for Paradise's sake and partly for his own. If he went, Jones would have little difficulty in saving his own face; if he did not, then their friends might lay at least a part of the blame on Jones. At length Paradise, his mild nature driven beyond endurance, turned on him and they quarreled bitterly and irrevocably. For once Jones heard the truth about himself. Paradise told him that he was a false friend and that he never wished to see or hear from him again. These were the last words that were ever spoken between them. Jones rose and departed in anger and injured dignity, meditating not so much revenge, as self-justification. They were to amount to the same thing.

In spite of what he had said, Paradise did not entirely give up his intention of going to America. About the time Jones left Nantes, the South Carolinian, Henry Laurens, not long since released from his two year's imprisonment in the Tower of London, arrived there, intending to sail for America. Overcoming his repugnance to Nantes, Paradise arranged to make the voyage to America with Laurens and remained there several weeks longer before his hopes were dashed again. Laurens received warning of a possible second capture if he should venture on the high seas and prudently decided to postpone his journey.[26] It was then that Paradise finally and definitely abandoned his plans and returned to Paris.

There he found that Franklin's mind had already been poisoned against him by one of Jones's smooth, resounding letters. According to this letter Jones had promised Paradise to return to Nantes in three weeks,

but had "importuned" him with "fruitless intreaties"
to go on alone if he should fail to return. All his arguments had been met with a "strange pertinacity" on the
part of his friend. Jones took pains not to draw too bad
a picture of Paradise for Franklin to believe, putting
the emphasis rather on his own good intentions than on
Paradise's alleged weakness. He was also careful not
to burn the bridge of Franklin's favor behind him. He
said that he was going to England for a time, but if on
arriving he found that the English were still "too
indolent or too dastardly to preserve their popular
rights" he still intended to set out for "the land of
virtue and liberty."[27] All this being interpreted meant
that if any hitch occurred about the Indian judgeship,
he still wanted Franklin's backing should he decide
after all to go to Pennsylvania.

To his friends in England—Baron Eyre, Dr. Shipley, Lord Althorpe, and others—Jones defended his
desertion of Paradise so eloquently as to make himself
appear to be the injured party, and it is plain that
before long he even believed this himself. Paradise, he
declared, was "timid," "imbecile," "enervated by dread
of some imaginary danger." How could he put any
dependence on a man who "had none upon himself"
and who was even now, so he told Edmund Burke,
"feeding himself upon vain hopes" in Paris?[28] The
insidious thing about these statements was that they
contained the grain of truth that caused them to be
swallowed by men like these who knew Paradise but
superficially. Jones's instinctive cleverness taught him
just how far to go and in what directions. In saving
himself, he did not hesitate to damn his former friend.
He was brilliantly successful in both.

At least once after he reached England his armor of
self-justification was penetrated by the pangs of re-
morse. Late in October, he received a letter from the
brilliant, accomplished Georgiana, Duchess of Devonshire—a cousin of his future wife. She said that she
had just received as a present a copy of Jones's *Ode in
Imitation of Callistratus.* "I wish I understood Greek,"
she wrote, "that I might read something Mr. Paradise
has written at the top of it."[29] She copied the two lines
out in her letter:

$$\text{Αι χαριτες τεμενος τι λαβεῖν ὅπερ ουχι}$$
$$\text{Πεσείη, Ζητουσαι, ψυχηι ευρον Ἰωνιουου.}$$

"The Graces, seeking a shrine that would never
decay, found the soul of Jones.

Only Jones could feel the depth of irony now held by
these two lines.

Jones's story can be ended succinctly. After declaring, for the benefit of the conservative Lord Thurlow,
that he was "no more a republican than a Mahomedan
or a Gentoo,"[30] he obtained his Indian judgeship in
March, 1783, with a baronetcy thrown in. And now,
all "prudent attention to worldly interests" having been
paid, he married his Anna Maria in April and departed for India on a frigate which by some sardonic
chance had been christened the "Crocodile." Once
arrived there he apparently had but one bad moment.
This was when Burke threatened to recall him if he
sided with Warren Hastings. This threat would have
placed almost anyone else in an embarrassing dilemma,
for Warren Hastings was one of Jones's most intimate
friends. But the supple mind that had mastered twenty-

eight languages was equal to the occasion. He wrote
Burke an elaborate letter declaring that he would
weigh the evidence carefully and then would act "independently," according to his own opinion of Hastings'
guilt or innocence.[31] Afterwards, however, he prudently forbore expressing any opinion or taking any action,
and so it is impossible to say what conclusion he
reached.

He never lost his verbal enthusiasm for America and
"liberty." From Chrisna Nagar in Bengal he wrote to
Arthur Lee in 1788:

> ... The interesting picture you give of your country,
> has both light and shade in it; but though some rocks
> and thickets appear to obstruct the foreground, I see
> the distant prospects brighten, and have a sanguine
> hope that I shall live to admire your constitution, in
> all the blaze of true liberty and universal justice. If
> young Englishmen had any English spirit, they would
> finish their education by visiting the United States,
> instead of fluttering about Italy; and strive to learn
> rather political wisdom from republicans, than to pick
> up a few superficial notions of the fine arts, from the
> poor thralls of bigotry and superstition. If I live, I
> seriously intend to make the tour of your states, before
> I retire to my Sabine farm; and my wife, who is much
> better than when I wrote last, often speaks of the
> scheme with delight.[32]

But Jones's "serious" intention of visiting the United
States was again prevented, and this time there can be
no question of the sincerity of his reason. On the eve of
his departure from India he quite suddenly died.

As to Paradise, he remained in Paris as long as he
could, dreading to face the consequences of his failure
to go to America and the interpretation of his conduct

that Jones had spread abroad in England. His confidence in himself, never very great, was pathetically weakened by his experience, and henceforth his malady of hypochondria grew on him apace. At length in early September, when he could postpone it no longer, he returned, a bitterly disillusioned and humiliated man.

CHAPTER IX

Levée Paradisiac

BACK in London at his house in Charles Street
Paradise fell into his former way of life. Five
years were to pass before he made another
serious effort to go to America. In Paris he had received some reassurance from Franklin and Jay.[1] They
told him that by now it was fairly certain that the terms
of the peace would include provision for indemnity to
both American and British property owners. It seemed
entirely probable that Paradise would have his property restored to him by the State of Virginia and that
he would also receive payment from the British government for the stolen slaves. Meanwhile the estate
was in good hands and the revenues from it were being
deposited in the funds of Virginia. Perhaps after all
his failure to go would not prove so very disastrous.
There was, however, more kindness than truth in
Franklin's reassurance and Paradise must have realized
that he ought to go. By presenting himself in Virginia
at this time as a *bona fide* citizen of the State, he could
have obviated many of the complications that were to
harrass and mortify him from now until the end of
his life.

His relations with his wife became more strained
than ever. She could now with more justice lay on him
the blame for their lack of funds and for the tangled
state of their affairs, and she continued to spend even
more recklessly than before the money they did not
possess, making her husband's dilatoriness her excuse

for anything she chose to do. From now on the clash of their ill-matched natures began to be reflected in incidents that grew more numerous and more violent as the years passed.

On at least three different occasions he actually made the effort to live apart from her. One of these occurred a year and a half after he had returned to England from his ill-fated journey with Jones. Franklin was informed of it in a letter from Dr. Price: "You probably will remember Mr Paradise, a friend of Sr Willm Jones and a very worthy man, who has considerable property in Virginia and to whom you have been kind. He has lately been in great trouble. The folly, intemperance and extravagance of his wife produced for some weeks a Separation between him and her and made him the most unhappy man I ever saw. But they are now come together again."[2] Franklin's answer shows that by now he had come to accept the unsympathetic view of Paradise that Jones had encouraged with such industrious pains. "Poor Paradise whom you mention I respect and pity. But there is no helping him. He seems calculated by Nature for Unhappiness and will be equally miserable whether with or without his wife, having no firmness of Mind. I doubt his Property in Virginia may suffer by his Irresolution."[3]

At first the property did not suffer as much as might have been expected. After the signing of the Peace Treaty in the early part of 1783, the estate was released from confiscation and once more the Paradises began to receive the income from it. During the time it was under the control of the State, a sum of a little less than a thousand pounds had been accumulated and was now being held in Virginia bonds, presumably bearing interest.[4] The worthy Cary Wilkinson, who had continued to be the manager throughout the war, now died and was succeeded by his nephew, William Wilkinson. The arrangements were to be continued as before. Tobacco was to be shipped to a merchant in London and there exchanged in part for such English merchandise as was needed in Virginia and in part for English currency to be paid as an income to Paradise. It was hoped at the beginning of this new arrangement that the thousand pounds owing from Virginia would soon be paid. This would enable the Paradises to free themselves from debt, and if all went well they could continue their former style of living on the same income as before.

Almost from the first, however, things began to go badly. The shipments of tobacco became more and more irregular. Times were bad in Virginia, as in all the rest of America. Prices were high, and the currency of the various States, under the Confederation, became so depressed as to be almost valueless. Land values in eastern Virginia declined precipitately. It was soon clear that the whole country was suffering from what we would call today a post-war economic depression. A series of crop failures on the Paradises' land, owing partly to unfavorable weather and partly to the lack of slaves, brought their income down to almost nothing. It became more and more apparent that the debt from the Virginia funds would not be paid for many years, if ever. To make matters still worse, the payment of indemnities to British and American subjects that had been stipulated in the Peace Treaty was, owing to

certain disagreements that had afterwards arisen between the two governments, indefinitely postponed.

Now if ever, it would seem, was the time for the
Paradises to reduce their expensive scale of living. On
the contrary they lived, if anything, more extravagantly
than before. It is difficult to judge exactly where the
blame lay, since each of them bitterly accused the other
of extravagance. It is only fair to Paradise, however,
to say that while there are many known instances of his
wife's extravagance there is no such evidence concerning him; his needs were of course far simpler than hers.
They had both from childhood been accustomed to
luxurious living and it is perhaps more than could be
reasonably expected of them that, as long as there was
any hope of future prosperity, they should give up the
fine house, the servants, the carriage, and other acces-
sories of the only sort of life they had ever known,
much less the balls and evening parties and dinners
which to Mrs. Paradise were the very breath of her
existence.

The continuance of all this could only mean debt,
and still more debt. Going into debt was easy enough
for people like the Paradises, whose reputation for
wealth had been so long and so securely established;
and the English tradesmen of the eighteenth century
were proverbial for their trustfulness to people who
possessed the proper credentials. But it was not only
to tradesmen that Paradise went into debt. Borrowing
from a friend was opposed to all of his instincts and
principles, and yet he did it. Seward, Count Zenobio,
Dr. Warren, Dr. Bancroft, and afterwards Thomas
Jefferson,—all of them became his creditors. Within
four years after his return from Paris, every possible

resource had been exhausted; even his treasured library, bit by bit, had been sacrificed to continue the almost hopeless pretense of keeping up appearances.

In spite of these internal conflicts and tottering finances, the Paradise house continued to hold the distinguished place it had achieved already in the social and intellectual life of London. The scholarly accomplishments of its host, with his exotic background and education and his wonderful gifts of sympathy and understanding, continued to win for him the friendship of outstanding men of intellect in the London of the day. Its hostess displayed on most occasions the gracious manners, the well-modulated voice and elegant presence demanded by her position. By means of the more or less desperate expedients to which they were willing to reseort, the house continued to be famous for its open-handed hospitality.

It was only natural during and after the war that more and more emphasis should have been placed upon the Paradises' Americanism, both by their friends and by themselves. They had from the first been stout defenders of the American colonies—she from the unshakable loyalty that was one of her admirable traits and he from political conviction. As the quarrel with the mother country approached closer to its climax, they had stood out ever more conspicuously among the exponents of Americanism in London. Lucy became famous in society as a "strenuous American republican" and Paradise's views, though stated less vociferously, were rendered even more effective by his having become, during the war itself, a naturalized American citizen. Thus it came about that the Paradise house in Charles Street, already long known as a social center for European foreigners, became during the closing years of the Revolution and the four or five years after it the private house at which Americans and the friends of America could most readily find a welcome. The "levée Paradisiac" was spoken of with gratitude and affection and Lucy Paradise achieved an old ambition —that of becoming for almost a decade the outstanding American hostess in London.

Among the numbers of Americans who began to visit London after the war was a group of young men in their twenties, the sons of wealthy or otherwise prominent families, who either came to complete their education abroad or else to fill minor diplomatic posts at Madrid or Paris or London. Wherever their various missions took them, they all at some time during their stay abroad managed to visit England. There was William Short, the lovable young Virginian with a lively sense of humor and a talent for gallantry. There was John Brown Cutting of Boston, clever, literary, and very gay, who was a student of law at the Inner Temple. Cutting was the boon companion of Mrs. Paradise's cousin, Thomas Lee Shippen, who was also an Inner Templar. Shippen was introduced into the Paradise household by Arthur Lee, one of his favorite uncles, who wrote to him soon after his arrival in London: "By this time I presume you are domesticated wth M^r & Mrs Paradise. He always appeared to me, a worthy man, & if time should have moderated the passions of the Lady which used to mislead [her] into not very amiable excesses, it will be a very agreeable family to you. . ."[5] The third member of what Thomas

Jefferson referred to as the "triumvirate," when they were all traveling under his instructions on the continent, was John Rutledge, a nephew of Governor Rutledge of South Carolina. Although a little dull, he was prized by the others for his accommodating nature and his good fellowship. Far more sober and circumspect were the two ministerial secretaries who arrived at London in the train of John Adams and his family. William Stephens Smith and David Humphreys were both young colonels who had seen service in the war. Humphreys, a native of Connecticut and a graduate of Yale, was a poet who was admired by his contemporaries for his patriotic odes. To judge by the comments on him from the acid-tipped pen of Miss Abigail Adams, he was a brusque, pompous man, not at his best in the society of young ladies. With a characteristic lack of humor, he wrote and published while in London a "Poem to the Happiness of America," the purpose of which, he said, was to counteract the "unfavorable sentiments" of the British toward his native country. Humphreys, like so many other Americans, was made to feel welcome at the Paradise house in Charles Street, where he would sometimes dine and afterwards accompany his host to a meeting of the Royal Society. It was possibly in London that the American painter, John Trumbull, also a member of the Paradise circle, painted a picture of the most important scene in Humphreys' life. This was when he marched into the State House at Philadelphia on November 3, 1781, to present to Congress the British flags that had been captured at Yorktown. Washington, who loved him as a son, had selected him from among

all his officers for this "highest honor within his gift."
Such were the principal members of the set of younger
Americans who enjoyed the hospitality of the Para-
dises' home.

A part of the charm of the Paradise house was the
refuge it provided from the unaccustomed formalities
of English life, and from the hostility which the English displayed, at this time especially, toward Americans. It was for these younger men in particular, who
were eager and friendly by nature, that the gratuitous
rudeness of the English was so baffling and distressing.
Quite naturally, as their dislike of the English grew,
their affection for their own country increased. "I felt
myself entirely an American," wrote Thomas Lee
Shippen to his father some months after his arrival in
England, "I panted for my native Country—The dis-
tinctions which prevail here are surely not founded in
nature, and reason most loudly deprecates them. . ."[6]
The relief and pleasure felt by them all at being
received into the friendly atmosphere of a house like
the Paradises' was expressed by young Shippen: "There
are few places . . . where I breathe a salutary air and
where I am satisfied and at ease. The house of M^r
Paradise is . . . among this number. There I am in
America. A crouded levee of foreigners of distinction
make the society variegated and agreeable and the most
perfect sociability and ease of manner are found there.
One of the most pleasant days I have passed was that
before yesterday." He called at Charles Street between
one and two o'clock and found several French and
Italian noblemen present whom he accompanied with
Mr. Paradise to a nearby exhibition of paintings, after
which they paid several calls. At four they returned to

the Paradise house, dined "a la Virginienne" at five, and "concluded the evening at Mr Rucker's in a weekly American party."[7]

Like all socially prominent Londoners, the Paradises kept free a regular evening each week on which they were at home to all their friends. Sunday was the day on which they held their levees, and it was principally then that they entertained their American friends. It was not until 1785, when John Adams's wife and daughter joined him in London, that an official sanctuary for Americans was established at his house in Grosvenor Square. The distance from there to Charles Street was not very great and it was not long before the Paradises and the Adamses were on visiting terms. They kept up friendly relations during all the time they were in London together, and after the Adamses returned to the United States, Mrs. Adams and Mrs. Paradise corresponded with each other. Not long after arriving in London Miss Adams was married to Col. Smith, her father's secretary. The Smiths lived in Wimpole Street and were thus near neighbors of the Paradises. "We took tea with Mrs. Paradise," said Abigail Smith in her journal. "Met Count Lusi and two others, Greeks. The Count was very inquisitive about America, the manners and customs. . . He complains of the unsociability of the English; and inquired respecting the manners of the Americans; and said when the King of Prussia sent a minister to America he would ask to go. I confess I do not think he would be pleasing to the Americans."[8] Mrs. Smith was an extremely caustic, critical young lady, who prided herself on her wit. "I thank you for rolling Mr. Paradise so well up in your letter," wrote her husband while absent on a diplomatic mission, "and then stretching him out again." [9] Rolling a person up meant making fun of him and Abigail had evidently given her talent for ridicule full play with the eccentricities of Mr. Paradise. Neither she nor her mother cared very much for the majority of people they met in England. At one of Mrs. Paradise's parties, Abigail Smith saw "Many ladies whom I did not know even by name—one . . . an elegant woman and well dressed for an English lady. Pardon me, ladies—but I cannot acknowledge that I think in general you discover a large share of elegance or taste; there was another lady, Mrs. Maria Cosway. I had heard of her, and had seen several of her performances in the exhibitions of painting. . . The singularity of her taste struck me, as well as everyone else." [10] Mrs. Cosway, an Italian by birth, was the wife of the "macaroni" miniature-painter, Richard Cosway. She herself was a portrait painter and a well-known musical amateur whose parties at her house in Pall Mall were attended by everybody from the sculptor Nollekens to the Prince of Wales. Her charm was of the kind that attracted men and aroused the dislike of women. Thomas Jefferson, who saw her at the Paradises' when he visited London, corresponded with her for many years; it was to her that he addressed his famous "Dialogue of the Heart and the Head."

During the winter season of 1786, the American group in London made up a party for a visit to Bath. "Not to spend a fortnight or a month [at Bath]," said Mrs. Adams, "at this season of the year, is as unfashionable as it would be to reside in London during the summer season." The party consisted of Mr. and Mrs. John Adams, Col. and Mrs. Smith, Mr. and Mrs. Rucker—the most intimate friends of the Adamses in London—a Miss Ramsay, Thomas Lee Shippen, Mr. Murray, Mr. Bridgen, and John Paradise. Mrs. Paradise and her eldest daughter had a good reason for remaining in London. The only member of the party who was not an American was the Venetian, Count Zenobio, the friend of Paradise who was as American as liberal political views could make him. The group of friends set off from London in a long cavalcade, for they carried their servants with them, and made the three-day journey together.

At Bath, the social advantages of being in a group were great, for as Mrs. Adams expressed it, "when we went into the rooms, we at least had a party to speak to." On the whole the jaunt was successful, judging from the accounts of it that were given by young Shippen and Mrs. Adams.

Mrs. Adams's letters from Europe, especially those to her sister Mrs. Cranch, are an amusing mixture of appreciation and enjoyment on the one hand and of censure and didacticism on the other. Hers was a dual nature. Her Puritan up-bringing and her forthright Americanism, so intensified by her experience with a hostile English society, were superimposed upon a nature that was gay, witty, and inherently pleasure-loving. "I will now give you some account of my late tour to Bath," she wrote, "that seat of fashionable resort, where, like the rest of the world, I spent a fortnight in amusement and dissipation, but returned, I assure you, with double pleasure to my own fireside, where only, thank Heaven, my substantial happiness subsists. Here I find that satisfaction, which neither satiates by enjoyment, nor palls upon reflection; for, though I like sometimes to mix in the gay world, and view the manners as they rise, I have much reason to be grateful to my parents, that my early education gave me not an habitual taste for what is termed fashionable life. . . I, however, passed through the routine, and attended three balls, two concerts, one play, and two private parties, besides dining and breakfasting abroad."[11]

The party at Bath soon joined forces with other Americans, among whom was John Boylston of Massachusetts, "one of the nicest bachelors in the world," who invited them to tea and to an evening party in his apartments. Boylston had resided in England during the war, but had testified his devotion to his country by his benefactions to American prisoners. Another acquaintance, which was of the greatest interest to Paradise, was formed with George William Fairfax, formerly of Virginia, where he had been appointed in 1767 to succeed Mrs. Paradise's father, Philip Ludwell, on the Governor's Council. Fairfax was a cousin of the sixth Lord Fairfax, the great landed proprietor of the Northern Neck. Already the possessor of a large estate in Virginia, he had been called to England in 1773 to take possession of property which he had inherited in Yorkshire, and on his voyage up the Thames had passed a certain vessel bearing a cargo of tea which in Boston was put to a use for which it had not been intended. Like Paradise, Fairfax had failed to return to Virginia at the summons of the General Assembly, and as a result his property there was confiscated and he was without the income from it for ten years. It was during this time that he had retired to Bath and lived

there so well within his English income that he was
able, like Boylston, to contribute sums of money for the
benefit of American prisoners in England.[12] It was
possibly through the encouragement of his example and
advice that Mr. and Mrs. Paradise also retired to Bath
some years later in an effort to live more cheaply during
the crisis which their affairs had reached.

Bath was still the leading English resort and at the
time the American party was there was reported to
have no less than fourteen thousand visitors. "By this
you may judge what a place of resort it is," wrote Mrs.
Adams, "not only for the infirm, but for the gay, the
indolent, the curious, the gambler, the fortune-hunter,
and even for those who go, as the thoughtless girl
from the country told Beau Nash, (as he was styled,)
that she came, *out of wantonness*. It is one constant
scene of dissipation and gambling from Monday morning till Saturday night. . ." The wickedness of it all—
in retrospect—prompted in Mrs. Adams some extremely serious reflections after her return to London. "What
is the chief end of man?" she ruminated (unconscious-
ly quoting the Presbyterian *Shorter Catechism*), "is a
subject well worth the investigation of every rational
being."[13]

Thomas Lee Shippen's excuse for a visit to Bath was
the necessity he unfortunately had of consulting Dr.
John Fothergill, a famous physician there and a
nephew of Franklin's Dr. Fothergill. Young Shippen
was now in his most American phase and was persuaded
that he could find no pleasure in anything that was
English. He followed the literary fashion which
Smollett had set by writing his father a satirical description of Bath, of its fantastic invalids and "origi-

nals," and its men and women of society for whom he expressed a "republican" contempt that was only skin deep. Like most others who used the waters, he professed a cynical disbelief in their curative properties. Young Shippen's intimacy with the Paradises, which began about the time of this visit to Bath, became of the greatest significance to them and to him during the crisis in their domestic affairs which was now rapidly approaching. Of all the younger members of the "levée Paradisiac," it was he on whom both Mr. and Mrs. Paradise depended the most for friendship and for confidential advice.

CHAPTER X

Excellency Meets Majesty

MANY of the Americans who flocked to London
during the seventeen-eighties were merchants
seeking to renew the trade relations with the
English which had been interrupted by the war. It was
to be many years before America freed herself from
the habit of trading almost exclusively with the British.
This was especially true of the Virginia planters, who
found it inconceivable that they should ship their
tobacco to any other than an English port and there
receive in exchange for it the English goods to which
they had been so long accustomed. "Our countrymen,"
wrote Mrs. Adams not long after her arrival in 1785,
"have most essentially injured themselves by running
here in shoals after the peace, and obtaining a credit
which they cannot support. They have so shackled and
hampered themselves, that they cannot extricate themselves. Merchants, who have given credit, are now
suffering, and that naturally creates ill-will and hard
words."[1] England, without having fulfilled the terms
of the Peace Treaty which required her to abandon our
western trading-posts, already possessed the bulk of
American commerce and knew that she could hold it,
owing to our insatiable demand for British goods. As an
excuse for her failure to live up to the treaty she claimed
that America had not fulfilled her promise of satisfying
the war debts of British subjects. Since it was impossible for us to do so, with our currency depressed and our
trading posts still in the hands of the British, the situa-

tion had reached a deadlock which continued unbroken
for years. The result of it was a one-sided, financially
destructive commercial relationship which crippled the
merchants of both countries. Much of the hostility
toward America at this time is traceable to the disagreements between the English merchants and the
Americans who went to London in such disproportion-
ate numbers.

It was partly, in the hope of alleviating this situation
that Thomas Jefferson, in answer to a summons from
Adams, set out from Paris on the 6th of March, 1786,
in the company of Col. William Stephens Smith, who
had been sent to escort him.[2] This visit to London, the
only one that Jefferson ever made there, was destined to
bear only negative political results. He failed distinctly
in the furtherance of all three of the diplomatic missions which brought him thither. And more than that,
the hostile reception accorded him both publicly and
privately by the English confirmed him strongly in the
dislike that he had already conceived of them. His
attitude toward England remained unfriendly throughout the rest of his career. In happy contrast to the
reception which he met with elsewhere, the kindness
and hospitality accorded him at the Paradise house in
Charles Street made upon him a deep and lasting
impression. From John Paradise's point of view, this
visit of Jefferson's was the most auspicious event that
could possibly have taken place. It enabled him to
form a friendship which personally was one of the most
gratifying he ever made, a friendship which brought
more order and peace into his unhappy life than any
other factor whatsoever.

As our Minister to France on an official visit to

HIS EXCELLENCY THOMAS JEFFERSON.

From a portrait by Peale. Reproduced with the permission of the New York
Historical Society.

HIS MAJESTY GEORGE III.

Silhouette-engraving by Stadler. In possession of Mrs. Archibald Bolling Shepperson.

England, His Excellency Thomas Jefferson could not
of course ignore the customary diplomatic courtesy of
requesting to be presented to the King, and on Wednesday, March 15, Adams arranged for him to attend the
levée at St. James's.[3] Here any hope he had ever entertained of forcing a "decisive answer" from the British
Court on the subject of treaty settlements and trade
relations received a speedy check. George III well
knew that Thomas Jefferson was the author of that
Declaration by which America had asserted her independence; and his conduct, unpardonable as it was
toward an official representative of a recognized country, is understandable in such a man at such a time.
Mary Tudor had "Calais," George III had "America"
engraven upon his mind and conscience. Gradually
approaching the great American statesman as he made
his way along the circle of attending courtiers, his red
face with its white eyebrows fixed in the expression of
politeness which the occasion demanded, he at length
reached him and permitted him to be presented. Every
eye in the room was upon the group, as, with deliberate
forethought, he turned his back and passed on to the
next in line.[4]

In turning his own back on Jefferson, the monarch
turned England's back as well. From then on few
Englishmen of rank and none of official position would
converse with Jefferson or even speak to him if it could
be avoided. "On my presentation, as usual, to the King
and Queen at their levées," Jefferson wrote many years
later, "it was impossible for anything to be more un-
gracious, than their notice of Mr. Adams and myself.
I saw, at once, that the ulcerations of mind in that
quarter left nothing to be expected on the subject of my

attendence; and, on the first conference with the Marquis of Caermarthen, the Minister for foreign affairs, the distance and disinclination which he betrayed in his conversation, the vagueness and evasions of his answers to us, confirmed me in the belief of their aversion to have anything to do with us. We delivered him, however, our *Projet*, Mr. Adams not despairing as much as I did, of its effect. We afterwards, by one or more notes, requested his appointment of an interview and conference, which, without directly declining, he evaded, by pretences of other pressing occupations for the moment. After staying there seven weeks, till within a few days of the expiration of our [joint] commission, I informed the minister, by note, that my duties at Paris required my return to that place, and that I should, with pleasure, be the bearer of any commands to his ambassador there. He answered, that he had none, and wishing me a pleasant journey, I left London the 26th, and arrived at Paris the 30th of April."[5]

Jefferson was almost equally unsuccessful in the two remaining official affairs that had prompted his visit to London. It is true that his and Adams' conferences with the Chevalier Louis de Pinto, the Portuguese Ambassador to England, terminated in a provisional trade agreement with Portugal.[6] Owing, however, to the interference of Great Britain this agreement was for the time being refused validation when it was referred to the Portuguese Court.[7]

The immediate occasion for which Adams had summoned him was the arrival in England of Abdrahaman, the Tripoline minister to England, who was authorized to treat with the Americans concerning the tribute so

notoriously demanded from the United States by the
Barbary Powers, (as well as from most European
nations,) for immunity from piracy. Even before Jefferson's arrival, Adams had done his diplomatic best
to prepare a friendly atmosphere for their conference.
"Pappa made a visit this eve to the ambassador from
Tripoli," wrote his daughter Abigail. "By a little
Italian and French, with some Lingua Franca, they got
into conversation and understood each other wondrous-
ly. A servant soon brought two long pipes, with two
cups of coffee. Pappa took both; and smoked away,
taking a sip of coffee, and a whiff at his pipe; the
ambassador did the same. At last, one of the secretaries
cried out in ecstasy to pappa: *'Monsieur vous etes un
veritable Turk.'*"[8] After Jefferson came the two patriots
continued to smoke Abdrahaman's hookahs for their
country's good, but nothing came of it. We continued
to pay the tribute, which eventually amounted to
$2,000,000 annually, until, during his administration as
President, Jefferson threatened war and the bondage
was broken.

The leisure time that was in a sense forced upon
Jefferson during his London visit was spent in various
ways. Although he was opposed in general to the purchase of British goods by Americans, he found himself
unable to resist the superior bargains that London
offered over Paris. For himself he bought "A set of
table furniture, consisting of China, silver and plated
ware"; some "small tools for wooden and iron work,
for my own amusement"; and a box of books.[9] On his
return he ordered English harness for his two carriage

horses, which was to be "plated, not foppish, but genteel."[10] For his sister Nancy Jefferson, soon to become
Mrs. Hastings Marks, he bought "two pieces of linen,
three gowns, and some ribbon."[11] To Charles Thomson
and to Richard Henry Lee he sent one of the newly-
invented lamps, which would burn cheaper oil than the
old ones and much less of it. "The spermaceti oil is
the best," he wrote Thomson, "of the cheap kind."[12]
While in London he also arranged for Cavallo to make
for him a portable copying-press for making letter-
press copies of his correspondence. It was made from
his own design and proved to be so successful that in
Paris he had several more made. One he presented to
Lafayette, and others he furnished at cost for his
friends in America who desired them. One of them
went to James Madison.[13] Other commissions for pur-
chases after he left London were given to Col. Smith
and Dr. Bancroft; the most important of all his pur-
chases was arranged for him by Paradise.

Jefferson intended to return to Paris about the first
of April, but after writing his secretary to expect him,[14]
he was persuaded to join Adams in a tour of some of
the English country estates and places of historical
interest. At Stratford-upon-Avon, when they were
shown an old wooden chair supposed to have belonged
to Shakespeare, the two future Presidents of the United
States dived into their pockets and produced pen-knives
with which they each whittled a piece for a souvenir.
Adams meticulously observed in his diary that this was
"according to custom."

"Edgehill and Worcester," wrote Adams, "were
curious and interesting to us, as scenes where freemen
had fought for their rights. The people in the neigh-

borhood appeared so ignorant and careless at Worcester, that I was provoked and asked, 'And do Englishmen
so soon forget the ground where liberty was fought for?
Tell your neighbors and your children that this is holy
ground; much holier than that on which your churches
stand. All England should come in pilgrimage to this
hill once a year.' This animated them, and they seemed
much pleased with it. Perhaps their awkwardness before might arise from their uncertainty of our sentiments concerning the civil wars."[15]

Jefferson's interest was in the architecture and especially the gardens, and he carried with him a copy of
Whately's popular book on English gardens which
they made the guide-book for their tour.[16] They visited
nearly all of the estates which Whately described in his
book, including Woburn Farm, Caversham, the Leasowes, Hagley, Paynshill, Blenheim, and High Wycombe. Jefferson's observations were directed "chiefly
to such practical things as might enable me to estimate
the expense of making and maintaining a garden in
that style."[17] Although his notes are mainly statistical,
with careful figures of costs and dimensions, there is an
occasional flashing comment that shows he was alive to
the beauty of what he saw. He found the dwelling-
house at Paynshill ill-situated and the architecture
"incorrect," but observed in the grounds "A Doric
temple, beautiful." At Blenheim: "The water here is
very beautiful, and very grand." At Hagley, the residence of Lord Wescot, he observed in one of the stone
recesses on the bank of a stream "a Venus predique,
turned half round as if inviting you with her into the
recess." Of such things as this, Adams disapproved.
"The temples to Bacchus and Venus are quite unneces-

sary," he remarked drily, "as mankind have no need of artificial incitement to such amusements." He hopes "It will be long . . . before ridings, parks, pleasure grounds, gardens, and ornamented farms grow so much in fashion in America."[18]

After returning from this extended tour, Jefferson made several short excursions to places in the neighborhood of London, sometimes with Smith, sometimes with Paradise for a companion. He visited Moor Park, Hampton Court and also Kew, which had the most famous botanical gardens in Europe. On April 20th, he and the entire Adams household went on an all day jaunt to Osterly, "to view the seat of the late banker, Child." The house and grounds were elaborate and impressive, but John Adams lugubriously remarked that "The beauty, convenience, and utility of these country seats are not enjoyed by the owners. They are mere ostentations of vanity; races, cocking, gambling, draw away their attention."[19] Jefferson judged things from a different point of view. Although he did not care for English architecture, which he considered bad, or for English manners, which he considered worse, he had nothing but praise for the gardens: "The gardening in that country is the article in which it surpasses all the earth. I mean their pleasure gardening. This indeed went far beyond my ideas."[20]

Jefferson's social pleasures in London were restricted exclusively to the American set. It was naturally with the Adamses, with whom he had already formed a close personal friendship in Paris, that most of his time was spent and through them that most of his new acquaintances were made. After Grosvenor Square, it was

Charles Street that welcomed him most hospitably and showered upon him the "multiplied civilities and kindnesses" for which he thanked and generously rewarded his host and hostess there. At the house of John and Lucy Paradise he could, like the homesick young Shippen, dine "a la Virginienne" and end the evening in an American party, or accompany his host to a meeting of the Royal Society.

The first occasion of his dining there was the afternoon of Thursday, March 30th.[21] This was also the date of the most "uncommonly splendid" social event which London afforded during his visit; that night the popular French Ambassador, Count d'Adhémar, was giving his annual ball. The arrangement was that after dinner the Paradises and their guests should attend the ball as a party. Mrs. Paradise, who was marvelously impressed with Mr. Jefferson, had adroitly selected an occasion on which her social gifts could be displayed to the best advantage. She was a graceful, accomplished dancer and was far more adept in the small talk and social amenities of an occasion like the present than in the intellectual exertions demanded by an evening of conversation. At thirty-five, she was still a beautiful and attractive woman, especially when she wore the elegant company manners which she undoubtedly put on for the man whom she considered "the First Character in Our State, and I shall add the First in the Continent of North America."[22] Jefferson embodied for her all the ideal conceptions of her "dear Virginia." His deferential, charming manner toward women, so like her father's, recalled the old Virginia, and his liberal politics suggested the new; both were appealing to her. Not only was he a potential friend of great

power and influence, but he became more and more in
her eyes an object of reverence and even of affection.

The company at dinner was small and carefully
selected. The Adamses of course were there, with Col.
Smith, and also Dr. Edward Bancroft, an American-
born friend who had already interceded with Jefferson
on the Paradises' behalf. To add color and variety to
a group that was otherwise strictly American, the Ambassador from Russia and Countess Woronzow were
invited and also Count Soderini, the Minister from the
Venetian Republic. The dinner began at five and at
eight the guests retired to their homes to dress, the
party reassembling an hour later at the Embassy.

The French Embassy, fronting on St. James's Park,
was the most splendid in London, with a ballroom that
accommodated five or six hundred people, with plenty
of room for minuets and country dances. "It is most
elegantly decorated," wrote Mrs. Adams, "hung with a
gold tissue, ornamented with twelve brilliant cut
lustres, each containing twenty-four candles. At one
end there are two large arches; these were adorned
with wreaths and bunches of artificial flowers upon the
walls; in the alcoves were cornucopiæ loaded with
oranges, sweetmeats, &c. Coffee, tea, lemonade, orgeat,
&c. were taken here by every person who chose to go
for them. There were covered seats all round the room
for those who did not choose to dance. In the other
rooms, card-tables, and a large faro-table were set: this
is a new kind of game which is much practised here."[23]
At eleven Mrs. Fitzherbert arrived, escorted by the
Prince of Wales to whom she was then united by a
morganatic marriage. Many other "very brilliant ladies
of the first distinction were present." Sixteen of them,

all court belles, appeared in a uniform dress and this, said *The London Chronicle*, "greatly contributed to the brilliancy of the spectacle."[24] In conforming to the fashion, as she assuredly would have done, Mrs. Paradise wore a silk waist, a painted tiffany coat decorated with beads, a satin petticoat trimmed with velvet ribbon, and an enormous hat with feathers, turned up at the side, perhaps with diamond loops and buttons of steel. Mrs. Adams was "full gay" in a blue *demisaison* with a satin stripe, sack and petticoat trimmed with white floss, and a full-dress court cap without the lappets. Her jewelry was a pair of pearl ear-rings and three pearl pins. Her head-dress was adorned with two black and blue flat feathers which cost her half a guinea apiece—"but that you need not tell of."[25] She carried a bouquet of roses.

Thomas Jefferson, with his tall, angular figure, his reddish hair sanded with grey, and his intellectual, distinguished countenance, must have appeared as he felt—in violent contrast to all around him. Although he certainly did not play cards—card-playing was not even permitted in his home—he probably danced a minuet with his hostess, Mrs. Paradise, who was so famous for demanding this attention from the gentlemen in her train. There were few men outside of their party with whom he was encouraged to converse. Among these few were the Marquis of Lansdowne and the Earl of Harcourt. "These two noblemen," said Adams sarcastically, "ventured to enter into conversation with me. So did Sir George Young. But there is an awkward timidity in general. This people cannot look me in the face; there is conscious guilt and shame in their countenances when they look at me. They feel that they have behaved ill, and that I am sensible of it."[26] Jefferson and the Adamses left before supper, at one in the morning, as Miss Adams was suffering from a cold.

The friendship that began between Jefferson and John Paradise on this visit was soon to develop into an intimacy based on common interests and on certain fundamental traits of character which the two men shared. Underneath Jefferson's calm, rather austere exterior, he was an extremely sensitive man who was keenly alive, as he himself confessed, to praise or blame even from inconsequential persons. No one could have been more sympathetic toward the misfortunes of other people. In all this Paradise resembled him, except that where Jefferson was strong, he was weak. It was in part this very weakness that encouraged the friendship of the generous-spirited Jefferson. The tastes of them both were essentially intellectual. Jefferson's interest in learning was never slackened throughout his long and crowded life, and with Paradise scholarship and the conversation of learned men were ever a ruling passion. In political principles they were entirely in accord even before they met. Here of course Jefferson was the leader; but Paradise soon showed himself to be a gifted disciple, disposed by half a lifetime of practical liberalism to embrace the democratic principles which Jefferson could so brilliantly elucidate. In short Jefferson found in Paradise a well-rounded, cultivated European mind, receptive and eager, flatteringly predisposed toward the new-world philosophy of which he was the great exponent. With Paradise such free and enlightened conversation was possible as Jefferson had seldom enjoyed since those early student days in Williamsburg, when his own ideas were being forged in talks with

Virginia's brilliant Governor, Francis Fauquier, and the liberal, cultured Scotsman, William Small, Professor of Mathematics and Philosophy at William and Mary College. Paradise, already an American citizen, was the type of European whom Jefferson felt should be encouraged to settle in America. Married as he was to a Virginia woman with an imposing family background, he must settle either on her estate near Williamsburg or else, so Jefferson was fain to persuade him, further inland in his own beloved foothills of the Blue Ridge Mountains.

Jefferson's interest in the problem of Paradise's estate in Virginia had had its beginning some months before he came to London in a letter from Dr. Edward Bancroft, written at Paradise's request. The letter had been a strongly-worded one in which Paradise and his misfortunes were set forth in terms that were friendly but strictly just; Jefferson's assistance was asked in obtaining the payment of the thousand pounds that were owing from the state of Virginia. "I[n] Conveying you this request I know not how far it may be practicable to obtain payment to *any individual particularly*, from these or any other Considerations: I am however so Confident of Mr Paradise's merit and so anxious for his releif from Embarrassments, the more distressing, because he has been so little used to them, that I cannot refuse joining my intreaty to his that you will favour him with your Countenance & interference as far as you can with propriety."[27] This letter remained unanswered for three months—a thing almost unprecedented with the methodical Jefferson. Bancroft, as well as Paradise, became alarmed. Perhaps Jefferson, who was known as the opponent of special privilege, had been offended. Bancroft then wrote an extremely clever letter which served at once as an apology in case he had offended, (if he had erred it was in his "sensibility" rather than in his judgment,) and a reminder in case Jefferson had merely forgotten.[28] Both were unnecessary. Jefferson had not been offended and several days before Bancroft's second letter reached him he had written about Paradise's debt to his influential friend in Virginia, James Madison of Orange. In enclosing Bancroft's letter, he had said characteristically, "I add my solicitations to his, not to ask anything to be done for Mr. Paradise inconsistent with the justice due to others, but that everything may be done for him that justice will permit."[29]

The contrast between this brief, conventional message and the letter which Jefferson wrote to Madison from London after he had known Paradise for six weeks is some indication of the value which he had already begun to set upon their friendship: "I wrote you in a former letter on the subject of a Mr. Paradise who owns an estate in Virginia in the right of his wife and who has a considerable sum due him in our loan office. Since I came here I have had opportunity of knowing his extreme personal worth and his losses by the late war." He then described in detail the circumstances of Paradise's loss of fortune and added, "His situation is now distressing and would be completely relieved could he receive what is due him from our state. He is coming over to settle there. His wife and family will follow him. I never ask unjust preferences for anybody; but if by any just means he can be helped to his money, I own I would be much gratified. The goodness of his heart, his kindness to Americans before, during and since the war, the purity of his political and moral character, interest me in the events pending over him and which will infallibly be ruinous if he fails to receive his money. I ask of you on his behalf that in pursuing the path of right you will become active for him instead of being merely quiescent were his merit and his misfortunes unknown to you."[30]

On April 26, the day after this letter was written, Jefferson set out for Dover on his way to Paris. He returned as he had come, in his own carriage. Paradise accompanied him as far as Greenwich. On the 28th he had the leisure to visit "the successor of Sterne's monk"[31] in Calais, to whom he gave a small gratuity: Jefferson was an enthusiastic admirer of Sterne and considered that his writings formed the best course of morality that ever was written. He arrived in Paris on April 30th, and although he had written Mrs. Paradise a civil note of thanks before leaving London, he lost no time in opening a correspondence with his new friend, John Paradise:

Paris May 4. 1786.

Dear Sir:

I arrived at Dover a little before midnight of the day I parted with you at Greenwich, and was detained there a day & a half by bad weather & unfavorable winds. however I had at length an excellent passage of three hours only, and was able to get to Paris on the 5th day of my departure from London. I find nothing here very remarkable. the Cardinal de Rouen [Rohan] is still the great topic. he continues in the Bastille as does Cagliostro, nor do I hear of any probability of their getting out soon. it is thought here that the King of Prussia [Frederick the Great] is in a situation in point of health which must end soon & fatally. I reflect with great sensibility on the multiplied civilities &

kindnesses I received from yourself, mrs & miss Paradise, and beg of them and yourself to accept my very sincere thanks, with assurances of my high esteem. I shall hope to be honoured sometimes with your letters, and particularly when you shall have fixed the date of your departure for Virginia. in return I shall take the liberty of sometimes troubling you with the occurrences of this place. I am with the highest esteem Dr Sir

Your most obedient humble servant

Mr Paradise   Th: Jefferson[32]

Paradise's reply shows that he was keenly sensible of his good fortune in forming such a friendship:

London
May 23, 1786

Dear Sir,

I received in due time Your Excellency's very obliging letter of the 4th instant, which I beg leave to assure you gave me inexpressible satisfaction, both as it conveyed the intelligence of your safe arrival at Paris, and likewise because it afforded me fresh marks of your kind and invaluable friendship to me and my family. I shall ever consider the acquisition of this friendship as one of the most fortunate circumstances of my life, and earnestly wish that opportunities may frequently offer in which I may have it in my power to give you convincing proofs of the sincerity of this profession. My voyage to Virginia remains still uncertain, as I have not yet received any letters from my steward. As soon as I hear from him and am able to take some resolution upon this matter, you, my dear Sir, will certainly be the first to whom I shall communicate the steps that I shall propose to take, not doubting that I shall be favoured with your friendly advice and assistance. Mr. Cavallo has delivered according to your direction the printing press to Colonel Smith who discharged the expense attending it, which, to my great surprise I find, amounts to five Guineas. The Colonel, however was so well pleased with it that he ordered one to be made for himself. Doctor Price, whom I had the pleasure of seeing last night, desires to be particularly remembered to you. My wife and daughters join likewise in best respects to you and your amiable family, and I have the honour to be with the greatest deference

Your Excellency's
Most obliged humble serv[t]

John Paradise.[33]

CHAPTER XI

A Harpsichord for Monticello

THOMAS JEFFERSON'S second letter to Paradise, filled with requests for favors to himself and proposals for Paradise's welfare, was written before he had received an answer to the first:

Paris May 25. 1786.

Dear Sir

My constant occupation in London put it out of my power to avail myself of your friendly offers to instruct me in the modern pronunciation of the Greek, or rather in the pronunciation of the modern Greeks. yet I so ardently desire to become acquainted with this that I am induced to make you a most unreasonable request, that is to give me some written instructions on the subject. I do not mean to trouble you with writing a treatise for me. would you do this for the public you would render them an acceptable service, but for myself I will only ask you to write down the Greek alphabet & the diphthongs, and opposite to each letter or diphthong, to express it's power in Italian orthography, adding perhaps an example or two of a greek word, in Greek letters, & then in the Italian letters of equivalent sound. I fix on the Italian rather than English orthography, because in the latter language the same letters have very different sounds in different words: where the sound of the Italian letters is always the same in the same situation. I have yet another favour to ask which is to get Kirkman to make for me one of his best harpsichords with a double set of keys, and the machine on the top resembling a Venetian blind for giving a swell. the case to be of mahogany, solid not vineered, without any inlaid work but deriving all its beauty from the elegance of the wood. I would wish entirely to avoid a complication of stops, wishing to have such only as are most simple & least liable to be put out of order as the instrument is to go to a country and to a situation where there will be no workmen but myself to put it in order. when done I shall be glad to have a celestini apparatus put to it by Mr. Walker. I hope by that time he will have brought to perfection some method of giving it movement by a spring or a weight, or by some other moves than the foot or hand. I confide so much in Dr Burney's judgment & knowlege of musical instruments, and his interest too with Kirkman, that tho' I have no right to ask either myself. from the momentary, yet pleasing, acquaintance I contracted with him, I will however resort to your better acquaintance to interest him in advising or directing for the best. on receiving advice of the time when the instrument will be ready, I will take care to place the money in time in London & to direct it's package & conveiance.

The mass of letters & business which had accumulated during my absence has kept me closely employed till now. I have seized the first moment of leisure to write letters to my friends in Virginia which I will pray you to deliver personally. I took the liberty of recommending to you an interior situation in Virginia. the principal reason was that the thunder in the lower parts was peculiarly disagreeable to you. long experience & residence in the lower as well as upper parts of the country enable me to assure you that the difference is very great. in this I shall be contradicted by no man of observation who has lived in both parts as I have done. I can further assure you that since my return to Paris we have had as severe thunder as I almost ever heard in the upper parts of Virginia. to this reason for preferring the upper country I will shortly sketch several others 1. the heats are less 2. not subject to fevers & agues & other bilious complaints 3. the stile of living is more oeconomical 4. in being distant from your principal estate it's operations will be less disturbed, and your time more at your own command. all this however will be contraverted by the good people in and about Williamsburgh who will wish to fix you in their neighborhood: you will be best able to judge for yourself after you shall have seen both parts of the country. I shall be happy to hear that you avail yourself of the good season to make the passage, that you have it safe, speedy & pleasant; after your arrival I know all will be well & shall have no other anxieties.

We have little new worth communicating. the Cardinal de Rohan's memoir has appeared, but we do not see when his affair is to be ended. rumors are still as incertain as they are unfavorable as to the situation of the K. of Prussia. present me affectionately to mrs and miss Paradise & be assured of the sincere esteem with which I have the honour to be Dear Sir your most obedient humble servant

Th: Jefferson[1]

P. S. May 30. 1786. some interesting business having for several days prevented my finishing the letters which accompany this, I have in the mean time received your favour of the 23. I owe you many thanks for the favourable sentiments you are pleased to express therein. they are more the effect of your own goodness than of any merit of mine. in fact, I am the gainer by this acquaintance: and I shall be happy to find occasions of convincing you that I view it in that light. the trouble I give you in the preceding part of this letter is but too opposite a proof that you are the loser.

Mr Paradise

Of the letters of introduction which Jefferson enclosed, the one to George Wythe, who had been his law instructor at William and Mary College, gives the best

account of Paradise. Wythe was one of his oldest
friends and Jefferson had always regarded him as
among the most enlightened and intelligent of men:

Paris May 29. 1786.

Dear Sir

This will be handed you by mr Paradise, a Graecian
& honest man by birth, a gentleman & man of learning
by education, & our countryman by choice the most
rational of all titles. I need not say more to ensure him
all the services you can render him. he has a heart
which will repay your attentions with overflowings of
gratitude. probably he will want your counsels, perhaps
too your encouragement to do what you shall find for
his interest; for he is of a temperament disposing him
to recoil from difficulties rather than meet & surmount
them. this is a false calculation, for by shrinking from
a small pain, it often recurs upon us from another
quarter with double force. his interests & inclinations
would have led him to Virginia, but a singular dread
which he has of thunder and the informations he had
gathered that it is formidable about Williamsburg
seemed to leave him fixed in England. I told him that
many years residence both in the lower and upper country, & particular observations enabled me to tell him,
that there was infinitely less in the latter than former.
he goes to try this, & the result on his sensations will
determine him ultimately. present me affectionately to
mrs Wythe & be assured of the sincere esteem with
which I am

Dear Sir your friend & serv[t]

mr Wythe   Th: Jefferson[2]

Jefferson's request to Paradise to teach him modern
Greek, besides reflecting his desire for knowledge of
all sorts, was based on a favorite idea of his which is
expressed in another letter to Wythe, written more than

a year later when Paradise was actually in Virginia:

. . . Constantinople is the key of Asia. Who shall
have it is the question? I cannot help looking forward
to the reestablishment of the Greeks as a people, and
the language of Homer becoming again a living language, as among possible events. You have now with
you Mr. Paradise, who can tell you how easily the
modern may be improved into the antient Greek. . .[3]

This idea seems less visionary when we recall that at
this time the subject of Greek independence from
Turkey was a live one, although it was not to reach a
culmination until nearly forty years later. The English
poet Byron, born a year after this letter was written,
lost his life while fighting for Greek freedom in 1825—
a year, it will be remembered, before Jefferson himself
died.

The Dr. Burney whose assistance Jefferson had requested Paradise to engage in the purchase of the
harpsichord was Dr. Charles Burney, the leading English musician of his day and the father of the famous
novelist, Fanny Burney. This kindly man, whose very
failings were amiable, was a devout Tory, proud of his
friendship with Dr. Johnson, of his membership in the
Literary Club, and of the personal notice that had been
taken of him by the Händel-loving monarch, George
III. His only faults were his vanity, which was easily
brushed aside, and his love for the society of lords and
other great men. Tory prejudice became submerged in
natural kindliness when he received Paradise's appeal,
and he immediately replied to him:

[London]
June 19th 1786.

Dear Sir:

I beg you will acquaint Mr Jefferson that he flatters me very much by his remembrance, & that I shall have great pleasure in executing the commission with Kirkman. I went to him immediately on receiving your Note, and have bespoke a double Harpsichord of him, which is to fulfill, as nearly as possible, every Idea & wish contained in Mr Jefferson's Letter. The machine for the Swell, resembling a Venetian-blind, will be applied; The Stops & machinery for moving them & the Swell will be perfectly simple & unembarrassing to the Tuner, the Lid of the Case will be of *solid* mahogany; but the sides cannot if the wood is beautiful: as the knots & irregularities in the grain, by expanding & contracting different ways, will prevent the Instrum^t from ever remaining long in tune; but Kirkman will answer for securing the sides from all effects of weather & climate, by making them of well-seasoned Oak, & veneering them with thick, fine, long mahogany, in one Pannel. By this means he has sent Harp^{ds} to every part of the Globe where the English have any commerce, & never has heard of the wood-work giving way. The Front will be solid, & of the most beautiful wood in his possession. The Instrument will be ready to deliver in a^{bt} 6 weeks; & the price, without Walker's machine, and exclusive of Packing-case & Leather-cover, will be 66 Guineas. The cover & packing-case will amount to a^{bt} 2 G^s & ½. A desk to put up in the Harp^d will not be charged separately, but be reckoned a part of the Instrum^t.

With respect to Walker's Celestine stop, I find that Kirkman is a great enemy to it. He says that the Resin used on the silk thread that produces the tone, not only clogs [the] wheels & occasions it to be frequently out of order; but, in a short time, adheres so much to the strings as to destroy the tone of the instrument. This

may be partly true, and partly [his] prejudice. I am
not sufficiently acquainted with this Stop to determine
these points; but I will talk with Walker on the subject,
& try to discover whether he admits the difficulties or
can explain them off; & whether he has found out any
such method of giving motion to his *Bow-string* as that
suggested by Mr Jefferson.

Ma Lettre tire en longueur; but being unfortunately
out of the reach of a conversation with your very intelligent correspondent *viva voce*, I was ambitious to
let him know that I entered heartily into the business
in question, & give him all the information in my
power on each particular article of his commission.

I am, dear sir, with very sincere regard,
& most respectful Compliments to
Mr Jefferson, your obed^t
and most humble Servant

Chas Burney.[4]

Although Jefferson was not a performer on the harpsichord himself, he well deserved Dr. Burney's intima-
tion that he possessed a "very intelligent" knowledge of
the instrument. While in Philadelphia he had become
acquainted with the musician Francis Hopkinson, a
signer of the Declaration of Independence, with whom
he had had much discussion and much correspondence
on the subject. Hopkinson had perfected an invention
for improving the quilling of harpsichords only to find
that the same idea had been hit on and put into practice
in England shortly before.[5] Jefferson had done all he
could to establish his friend's invention in Paris, even
to interviewing the leading French musicians and pub-
lishing his treatise in French. But when he went over
to England, he discovered that the invention had indeed
been made independently there: "I have just returned

from a trip to England," he wrote Hopkinson from
Paris on May 9, 1786. "I was in the shop of Mr.
Broadwood, the maker of your Harpsichord, and conversed with him about your newest jack. He shewed
me instruments in his shop with precisely the same
substitute for the quill, but I omitted to examine
whether it had the same kind of spring on the back. . .
I wait till I hear more particularly from you as to your
last improvement before I order a harpsichord for my
daughter."[6] It is evident that with his customary
thoroughness Jefferson had made a study of the manufacture of harpsichords both in England and France
before making his purchase. It was while in England
that he had become acquainted with Walker's "divine"
Celestine stop, and we see from his letter to Dr. Burney
that he was determined to have it:

Paris July 10. 1786.

Sir
    I took the liberty, through mr Paradise, of asking
your advice in the matter of a harpsichord. he has
transmitted me a letter you were pleas'd to write him
on that subject. the readiness with which you have
been so good as to act in this matter excites my utmost
gratitude, & I beg you to accept of my thanks for it.
the objection made by Kirkman to the resin of Walker's
bowstring has some weight, but I think by wiping the
strings from time to time with a spunge moistened in
water or in some other fluid which will dissolve the
resin without attacking the metal of the strings, the evil
may be relieved. it would remain to use Walker's stop
sparingly: but in the movements to which it is adapted
I think it's effect too great not to overweigh every objection. that it should be worked however either by a
weight or a spring is very desirable. the constant
motion of the foot on a treadle diverts the attention &

dissipates the delirium both of the player & hearer. whenever either yourself or mr Paradise will be so good as to notify me that the instrument is ready, with information of the cost of that, it's appendages, packages & delivery at the waterside, I will send by return of the post a banker's bill for the money with directions to whom to deliver it. are organs better made here or in London? I find that tho' it is admitted the London workmen make the best harpsichords & piano-fortes, it is said the best organs are made here. I omitted in London to visit the shop of any organ-maker, but you are so much the better judge, that your decision would be more satisfactory. indeed if it would not be too great a liberty I would ask the favor of your description of a proper organ for a chamber 24 feet square & 18 feet high, with the name of the best workmen in that way in London. I feel all the impropriety of the freedom I am taking, & I throw myself on your goodness to pardon it. the reading your account of the state of music in Europe had prepared me to expect a great deal of pleasure from your acquaintance, and the few moments I was so happy as to pass with you, were a proof that my expectations would have been fully gratified, had not the shortness of time which obliged me to hurry from object to object, deprived me of opportunities of cultivating your acquaintance. I must be content therefore with offering you my hommage by letter, & assuring you of the esteem & respect with which I have the honour to be Sir

> Your most obedient
> & most humble servant
> Th: Jefferson[7]

Burney's reply to this was through Paradise, who, in a letter of July 28, says: "Doctor Burney, who was with me a few days ago, desired me to acquaint you, that, in consequence of the letter with which he has been honoured by you he went to Kirkman's to enquire what state the double harpsichord was in, which he had bespoken for you; and though he found it on the stocks, he was informed that it would be near a fortnight before it could be played on in the way of trial. This being the case the Doctor will postpone his answer to your Excellency's letter till it is finished, and ready for Mr Walker's Machinery, with whom he will have a conference previous to the instrument's being placed in his hands; the result of which shall be communicated to you, as well as the Doctor's opinion of the comparative excellence of French and English organs. He went out of Town the day after I had the pleasure of seeing him, for about a fortnight, and begged that these particulars may be communicated to you as a preface to the letter which he shall write at his return."[8]

This was the last word which Jefferson received on the subject of his harpsichord for more than three months. The following letter from Paradise partly explains the delay:

London
November 10, 1786

Dear Sir,

Doctor Burney has just this moment been with me to acquaint me that the harpsichord that was bespoken for you has been finished by Kirkman for a considerable time, and is now in the hands of Mr. Walker, who is affixing to it his celestine stop, upon a new construction, according to your Excellency's wish and idea. The Doctor has been in daily expectation ever since his arrival in Town, of hearing from Mr. Walker that the instrument was ready for trial with his new machine for the celestine stop. He has postponed writing to you till he could speak of all the particulars belonging to this harpsichord, which he is ambitious should be as complete as possible. He intends calling again tomor-

row upon Mr. Walker in order to see what forwardship
it is in, and if finished, will give you an account of it
by the next post. I hope soon to have the happiness of
seeing you. Mrs. Paradise and my daughters join me
in every good wish to you and your amiable family, and
I have the honour to be with the greatest respect y^r
most faithful and oblig^d serv^t

John Paradise.[9]

Hearing no further word for more than another month,
Jefferson made inquiries from William S. Smith,[10] who
was now his accommodating London agent for all sorts
of practical matters. But nothing satisfactory was
learned until the arrival of the long-expected letter
from Dr. Burney:

London, Jany 20th
1787.

Sir

Few things have given me more concern than the not
being able sooner to give you a satisfactory acc^t of the
Harp^d & its Machinery, wch I had the honour to be-
speak for you, last Summer. I visited Kirkman from
time to time whenever I came to town, & saw the In-
strum^t in every Stage of its construction. The wood was
chosen with great care; the Lid is solid, as you desired,
& no part has been veneered or inlaid that c^d possibly
be avoided, or wch c^d receive the least injury from the
vicissitude of climate. I got the Instrum^t out of Kirkman's hands very completely finished, as far as concerned his part of the business, in autumn; & by a little
management prevailed on him to send it to Walker,
with tolerable good-humour. Walker undertook to
place his Machine for the Celestine Stop upon it, with
great readiness, finding for whom the Instrum^t was
made: as I discovered that he had had the honour of
conversing with you ab^t the difficulties & objections on
the subject of his Stop. I was glad of this, as it made

him more alert & solicitous to execute his part well.
He told me that he had little doubt but that he c^d put
his machinery in motion by clock-work, with very little
use of the Pedal. I let him alone to meditate & work at
his leisure till the Month of November; when I began
to be uneasy lest you sh^d imagine the commission had
been neglected on my Part. Walker was still in high
spirits ab^t the success of his new Machine, & only
waited for the Clock-makers part of the Work. Last
month the new Machine was applied; & though infinitely superior to the old, the motion given to it by a
single stroke or pressure of the foot, was not so desirable as I wished, or as Walker expected. He had difficulties in placing, & covering his Machine, after it was
made; as well as in regulating its operations. At length,
after long delays, some occasioned by real difficulties,
& others by having, like all his brethren, project[ed]
too many pursuits at a time, the Machine has rec^d all
the perfection he can give it. He has promised to describe its powers, & the means of exhibiting them, in a
paper wch will accomp^y the Instrum^t. The Resin will,
he says, be easily brushed off the strings, if adhesion
from damp is not suffered to take place, by neglecting
to clean the strings too long: As a Harp^d I never heard
a better instrum^t or felt a more even & pleasant touch.
The Tone is full, sweet, & equally good through the
whole Scale. And as to Walker's Stop, it is much more
easily used than any I ever tried. It will not suit things
of execution, but it is not confined to mere psalmody, as
was the Case at the first invention. The machine or
musick-bow is sooner & more easily brought into contact, than formerly, & is not so subject to produce a
Scream by over pressure of the Keys. It is perfectly
sweet, & at a little distance *Organic*: that is, [it] re-
minds one of the best & most expressive part of an
Organ, the Swell. On the degree of pressure depends,
not only the durability of tone, but its force. It will
require much exercise to find out, & display, all the

beauties of this stop. You, Sir, are speculative Musician sufficient to know the truth of this assertion, & to avail yourself of it. As to the Question you ask concern^g the superiority of organs made in England or France? I can only answer that as far as I have seen, heard, or examined, the mechanism of the English is infinitely superior, as well as the tone of the solo-stops. Green the or^g builder here, is a very ingenious & experimental man, & not only makes dayly discoveries & improvements himself, but readily adopts those that may be made or recommended to him by others. *pour la forme* & ornaments, the Fr. will doubtless beat us; mais, *pour le fond*, I think we always *had*, & still *have* it all to Nothing against the rest of Europe: We are notorious for want of invention—yet give us but a principle to work on, & we are sure of leaving an invention better than we find it. I write now in too great a hurry to describe the contents of such a Chamber or^g as you have in meditation. Ab^t £100, w^d I think supply all that is wanting in such an Instrum^t, sev^l stops, well-varied, & chosen, will produce better Effects in a small space, than crowds of such course or unmeaning pipes as are usually crammed with Chamber organs of any size. If I can be of the least further use in this or any other commission in my Power, I beg you not to spare me, being with great respect & regard, Sir

> your obedient
> & most humble Servant
> Chas Burney.[11]

The matter was ended, as far as Dr. Burney was concerned, by Jefferson's letter of thanks:

> Paris Feb. 12. 1787.

Sir

I have been honoured with your favor of the 20th of January, and am now to return you my sincere thanks for your very kind attention to the instrument I had desired. your goodness has induced you to give yourself a great deal more trouble about it than I would have presumed to propose to you. I only meant to intrude on your time so far as to give a general instruction to the workmen. besides the value of the thing therefore, it will have an additional one with me of the nature of that which a good catholic affixes to the relick of a saint. as I shall set out within three or four days on a journey of two or three months, I shall propose to Col° Smith, if the instrument is not already embarked, not to send it till about the 1st of April when it will be less liable to be injured by bad weather. a friend of mine in America (the same who improved the quilling of the harpsichord) writes me word he is succeeding in some improvements he had proposed for the Harmonica. however imperfect this instrument is for the general mass of musical compositions, yet for those of a certain character it is delicious.—we are all standing a tip-toe here to see what is to be done by the assembly of Notables—nothing certain has yet transpired as to the objects to be proposed to them. the sickness of the ministers continues to retard the meeting. I have the honor to be Sir

your most obedient
& most humble servant

Dr Burney   Th: Jefferson[12]

Jefferson was absent from Paris on his tour of France and Italy from February 28 to June 10. During this time he received many letters from his daughter Martha, (then in the convent school à l'Abbaye de Panthemont near Paris,) asking what had become of her harpsichord. "I have not heard any news of my harpsichord," she wrote him on April 9; "it will be really very disagreeable if it is not here before your arrival. I am learning a very pretty thing now, but it is very hard."[13] The young girl had made several more such inquiries before her father informed her that he had written instructions to London for the harpsichord not to be sent before April or May.[14] Encouraged by this, she learned several new pieces to play to her father in his return.[15] Hearing this, Jefferson replied from Nantes, June 1: "I forgot, in my last letter, to desire you to learn all your old tunes over again perfectly, that I may hear them on your harpsichord, on its arrival. I have no news of it, however, since I left Paris, though I presume it will arrive immediately, as I have ordered. Learn some slow movements of simple melody for the Celestini stop, as it suits such only."[16] The disappointment of both Jefferson and his daughter must have been keen indeed when the harpsichord not only failed to arrive on his reaching Paris, but had still not reached them on the 31st of August. He wrote to Smith and begged him to see what had become of it.[17] No explanation remains as to its fate during all those months; but that it finally did arrive we have proof in a letter from Jefferson to Francis Hopkinson, thanking him for the gift of a book of his songs: "I will not tell you how much they have pleased us, nor how well the last of them merits praise for its pathos, but relate a fact only, which is, that while my elder daughter was playing it on the harpsichord, I happened to look towards the fire, and saw the younger one all in tears. I asked her if she was sick? She said 'no; but the tune was so mournful.'"[18] The Celestine stop was doing its work only too well!

During all this long-drawn-out correspondence regarding the harpsichord, Jefferson was becoming ever more interested and involved in Paradise's Virginia affairs. In London he had urged upon Paradise the necessity of going to Virginia and in this he had been supported by Dr. Bancroft and Mrs. Paradise. On his return to Paris he was fully persuaded that Paradise meant to go at once and probably remain there as a citizen. This was undoubtedly Paradise's sincere intention at the time; but his wife, who knew him better than Jefferson possibly could, realized that the most strenuous measures would be required to strengthen his resolution and bring him to the actual point of carrying it out. His dread of making the voyage, the increasing frequency of his attacks of nervous debility, and above all his natural disposition to postpone whatever was disagreeable to him might cause him to delay and eventually abandon altogether this step that was now so essential to their welfare. Mrs. Paradise determined to take an active part in their affairs. Jefferson had aroused in her the intensest admiration and she threw herself without reserve upon his confidence in a series of voluble, repetitious, badly-spelled letters, the first of which reached him within two weeks of his return to Paris:

1786, May 5

Sir

I hope before you shall have received this letter, your Excellency will be safe arrived, and found your amiable daughter in perfect health to whom, I beg you will make all our Compliments. Your very kind letter, I received on the morning of your Excellency's departure, for which, I return you a thousand thanks, as it gave me great comfort and brought me the pleasing assurance of your Excellencys doing every thing you could for to promote mine and my familys welfare. It is not in language to express to your Excellency the feelings I had upon the occasion, to see myself supported by the First Character in Our State, and I shall add the First in the Continent of North America. The Ware, and the very ill state of Mr Paradises health, have brought very great afflictions upon me, as your Excellency well knows. But I trust with your kind, and friendly assistance, to be brought to that state of tranquillity I once enjoyed. The assistance, I ask of your Excellency is to take the trouble to write to Mr Paradise in the strongest terms to advise him to go by the very first opportunity. How happy should I be could I accompany him, but that my own reflections tell me, it would be very improper at this time, as it would have a very bad appearance in the eyes of his creditors, who would conclude immediately that we were run-a-way. Mr Paradise and myself who have during the whole time of the Ware keept up our credit in this Country, must not now let it sink, by any mean or bad action, he is a Man of Strict honesty, and would shudder at the thought of any action which would at once blast his name, and that of his family's. The only thing he wants is to take resolution to undertake the voyage, and I know of no one more capable of giving him that, then your Excellency. Ships have arrived, since your Excellency's departure, but they have not brought us one line, what the mean[ing] can be of it I cannot tell. The Steward must have independent of the money in the Loan office, abo[ut] Two Thousand Pound, and that Money he must have had for Some time. I cannot say enough in the praise of Dr Bancroft who seems to interest himself heartily in mine and my familys welfare. When your Excellency does Mr Paradise the hon[or] to write to him, I shall esteem it a mark of your regard, if your Excellency would send him letters for Virginia to those Gentlemen who have shewed themselves true friends to our Cause during the Ware. I say the Ware, as that was the time, to see whether they were sincere friends to their Country. We have proved ourselves such, and was the same which has already passed to come over again, we would act in the same manner. By your Excellencys sending letters accompany'd with one from yourself it would make him think and finely determine to go.

Adieu

my Dear Sir

And believe me to be Your Excellencys

Most Obedient humble Servant

and Friend Lucy Paradise[19]

P. S.

I have to beg of your Excellency, that this letter may not be known to Mr Paradise. If your Excellency should honour me with a Letter, please to direct your letter for me, under cover to Dr Bancroft N° 12 Villiers Street York-Buildings.

London Charles S^t
May ye 5th 1786.

Jefferson's judgment allowed him to accede to Mrs. Paradise's request that their correspondence be kept private from her husband. His reply to her effusion shows that he understood her as well as he did Paradise and that he was also aware that at least a part of their difficulties were due to the lady's imprudence and extravagance. The interest that he continued to take in their affairs was not based on any illusion of either of them being other than they were. If Paradise's weakness of resolution was not at once apparent to him, Mrs. Paradise had not allowed him to remain long in ignorance of it. Jefferson was convinced, however, that much of this was due to certain unfortunate factors in his environment and especially to the lamentable condition of his financial affairs. His answer to Mrs.

Paradise shows that he believed these handicaps would be overcome by their removal to Virginia and he consequently was willing to urge it with all the eloquence at his command:

Paris May 29. 1786.

I have been honour'd, my dear Madam, with your letter of the 5th instant, and embrace the first opportunity which has offered by a private hand of sending to mr Paradise letters for Virginia. I shall be happy to hear he is gone there, because I believe he will be happier there than in England. it is a country where a rational & studious man may follow his inclinations with less interruption, & where a warm heart will meet with more genuine returns of friendship than in Europe. these circumstances would induce me to hope yourself & miss Paradise would also like it. but against these we must reckon a greater simplicity of manners, & a good degree of solitude more than you have been used to. the best means of getting an idea of this would be the fixing yourself a while in a country situation in England; where the state of society probably resembles that of your own country. if on trial you should like such a situation, you may safely venture to Virginia. if it be your purpose in all events to go to that country, I should suppose the sooner you go, the better; because you would doubtless prefer the settling your daughter in the same country with yourself, and she is now of that age when the affections will not await the movements of the parent. these may become engaged, and may occasion greater pain to you both, & greater inconveniences than those which would attend an early departure to America. I can safely assure you that you will find the state of domestic society there infinitely more replete with happiness than it is in Europe. mr Paradise's dislike of thunder storms will oblige you to settle in some interior part of the country where the manners will resemble still less those of Europe, and where the band of family society is drawn still closer. however he will have a great extent of country a great variety of societies to chuse among & prepare a settlement for you. that he may make a choice which shall be agreeable to you and that it may be followed with every circumstance of felicity to you both & to the young ladies is the sincere wish of dear Madam your most obedient & most humble serv^t

Th: Jefferson.[20]

Mrs Paradise

A month passed before Jefferson received any further word about the Paradises. At the end of June, however, each of them wrote to him, without the knowledge of the other. Both letters disclosed the important fact that the voyage to Virginia had been postponed, but neither revealed the true reason for it. Mrs. Paradise angrily attempted to lay the blame entirely on her husband:

June 25, 1786.

I return your Excellency a thousand thanks for your kind and friendly letter. I wish it was in my power to acquaint you that the time was fixed, and that we had taken our passage for our return to dear Virginia. Since you left us I thought proper (seeing the affairs of Mr Paradise grow worse, and worse every day, as my truly good friend Dr Bancroft will acquaint you) to write a letter to Dr Price to beg he would use his influence with him, to go, and take my daughter and myself with him. Mr Paradise promised Dr Price, and Dr Bancroft that he would go by the 15th of July, and if he could not support his family in his absence, he would take them likewise. He has a debt of above Two thousand pounds and as yet no Ship is arrived, and I fear his Creditors begin to be a little uneasy about their money. Mr Seward a friend of Mr Paradises offered to pay the Sum of Two hundread pound and above to one of his

Creditors if he would go directly, and take his family with him, he has refused him, and seems determined to stay in England at all events. I have ever since I was married been begging Mr Paradise to carry me home, and he from time to time have put me off. Was he a man that had Ten Thousand a Year, he ought to have granted my request, as it was neither unreasonable nor unjust. But in the Situation he is at present, without a farthing in this part of the world to support him, or his family, I think, I have a right to demand that if he will not go himself and take his family with him, he ought to let me go, and to have the whole management of my property. I wish your Excellency would give me your opinion upon this Subject. I forgot to tell you, that he had only his life Inter[est] in the Estate, as likewise, the Interes of [one unreadable word] money in the Funds of England. I must beg of your Excellency to write to me by the first oportunity. I am in great afflictio[n] as Dr Bancroft will tell you. He has re-ceiv[ed] the letters for which act of friendship, I retur[n] your Excellency my most sincere thanks. Adieu

Dear Sir

And believe me to be your Excellen[cy's]

most obliged humble Servant and frien[d]

L Paradise[21]

P. S. It was it is the wish of my heart to go home and therefore he will keep me here as long as he can—Be my *friend and Support*.

The letter from Mr. Paradise was in the unformed handwriting of his eldest daughter:

June 27, 1786

Dear Sir

I am so ill that I am obliged to have recourse to the assistance of my daughter to thank you for your very obliging letter, and to inform you that the plan con-

certed between your excellency, Dr. Bancroft and myself about my going to Virginia, is totally altered. I am
to go, but not till next spring, and then it will be with
my wife and children. How this alteration came to
pass you will learn from Dr. Bancroft, who is thoroughly acquainted with every circumstance concerning
this affair, and whose kindness to me and mine must
ever be remembered by us with the deepest sense of
gratitude. I have executed your commission with regard to the harpsichord, and I hope soon to be able to
give you some account of the modern greek language.
In the mean while I have the honour to be with the
greatest respect

Your excellency's

Most obliged humble servant

John Paradise.[22]

The true reason for Paradise's refusal to go to Virginia and for Mrs. Paradise's consequent anger was
told to Jefferson by Dr. Bancroft, who delivered both
these letters into his hands at Paris. There had been
another violent quarrel between them over the management of their daughter Lucy, who was now a young
lady of fourteen. Mrs. Paradise, with a foolish disregard of convention and more especially of her daughter's ardent, pleasure-loving nature, had insisted on
bringing her out at an absurdly early age. This she had
done despite all the opposition her husband could offer.
The consequence had been several near-elopements
with undesirable suitors which it had required all of
Paradise's tact and pertinacity to thwart, especially
since each of them had been half-connived in by the
imprudent, headstrong mother. The occurrence of the
third or fourth such incident in the early part of June
was what had made Paradise determine not to leave

for America until he could take his family with him.
In his present financial circumstances it was impossible
for them all to go. His reasons for postponing the
journey at this time, although of course Mrs. Paradise
would not admit their validity, were in fact only too
well grounded, and it was not to be many months before
the conduct of his wife and daughter was to prove
them so.

The result of Jefferson's and Bancroft's conferences
about their friend's affairs were revealed in letters
which Jefferson wrote to each of them on the same date.
His reply to Mrs. Paradise's appeal was formal and
circumspect. Perhaps he was already beginning to experience some regret at his hasty agreement to keep
their correspondence secret from her husband:

Paris July 10 1786.

Dear Madam

I have duly received the favour of your letter by
doct^r Bancroft and am sensible of the honour of the
confidence you are pleased to repose in me. I wish it
were in my power, more than it is, to promote those
measures which the interests of your family seem to
require. I have taken the liberty of writing to mr
Paradise on the subject, a liberty greater than perhaps
could be justified. were my right to interfere to be
measured by my good wishes, it would indeed be
boundless. Dr Bancroft & myself think that would mr
Paradise take a flying trip to this place we could aid
him in his determinations as to what is best to be done.
it is not too late for the present season; the expence of
the journey to him, coming as a single person, would be
small, & perhaps might be compensated by your care
at home. I submit this proposition to your better judgment. if you approve of it, you will of course give it
the weight of your influence. I pray you to present my

respect to miss Paradise, & to be assured of the esteem
with which I have the honor to be Dear Madam your
most obedient and most humble servant

                              Th: Jefferson[23]
Mrs Paradise

The more friendly tone of his letter to Paradise is an
indication of where his sympathies lay:

                              Paris July 10. 1786
Dr Sir
    I am honoréd with your letter by Dr Bancroft inclos-
ing one from Dr Burney for which I return you my
thanks and now trouble you with one to that gentleman.
I have had with Dr Bancroft much conversation on
your subject. we concur in proposing to you a short
trip to Paris, and in thinking it will relieve your health
and place you in a situation to decide on your plans
more according to the dictates of your own judgment.
he is lodged at the Place Louis XV. we could find for
you lodgings in the same quarter, & there would only
be the fine walk of the Champs Elysees between us.
I should certainly spare nothing to make your time
agreeable, and perhaps the Doctor & myself could aid
you in your determinations. the necessary expense of
the journey would be small, as would be the residence
of a single person here without a family. mr Trumbull
is setting out for this place & would be an agreeable
companion. you are the best & only judge however of
it's expediency. I shall be happy in every occasion of
serving you, & of testifying the sincerity of the esteem
with which I have the honour to be Dear Sir

        Your most obedient & most humble serv[t]

[Mr Paradise]   Th: Jefferson[24]

Jefferson confided these two letters to Thomas
Appleton, who was about to leave for London. He gave

them to Adams's son-in-law, Col. William Smith, who was instructed to deliver them privately. "I called at N° 28 Charles Street," Smith wrote Jefferson on July 18, "and delivered the letters separately agreeable to their address; the gentleman has put off every idea of his voyage untill the spring; what will be the consequence I cannot pretend to say. I fear the worst; but I can see no end to be answered by advising him, for he will ultimately follow his own opinions. The same thing which prevents him from going to America I suppose will keep him from visiting Paris, viz.: want of confidence in the prudence of his family during his absence. This is what no arguments will remove; it is riveted on his mind and sways his conduct. . ."[25] Although this was certainly Paradise's chief motive for not going, he was not yet able to bring himself to confide so mortifying a circumstance to his new friend, especially since there was another perfectly valid excuse which he could plead:

London July 28 1786.

Dear Sir;

Your very obliging letter gave me inexpressible satisfaction; as it afforded me convincing proofs of my holding that rank in your friendship, which it has ever been my ardent wish to enjoy. I entirely concur with your Excellency and with the inestimable Doctor Bancroft in opinion, that a trip to Paris would be productive of many good consequences. I thought so when the Doctor was in England, and mentioned it to Mrs Paradise more than once. But alas! my dear Sir, this trip, trifling as the expense may be with which it will be attended, I am at present totally unable to take, being, to speak the plain truth of the matter, literally ἀνάργυρος [without silver]. There are indeed friends,

and not few, who would willingly and cheerfully assist
me: but a very worthy Gentleman, with whom I have
lived in habits of the strictest intimacy for these twenty
years and upwards, has some time ago in a manner
forced upon me the loan of one hundred and fifty
pounds, which it has not yet been in my power to
reimburse; and the thoughts of my being dependant
upon him, though he has never given me the slightest
cause to feel the dependance, are so exquisitely torment-
ing to me, that for the future I am determined (and
Heaven and Earth will bear me witness that what I am
going to say comes from my very heart) sooner to
starve and become an ἑλώριον Κύνοις Οἰωνοῖσί τε Πᾶσι.
[a prey to dogs and vultures], than apply to a friend,
be he ever so dear to me, for pecuniary assistance. I
have, however, at last received two letters from my
Steward, one dated the 22d of April, the other the 26th
of the same month, in both of which he informs me
that he has shipped on board a vessel called the George
and commanded by Captain Walter Wallace, forty
four hogsheads of tobacco; that he would be able to
send fifteen or twenty hogsheads more by the first good
ship that should sail after the George; and that the
George was to sail the 1st of June. As soon then as this
blessed George arrives, and no words can express with
what anxiety we expect it, I shall be able to raise some
supplies from my merchant, and then will set off for
Paris without delay; for I really long to have one more
interview with your Excellency before I leave Europe;
as it is on you and you alone that all my hopes depend. . . . . My Wife and daughters join with
me in every good wish to you and your amiable family.
I beg to be remembered with the sincerest affection to
Doctor Bancroft, and have the honour to be with the
greatest respect

Dear Sir:
Your most obliged humble Servt

John Paradise[26]

Although Jefferson was now perfectly aware of the family difficulties which Paradise had refrained from mentioning, he tactfully avoided reference to them in his reply:

Paris Aug. 8. 1786.

Dear Sir

I have been honoured with your favour of July 20. & it's duplicate of July 28. I am glad that you concur in the opinion that a trip to Paris will be advisable and I shall be happy in the pleasure of your company here and in every occasion of serving you. perhaps you will find it convenient to come on the return of Dr Bancroft whom you will have seen in London before this.—we have obtained a regulation here obliging the farmers general to buy, from such individuals as offer, 15,000 hhds of tob° a year at 34^{tb}. 36^{tb}. & 38^{tb} the quintal, according to it's quality. if you could send your tobacco here in a *French* vessel it might obtain you that price which I apprehend to be more than is given in London. a port where there are manufactories of tobacco would be best, as there would be an abatement of 1^{tb}10^s the quintal in any other port. I have lately received a letter dated May 12. 1786. from my friend Col° Madison of Orange to whom I had written on your affairs. it contains the following paragraph. 'Doct^r Bancroft's application in favor of mr Paradise, inclosed in your letter, shall be attended to as far as the case will admit; though I see not how any relief can be obtained. if mr Paradise stands on the list of foreign creditors, his Agent here may probably convert his securities into money without any very great loss, as they rest on good funds, and the principal is in a course of paiment. if he stands on the domestic list, as I presume he does, the interest only is provided for, and, since the postponement of the taxes, even that cannot be negociated without a discount of ten per cent at least. the principal cannot be turned into cash without sinking three fourths of it's amount.' the question, you see then, is whether you be considered as a citizen or a foreigner? in *mind* I know you to be zealously a citizen, but in *body*, the law will consider you as a foreigner: because that has not only presented that the oath of fidelity shall be taken, but that it shall be taken before some *magistrate in the country*. this you have never had an opportunity to do. as you are therefore subject to any loss which the character of a foreigner might bring on you, so you ought to avail yourself of any benefit which it may bring. mrs Paradise's being born a citizen, saves the estate from confiscation. your being a foreigner entitles you to prompt paiment of the debt due to you. I would therefore press you strongly to avail yourself of this circumstance & to instruct your agent to claim paiment for you as a foreigner. he may safely apply to mr Madison for advice, & cannot obtain better advice. get paiment as a foreigner first, & then reward our country by becoming it's citizen. present me affectionately to mrs & miss Paradise & be assured of the esteem with which I have the honour to be Dear Sir your friend & serv^t

Th: Jefferson[27]

Mr Paradise

This legalistic-sounding advice of Jefferson's was surely equitable. Paradise had suffered in England by being thought an American, and in America his affairs had been thrown into disorder by his being thought an Englishman; it seemed only fair that he should be permitted to enjoy whatever benefits there might be in such a situation.

The unreasonably long delay in receiving the shipment of tobacco, which had been ready since the preceding April, is difficult to account for. In a moment of desperation Paradise had, against his principles, appealed for help to his brother-in-law, William Lee.

He had asked him to attend to having his tobacco shipped to London and consigned, not to a merchant there,
but to himself. Although Lee obeyed the letter of the
instructions, he was not able to disregard an opportunity to turn an honest penny and he had the tobacco
shipped by his own merchants, Donald & Burton of
Virginia and London. At the same time he wrote to
Paradise in the strongest terms, suggesting that he was
under obligations to Donald & Burton for having
undertaken the shipment (a thing which they for some
unexplained reason were reluctant to do), and that
therefore Paradise owed it to them to allow them to
handle the tobacco in London. This would of course
have meant a commission for William Lee as well,
although he does not trouble to mention this circumstance.[28] On the whole it was not an unfriendly act, but
Paradise seems to have regarded it as such on the
grounds that he had ordered the tobacco to be consigned to himself direct. He silently ignored William
Lee's request and when the tobacco at length arrived he
turned it over to his own merchant. This precipitated a
breach between them that was never fully to heal. The
"blessed George," with its badly-needed cargo, did not
arrive until the first of August, and Paradise seems to
have held Lee responsible for this long delay.

Soon afterwards, Mrs. Paradise wrote another of her
confidential letters to Jefferson, a letter which, inten-
tionally or otherwise, disregarded their most recent
correspondence:

Dear Sir
I had the honour to receive your Excellencys kind
and friendly letter of the 29th of May, for which I

return you a thousand thanks. The present situation of our affairs is truly distressing, as a debt of such an enormous size is not easily discharged. The Ship we expected arrived a few weeks ago, and brought only 44 Hogs^{hd} of tobacco, I say only 44 as it is not enough to pay the creditors and at the same time to support the family. The very valuable library we had has at different times been sold, and the last of them were disposed of about a month ago. Mr Paradise received your Excellencys letter, and likewise the letters for the gentlemen in Virginia, for which he told me, he was greatly obliged to you, and that had he had money he would have set out immediately on receiving your kind invitation. He has told me and our dear friend Dr Bancroft that he would positively go in the Spring and take his family with him. There are many months to the Spring, therefore if he could be advised, and prevailed upon to go in October, and he would go, I think it would be the wisest action he ever did. The merchant we have now got, is a very proper one, as he is perfectly acquainted with all my relations and likewise with our property: His name is Gist and he lives in America Square Crutched friers. To this gentleman if I was Mr Paradise I would lay open the whole of the debt I owed, and ask him if he would become the only creditor, I mean by that, if he would advance the whole of the money that would be necessary to pay all the creditors. I am of opinion he would, and then Mr Paradise could go very easely in October: For the longer he stays here the greater the distresses he must necessarily draw himself and his family into. This letter will be delivered into your Excellencys hand by Mr Voss a very amiable honest and good young gentleman and a native of Virginia. He has promised to deliver it to you himself and if it will not be intruding upon your precious moments, he will bring me your Excellencys Answer at his return. The truly kind and friendly part you take in my affairs I never shall forget

as long as I live, and I beg you will believe me when
I assure you that if there is an thing in this World I
can be of service to you, or your amiable daughters,
you have only to let me know it, and I will do it to the
utmost of my poor abilities,

And remain
Your Excellencys most
Obliged humble Servant

Lucy Paradise[29]

P. S
I beg no mention may be made of this letter to M^r P.
London Charles St
August the 15th 1786—

Jefferson's prompt reply indicates the thoughtful
consideration which he gave to these suggestions:

Paris, Aug. 27, 1786.

Dear Madam,—I am honored with your letter of the
15th inst. by Mr. Voss. I concur with you in opinion
that it is for Mr. Paradise's interest to go as soon as
possible to America and also to turn all his debts into
one, which may be to Mr. Gist or any other: upon
condition that the person giving him this credit shall
be satisfied to receive annually his interest in money,
and shall not require consignments of tobacco. This is
the usual condition of the tobacco merchants. No *other
law* can be more oppressive to the mind or fortune, and
long experience has proved to us that there never was
an instance of a man's getting out of debt who was once
in the hands of a tobacco merchant & bound to consign
his tobacco to him. It is the most delusive of all snares.
The merchant feeds the inclination of his customer to
be credited till he gets the burthen of debt so increased
that he cannot throw it off at once, he then begins to
give him less for his tobacco & ends with giving him
what he pleases for it, which is always so little that

though the demands of the customer for necessaries be reduced ever so low in order to get himself out of debt, the merchant lowers his price in the same proportion so as always to keep such a balance against his customer as will oblige him to continue his consignments of tobacco. Tobacco always sells better in Virginia than in the hands of a London merchant. The confidence which you have been pleased to place in me induces me to take the liberty of advising you to submit to any thing rather than to an obligation to ship your tobacco. A mortgage of property, the most usurious interest, or any thing else will be preferable to this. If Mr. Paradise can get no single money lender to pay his debts, perhaps those to whom he owes might be willing to wait, on his placing in the hands of trustees in London whom they should approve, certain parts of his property, the profits of which should suffice to pay them within a reasonable time. Mr. Voss gives me hopes of seeing Mr. Paradise here. I shall not fail to give him such information as my knowledge of the country to which he is going may render useful: nor of availing myself of every occasion of rendering him, yourself & family every service in my power, having the honour to be with sentiments of the most perfect esteem & respect, Madam, &c.[30]

The gap that occurs in Jefferson's correspondence with Paradise in the autumn of 1786 makes it seem probable that Paradise actually did visit him in Paris. If so, it was the only one of the present suggestions that was carried into effect. The debts were not turned over to Gist or to any other single creditor, but remained in their ever-increasing chaotic condition. The voyage to America was definitely given up until the following spring. Perhaps in private conversation Paradise was able to present to Jefferson his real reason for not wishing to leave London and to convince him of the validity of it. The question was not afterwards agitated between them for many months and then only after an event occurred which proved how right Paradise had been to remain upon the scene and do what was possible to mitigate the rash conduct of his irresponsible wife and daughter.

CHAPTER XII

Elopement à la Mode

"YOU have frequently heard of a Greek gentleman named Paradise who married Miss Ludwell of Virginia. By this lady Mr P. is related to me, and two daughters are the issue of the marriage. Miss Paradise was introduced into company at an age, when Passion generally triumphs over Reason unless properly restrained, and checks of any kind have been totally wanting. The consequence has been, that at the end of her sixteenth year as she now is she can scarcely number the courtships, adventures, intrigues (if so I may call clandestine tho' innocent stratagems with her admirers) in which she has been engaged. The most serious and important of all was reserved to the time when your son by consanguineal as well as national ties, became so intimately connected with the family that nothing of consequence which befel them could be altogether indifferent to him. The house of Mr P. has been for a number of years the crouded rendezvous of foreigners of distinction, and on Sunday Evenings open to almost every stranger. This circumstance while it bespoke great hospitality and kindness on the part of M^r P has subjected him and his family to great risk and inconvenience, and considering the age and disposition of the young lady, was pregnant with alarming danger. No less than 4 foreign noblemen are said already to have paid their addresses to her, and Genl Harrison of Virginia offered her his hand at 14. Though the father's vigilance saved her

from elopement with the latter, and broke off all connections with the rest, the transaction left behind it
sentiments and opinions ill suited to a girl of her time
of life and sowed the seeds of the affair which I am
now going to relate. Count Bozziza, a Venetian noble
of Senatorial rank is one of those who during the last
6 months have composed the levee Paradisiac; and
Mademoiselle, who at this time had persuaded herself
that a *lover* was to a lady of 16 a sine qua non, an
indispensable matter of course, cast her eyes upon him.
Attentively to look out for a husband and having found
an object, to lay hold of and secure it, had been long
inculcated by Mamma, and it was the religion and
morality of the young lady to govern herself by maternal precepts. The Count was adjudged worthy of Miss
Lucy's hand, and became the burden of her song.
Without entering into the particulars of the courtship
which I have had since detailed to me both by the
Count & the young lady Mr P. and Madame and which
of themselves would fill a volume let us proceed to that
crisis when upon the father's peremptorily refusing his
consent, the young couple determined to proceed without it to the goal of matrimony. . ."[1]

The young man of twenty-one whose intimacy with
the Paradise family enabled him to write his father so
well-informed an account of their elder daughter's love
affair was Thomas Lee Shippen. His "consanguineal"
relationship with Mrs. Paradise was through his
mother, who was born Alice Lee and whose marriage
to Dr. William Shippen had taken place in London
twenty-five years before in the presence of Mrs. Paradise's father.[2] Young Shippen was thus related to Mrs.
Paradise both by blood and by marriage. When he

arrived in London to study law at the Inner Temple
and proved to be "as genteel, well-bred a youth as any
one from our country,"³ Mrs. Paradise reckoned the
kinship by the Virginia method and declared it to be
even closer than it was. She opened wide for him the
doors of the house in Charles Street and it was not long
before he was on easy, friendly terms with the entire
Paradise family and with the American set of which
they were the center.

Although Shippen's home was in Philadelphia, almost half his life had been spent in Virginia. He had
been sent there for his elementary schooling, and there
he had begun the study of law under George Wythe,
at William and Mary College. He of course had
visited his mother's old home, Stratford Hall, the first
sight of which had moved him to tears by its grandeur
and associations. At Green Spring he had made a close
friendship with his uncle's young son and heir, William
Ludwell Lee. At Westover, Shirley, Nesting, and
many other Virginia places he had found the gay
society that his pleasure-loving nature adored and it
was with reluctance that he had obeyed his father's
command to come to London for the completion of his
legal education.

It would be hard to imagine a more homesick young-
ster than he was on his first arriving. His parents and
his two uncles, William and Arthur Lee, all of whom
had spent years in London, gave him introductions to
many of their former associates; but these, although
some of them later proved friendly, were at first inclined to hold themselves aloof and the young Ameri-

can's impressions of English hospitality were far from
pleasant. The only Englishman whom he found congenial at the first was John Wilkes, who many times
invited him to dinner at Dilly's and entertained him
with his wit and his reckless talk. Wilkes and his crew
were unblushing libertines, but young Shippen un-
blushingly enjoyed their society for a time at least.
Another welcoming hand was that of the Scotchman,
James Boswell. "I met with a Mr Boswell at Mr Dilly's
table some time ago," Shippen wrote his father, "who
mentioned you with great respect and consideration; he
said that he had known you intimately at Edinburgh,
and had passed many jovial & agreable days there in
your society. He is the gentleman who has made himself famous lately in the world of letters by his history
of Corsica, and his tour to the Hebrides, which he
performed in company with Dr S. Johnson. . ."[4] Some
time later he wrote his father that "the good Boswell
gave me a dinner not long since in celebration of the
happy scenes he had passed with my father—he is very
fatherly and polite."[5] Such instances of friendliness
among the British were, however, extremely rare at
this time and Shippen very naturally gravitated into
the American circles of the Adams and Paradise households. There his attractive personality won him easy
success. The ladies, especially, found him charming
and constantly commanded his services on social occasions. Mrs. John Adams and her daughter, when
they gave a large party, "engaged Mr. Shippen as an
assistant."

On the evening of the 9th of February, 1787, the
corps diplomatique gave a ball in the Festino Rooms
in Hanover Square, which they annually hired for the

occasion. The Adamses were of course invited, but Mr.
Adams "preferred the society of Grotius in his cabinet
to that of the Diplomatics," as Shippen wrote his
sister, and transferred his ticket to his young friend,
"who not only had no scruple against dancing but
wished very much to be of the party." As Mrs. Adams's
escort, he represented "la seule personne de Monsr
Adams." They arrived at the Festino Rooms at nine
o'clock, an hour too early, in the company of Col.
Smith and Mrs. Rucker. "The two principal rooms
are very lofty and spacious," wrote Shippen, "capable
of containing with ease 300 persons each. The dancing
room is ornamented on all sides by mirrors of a thous-
and different shapes and sizes which are themselves
adorned by parti-coloured festoons and gilded frames.
The cieling is handsomely painted, and the upper parts
of the sides are diversified by statuary. The Supping
room is not unlike the temporary building which the
Chevalier de la Luzerne erected in Philad^a in com-
memoration of the Dauphin's birth. It is not quite so
large, but it is hung with the richest tapestry. . ."
Shippen soon discovered his friends the Paradises and
of course paid Mrs. Paradise the customary tribute of
dancing a minuet with her. After he had danced another set with Miss Paradise, his eye happened to fall
on a "young and blooming damsel" who sat unoccupied
and alone upon a bench. "I found her lovely and
interesting, her face was a compound of ineffable
sweetness and penetrating sagacity . . . I was convinced
that her temper was that of an angel . . . I could not
resist the temptation of sitting down beside her, and
we entered into conversation." With this Arabian-
Nights beginning he makes a long story of his flirtation

with the young lady throughout most of the rest of the evening, apparently oblivious of the fact that he was supposed to be representing "la seule personne de Monsr Adams." At four A.M. he returned to his own group; the dancing continued until after five.[6]

Shippen's partiality for the other sex was very great indeed and is reflected in at least one incident of his professional career. It was customary for the students at the Temple to hold occasional debates at Westminster Hall. There in October, 1786, he took part in a discussion of "whether the conduct of Charlotte in receiving the visits of Werter after her marriage" was "consistent with female delicacy." He successfully upheld the lady's cause and won the enthusiastic applause of his audience of five hundred people.[7]

The intimacy which he formed with his cousins the Paradises continued to grow, as is shown by the increasing number of shillings he spent for cab fare between the house in Charles Street and his rooms in the Inner Temple and for tips to "Mr Paradise's porter."[8] Each member of the family learned to consider him as a special friend. His eagerness and his naive enjoyment of everything that was presented for his entertainment made him an ideal protégé for the worldly Mrs. Paradise.

On a Sunday afternoon late in January of 1787, he accompanied Mr. Paradise to an exhibition of paintings held by the wealthy virtuoso, John Udny of Teddington, one time British consul at Leghorn. His fine collection contained paintings by Titian, Corregio, Dominichino, Rubens, and Van Dyke. Just as Shippen's "fancy grew jaded," they were led up to two veiled pictures from which Mr. Udny himself drew

back the curtains. The first was of Venus in the Arms
of Cupid, by Guido. "The Venus was such a one as
Shakespeare's where he says we see Fancy outwork
Nature." His boredom was at once dispelled. "I was
fixed and rivetted, I could not for a considerable time
leave the spot or discontinue my adoring." However,
the relentless Udny drew back the curtain and then revealed the other painting, which was Corregio's half-
length painting of Christ wearing the crown of thorns.
With a rapid change of mood, Shippen declared that it
would immediately have made him into a Christian
even if he had been an Infidel before—"tho' less attractive to youthful blood" than the other.[9] This incident,
so unselfconsciously narrated in a family letter, forms
a good epitome of young Shippen's character. Easily
and quickly swayed, he was sympathetic to a fault and
perhaps too readily won to the opinion of the last
person with whom he had talked; but in this he was
completely without guile and when he offended, as he
sometimes did, it was always from an excess of good
will.

On the morning of Saturday, March 10, 1787,
Shippen received a peremptory summons to call on
Mrs. Paradise in Charles Street. He rightly suspected
that she wished to consult him regarding her daughter's
affair with Count Barziza, which had been going on
for months and now, as was clear to everybody, was
approaching some sort of a climax. He found her still
at breakfast and awaiting him in great excitement. She
soon revealed that the Count had proposed, that Mr.
Paradise had flatly refused his consent, and that the

lovers had determined to elope. Although her conversation with Shippen was self-contradictory and confused, it was clear to him that she not only approved
but was actually willing to assist them. "Mrs. P." he
wrote his father, "always actuated by tenderness and
zeal for her daughter's advancement, tho' not perceiving very clearly the combination of causes and effects,
without approving winked at the measure, and tho' she
was determined not to assist, yet did assist them in the
accomplishment of it. Indeed she went so far as to
send for me on the occasion, communicate to me the
whole minutiæ of the business, and endeavor to interest
me and all my resources, as she termed it, in her daughter's favour, telling me at the same time that she
dreaded the consequences and wished it could be
avoided. In the afternoon of the day on which the first
mention of the affair had been made to me, Miss P.
wrote me a very affectionate letter, stating that she had
been informed of her mother's making me a confidant,
that she highly approved of it, and imploring my aid
and counsel. With her letter she sent a very handsome
drawing of her own in a large gilt frame, supposing
that as in Morocco, so in the seat of Law-study, no
request accompanied by presents could fail of success.
In answer to this, I wrote a long and solemn epistle,
stating in the most alarming manner that I could, the
nature, circumstances, & probable effects of her per-
severing in the enterprize in which she had embarked,
considering the distance of the Country to which she
must reconcile herself, and this person being almost a
stranger to whom, in the most confidential and unre-
served manner she confided herself, her innocence and
her honor."[10]

Shippen's diary takes up the story at this point: "Sunday, March 11, 1787. (Inner Temple) Rose at 8, dispatched the letter which I had written yesterday to Charles Street and continued my common place of Evidc° until about eleven oclock when I was called to see a gentleman who was waiting for me in a coach and impatient to see me. I pulled off my robe de chambre and went to the Temple gate in my slippers, where instead of a gentleman three ladies had done me the honor to call upon me & offer me a ride in their carriage & here the finest scene took place yᵗ perhaps ever was imagined much less realized. Madᵉ [Paradise] & her two daughters were the party: & having now become the confidant of both mother & daughter, the budgets of both were opened upon me at once: perpetual interruptions loud and louder vociferations were echoed across yᵉ coach if not across yᵉ City, and I begged yᵗ they would drive over yᵉ bridge. To this they consented. And then yᵉ plans were laid before me. Letters upon letters were given me by Miss which had been written to her by yᵉ Count, all which I was to read tho' written in a very bad hand of French hieroglyphics, while she & her mother vying with each other who should talk loudest and who yᵉ fastest, were pouring in oceans of complaints, apprehensions, plans & determinations all wᶜʰ [were] inconsistent & contradictory, unreasonable & impracticable. While I sat listening with both my right hand & my lap filled with Miss's letters, very much engaged in decyphering them, they imagined that nothing would be easier than for me to read them all hear all their schemes and advise them upon every one of them & all in a moment. Law, Mamma, & Law, Miss P. were the exclamations when one conceived that ye other took up too much of my attention which that there might be no possibility of vacuum in it, Mrs. P. now pulls out a large parcel of papers containing her marriage settlement which she had purloined out of her husband's private Drawer with a false key, ye division of her father's estate, his last will, articles of agreement and separation &c &c &c. Three of these she begged I would look at while I had still some scores of her daughter's letters unperused and explain to her ye true construction. By all means. They filled my left hand and ye part of ye front seat of ye coach which was not occupied by Philippa & myself. I sat in ye middle of it & facing the two orators. To one I gave my right ear to the other my left. I kept ye papers of one lady in one hand; ye other hand was devoted to ye other lady—To satisfy them I read the papers two at a time and remarked upon each as I found time."[11]

"Had I considered the nature of the female character but for a moment," Shippen later wrote his father, "or put into practice, the little knowledge which my short lived experience had given me of women, I should have been quickly satisfied that to give advice to Miss P. in her situation unless it corresponded *exactly* with her determinations and preconceived opinion, was like the mastiff barking at the sea. I had taken considerable pains as I said before, to paint in the most awful colours the success of her design; In the instant of receiving my letter, she ordered the carriage, that she might concert with me the best and most certain means of effectuating it. Such is woman! and such always will be a young woman improperly educated! How much care and attention they require, how much ought

parents to bestow! Miss P. went to the length of persuading me to consent to an interview with the Count.
It was determined that he should wait upon me on the
following Tuesday & no conference allowed between
the two lovers. The hour of appointment came and the
Venetian employed two hours in disclosing every particular of his connexion with the young lady, from the
first dawn of his acquaintance with her until the moment I bade him tell it. There were some things into
which it was necessary for me to enquire before I could
speak to him with confidence, and he left me promising
to return on a particular day and at a certain hour, and
thanking me for the patience I had discovered in listening to him for so long and with so much attention."[12]

Shippen now turned his attention to the documents
which Mrs. Paradise had stolen from her husband's
escritoire and put in his possession—her marriage contract and her father's will. On these depended the vital
question of whether Paradise really could, as he had
threatened, disinherit his daughter if she eloped, and
Shippen's interpretation of them was impatiently
awaited by all three of the conspirators. His exami-
nation showed clearly that Paradise's interest in the
Virginia estate was only a life interest and that there
was nothing he could possibly do to prevent his daughter from inheriting her share. Late on Wednesday
evening he wrote this welcome news to Miss Paradise
in a letter, enclosing the stolen papers with it. The
letter contained, as Shippen wrote his father, "some
expressions of *duty and affection owing by a daughter
to a good parent* &c which tempered and qualified in
some degree the mention which I made of an elope-

ment."[13] It was dispatched to Charles Street early Thursday morning.

The person who received it was Mr. Paradise. Already suspicious, he guessed intuitively that the bulky packet addressed to his daughter contained some matter about which he ought to be informed. He hastily took it to Dr. Bancroft, who lived nearby in Charlotte Street, and after consultation the two men broke the seal and read the contents. These revealed to the outraged father that his daughter was planning an elopement with the secret connivance of his wife, who had gone so far as to rifle his personal papers to gain her end. In the stormy interview with his daughter which at once ensued, she openly defied him and declared that she would marry Barziza either with or without his consent. Paradise threatened what was then a parent's prerogative—that he would lock her up until she came to her senses. It was then the young girl gave her father the best of all possible reasons for consenting to the marriage; she told him that she had already, as she expressed it, "lost her virtue" to the Count. By no amount of coercion was Paradise able to discover whether this statement was true or whether it was merely a stratagem to gain her point. He decided that the safest course was to keep her in confinement until the truth could be determined. Realizing that Mrs. Paradise would certainly find means to release her, if he locked her up at home, Paradise appealed for help to one of his oldest friends and before the day was out the would-be Countess Barziza found herself a prisoner in the house of Richard Paul Joddrell in the City.

The next day young Shippen was summoned once more to the breakfast-table of Mrs. Paradise. He found

her alone, for Paradise, after the excitement of yesterday's crisis, had taken to his bed. Suppressing only the
fact of her daughter's confession, she told him of all
that had occurred. Almost insane with anger, she
plunged without intermission into a declaration of her
wrongs and of her determination to leave her husband.
"That you may better comprehend the mysteries of this
perplexed affair," Shippen told his father, "you must
know further that between M^r and Mrs P. there has
been a four years contention upon the subject of their
going to America, Mad^e violently urging to go in every
vessel: Monsr wishing still a little longer to postpone
it. In this I had often been called in. To him, I advised (and I was serious) compliance with his wife's
wishes; to her, composure and resignation to her husband's will. In this counsel pacification was my object.
Sometimes I had succeeded in placating them, sometimes had been involved in their confusion. But at the
time of this love embrarrassment of the daughter—
unexpectedly, because we all thought her much interested in it—the mother, perhaps supposing a storm
favorable to her design, took it into her head more
warmly than ever to press the execution of her favorite
measure and proposed separation from her husband,
or going alone, or any thing that might be a means of
compassing her darling object." Shippen, although he
was hugely enjoying all the excitement, was at length
obliged to take his leave to fill a previous engagement
with Count Barziza; he promised to return to dinner.

He was "under the hair dresser" at his chambers in
the Temple when Barziza arrived. "He shewed me a
number of letters which he had received the day before
from Miss P. in one of which she mentioned having

told her father that she had lost her virtue & I could not find out certainly whether this was a stratagem or not, but left y⁰ Count, determined to find out from the mother and if y⁰ story were true to use my utmost influence with P. to gain his consent &c—I agreed to meet Baz at 2 o'clock in Pulteney Street to inform him what had been done, and went again to Charles Street. Mʳˢ P. met me at y⁰ door. I expressed so much apprehension lest y⁰ information given by Miss P. to her father should be true that she seemed quite alarmed, and declared to me that it was nothing but a trick &c But not quite satisfied herself by my advice she wrote a letter to her daughter which I dictated desiring in a most solemn manner yᵗ she would declare whether she was virtuous &c. In the mean while I went up to see Mʳ P., who was at 2 o'clock enfoncé dans un lit affreux couvert de tabac. Most miserable indeed was his situation, in a state of complete intoxication with the instrument of his ruin standing beside his bed. To this he ever and anon recurred notwithstanding a violent fever which it had already occasioned and which confined him helpless to his bed. He thought now that it was necessary to his existence and I could not persuade him that it was certain poison. A great deal of conversation took place and I was surprised to find that drunk as he was he spoke so rationally. There was but one point in which I thought him absurd—It was my principal object to persuade him that in case what his daughter had told him were true he had no alternative, but must give his consent. He insisted that she should go to Virgᵃ and repent while he prosecuted for seduction of an Heiress &c." He found that Paradise in reading the

sage, if not entirely heart-felt, counsels in the inter-
cepted letter had drawn the best conclusions from them
and was now more his friend than ever.

Completely beside himself with the anguish of his
situation, Paradise could think of nothing—now that
his daughter was *"in salva et archa custodia"* at the
house of his friend—but how to escape from the incoherent recriminations of his wife. He promised to quit
the bottle, but only on condition that Shippen would
accompany him on a journey somewhere away from
London. He would not go alone; he could not remain
with Mrs. Paradise and stay sober; he implored Shippen to go with him to Oxford. There in the quiet
society of his scholarly friends he could hope to be
restored to health and reason. It was agreed that they
should set out early the following morning, and Shippen then left Charles Street for a second conference
with Barziza.

He found Barziza in his apartments in Pulteney
Street, sitting with the Venetian Minister, Count
Soderini. Confident that Paradise's consent would have
been gained, Barziza had begun to pack his belongings
and was surrounded with clothes and packages and
trunks. When Shippen informed him of Paradise's
inexorable refusal, he flew into a violent rage and began
to talk a great deal about *his* injured honor. Since
Paradise had already made inquiries about his character, he said, the refusal to sanction the marriage would
cast a reflection upon him to which he would never,
never submit. Shippen and Count Soderini used every
possible argument to convince him that no such in-
ference could be drawn. They reminded him that the
laws of England gave fathers a power over their daugh-

ters which they might exercise without accounting to anyone, and that Paradise had done no more than exert this power. But Barziza obstinately continued to rage about his damaged reputation, (completely unmindful of that of his intended wife,) until Shippen was obliged to leave him to his heroics.

"I now returned once more to Charles Street; and dined with Mrs. P. Mr. P. being too unwell to join our party. We talked over the favorite subject of Trans Atlantic joys and were comforted with the prospect. In the Evening Mr. P. came down and looked wretchedly. The only subject upon which he could either think or converse his daughter was again discussed, and after a great deal of argument & persuasion on my part being expended in vain he desired me to go and consult Dr Bankroft. To this I very chearfully assented and went to Charlotte Street. I soon found that ye D^r was with me in opinion—while I was here ye daughter's answer was brought to me, which I read to ye D^r—and after an half hour's conversation I went to tell Mr P. that his friend concurred with me. I now took my leave of Charles Street, promising to return the next morning and went to Grosnenor Square, where I found besides the [Adams] family my friend Cutting & Mr Trumbull—I played cards with this most amiable family until 11 o'clock and then came home accompanied by Mr Trumbull as far as Rathbone [Place]. As I perceived him to be in ye secrets of ye P. family I communicated to him what had passed in the morning and explained the peculiarity of my own situation—at the same time the confidant of the husband & wife of the father & ye daughter in ye most violent controversies between them all, & convulsions to which no period

was promised or apparent. I went quietly to bed waiting for what the morrow might bring forth."[14]

The next day, Saturday, Shippen arrived at the
Paradise's at ten o'clock, where he found Mr. Paradise
still in bed, but preparing to go as planned to Oxford.
At his insistence a post chaise was ordered. Mrs.
Paradise seems to have been singularly reconciled to
her husband's departure at this critical time. She prepared the morning chocolate for them, which Shippen
declared was excellent, and sent them on their way.
By five o'clock they had reached March's Tavern at
Salthill, where they dined. Although Paradise kept his
bottle in the carriage beside him, he abstained from
drinking from it. He could talk of no subject except
the disgrace and misery to which his daughter had
reduced him,—"of prospects blighted, hopes destroyed,
and all immeasurable ills blown thick upon him." At
Salthill he dictated a letter to Mrs. Paradise in which
he reaffirmed his position: that he would never give his
consent. They pressed on that night to the small village
of Henley, where they took supper at a tavern at twelve
and retired. Although still abstaining from his bottle,
Paradise placed it beside his bed. "Rest, or rather
sleep," says Shippen, "my companion found not, but he
passed a most miserable & sleepless night."

On Sunday morning, the 18th, they went on to Benton
for breakfast, "where we found a cold bad house with
nothing good in it and an ugly squinting waiter sent on
purpose as he thought to distress my poor hesterical
friend who had been attended by squinting people ever
since his acquaintance with the squinting Bazziza—
When we got into the carriage we discovered at a distance a man cloathed in a Turkish habit, walking

toward us. Mr P. asked him in the Turkish language
from what Country he came. This appeared to astonish
him and he vented his astonishment by an ejaculation
of this sort—In the name of God where did you learn
Turkish! They conversed in 5 different languages and
then we drove off leaving upon the minds of the mob
who had been drawn together by the singular appear^ce
of the stranger the impression of Mr. P wonderful
learning. The Turk had a ribband and some other
ensignia of *ordered* distinction which Mr P. supposed
he must have assumed as the Turks have no orders."

In Oxford at twelve o'clock they put up at the Angel
Inn. "Mr P. sent for his Doctor's cap & gown and both
of us asked the assistance of a hair dresser—A hair
dresser came and I made choice of a warm room over
the kitchen to be dressed in. Here after dressing I
prevailed upon the chamber maid to bring me a pail
of hot water & in the hot water I did myself ye honor
to bathe me from head to foot, and was thereby wonder-
fully refreshed." After their dinner—a haunch of
mutton, rabbits & fish, which with two sorts of wine
made it a "nobly good repast"—they set out to see the
walks, the Colleges being closed on Sunday. At first
they went to Christ Church Walk, "a most beautiful,
romantic & shady place," but they soon found that it
had ceased to be fashionable since Paradise's acquaintance with Oxford and therefore repaired to Eddington
Hill Walk, which "rivalled and surpassed" Christ
Church. There they met a great many students, heads
of colleges, fellows, professors and tutors. "Among the
four last classes my friend recognized a number of his
old acquaintances. In particular Mr Crowe ye public
orator of ye University Mr Crofts a fellow of Univer-

sity College and a compiler of a new dictionary a D^r
Stackhouse fellow of Queens and Mr Shergoure fellow
of Pembroke. They all expressed great satisfaction at
meeting their old friend, and severally invited him to
their apartments where they assured him in the Oxford
phraseology that they should be glad to wait upon him.
The Eddington Hill walk is upward of a mile and a
half in extent and exhibits greater variety and more
romantic prospects than any I have known. It is no
impeachment of ye Oxonian Taste that this walk has
superceded that of Christ Church in fashion—It is
remarkable also for a number of little stiles at y^e
distance of 200 or 300 yards in some places at a greater
distance from each other, put there I suppose to arrest
the progress of vagrant cattle. They give you some
difficulty in passing as it is necessary to go round in
order to get by them. This merely serves however as
the thistle to ye rose. We met at least 200 students tho'
ye most crowded hour was past before we began our
peregrinations." At half past two they found Mr.
Crowe awaiting them at the Angel Inn with an offer
to take them to hear a "chanting" at New College
chapel and an invitation to dine with him the next day
when he would be glad to show them the "curiosities"
of Oxford. At three they dined and set out to St. Peter's
in the East to hear a University sermon. But they
arrived "just as ye sermon was ended, lamented our
hard fate, and returned to the Inn." Here "we finished
the bottles of wine which were left at dinner, and prepared ourselves for a visit to Dr Noel the Principal of
St. Mary Hall (ye place where Mr P. was educated)
and M^r P's old master. The old gentleman received us
with great cordiality and did every thing that was

possible to raise my unhappy friend's spirits. He was sunk almost to a state of desperation and nothing could relieve him for a moment. Every thing that was said reminded him either of his wife or his daughter, they were both sources of intarissable [?] grief and melancholy to his distressed mind—We drank tea with Dr Noel and heard a cat & dog story from his wife: very interesting to me but Mr P. could not prevail upon himself to attend to one word of it, tho' she constantly addressed herself to him. We went from Dr Noel's to make 2 or 3 visits and returned at 8 oclock to ye Angel where we supped upon a roasted fowl and at eleven oclock retired to our chamber."

The next day was bright and brilliant, the air fragrant, and after a breakfast of strong coffee and well-roasted muffins they set out on a tour of the buildings, going first to the Bodleian. But Paradise was "weak and impatient" and they soon left. Here Shippen's account of the journey abruptly breaks off. They remained for several days more, however, during which they visited some of the country estates in the neighborhood of Oxford.[15]

Back in London within the week, Paradise was confronted with a *fait accompli*. Mrs. Paradise, his daughter, and Count Barziza had disappeared. In some way Mrs. Paradise had managed to free her daughter from confinement and the most hopeful presumption was that by now she was married to the Count. Paradise now turned to Bennet Langton for assistance, and the two of them held a consultation with Sir John Hawkins as to what legal steps could be taken.[16] However, before any action was possible the runaways returned. According to a letter from Dr. Bancroft to Thomas Jefferson, some sort of marriage ceremony had taken place:

Dear Sir

I have been deprived much longer than I expected of the Pleasure of seeing you in Paris, and I am afraid my business here will not permit my return to that Capital until the middle or latter End of May. It is however at the desire of Mr Paradise that I now address myself to you, as the present State of his mind (from the recent Elopement & marriage of his eldest Daughter to Count Barziza a Venetian Nobleman) joined to his general ill health renders him unable to write to you himself. Both M^r & Mrs Paradise seem convinced from past experience and the present contrariety of their tempers and dispositions, that it will be impossible for them to Live happily together; and it is therefore agreed that the Lady shall return to Virginia & be allowed a House in Williamsburgh, & three hundred Pounds Sterling p an. for her Separate maintenance, whilst Mr Paradise will probably fix himself in some more retired & Cheap situation than his present, perhaps at Oxford, or some place in France— But as this Plan precludes all probability of his going to America at least for some years, he is Sollicitous to Commit the Superintendance of his Affairs, & of his Stewards Conduct, to one or two Gentlemen, whose Situations are not two far removed from his Estate, & who are properly qualified, & may be induced, by their Care of his intrests to prevent the ill Consequences which might otherwise arise from his Absence. And as Mr Paradise has the utmost Confidence in your friendship, as well as in your Judgment of men & things in that Country, he earnestly intreats, as a favour of the highest importance that you will be so kind as to point out one or two Persons to whom he may with Propriety send a Power of Attorney for these Purposes, and that you would at the same time by Letter employ your good offices, to induce these persons to undertake the trust which he wishes to place in them. you are sensible that Mr Paradise is very much *disinclined* towards the Lee's and those who may be particularly Connected with them, and as Mrs Paradise is to receive her separate allowance without having any Concern in the Management of her Husbands affairs, he much wishes that the proposed Powers should be sent to persons out of this Connection—Mr Paradise requests me to assure you of the high esteem & sincere respect which he entertains for you and of his grateful sense of your former favours. permit me also to join the like assurance respecting myself, and believe me to be with the greatest truth

Dear Sir
Your most affectionate
& faithful Humble Servant

Charlotte Street   Edwd Bancroft[17]
Rathbone Place. London
March 27th 1787.

As to his daughter's marriage to Barziza, Paradise was obliged to give in. There could now be no question of her having been compromised—compromised with the shameful assistance of her mother. He did, however, demand that another ceremony should be performed, and accordingly a notice appeared under the caption of "Marriages" in all the London journals:

On Wednesday last [April 4] was married his Excellency Count Barziza, Patrician of Venice, to Miss Paradise, daughter of John Paradise, Esq; of Charles Street, Cavendish Square.[18]

All London knew the story behind that formal notice. The sharp tongue of Laetitia Hawkins, in whom her

father immediately confided, soon revealed the juicy
details that were not already known, and once more the
private affairs of John and Lucy Paradise became the
public property of their friends and enemies.

To Tom Shippen the whole affair had been like an
episode from one of the romantic novels which he liked
to read. The exciting week of secret correspondence
and "stormy interviews" in which he had played the
rôle of confidential friend to everyone concerned was
by far the most enjoyable experience of his young life.
He wrote hilarious accounts of it to his father and to
his favorite uncle, Arthur Lee, suppressing a few, but
only a few, of the most scandalous details, out of friendship for the Paradises. "I am much delighted with the
propriety & good sense of your conduct in Miss Paradise's affair," his father replied.[19] At Mrs. Paradise's
request, Shippen appealed to William Lee for advice
about her coming to Virginia, but William, still furious
with Paradise over the affair of Donald and Burton
and always impatient with Mrs. Paradise for what he
considered her high and mighty airs, was sour and
unsatisfactory: "The Ladies situation which you mention is very truely to be lamented and very difficult to
be releaved; for were I on the spot I should not know
what to advise unless it was that she should without
delay fix on her own Estate where she might at least be
comfortable and independant, tho not grand; but as to
this plan I apprehend objections will never be wanting
on one side or the other, those already made are too
childish to require refutation, for of what service can
a useless Carcass be to him that wants the yellow ore.
You seem to be pretty well acquainted with P. but I
question whether you have got to his bottom, his own

writings are very different from the strains of distress, therefore 'tis probable he conceal'd something from all about him from political reasons, and that is [that his] resources in the funds which he inherited are not yet exhausted, but of this you can form a better Judgment than me and let his situation be what it will any advice from me would be totally useless for I never ventured to give it but once and in that instance it was entirely disregarded and with the appearance of being treated with contempt, not with standing this, any thing that is in my power shall be cheerfully contributed to promote the happiness of the whole."[20] And with the deep breath that was no doubt necessary after he had completed this sentence, William Lee dismissed the Paradises to their fate.

Arthur Lee's attitude toward the Paradises had always been more friendly than William's, and he seldom failed to send them his affectionate greetings in his frequent letters to Shippen. He was obviously very much pleased that his young cousin had married a nobleman: "If the Venetian Count is not an imposter, Miss [Paradise] is very well off."[21] Shippen, among his other efforts to pour oil on the troubled waters, suggested to Barziza that he should write a polite letter to his new relation. To this letter, Arthur Lee replied in kind, but in writing of it to his nephew he inquired: "How did it happen that you said nothing about our noble relation when you enclosed his letter? Is he assuredly noble, with £2,000 per annum, and if so what could be the father's objection."[22]

The answer to this pertinent question is that Barziza was most assuredly a member of an ancient and noble Venetian family but that he very probably did not

possess an income of £2,000. The Barziza family was
one of the group forming that hereditary oligarchy
which for centuries had been in control of the so-called
Republic of Venice. The wealth which was the basis
and continuation of their undisputed power had been
derived from trade with the Levant. This trade had
been gradually wrested away from them—chiefly by
the British—and in the resulting decline of both wealth
and power the Barziza family, with many others, had
been involved. Much of the grandeur, however, still
remained and Count Antonio Barziza, of whom Paradise had been so reluctant to become the father-in-law,
belonged to the inner circle of patricians who were of
senatorial rank and his name was emblazoned on the
pages of that most exclusive of all registers, the Libro
D'Oro of Venice. He still possessed the family palazzo
in Venice and at Alzano, not far from Milan in the
Venetian province of Bergamo, he owned a country
estate for summer residence. Of all this Paradise was
well aware; but he was also aware, through his Venetian friends Counts Soderini and Zenobio, that the
Barziza fortunes were rapidly declining. There had
been no doubt in his mind from the first that the object
of the young Count's visit to London was to mend them
by marriage to a wealthy woman. This was undoubtedly Paradise's chief objection to the match. He naturally
did not wish his daughter to be married to a fortune-
hunter, especially when he knew that the expectations
of wealth were far higher than the fulfillment was
likely to be. He knew only too well from his own
bitter experience to what unhappiness a husband and
wife could be brought by disappointment and quarrels
over money. Immediately after the marriage Barziza

engaged an English lawyer through whom he insisted
on a settlement, but of course in the present state of
Paradise's affairs no ready money was available and
the Count was obliged to be contented for a time with
a strictly worded agreement that his wife or her heirs
should inherit a half of her parents' fortune at their
death. The later demands that Barziza made, as his
own fortunes continued to decline, were neither so
reasonable nor so easy for the Paradises to meet, and
before many years had passed even Mrs. Paradise was
forced to acknowledge that her daughter's choice and
hers had been a most unhappy one. The Count's squint-
eyed unattractiveness of appearance and his far from
prepossessing manner, which at first had been out-
dazzled by his worldly position, did not make his
cupidity, and certain other more personal disadvantages
which later developed, any easier to bear. Happily for
Paradise he was never to learn the full extent of his
daughter's payment for the distinction of being styled
the Countess Barziza.

Mrs. Paradise's sense of triumph over her daughter's
marriage did not blind her to the fact that there was
another field to gain before her victory should be
complete. Her determination to go to Virginia had by
now become an obsession. In this she was motivated
partly by a sentimental desire to return to her old home,
which she now envisioned as a far more desirable place
of residence than London, and partly by the real
necessity of someone's attending at first hand to the
affairs of the Virginia estate. On this purpose she now
bent every effort of her inexorable will. If her husband

would not go with her she would go alone; nothing mattered, now that her mind was made up, except that she should have her way. It seemed at first that she would be forced to yield to the compromise outlined in Bancroft's letter to Jefferson—but not for long. Her husband's resistance had been weakened rather than strengthened by his unusual effort at the time of his daughter's elopement, and his anger soon dwindled into nervous irritability. It was not very difficult for Bancroft to persuade him to a reconciliation and once more he renewed the bad but unbreakable habit of living with his wife. The reversal of their plans was announced in an exultant letter to Jefferson, written and composed by Mrs. Paradise, and bearing as a symbol of her victory the joint signature of "John and Lucy Paradise," also subscribed in her own handwriting:

London June the 22ᵈ 1787

Dear Sir

Before our departure for Virginia which is to take Place the End of this Month or the beginning of next, We take the liberty to trouble your Excellency with a few lines to thank you a Thousand and a Thousand times for the friendly part you have taken in our affairs, and to assure you at the same-time of our sincere attachment to you and your family. If when we are settled in Virginia you have any thing you wish to have done, we beg you will command us, as we shall think you confer an honour upon us whenever you signify your wish for us to serve you. On the 4ᵗʰ of April His Excellency Count Antonio Barziza a Patrician of the Republick of Venice and a Gentleman with a good Character, and fortune was Married to our Eldest Daughter. We take the liberty to acquaint you with this event in our family, that in case you sho[uld] at any time think proper to go to Italy, you should be sure to meet with persons

that would shew you all the attention that such merit
as yours deserves. The Counts Estates being at Berga-
mo he lives for the greatest part of the year there a[nd]
the other part at Venice. We gave a letter to them to
present to your Excellency in case they went to Paris.
We take the libe[rty] to send you the direction of our
Dear Daug[hter] in case you should chuse to honour
her with a Letter at any time.
Her Direction À Son Excellence
Madame la Comtess Paradise Barziza
À Bergamo
Italy. Venise

We all join in best Compliments to you and wish you a
long continuance of heal[th] and happiness. And believe us to be

Your Excellencys true and Sincere
friends John and Lucy Paradise.[33]

P. S.

I cannot pass over in silence without acquainting your
Excellency the truly Active part Our Dear friend D[r]
Bancroft has taken in our affairs. And if at any time
you shall have it in your power to Serve a truly Good
and Honest Gentelman, We beg, you will remember
this Gentleman, and by so doing, you will confer an
everlasting obligation upon us, your Excellencies true
and sincere friends

John and Lucy Paradise

CHAPTER XIII

A Passage Through America

IT had required the combined offices of Bennet Langton, Sir John Hawkins, and Dr. Bancroft to bring about the reconciliation between Mr. and Mrs. Paradise.[1] In June, 1787, Paradise's former resolution to go to America accompanied by his family was about to be carried out. The decision was for Mr. and Mrs. Paradise to go to Virginia, establish a home there and then send for their younger daughter Philippa, who meanwhile was placed in Mrs. Stevenson's boarding-school in Queen-square.[2] On hearing of their intention, Thomas Jefferson with customary kindness immediately set about writing further letters of introduction and recommendation to his friends in Virginia, letters which, it seemed, were at last to be put to the use for which they were intended. Passage was engaged on the "Juno,"[3] which was to sail late in July or in August, and the day approached when John Paradise, who for eighteen years had been contemplating this journey, was at last actually to sail for Virginia. Would fate, which had so often intervened before, again put a barrier in the way? It seemed not. All arrangements went well, and the most important, the settling of the young girl Philippa comfortably and happily in her boarding-school, was finally made. Friends were admonished to show her kindness during the trying months of separation from her parents, young Shippen being especially charged with the welfare of his little cousin. All of London was aware that at length Mr.

Paradise and his lady were sailing for Virginia to take up their abode on the famous estate. And then on the actual day of sailing an accident occurred which the superstitious must have seen as a premonition of disaster. The skipper of the "Juno," Captain John Allanby, fell and broke his leg. But after some delay another captain was appointed and the ship sailed, with Mr. and Mrs. Paradise actually among its passengers. The voyage was long and disagreeable, despite the fact that August was usually a good month for crossing, and the substitute captain turned out to be a "brute," as Mrs. Paradise expressed it.[4] It was not until the latter part of September that Lucy Paradise again set foot upon her native soil, after twenty-seven years of absence, and that John Paradise for the first time saw the land of liberty and his adoption.

How must America, and especially Virginia, have appeared to one like John Paradise, who had spent his entire life in an atmosphere of European culture and wealth? Travelers from abroad[5] were impressed first of all with the wooded appearance of Virginia's shores. Out at sea, if the breeze were right, the odor of pines could be plainly discerned and a closer approach soon revealed its source in the heavy blanket of pine forests that darkened the shores of Cape Charles and Cape Henry and of the harbor of Hampton Roads itself. To unaccustomed European eyes the wooden structures in Norfolk, Yorktown, and Williamsburg were a startling and by no means attractive feature. The small storey-and-a-half residences and shops appeared mean and ill-constructed. To the critical European it was

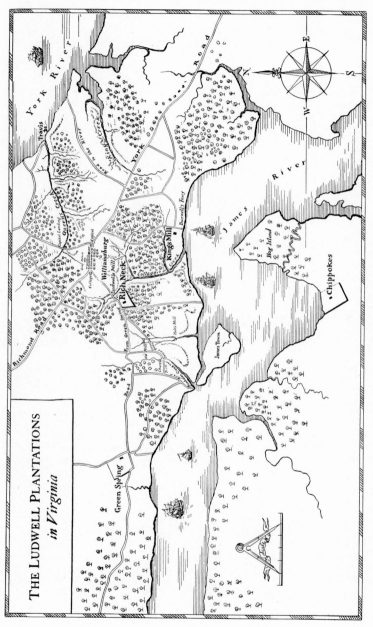

THE LUDWELL PLANTATIONS IN VIRGINIA.
A map showing the principal Ludwell properties.
Drawing by Elmo Jones.

something of a shock to discover that such small and insignificant buildings housed the most respectable inhabitants of the towns. In contrast to the neatly cultivated fields of France and England, the occasional patches of cleared ground cut out of the surrounding forest seemed ragged and wild, and the absence of fences, except for the crude though picturesque "snake" fences composed of rough-hewn rails, must have done little to mitigate the impression of a raw and undeveloped, though naturally beautiful, wilderness.

The natural aspects of Virginia presented much that was exotic to European eyes. The fields of growing tobacco were unfamiliar to them, accustomed though they were to the manufactured product. Many of the native trees, such as the dogwood, the sassafras, the tulip poplar, the liquid amber, and dozens of shrubs and wild-flowers were new and strange. To northern eyes such as theirs the slow-moving, muddy streams of eastern Virginia, their banks overgrown with vines, brambles and shrubs, the swamps with their ruddy water studded with cypress "knees," the wide sky, and the brilliant, blinding sun gave all the feeling of the tropics. Even the birds—the red-bird or "Virginia nightingale," the incredible humming-bird, and especially the mocking-bird, whose liquid notes charmed all who heard it—added to this feeling of remoteness and other-worldliness.

A surprise was in store for the unsuspecting traveler who allowed himself to be momentarily deceived by outward appearance. Some years after the Paradises' visit to Virginia, their grandson, a young viconte, fresh from his native Italy, attended a ball in Williamsburg. He saw with amazement that the young ladies present were, some of them, beautiful, and all of them well-dressed with charming, graceful manners. "How can such houris come out of such hovels?" the young man remarked imprudently, for one of the young ladies overheard and vowed a revenge which she effected by soon after becoming his wife and presenting him rapidly with ten children.[6]

Williamsburg was of course the Paradises' destination and in spite of the recent quarrel with William Lee they were received by him at Green Spring, Lucy's old home. Disagreements and differences were for a time forgotten in the excitement of their arrival and their first ten weeks in Virginia were spent there. It was convenient to Williamsburg and to the Paradise possessions of Rich Neck, Archer's Hope, and a half a dozen other farms on the near side of the James and it was only a few miles away from the ferry that would carry them across the river to the most opulent of all their possessions, Chippokes, in Surry County.

The contrast between the Virginia Lucy Ludwell had known as a child and the Virginia that Lucy Paradise beheld in 1787 was at once apparent. Eastern Virginia had been economically depressed, except for a few fitful periods of prosperity, ever since the high taxes of 1763 had first made tobacco a less profitable crop than it had ever been before. Virginia as a whole had suffered. Her great advantage before the Revolution had been her trade with England. As a colony she had been closely associated economically, as well as socially, with the mother country. Her many creeks and rivers, including the Chesapeake Bay, had served at once to isolate her from the northern colonies and to put her in easy contact with England by the sea. Trade with the

CHIPPOKES, SURRY COUNTY, VIRGINIA.

Inherited by Mrs. Paradise from the Ludwells.

Courtesy of present owner, Mr. Victor Stewart, and of Fairchild Aerial Survey.

rest of America was slight and sporadic; that with England was regular and direct. The Virginia planters could, if they chose, market their tobacco at Yorktown itself, where English merchants awaited it with English goods to give in exchange. Or if they preferred, the tobacco could be shipped to England and marketed there by a Virginia merchant, who would fill the ship for its return journey with luxuries and necessities not obtainable in Virginia. The men would send the list of their requirements to the merchant himself; their wives would send theirs to the merchant's wife. Thus almost up to the Revolution a highly satisfactory relation had existed between England and Virginia, a relation that was to be completely broken off by the war and never resumed again.

The wealthy, slave-owning class that had been made possible in Virginia by the profitable tobacco trade dates the beginning of its decline, not from the War Between the States, but from the Revolution itself. The loss of trade with England was an immediate cause, but more deep-seated than this were the inexpert methods of farming which resulted in ever poorer land and worst of all the institution of slavery, which thoughtful Virginians had long realized as an economic and social evil. Virginia's efforts to free herself from this incubus, by gradually freeing the slaves themselves, had begun long before the Paradises' arrival; but even if this evolutionary solution had not been unwisely interrupted by "reformers," its good results could not have begun to show themselves for many years. Indeed the immediate hardship on individuals who, like Lucy Paradise's nephew, freed their slaves, was a part of the burden that Virginia was bearing at this unhappy time.

That it was an unhappy time for Virginia, and especially for eastern Virginia, is testified to by every one of the European travelers who visited the country during this period.

Williamsburg and Yorktown and the great estates in their vicinity had suffered most of all. The ravages wrought by the British as well as by the friendly French and Americans during the battle of Yorktown and the months preceding it were still apparent. In private as well as public buildings, troops had been quartered, horses stabled, and enemy depredations committed. In addition to having been a storm center of the Revolution, Williamsburg had suffered another irreparable set-back. In 1779 it had been decided to move the capital of the State further inland for the sake of safety. Up until then Williamsburg had enjoyed an importance out of all proportion to its size— its population was never more than 2,000—in being the social and political center of Virginia. The removal of the capital to Richmond, the destruction by fire of the Governor's Palace, its most pretentious building, and the run-down condition of the neighboring estates had combined within a few years to reduce its population to twelve or thirteen hundred people, half of whom were Negroes. By 1787 it had dwindled into a country village. The merchants, inn-keepers, artisans, dressmakers, and public entertainers, either moved to Richmond or remained where they were in unemployment and increasing poverty. The bi-weekly market, the College, at that time consisting of eighty students and three or four professors, and the insane asylum were the only sources of revenue that the town contained. The fine old Capitol was falling into ruins and even

the statue of Lord Botetourt which occupied its peri-
style had been cracked and mutilated by the revolutionary fervor of hoodlums.[7] The unpaved streets were
ankle deep in sand and dust, and the whole town wore
an air of abandonment and desolation.

The Virginia houses in which the Paradises spent
the greater part of their time reflected outwardly the
same falling off from former splendor as did Williamsburg. Very few of them were in an even tolerable state
of repair. Ready money was scarce in all the States, but
it was scarcer in Virginia than in any of the others,
owing to the greater loss in foreign trade. In eastern
Virginia, there was less money than in any other part
of the State; even land, which in other regions had
increased three and four times in value, remained at
the same figure as before the Revolution. But although
the upper class Virginians lacked the money to buy
fine clothes and other luxuries or to repair their houses
and furniture where this required an outlay of cash,
they still had the houses themselves, with the superior
equipment from former and more prosperous times.
They had the land on which to raise their own food
and they had slaves to work the land and act as household servants. "You will find," writes La Rochefoucauld de Liancourt, ". . . very frequently a table, well
served, and covered with plate, in a room where half
the windows have been broken for ten years past, and
will probably remain so ten years longer."[8] Thus they
were enabled to live much as they had before, with the
comforting assurance that while they were growing
poor, they were growing poor slowly. They possessed
above all a morale—an *esprit de corps*—happily transmitted to their descendants of a hundred years later,

which enabled them to ignore material deficiencies and,
as it were, stare poverty out of existence by nourishing
their self-respect and pride on the consciousness of what
they were rather than what they possessed.

Such a state of things must have been disillusioning
indeed to the two travelers from England who arrived
in Williamsburg that early autumn day of 1787. Lucy's
enthusiastic childhood recollections had doubtless encouraged higher expectations than the decaying Williamsburg had been able to fulfill. Even at Green
Spring there was little alleviation for disappointed
hopes. Cornwallis's troops had occupied and robbed
the rambling old house at the time of the Battle of
Green Spring. In 1782, having been unoccupied for
more than twenty years, it was in a "ruinous" condition,
its long balcony sagging despite its props,[9] and within
a few years after the Paradises' visit it had to be torn
down and replaced with a modern structure. William
Lee was living there a widower's life with his two
young daughters and his even younger son, William
Ludwell Lee, who, as his father said, was growing up
like an "uncultivated asparagus." The fact that William Lee had been blind for a year and a half was
another unhappy discovery that greeted the Paradises
on their arrival. Nevertheless his friendly welcome did
much to atone for this and other unpleasant circumstances and at the end of six weeks Mrs. Paradise was
able to write Jefferson a reasonably cheerful account
of their visit to Green Spring and of the hospitality
which had been shown them there.[10]

The lack of actual details about the Paradises' visit
to America is more than made up for by the evidence

both then and later of the friendships which they
formed with outstanding Virginians and other Americans. Mrs. Paradise's connections insured that she and
her husband were made welcome in the best society
which Virginia afforded. It was owing to Jefferson,
however, that John Paradise was at once enabled to
make the particular kind of friends he individually
preferred. In his enthusiasm for his friend Jefferson
had written glowing letters of introduction to all the
members of his intimate circle and in this, it is needless
to say, were included the most intelligent, least provincial, and best-educated Virginians.

At the College in Williamsburg was George Wythe,
Jefferson's friend from his own days there, a Signer of
the Declaration of Independence, and now recognized
as Virginia's leading jurist and foremost classical
scholar. As "Professor of Law and Police," he occupied the earliest chair of law at any American college.
In 1787 he was sixty-one years of age and his prestige
and influence were very great. Austere, unostentatious,
methodical, he was nevertheless a man of polished,
courteous manners and one of the most ethical of law-
yers, who would relinquish a client and return his fee
if, during a case, he discovered that through deception
or some mistake of his own he had embraced an un-
worthy cause. Through Jefferson's introduction, he and
Paradise met and became immediate friends. In this
friendship Mrs. Paradise was also included and on the
death of Wythe's wife, which occurred soon after the
Paradises' arrival, she offered him such kindness and
consideration as were, he told John Page, of great
comfort to him.[11] It was a little more than a year after
the Paradises' return to Europe that Wythe was chosen

by the General Assembly as Chancellor of Virginia, a fact which Paradise, of whom he had become the "inestimable" correspondent, was able to communicate to Jefferson, who had not heard it.

Another friend at William and Mary College whom Paradise made through Jefferson was Charles Bellini, Professor of Modern Languages. As it happened, he also occupied the first chair of its kind in an American college. His opinion of Paradise is expressed in a letter to Jefferson: "He is certainly as you describe him, a man of very amiable character, who possesses all the qualities which constitute the man of letters and true gentleman, whose acquaintance and friendship are precious acquisitions to every intelligent person. But it would have been much more advantageous to me had I been recommended to him, instead of recommending him to me. I regret very much that adverse circumstances at this time, together with the constant infirmities of my wife, prevent me from showing to this very worthy gentleman all the attentions and civilities that his merit and my inclination exact, and to cultivate his valuable and edifying conversation."[12] Bishop James Madison, Professor of Moral Philosophy and Mathematics and President of William and Mary, also made the acquaintance of the Paradises,[13] and John Paradise was admitted to the Board of Visitors of the College.[14]

Jefferson of course introduced Paradise to his oldest friend, John Page, with whom he maintained an unbroken intimacy. Page was the owner of Rosewell, in Gloucester County, one of the most magnificent of all the Virginia plantation houses. He was twice married; first to Alice Grymes, a cousin of Mrs. Paradise's, by whom he had twelve children; and second to Margaret

Lowther, a Scotch lady, by whom he had eight more. As his marital activities would seem to indicate, he was of a nature pre-eminently social although he was also a man of intellect and achievement. He was a member of the Virginia Assembly and of the Congress of the United States and was three successive times elected Governor of Virginia. He said himself that the knowledge he had was not very profound because, unlike Jefferson, he was incapable of shutting himself off from social activities when he wished to study. One of his interests was astronomy and his successful calculation of an eclipse of the sun won for him the nickname of "John Partridge." He also performed experiments in the measurement of the fall of rain and dew. He and Paradise immediately became friends. "I am much obliged to you for your introduction of him," Page told Jefferson. "He supports the Character you gave him wherever he goes. We think him a great Acquisition to our Country & to Wmsburg in particular."[15]

Page and Wythe and Bishop Madison were all members of the Society for the Advancement of Useful Knowledge which had been founded in Williamsburg in 1773.[16] Its activities were interrupted by the Revolution but by the time of Paradise's visit they had been resumed and prominent scientists from all over the United States belonged to it: Dr. Benjamin Rush of Philadelphia and Benjamin Franklin and even Franklin's English friend, Dr. Lettsom of London. Thomas Jefferson was offered the Presidency of the Society at the time of Paradise's visit to Williamsburg but was obliged to decline, not knowing when he would return from France. A letter written by Paradise from Williamsburg to Sir Joseph Banks, President of the Royal

Society, reflects the interest which he held in common with his friends in the Virginia organization:

Dear Sir,

Agitated and hurried as I was when I was preparing to leave England, I found myself totally unable to wait on you with the dissertation of M[r] Knight, which you were so good as to lend me. I, therefore, left it with Doctor Bancroft, who kindly undertook to deliver it himself into your hands with my best acknowledgments. If you think me capable of being of any service to you here, command me freely; and be assured that your commands will ever be received by me with infinite pleasure, as your civilities will ever be remembered with the greatest gratitude. There is scarcely, I suppose, anything either in the animal or vegetable kingdoms here that would be an object of curiosity to you: But as the mineral is far yet from being thoroughly explored, should I meet with anything remarkable in it, I shall most certainly take care to send it to you. I wait with impatience to hear of the fate of my most excellent tutor, the archbishop of Cherson, which, as his merit is known to you, I have great reason to flatter myself, will prove prosperous. Be pleased to present Mrs. Paradise's and my respectful compliments to Lady and Miss Banks and believe me to be with the greatest deference, dear Sir,

Your most obliged humble servant

John Paradise[17]

Williamsburg in Virginia
Nov. 22. 1787.

Among Paradise's younger Virginia friends was William Nelson, Jr., a nephew of Governor Thomas Nelson. He was now at the beginning of his career as a lawyer and a politician, and he found in Paradise a sympathetic, enlightened confidant for his hopes and ambitions. Nelson was deep in love at the time and Paradise also listened to his confidences about his sweetheart. "He is really an amiable & as far as I can judge, a learned man," Nelson wrote Jefferson's secretary, William Short, after Paradise's return to Europe, ". . . Where is he settled and what is his situation? We flattered ourselves with the hope of a valuable addition to our society in Wmsburg, in his family, when he was suddenly called from us."[18] The friendship between them was carried on for some years, Nelson having been chosen Paradise's legal representative in Virginia. "Remember me to Mr Paradise in the most affectionate manner," Nelson again wrote Short, "& to his lady in the proper style—This you at Paris must know better than I do in Virginia."[19]

The Paradises remained at Green Spring on friendly terms with their difficult host until the middle of December when they set out for a round of visits to relations and friends in the northern part of the State. The success of their enterprise seemed now to be assured. They liked Virginia and Virginians liked them. Mrs. Paradise was pleased and flattered with the reception that had been given them by her cousins and her father's old friends; Paradise was more than satisfied with the intelligent society among which he had been introduced by Thomas Jefferson. Such news as they had received from their daughter Philippa in England was entirely encouraging. She was in perfect health and happily situated in her school. They had found their own affairs in Virginia somewhat better than the scanty remittances to England had led them to expect. So it was that when they started on their journey to the north it was with every intention of returning

to Williamsburg to settle there, either in the Brick
House in Williamsburg, (which they would rent from
William Lee), or else on one of the nearby plantations
—possibly Rich Neck, where Lucy's grandparents had
resided before they moved to Green Spring.

The sort of visit which the Paradises were now beginning was a social institution in Virginia. Except for
gatherings "in public times" at Williamsburg during
the days of the Royal Governors, Virginia had never
developed an urban center comparable to Philadelphia
or New York. Richmond was destined never to attain
the importance that Williamsburg had held in this
respect and from the Revolution onward Virginia
social life revolved around the plantations themselves.
The abundance of food and servants, the simplicity of
manners which allowed half a dozen people in a
room with three or four in one bed, and the hearty,
old-fashioned hospitality for which Virginians were
famous, permitted visits which lasted from a week-end
to a month, not from individuals or couples, or even
families, but from large groups of friends, who moved
in snow-ball fashion from one large house to another,
frequently being joined by the host and hostess of the
plantation they had been visiting when they moved on
to the next. If the party grew too large to be accommodated in the main house, the gentlemen were put up
in the "office," a separate building in the yard which
seems to have been used more for hospitality than for
business; or else they slept at a neighboring plantation
and rode horseback to and fro. The entertainment consisted of plenty of food and drink, dancing—minuets
and country dances were still the vogue—riding, hunt-

ing, games and charades and midnight feasts and frolics
for the young, cards, cock-fights, and excursions to the
races at some nearby village or estate. Manners in
Virginia were formal and stereotyped on the surface,
with bows and scrapes and elaborately conventional
phrases of greetings and farewell; but in Virginia, as
in England, this surface formality was quickly dis-
carded among friends and the laughter became as
hearty as the jokes were practical and the games
uproarious.

"I must tell you of our frolic after we went in our
room," wrote a young Virginia lady from Bushfield,
one of the many Washington estates in the Northern
Neck. "We took it into our heads to want to eat; well,
we had a large dish of bacon and beaf; after that, a
bowl of Sago cream; and after that, an apple pye.
While we were eating the apple pye in bed—God bless
you! making a great noise—in came Mr. [Corbin]
Washington, dressed in Hannah's [Mrs. Corbin Wash-
ington] short gown and peticoat, and seazed me and
kissed me twenty times, in spite of all the resistance
I could make; and then Cousin Molly. Hannah soon
followed, dress'd in his Coat. They joined us in eating
the apple pye, and then went out. After this we took it
in our heads to want to eat oysters. We got up, put on
our rappers, and went down in the Seller to get them:
do you think Mr. Washington did not follow us and
scear us just to death. We went up tho, and eat our
oysters. We slept in the old Lady's room too, and she
sat laughing fit to kill herself at us. She is a charming
old lady—you would be delighted with her. I forgot to
tell, Mr. Beal attended us here. I have been makeing
Molly play on the forti-pianer for me; she plays very

well. I am more and more delighted with her. She has just returned from the Fredericksburg races, and has given me a full account of them."[20]

The lively young lady who kept this journal was Miss Lucinda Lee, a cousin of Mrs. Paradise's, who was visiting the very houses and people whom the Paradises visited themselves: Chantilly, the home of Richard Henry Lee; Stratford, whose owner was Philip Ludwell Lee; Lee Hall, whose master was the family counsellor, "Squire" Richard Lee; Leesylvania, which had been the home of Mrs. Paradise's aunt and uncle, Mr. and Mrs. Henry Lee, the parents of "Light Horse Harry"; and Menokin to which the wisest and most charming of all the Stratford Lees, Francis Lightfoot, a Signer of the Declaration, had retired to private life after distinguished service in the Revolution. Not only the Lees, but the Washingtons, the Balls, the Brents, the Spotswoods, the Gordons, and many other families of memorable Virginia names kept open houses in this hospitable region.

On leaving Green Spring the Paradises' first destination was another of the many Lee estates, Belleview, a few miles from Fredericksburg. This was now the home of Thomas Ludwell Lee, Jr., nephew of William Lee and Mrs. Paradise's near cousin. Although nephew and uncle were on the best of terms, the inexorable William never allowed kinship to interfere with business and had instructed the Paradises to present young Lee with a bill for money due as well as his affectionate greetings.[21] Since Mrs. Paradise had brought her maid, as well as the other impedimenta of a fashionable lady of London, they necessarily traveled by coach or carriage. One would like to be able to conjecture the thoughts of this remarkable pair as they started out on the westward road from Williamsburg. Reassurances of friends to the contrary, it must have seemed like an emigration into the wilderness. At this season of the year there were probably no thunderstorms, but no doubt the lively imagination of Paradise discovered wild Indians lurking in every copse; even the Negroes must have appeared as a menace to his unaccustomed eyes.

Their road led them through what is today the town of Toano, where there was an ordinary, and thence to West's Point, now West Point, where the Pamunkey and Mataponi Rivers unite to form the York. Before crossing the Pamunkey by William's Ferry, they saw the home of Major Chamberlayne, which stood just beside it. With a visit to Mount Vernon in prospect, it is impossible that one of Mrs. Paradise's match-making proclivities could have failed to be thrilled by the associations which this spot evoked. Major Chamberlayne's house was well known as the scene of the first meeting between the brilliant young Colonel, George Washington, and Mrs. Paradise's cousin, Martha Dandridge Custis. The rather prosaic courtship of this now world-famous couple had been glorified into a romance, and Mrs. Paradise was soon to have an opportunity of recounting her childhood recollections of it to General and Mrs. Washington themselves.

George Washington's succinct, business-like diary gives us few circumstances of the visit of Mr. and Mrs. Paradise to Mount Vernon."[22] An entry for Sunday, December 30, 1787, records that about eleven o'clock that day "Mr. Paradise and his Lady, lately from England but now of Williamsburgh, came in on a

visit." They remained for four days. During a part of
that time Mrs. David Stuart and her daughter Miss
Nancy Stuart were also guests. These ladies spent the
night of December 31st at Mr. Lund Washington's,
returning to Mount Vernon after breakfast the following morning. Their place was taken by Charles Lee of
Alexandria who came for dinner on the 31st and remained until the following day. Apparently Washington found the society of Mr. and Mrs. Paradise agreeable, for instead of going about his affairs as he usually
did even when guests were in the house, he records that
he stayed at home during the whole of their visit.

It requires no great stretch of the imagination to conjecture what were the subjects of conversation between
John Paradise and George Washington at this time.
It would be hard to conceive of a person who possessed
more of the kind of information that Washington
would welcome than did his intelligent and sympathetic
guest. The intimate terms on which Paradise stood
with America's most important representatives abroad,
Thomas Jefferson and John Adams, made it possible
for him to give Washington news of them that could
not permeate the formal official letters—intimate, personal details about their lives, their relationships with
the English and the French, and perhaps about their
hopes and half-formed schemes for developing our
foreign relationships. Paradise's familiarity with the
European background and his many contacts and
friendships with foreign diplomats like Woronzow and
Soderini and Freire made him the ideal purveyor and
interpreter of foreign news. On domestic affairs there
could be but one topic of conversation—the ratification

of the Federal Constitution that had been drafted a few months before in Philadelphia. Of all subjects this was the one at this time closest to Washington's heart. It is highly probable that here, too, Paradise had information that could be of interest. His recent sojourn in Virginia had brought him in contact with almost every one whose word was of importance on this momentous issue, especially George Wythe and Richard Henry and Francis Lightfoot Lee. Virginia's decision was of the first importance, and it was extremely uncertain whether she would ratify or not. Washington was awaiting developments at Mount Vernon while using all his influence in Virginia in favor of ratification. Richard Henry Lee, whose influence in Virginia was almost as great as Washington's, waited at nearby Chantilly but with opposite hopes, for much to the fear and resentment of Washington, Lee bitterly opposed ratification. It must have been bewildering to John and Lucy Paradise to find their friends and connections so sharply divided: William and Richard Henry Lee were against while Francis Lightfoot was for; among their new friends William Nelson was against and George Wythe for; speculation was rife throughout Virginia as to which side Thomas Jefferson would have taken had he been at home. The State convention of 1788 did not decide the question until July 27, three months after the Paradises departed, and they heard the subject canvassed at every Virginia table at which they dined. But as at Chantilly and Mount Vernon, everything that was said at one table was contradicted at the next and it is doubtful if strangers like the Paradises were made any the wiser. As it happens, though,

John Paradise did predict the general result to Jefferson on his arrival in Paris—a prediction that proved to be correct.[23]

It was an added pleasure to Mr. and Mrs. Paradise in their visit to Mount Vernon to find their old friend David Humphreys established there as a member of the household, and to have him carve their meat for them, as was his custom, at the table of the Father of his Country. No doubt the satisfaction was shared by Humphreys, who must have recalled with gratitude the kind attentions which the Paradises had paid him while he was in London.

On Wednesday, the second of January, Col. Humphreys and Washington accompanied the Paradises on their eight-mile drive to Alexandria, where the whole party dined at the house of Mr. Charles Lee,[24] a kinsman of Mrs. Paradise who was now the Collector of the Port of Alexandria and was later to succeed Edmund Randolph as Attorney-General of the United States.

The remainder of the Paradises' social pilgrimage cannot be related. On January 25, William Lee, who was expecting them to return to Green Spring, wrote his nephew that they had not yet arrived.[25] His tone indicates that he was somewhat uneasy at the delay, not perhaps from any overweening anxiety to see them but because of a certain black-sealed letter that had arrived from London which bore the handwriting of Thomas Lee Shippen. A similar letter had already been received by Dr. Shippen in Philadelphia and the unaccustomed blackness of the seal had been accounted for by a simple statement in the post-script: "I am in mourning for my poor little cousin Paradise whom her parents left behind when they went to Virginia."[26]

This was the news which greeted John and Lucy Paradise when they arrived some time in February at Green Spring. It is impossible to conceive of anything more shocking. The child had been to all appearance in perfect health when they had left her, and since their arrival they had received word of her continued health and happiness. Shippen's letter had been sent from London on November 6, five days after the event, but they, owing to their absence did not receive it until almost three months later. No doubt Shippen softened the tragic story as far as possible—his letter has been lost—but the facts are succinctly told in the *Gentleman's Magazine*. Here there is no suppression of harrowing details:

November 4. At the boarding-school of Mrs. Stevenson, in Queen-square, aged 13, [died] Miss Paradise, daughter of John P[aradise], esq; late of Charles-str. Cavendish-square, well known as the friend of Sir Wm. Jones; and, from his many accomplishments and amiable qualities, well worth wishing as a friend by every body. In this daughter's constitution and habits there was no noticeable particularity. She had hereditary good health, and, living as children do, in the order and proper simplicity of a school, that health, originally good, was not likely, by any subsequent errors, to become worse. She was visited by a valuable family friend; and, after receiving from him some little endearments, which gratified her much, she took her leave of him, overjoyed; and running up stairs, before she reached her room, dropped down dead. Sir Paul Joddrell was called in, and saw her in a few minutes; but saw no hope of returning life. Had it been a case of animation suspended only, the speed as well as skill of his administrations must have done all that skill, the best administered, could do. It not being possible to counteract death, all that remained was to see what had caused it. This operation, much oftener useful than imagined, and in such extreme cases, morally almost indispensable, was performed by Mr. Farquhar. A rupture of some superior artery being the apprehension, they were all examined, and were all found entire. There was no extravasation any where; nor any appearance in the brain morbid at all, or preternatural. The muscular texture of the heart alone had been affected. That had suffered with such violence that the cause of death became at once decided, and was pronounced 'a spasm of the heart.' The physicians who assisted were, Dr. Warren and Sir P. Joddrell.—Mr. and Mrs. P[aradise] are now in America, on the necessary care of their property, which is chiefly there. The packet now sailing from Falmouth is charged with this melancholy news.[72]

In the first wildness of their grief they determined to set out for England. Without fully considering what they were doing they started for the port of Yorktown to sail on the first vessel that would take them. On the road they were met by their friend William Nelson, Jr. to whom they told the cause of their grief, and of their intention to sail at once.[28] Whether because they found no ship, or whether on reflection they realized that certain indispensable matters remained to be attended to, or whether for some other reason of which we now have no hint, the fact is that they did not sail from Yorktown. Perhaps after all their main object, without realizing it, was to escape the well-meant attentions of consoling friends. Perhaps at some inn at Yorktown or during some walk along the sparkling waters of the

river there, the pathetic, grief-stricken pair found the
courage to turn again and face the world.

The Paradises remained in America for more than
two months after they heard the news of their daughter's death. Abigail Adams Smith, who returned with
her husband in the early spring of 1788, saw them in
New York. Always interested in the Paradises without
being in the least sympathetic with them, she retailed
to her mother the latest rather cruel gossip concerning
the eccentric pair: "Mr. and Mrs. Paradise, embarked
in the last French packet for France, both of them as
insane as ever; they had heard of the death of their
daughter, and pretended that this was the cause of their
return to Europe, but I am told they found their estate
more productive than they expected, and are going
back to bring action against Mr. L—, for the produce,
which has regularly been deposited in his hands."[29]
This malicious rumor seems to have been largely without foundation, although it is easy to understand why
false statements should have been circulated concerning
people whose conduct was as erratic as that of the
Paradises. They had come to Virginia with the avowed
intention of remaining permanently. Why then should
the news of their daughter's death, tragic as it was, have
caused them to abandon their plan? It required a
better knowledge of their characters than was possessed
by an unfriendly acquaintance like Abigail Smith to
interpret their seemingly unreasonable behavior. Their
impulsive effort to sail at once from Yorktown had
been followed by an agonized visit of two or three

weeks to Green Spring, where a violent quarrel took place with William Lee.[30]

It is extremely likely that, as rumor stated, this quarrel concerned the management of the estate; but it is highly unlikely that the insinuation of Lee's withholding a part of the Paradise's income had any truth in it. Lee was certainly an avaricious man but there is every reason to believe him honest. He had always attempted to take a hand in the management of the Paradises' share of the Ludwell property and John Paradise's determination that he should not had been one of the sources of the many disagreements between them. If Paradise had been stronger, the matter could have been settled once and for all at the beginning of their association; but his gentle nature had prevented him from expressing himself in the strong terms required for a man so insensitive as his brother-in-law, and William had continued to interfere periodically, not realizing that beneath all Paradise's soft exterior there was a layer of hard, stubborn resistance which was all the more impenetrable because it was passive. Thus for the sake of profitable commissions for himself and his friends, William Lee had overstepped himself more than once, offering advice when it was not demanded and acting in the disposal of Paradise's tobacco when he had not been authorized to do so. Paradise had been partly to blame, for in a moment of desperation he had been unwise enough to appeal to Lee for help. This had given the eager merchant all the encouragement he needed to go ahead and act without authority, and thus was precipitated a quarrel that was never to be made up.

None of the circumstances of this second visit to

Green Spring are in existence. It must have come to its sudden and disagreeable end about the middle of February, for on the last day of that month the Paradises were in Philadelphia. Perhaps then this unhappy relationship with their nearest kinsman was in part the cause of their considered decision to leave Virginia, although it was absurd to report, as Abigail Smith did, that they were returning to Europe in order to instigate a law-suit. "The death of their daughter," said the Paradises' new friend William Short soon after their arrival in Paris, "seems to have been the cause of their quitting Virginia—they declare themselves much attached to it & I believe are so—probably this melancholy intelligence rendered them unhappy where they were, and induced them to change their place in hopes of changing sensations."[31] This judgment was undoubtedly correct as far as it went; Short did not then know that they had requested the Countess Barziza to meet them in Paris and that their return had been motivated in part by a desire to be near their one remaining child.

The route from Virginia to New York, in those days of muddy roads, dangerous fordings of streams, ferries, and bad inns, although it required ten times as long to traverse, was almost identical with the principal route today. Travelers from eastern and southern Virginia went to Fredericksburg and thence through Alexandria, Baltimore, Wilmington, Philadelphia, Princeton, Elizabeth, and Newark to New York.

Mr. and Mrs. Paradise remained in Philadelphia long enough to pay two visits. The most important of these was naturally to Paradise's old friend and benefactor Benjamin Franklin, now in his eighty-third year. At the time Franklin had just recovered from an illness owing to a fall on the steps that led to his garden. He had suffered a sprained wrist and a return attack of his ancient enemy the stone.[32] It had been more than five years since Franklin had bade Paradise farewell but various circumstances had kept the memory of him alive. Reminders had come in the form of letters from Dr. Richard Price, whose liking and respect for Paradise were uninterrupted. Another reminder had been Franklin's grandson, the social and dandified William Temple Franklin. When this young man had visited London in the autumn of 1784, none of his grandfather's friends was more cordial than Paradise, who eagerly seized this opportunity of repaying the kindnesses he had received in Paris. "I drank tea t'other day with Paradise & family—they are exceedingly grateful for the Services you have rendered [them],"[33] William Temple wrote his grandfather, and in another letter he mentions a dinner at the Paradise house with Dr. Blagden and other members of the Royal Society.[34] Only a few months before Paradise arrived in Philadelphia, Franklin had received the news of his sailing for Virginia: "His accomplishments as a scholar, and his excellent principles as a citizen, must make him useful there, and I hope also happy," wrote Dr. Price.[35]

Paradise's visit to the house of the old philosopher again brought him into a highly congenial atmosphere of scholarship, politics, and scientific discussion. Franklin at this time, owing to his painful malady, was unable to walk more than a short distance, even when he was comparatively well. For necessary occasions, as when his presence as President of Pennsylvania was absolutely required, he had provided himself with a

sedan chair in which he was carried. In consideration
for his infirmity and out of respect for him, the members of the Philosophical Society and of the Society
for Political Enquiries held their meetings in the din-
ing-room of his residence on Market Street. "My
friends indulge me with their frequent visits, which I
have now leisure to receive and enjoy," he said.[36] Thus
it was a fortunate time for Paradise to pay his visit.
He was able to take a favorable account of Franklin's
health to Dr. Ingenhousz and other friends in Paris,[37]
and was entrusted by Franklin with a letter to Madame
Helvetius: "M. Paradise, the Gentleman who will
have the Honour of delivering this Letter, intends to
reside some time in Paris, and acquaints me that he has
ordered some Cardinals to be frequently sent to him
from his Estate in Virginia, and that if any of them get
to Paris alive you shall be sure to have one. He had the
Pleasure of seeing you formerly with me at Passy."[38]
This custom of sending cardinals, or red-birds, from
Virginia to Europe had been in existence for at least
three quarters of a century. By the time of the Revolution, it had become a rage among the ladies of both
England and France to possess one or more of these
birds. Usually, however, the attempts to transport them
was fatal, as for some reason they seemed unable to
survive the long sea voyage. Madame Helvetius must
have been particularly fond of birds, for not long before Franklin had offered to give her, as an inducement
for coming to America, "1000 Acres of Woodland out
of which she might cut a great Garden and have 1000
Aviaries if she pleased."[39]

Franklin was to perform one more service for Paradise before his death two years later. In the summer of

1789, a law-suit arose in Virginia in which it was
necessary for Paradise's interests that his oath of allegi-
ance to the United States, taken before Franklin in
Paris, should be attested to. William Nelson, Jr., as
Paradise's lawyer, requested a statement from Franklin. He replied with commendable promptness, enclosing a copy of the oath, together with a sworn statement
of his own that it had been taken and the hope that it
might "arrive in time to serve M[r] Paradise."[40]

The last day of February was spent at the home of
Dr. and Mrs. William Shippen, now among the most
distinguished residents of Philadelphia. Having served
as Chief Surgeon of the American army during the
Revolution, Dr. Shippen had afterwards established
himself in medical practice in Philadelphia and some
time before the Paradises' visit had begun his lectures
on anatomy which resulted in the founding of the
school of medicine at the University of Pennsylvania.
"We were surprised two days ago," Dr. Shippen
wrote his son, "by the arrival of your old Friends M[r]
and M[rs] Paradise, who spent yesterday with us, they
seemed truly distressed & miserable, by the loss of their
daughter—could talk of nothing with pleasure, when
you was not the subject—they seemed really pleased &
interested when I read your opinions of our new Government, your description of Littlepage & gratitude to
Oxford of which he said he would write his friends
there."[41] Dr. Shippen added that the Paradises were
on their way to Paris where they expected to meet their
daughter and accompany her home to Italy. They were
most anxious for Shippen to join them, and the doctor
approved, if his son could manage the journey without
too great expense. Since both Dr. and Mrs. Shippen

had spent years in London during the seventeen-sixties, there could have been no lack of subjects for conversation. But most of the talk, as Dr. Shippen said, was about his son, whom the Paradises had seen so recently and known and liked so well.

Mr. and Mrs. Paradise spent their last weeks in America at New York, which, in the winter and spring of 1788 was the center of the social and political life of the country, being at this time the scene of the final meeting of the Congress of the Confederation. The uncertainty concerning the adoption of the new Constitution, which caused this period to be known as the "Year of Suspense," very naturally slowed down the activities of the Congress, whose members must have felt the futility of undertaking anything constructive in the face of a complete reorganization of the Federal government. "Congress are sitting," wrote Abigail Smith to her mother in May; "but one hears little more of them than if they were inhabitants of a new-discovered planet."[42] Nevertheless, the fact that Congress was in session, however inconsequential their procedures, meant that New York was filled with the most prominent men and women in the country, who in the absence of more serious pursuits directed their energies to social affairs and gave New York the liveliest season it had enjoyed since the beginning of the Revolution.

It is difficult to conceive of New York City as ever having been a town of less than thirty thousand people, with its residential center on lower Broadway in the neighborhood of Wall Street. Owing to their recent bereavement, Mr. and Mrs. Paradise naturally did not take a very active part in the social life there, yet they discovered a number of old friends and ac-

quaintances and also made some new ones. Arthur Lee
was at this time residing in New York, and Richard
Henry Lee had very recently been there as President
of the Congress. His successor, Cyrus Griffin, was also
from Virginia. The Paradises were received by the
Griffins at their residence at the White Conduit House,
near the Hospital, and on departing, Paradise was
commissioned by Griffin to carry to Jefferson printed
copies of the debates of Congress and the Constitutional
Convention and other pamphlets of political interest,
probably including such numbers of *The Federalist* as
had then appeared.[43] James Madison, not knowing that
Griffin had done so, also attempted to send the same
material to Jefferson; but his packet arrived after
Paradise's departure.[44]

Among the most prominent social leaders in New
York at this time was Mrs. John Jay, who, in contrast
to her sober husband, was gay and pleasure-loving.
The Jays lived in a granite-faced double house on
Broadway, just below Wall Street and the receptions
and dinners which they gave there were very distinguished indeed. A few years after this, when Jay was
appointed Special Commissioner to England, the Paradises were enabled to return in London the hospitality
which had been accorded them in New York, Jay's
former suspicions of Paradise as a British spy having
long since been allayed.[45] Other New York acquaintances of the Paradises were Sir John and Lady Temple,
the British Consul General and his wife. Born in
Boston, Sir John had inherited his title from an English great-grandfather. Lady Temple was the daughter
of Governor James Bowdoin of Massachusetts, to
whom Paradise had been given a letter of introduction

by Franklin on his intended journey to America in 1782.

The couple with whom the Paradises became more friendly than with anyone else whom they met in New York were General and Mrs. Henry Knox, to whom they were in all probability introduced by the Washingtons. Knox had been Secretary of War under the Confederation and had later served in Washington's cabinet; he had won great fame at the battles of Trenton and Yorktown and was deeply beloved of Washington, who wept as he embraced him farewell, first of all his generals, at Fraunces' Tavern in New York. Mrs. Knox was one of the most intimate friends of Martha Washington. The Knoxes loomed large in American life, both socially and physically. It is said that the General at one time weighed almost three hundred pounds and that his wife was not far behind him. He was a full-blooded, florid man, of "Bacchanalian figure," with a pompous manner and an incurably sanguine disposition. His talk was forceful, often profane, and extremely brilliant. Mrs. Knox was a "lively and meddlesome but amiable leader of society, without whose coöperation it was believed, by many besides herself, that nothing could be properly done, in the drawing-room or the ballroom, or any place indeed where fashionable men and women sought enjoyment."[46] General Knox's house was at No. 4 Broadway; it was a four-storey brick building containing a number of reception rooms to accommodate the large parties which he and his wife were accustomed to give. Mrs. Paradise and Mrs. Knox had both been christened "Lucy" and it can be seen that they also possessed many characteristics in common; however, the contrast between the diminutive, elegant figure of Mrs. Paradise and that of her friend (which was so enormous as to "frighten" Abigail Smith) must have caused a smile whenever they were seen together. Mrs. Knox loved to dance and as her friend Mrs. Washington did not she was often seen to open a ball with the Father of his Country, a sight which may have caused an even broader smile, although Washington himself was an unusually graceful dancer. Mrs. Paradise seems to have been closer drawn to this friend than to any other whom she made in America and never ceased to speak affectionately of her.

Public amusements were plentiful in New York during the spring of 1788. Sheridan's opera "The Duenna" was performed with Mrs. Henry in the leading rôle. Signor Carli presented some "wonderful performances in balancing," with a Negro man and a small white boy as the principal performers. "The School for Soldiers; or, The Deserter" was offered and adjudged "a most affecting performance & admirably executed; a very crouded house & many weeping eyes." Miss Eccles gave a public concert on the harpsichord.[47] The event of the season, however, was not a planned performance, although it was an extremely dramatic one. This was the famous "Doctor's Riot," of which John Paradise was an eyewitness about ten days before he sailed. A great many accounts of this incident, which vary extensively in detail, have come down to us. The story that Paradise told Jefferson when he saw him in Paris was retailed by Jefferson in a letter to William Carmichael in Madrid:

. . . a riot has taken place in New York which I will state to you from an eye witness. It has long been a practice with the Surgeons of that city to steal from the grave, bodies recently buried. A citizen had lost his wife. He went the 1st or 2d evening after her burial, to pay a visit to her grave. He found that it had been disturbed and suspected from what quarter. He found means to be admitted to the anatomical lecture of that day, and on his entering the room saw the body of his wife, naked & under dissection. He raised the people immediately. The body in the mean time was secreted. They entered into & searched the houses of the physicians whom they most suspected, but found nothing. One of them however, more guilty or more timid than the rest, took asylum in the Prison. The mob considered this as an acknoledgement of guilt. They attacked the prison. The governor ordered militia to protect the culprit & suppress the Mob. The Militia, thinking the mob had just provocation, refused to turn out. Hereupon the people of more reflection, thinking it more dangerous that even a guilty person should be punished without the forms of law, than that he should escape, armed themselves and went to protect the physician. They were received by the mob with a volley of stones, which wounded several of them. They thereupon fired on the mob & killed four. By this time they received reinforcement of other citizens, & of the militia horse, the appearance of which in the critical moment dispersed the mob. So ended this chapter of history, which I have detailed to you because it may be represented as a political riot, when politics had nothing to do with it. Mr. Jay & Baron Steuben were both grievously wounded in the head by stones. The former still kept his bed, & the latter his room when the packet sailed which was the 24th of April. . .[48]

The dramatic discovery of his wife's corpse by the citizen is denied in some accounts, which state that the identity of the corpse was never established. Jay's wound was at first thought to be serious; he was knocked unconscious by a stone which hit him almost between the eyes and had to be carried off the field of action. However, it was soon discovered that his skull had not been fractured, as was thought at first, and he escaped with no greater injury than a pair of well-blackened eyes. President Duer, in front of whose house the scene occurred, afterwards told a rather ludicrous story of Baron von Steuben's wound: "At the moment of receiving it he was earnestly remonstrating with Governor Clinton against ordering the militia to fire on 'the people,' but as soon as he was hit his benevolence deserted him, and as he fell he lustily cried out, *'Fire, Governor! fire!'*" The old veteran was carried into Duer's house, where his wound was attended to.[49]

The visit of John and Lucy Paradise to America was marred and brought to an end by the sudden death of their daughter. Except for this, the impressions which they carried with them as they sailed from New York, April 24, on the French packet,[50] must have been very pleasant ones indeed. Paradise had been accepted everywhere at his true worth. His gifts as a scholar were recognized by all the many intellectual Americans with whom he had come in contact—Wythe, Page, Bellini, and both the Madisons, not to mention his old friend Franklin, to whose circle he was well known. The numerous acquaintances whom he and his wife had made—for her it was rather a renewing—were with people of the very highest social position in Virginia, as well as in Philadelphia and New York. The impression which they had created was everywhere favorable, and although their eccentricity was noted by more persons than Abigail Smith, there are a number of letters remaining which attest that they were on the whole well liked and highly respected. It is one of the many ironies of their joint life that the happiness which was so well within their grasp should have been so lightly and impulsively cast aside. Poor Paradise! From now on Franklin's estimate of him was proved to be correct. His lack of firmness was more and more in evidence, and the unhappiness for which he seemed to have been calculated by nature increased a hundred-fold.

CHAPTER XIV

Mr. Jefferson's Great Young Man

AS Jefferson's secretary, William Short had long been acquainted with the affairs of John and Lucy Paradise and when they arrived in Paris in the latter part of May, 1788, he was both eager and curious to meet them. His humor enabled him to perceive behind Jefferson's straightforward, sober characterization of them a pair of "originals" whose company would be diverting. From Smith and John Brown Cutting and also from Tom Shippen, who had just been to Paris on a visit, he had heard much of Mrs. Paradise's exaggerated manners and actions and of her scholarly husband's helpless thralldom to her whims. Short's strongest motive for seeking them out as soon as they arrived was his eagerness to learn the news from home. He knew that Mr. Paradise was fresh from conversations with many of the principal persons concerned in the burning question of the hour—the new Constitution and its chances for adoption in the various States; Paradise could tell him how Virginia stood. Above all he could learn from both of them the latest gossip about his friends in Williamsburg and the surrounding counties. Short had been born and reared at Spring Garden, in Surry County, not far away from Mrs. Paradise's plantation of Chippokes. His interest in Virginia and all that concerned his friends there was as keen as when he had come to Paris four years ago.

"Mr. Jefferson thinks him the greatest young man he knows," wrote Thomas Lee Shippen, "and all the world think him the best."[1] But that was not the whole truth about William Short. It left out of account the unusual personal charm that had won for him such an enviable position in the French society of the last days of the monarchy, where greatness and goodness were not perhaps the sole criteria of success. Slim and erect, with attractive rather than handsome features, this young aristocrat from Virginia had won his social laurels without effort and wore them without self-consciousness. The rare combination of intelligence and ready wit and his gift for sympathetic understanding of others were indicated in his flashing eyes and well-formed, mobile mouth; he was a young man whom most people could love as well as admire. Not all his laurels were the social ones which he so wisely cherished; his great ambition was for a diplomatic career and in this he was justified by past accomplishments and by very hopeful prospects for the future. At William and Mary College, from which he graduated at twenty, he had been one of the founders of the Phi Beta Kappa Society and subsequently its president. He had entered politics at once and was elected to the Virginia Council at the early age of twenty-four. In Europe he was sent by the American Commissioners to The Hague to assist in the negotiation of a trade agreement with Prussia, and the success of this, our first trade treaty with a foreign nation, was largely attributable to him.[2] Afterwards, in 1785, he had become Jefferson's secretary in Paris, with the distinct hope on Jefferson's part and on his own that he would become the American Minister to France on Jefferson's retirement.

Short's best friend in Virginia was the same William Nelson with whom Paradise had become so friendly.

On May 30, Short wrote to him that he had seen
Paradise three times in the past four days,—"merely to
question him about Virginia"—and had spent hours
with him each time. "You will say I might have
learned a great deal in those hours—it is true; but a
large deduction is to be made because Madame was
present. . ." Short accused Nelson to Paradise of having been a slow correspondent and Paradise defended
him on the ground that he was in love: "Mrs. Paradise
was clearly of the opinion that the excuse was a sufficient one; on the whole you were condemned by the
good Paradise, who loves you most sincerely." Short
was clearly delighted with his new acquaintance: "The
good Paradise (for he certainly seems to me from an
acquaintance of four days one of the best creatures on
earth) has been able to answer all my questions respecting the federal and antifederal dispositions of my
friends in Virginia—he tells me you are strongly in the
latter class & for that reason did not chuse to be a
member of the convention." Even so, Short's voracious
appetite for Virginia news had not been entirely satisfied: "Why did you not send me the Virginia newspapers by Paradise—I learned from him a great many
little anecdotes of deaths, births, marriages, sales of
property, rising and falling in the world &c &c but
from the newspapers I sh^d have learned still more."[3]

With the generosity characteristic of a time when
private letters so often took the place of newspapers,
Short shared with his younger American friends then
travelling in Europe the excitement and interest of the
Paradises' arrival. Shippen and John Rutledge of
South Carolina were on a tour through Holland, Belgium and Germany. The journey had been planned for

them by Jefferson down to the minutest detail of what
sights to see, what inns to stay in, and what wine to
order. On the advice of the Marquis de Lafayette,
they had assumed military titles and uniforms as safer
and "more economical."[4] To "Captain" Shippen and
"Captain" Rutledge, Short addressed letters on May 31.
The letter to Rutledge contained Paradise's story of the
riot in New York. That to Shippen contained some of
the news from Virginia and also an account of the
Paradises themselves: "Mr Paradise & his lady arrived
here a few days ago. they sailed from N. York on the
French packet—how long they will stay—what their
schemes, or whither they will go I cannot say."[5] At the
same time Short wrote his cousin, Fulwar Skipwith, in
Dijon: "By Mr Paradise who arrived here a week ago
with his lady from N. York, we learn that the constitution w^d probably be accepted in Virginia—the committee is probably now deliberating on it."[6] Skipwith,
who had known the Paradises in London, replied:
"Where in the name of Prudence can M^r P[aradis]e &
his lady be now driveing to? I fear they are mad however be pleased to make my respects to them."[7]

Throughout the summer Short's acquaintance with
the Paradises was greatly improved, and the "peculiar
talent for prying into facts" with which Jefferson accredited him soon taught him that they were too distracted
to have any plans at all. They had come to Paris intending to meet the Countess Barziza there, but her
retirement and the subsequent birth of her son had
prevented this. There was indeed some talk of their
going to Italy to visit her; however, they seemed
incapable of reaching a decision on this or any other
subject without the advice and direction of the ever-

friendly Jefferson. As their dependence on him increased, so, inevitably, did Short's knowledge of their affairs. The constant interchange of visits and dinners, at which Short was generally present, enabled him to study their characters at his leisure. Paradise, he soon observed, was a different and a much more impressive man when he was unburdened by the presence of his wife. This was indicated on such occasions as Mr. Jefferson's Fourth of July banquet for the American gentlemen in Paris (including Lafayette),[8] and at a dinner in honor of Dr. Ingenhousz to which only men were invited.[9] On these occasions Paradise really lived up to Mr. Jefferson's enthusiastic description of him. As to Mrs. Paradise, her extravagancies and inconsistencies made her a puzzle to even so acute an observer as Short. One fact about her he noted with secret amusement—the unnatural diffidence in her manner when Mr. Jefferson was present. This and a certain expression in her eyes as she gazed upon him told Short more about her feelings than perhaps even Mrs. Paradise was aware of. Certainly Jefferson suspected nothing. But Short wisely kept his own counsel. He knew that Mr. Jefferson was too suave and tactful a man ever to be caught in a situation from which he could not gracefully retire, even if Mrs. Paradise's gratitude toward him should develop into a softer emotion.

Bad news from London soon countered any cheerful discoveries which the Paradises had made about their estate in Virginia. The long-suffering creditors had at length grown restless and there was actually talk about their combining forces to demand a payment of the

JEFFERSON, THE PRIDE OF AMERICA.
Reproduced from original engraving in the Alderman Library, University of Virginia.

debts. Much as Short liked Paradise and much as he
enjoyed his association with so intellectual and learned
a man, he was soon obliged to acknowledge him to be
the most incredibly helpless person he had ever seen.
As the situation in London grew more involved, Paradise seemed ever more incapable of making any effort
to correct it. Mrs. Paradise's continuous railings about
her husband's inefficiency began to seem more justified.
By the middle of July the problem of meeting the
current expenses of himself and his wife in Paris had
obliged Paradise to begin to borrow money from Mr.
Jefferson. Short could but wonder at the kindliness and
patience with which these demands were met. He
knew that Jefferson's statement of his "limited means"
in the following letter to Paradise was far from being
exaggerated:

Paris Wednesday evening July 16. 1788.

Will any of your occasions for money, my dear Sir,
admit of being put off a few days? mr Grand will
indeed furnish the 50 Louis you desire, on my order;
but it will be on the condition, always understood between him & me, that I repay it punctually the 1st day
of the next month. the 100 Louis he has before furnished you, I repaid him the 1st day of this month. since
that I have been obliged to get him to remit 80 pounds
for me to London, and I have a quarter's rent which
became due yesterday. these anticipations, with current
calls, will take the whole of the monthly sum I am
authorized to draw, the 1st day of every month. if any
of your calls can be put off to the first week in next
month, it will give me another month to provide the
reimbursement. if they cannot, I will not let you suffer,
but will give you an order for the whole or a part as
you shall find indispensable, and will endeavour to find

some expedient to reimburse mr Grand, without which
it would be the last order of mine he would ever pay.
be so good as to write me candidly, my dear Sir, and to
be assured of every help my limited means will permit,
as well as of the sentiment of sincere esteem with which
I am Dear Sir

your affectionate friend & servant

Th: Jefferson[10]

Mr Paradise.

This letter was crossed by a second request from
Paradise, to which Jefferson at once responded:

July 17. 1788.

My dear Sir

When your letter was delivered me this morning, my
servant had just set out with one to you. I am waiting
till I hear from you and know what your wants may be
which you wish to have furnished immediately, and
which shall accordingly be furnished. have you heard
that the royal thunder has fallen on the Marquis de la
fayette?

Your's affectionately

Paradise John   Th: Jefferson[11]

Shortly before this it had been agreed that the
Paradises should visit Italy; the burden of making the
decision for them as well as the practical arrangements
had as usual devolved upon Jefferson. Although they
were not to go until September, there were business
matters to be arranged both in England and America,
money to be procured from some source, and letters
to be written on these and other subjects. In all of this
Jefferson took the initiative and the responsibility.
Among the mass of correspondence which Short had
presented him on his return from a continental tour

late in April had been letters from both the Count and the Countess Barziza, profusely thanking him for the part he had played in the success of Mr. and Mrs. Paradise's visit in Virginia. Now that the visit to Italy was in prospect, Jefferson set to work to answer these letters.[12] Perhaps he hoped that some of the burden of her parents' care might be shifted from his shoulders to those of the Countess and her husband.

For so ardent a republican, Jefferson was surprisingly punctilious in matters of formal courtesy to titled foreigners. How should an Italian countess be addressed? "Excellency" was proper for a count, but if his wife was a foreigner and a commoner did she share the title? Short could not answer with certainty, so Jefferson dispatched a note to Paradise, who replied with great solemnity:

Mr Paradise presents his best respects to Mr Jefferson, and, in answer to his excellency's note, informs him that the true form of addressing a letter to his daughter is A Madame la Comtesse Barziza, née Paradise a Bergamo, par Milan—Though Count Barziza, and those; whose letters to her Mr Paradise has seen, give her the title of excellency, to which she has no right, until her name be enrolled in the golden book. Mr Paradise thinks that the most expeditious way of sending a letter to Bergamo is by the way of Milan. As to the marriage settlement he begs leave to refer his excellency to Mrs Paradise's letter.[13]

Jefferson's letter to the Count is a model of formal proprietary: Paris July 8. 1788.

The letter of March 18, which your Excellency did me the honour to write me arrived during my absence on a journey through Holland & Germany, and since my return my attention has been necessarily engaged by objects of business which had accumulated during my absence. the friendly reception of mr and mrs Paradise in Virginia, which you kindly ascribe in some measure to my letters, was in truth owing to their merit alone, which had been too well previously known to need any testimony from me. my only merit consisted in wishes to serve them. this I shall long preserve, as it is the necessary effect which their virtue must produce on the minds of all who know them. I sincerely congratulate your Excellency on their safe arrival in France, and on your prospect of seeing them in the course of the present season in Venice, where their happiness will be perfectly reestablished by being witnesses to that of your Excellency and of your worthy spouse their daughter. that this may long continue and increase is the sincere prayer of him who has the honour to be with sentiments of the most perfect respect & attachment, Your Excellency's

most obedient & most humble servt

H. E. Count Barziza   Th: Jefferson[14]

To the Countess, although he carefully withheld from her the as yet unmerited title of "Excellency," Jefferson wrote a much more friendly and personal letter. His sympathetic understanding of Paradise is nowhere better revealed:

Paris, July 8, 1788.

Madam,—The letter of March 15, which you did me the honor to address me, came during my absence on a journey through Holland and Germany, and my first attentions after my return were necessarily called to some objects of business of too pressing a nature to be postponed. This has prevented my acknowledging as soon as I could have wished the honor of receiving your letter. The welcome reception which Mr. and

Mrs. Paradise met with in Virginia was due to their own merit which had been well known there before their arrival, and to the esteem for your family entertained in that country. You would experience the same, Madam, were any consideration to tempt you to leave for a while your present situation to visit the transatlantic seat of your ancestors. Heaven has already blessed you with one child, for which accept my sincere congratulations. It may perhaps multiply these blessings on you and in that event your family estate in Virginia may become a handsome and happy establishment for a younger child. It will be a welcome present to a country which will continue to think it has some claims on you. I felicitate you on the prospect of seeing Mr. and Mrs. Paradise at Venice. The happiness of your situation, your virtues and those of the Count Barziza will contribute to re-establish that tranquillity of mind which an unhappy loss has disturbed and continues to disturb. Sensibility of mind is indeed the parent of every virtue, but it is the parent of much misery too. Nobody is more its victim than Mr. Paradise. Your happiness, your affection and your attentions can alone restore his serenity of mind. I am sure it will find repose in these sources, and that your virtues and those of the Count Barziza will occupy his mind in thinking on what he possesses rather than on what he has lost, and in due time deliver him up fully to your affections.

I wish to you, Madam, a continuance of all those circumstances of happiness which surround you, and have the honor to be, with sentiments of the most perfect esteem and respect, Madam, your most obedient and most humble servant.[15]

The son and heir with which "heaven" had blessed the young countess rendered it necessary for some official statement concerning her own family and position to be in hand. The imposing document which Jefferson drew up, to which he affixed the great seal of the United States, was calculated to win for her the coveted right to have her name inscribed upon the Golden Book of Venice:

We, Thomas Jefferson, minister plenipotentiary for the United States of America at the court of Versailles, certify to all whom it may concern:

That we are personally and well acquainted with the family of mrs. Lucy Paradise, wife of John Paradise esquire, with their connections and condition:

That the said Lucy was born in the state of Virginia, in the lawful wedlock of her parents, of a Christian family and educated in the Christian religion:

That her father, the honourable Philip Ludwell esquire, was a native of the same state of Virginia, was a member of the Royal Executive council, of the General Court, the supreme judicature of the state and a Visitor of the College of Williamsburg of public foundation:

That her grandfather, the honourable Philip Ludwell esquire, was President of the said state, that is to say, the viceregent & representative of the king during the absence of the governor, & in cases of inter-regnum:

That her great grandfather, the honourable Philip Ludwell esquire, was Governor of the neighboring state of Carolina, that is to say, the immediate Viceregent & Representative of the King in ordinary and extraordinary:

That her mother was of the family of Grymes: her uncle on the mother's side, the honourable Philip Grymes esquire, was Receiver general of the King, a member of the Royal executive council, and of the General court, the supreme judicature of the state:

That her grandfather on the same side, the honourable Philip Grymes esquire, was Secretary of the state, a member of the Royal executive council, and of the General court, the supreme judicature thereof:

And that her ancestors in general, both on the side of the father & mother, have been of the most distinguished in that country from its first settlement, for their wealth, and the honours & offices they have filled:

That in that country no distinction of ranks has ever been admitted at all, much less to be made hereditary:

And all this we certify of our own knowledge, so far as the facts are of our own times, and so far as they are of earlier times we have learnt them from the public records & history of the state, & from the constant uncontradicted reputation of that country, of which we are native born.

With respect to the said John Paradise esquire, heretofore resident in the kingdom of Great Britain, lately removed to Virginia and become of our personal acquaintance, we can certify his personal worth only, which is great, and his condition, which is that of a gentleman, & citizen of the state of Virginia, invested with all the rights of that character, capable of all the offices & honours of that country, and received a Visitor of the same College of Williamsburg of which his father-in-law, Philip Ludwell before named, was a Visitor; his family is unknown to us but by reputation, whe— [illegible] represented it as well distinguished by wealth and [illegible] in England.

Given under our hand and seal at Paris, in the kingdom of France, this 6th day of July, in the year of our Lord, 1788.

Th: Jefferson.[16]

A temporary respite from financial worry had been given to Paradise by Jefferson's loan and by a remittance which arrived some time later from Anderson, his merchant in London. There came an occasion on which he was actually able to do a small favor for his benefactor. One day in the early part of July, he and Jefferson were caught in the rain and Jefferson, improvident for once, was not only without an umbrella but without the money to buy one. Paradise lent him thirty-six francs to make the purchase. Of course it was promptly returned.[17]

With characteristic optimism, Paradise allowed himself to put off the dreaded task of formulating some plan for placing his affairs on a permanent basis. It was absolutely necessary for him to do this before he should go to Italy, not only because of the need for ready money but because the demands of his London creditors were becoming ever more insistent. To Mrs. Paradise's strident demands for action he was entirely deaf; she could not even induce him to acknowledge Anderson's remittance. Driven at length to desperation, she appealed to Jefferson:

My dear Sir

As I find, I shall never be able to Speak to Your Excellency I thought it best to write to you. Mr Paradise is an honest man, and a man who has had a very good Education, but alas with all that, he never has, Since I have been Married given him self the proper time to think upon his affairs as he ought and that is the true reason of my past, and present suffrings. He thinks only of the present moment, and as for the future, that may take care of its Self. That my dear Sir you will allow with me, will never do. He is a man that spends or throws away a great deal of money without thinking of it, or of the consequences. Had, I seen any alteration since our return to Paris, I would have thought that my Sufferings was almost at an End; but that not being the case, I have been obliged to trouble you from time, to time. As this will be the last Letter, I hope, I shall have reason to write to your Excellency upon my affairs, you will pardon me taking up Your time, and thoughts. *You have it in your power to arrainge my affairs with M^r. Paradise, in such a manner that I shall* altho' at present deprived of the greatest part of my Income, be at least certain of not being brought to more want, then, I at present Suffer. What I want (of the friendship you have for me) is, to Speak openly to Mr Paradise, and tell him, if You was in his Situation You would, now, you was agoing to Italy, employ your time in writing something useful for Virginia, and you would advise him as his best friend to permit me to receive and take care his money affairs. He has not written a word about my receiving the Dividends to Mr Anderson which makes me very unhappy. And until he does either write to him to remit to me the whole of the Dividends every Six months which is £92 10^s supposing Count Zenobio not to receive any part of the above sum, or write to Mr Anderson to remit to me every Six months the Sum of £120 arising from the Tobaccoes, and you see he has done it, I shall not be easy. *I beg in the name of God* that you will tell him, he will forfeit your friendship and good opinion of him if he does not directly write the Letter to Mr Anderson in the strongest terms and shews it to you. Tell him at the Sametime, was you him, you would do it directly. as you could not be easy until you had made your Wife happy. Pray, Pray My dear Protector lose not a Mome[nt] to see this important business finished. And for which, (as, I know you will succeed, if you take the business up heartily) *God* will bless your family and I and my dearest Children will have reason to Pray for You and Yours for Ever——

I am Your Greatly
Obliged Hum^b Servt
and Friend

August the 2^d 1788   Lucy Paradise.[18]

The kind heart of Jefferson could not fail to respond
to such an appeal as this. He of course did not consider
for an instant Mrs. Paradise's proposal that he advise
her husband to resign their affairs into her hands. Such
a measure would have been, for the eighteenth century,
simply out of the question, even had Mrs. Paradise
been less glaringly incapable than she was. But he
began at once to consult with Paradise on a plan for
paying the debts and on arrangements for the management of the estate in Virginia. His tact in negotiating
the whole delicate matter drew anew the admiration of
his young secretary, William Short. Never once did
Mr. Jefferson suggest to Paradise by word or by impli-
cation that he was incapable of attending to his own
affairs or reproach him for neglecting them. It was
always, "Do thus and so—if it meets with your judgment," or "Be so good as to make what alterations you
would chuse." Nevertheless, it was always from Mr.
Jefferson, Short observed, that the proposals came and
it was always Mr. Jefferson who put them into effect,
for Paradise at this time could hardly be brought to
sign his name to an important paper. The results of
several weeks of conference were summed up in a letter
from Jefferson to Dr. Bancroft:

Paris Aug. 24. 1788.

Dear Sir

Mr Paradise having been rendered, by the loss of his
daughter, incapable of arranging his affairs while in
Virginia, he has stopped at this place in order to do
this. he will inform you by the present post of the
arrangements he has taken. in the first place he has put
the Virginia estate under the care of Col^o. Nathaniel
Burwell, one of the most skilful managers in that country, and of untainted integrity. this estate yeilds from

800 to 1000 £ sterling a year, clear, and with the money in the English funds will be about 1000. or 1200 £ a year. of this mr Paradise reserves for his & mrs Paradise's subsistence 400£ a year, the residue to be applied to the paiment of his creditors. in aid of this fund he has applied three additional resources. 1ˢᵗ the sum of £1000. due to him from the state of Virginia. I am not well enough acquainted with the funds of that state to say when this money will be paid. but I know they have made great progress already in the paiment of their state debt, & that they expect to pay the whole in a very short time. still we must count this article unfixed in point of time. 2ᵈˡʸ a debt of 800 £ sterling due to him from mr Norton, and for which judgment is supposed to have been obtained. this therefore will come in during the present year. 3ᵈˡʸ a valuable wood called Chipoaks, which has been hitherto preserved in the family untouched, and which is of itself more than equal to the paiment of the whole debts. this he has ordered to be cut, till, with the income & credits beforementioned, his whole debts shall be paid off. mr Paradise in the mean time proposes to travel oeconomically, staying longest where he can be cheapest. mrs Paradise will remain with her daughter at Venice. she is to have 130£ of the 400£ reserved for their subsistence; and on account of the distance of her situation, and a desire that she should not suffer, mr Paradise has thought it best that her portion should be paid out of that part of his revenue which is the most punctually paid, that is to say the English funds. to 30£ a year from the same fund his friend Count Soderini [this seems to be a mistake for Count Zenobio] is entitled. there will remain a small balance of £35. for himself, to which 240£ is to be added by remittance from Colᵒ Burwell to mr Paradise. the rest of the profits & proceeds of the estate Colᵒ Burwell is to remit to yourself & mr Anderson who, as mr Paradise hopes, will still continue the friendly office of receiving and distribut-

ing this among his creditors, and of managing every thing for him which is to be done in England. it appears to me that under this arrangement the paiment of his debts must be effected in two or three years, tho' I have persuaded him to make such allowance for accidents as to suppose it will be five years, & to make up his mind for living in this state of exile for that term. he has done so, and I am persuaded he will do anything for the satisfaction of his creditors: I am so much persuaded of this that I will undertake to engage him always to do whatever further they and you may think necessary. I should think it extremely desireable that the larger creditors should consent to the application of so much of Norton's 800£. as would sweep off all the smaller ones. that sum for instance so applied would pay off the whole of the creditors except the six largest, who would by this means render the affairs much more manageable for them & for you. the arrangements made by mr Paradise are by a power of attorney to Col° Burwell, sealed, & indented, & requiring expressly such solemnities for it's revocation as guard it not only against the influence of others, but in a great degree against any momentary will of his own. it amounts in fact to a deed of trust which, were he to think of changing any of it's dispositions, would require at least a twelvemonth to comply with the formalities to which the deed binds him. this would give time to his judgment to correct itself. having been principally consulted by him in this business I thought it proper to give you a full view of his arrangements & to that will only add assurances of the esteem, and attachment with which I am Dear Sir your most obedient humble servant

Th: Jefferson[19]

Dr Bancroft

Jefferson not only conceived this admirable plan, he drew up the power of attorney for Col. Burwell, sent

it to Paradise for revision, copied it out in his own
hand, and sent it to Virginia with a long letter of
explanation.[20] The only important step which he left
Paradise to take for himself was to write the confirma-
tory letter to Bancroft. But this letter did not go by the
"present post," as Jefferson supposed. It was almost a
month later, when Paradise was on his way to Italy,
that Jefferson received a reply from Bancroft stating
his approval of all the steps that had been proposed,
but saying that he had been unable to act because he
had received no word from Paradise!

Meanwhile the fluent pen of Mrs. Paradise continued
to pour out more and yet more letters to Jefferson.
Like Mr. Micawber, she never lost an occasion to write
a letter, although she and Jefferson were living in the
same city and were in frequent personal intercourse:
"I hope you will pardon my troubling you with my
Letters so often, but, Indeed, I do not know the reason,
but when, I have the honour, and happiness of conversing with you, I cannot speak often, what, I would wish
to say. . ."[21] If her conversation was any more incoherent than her letters, Jefferson must have been puzzled
indeed. She was full of all sorts of business proposals,
of which perhaps the most wildly impractical was that
her son-in-law, Count Barziza, should make himself
responsible for all the debts. This, she thought, would
be "a very good thing for all parties." Each letter contained enconiums on Jefferson and protestations of
gratitude for what he had done: "What happiness
should I enjoy, could I see Mr Paradise as thoughtful,
regular, active and Industrious as you are. . . I do
assure you my dear Sir I am not ambitious, what I
want, is to see our affairs in a regular train to live a

quiet regular Life and doing as much good as I can to those Friends, who when I stood in need of their advice and assistance served me and my family with all their hearts. The Almighty has been pleased to raise up your Excellency to regulate my affairs so as to bring them into the train I could wish. He has also attach-[ed] Mr Paradise to you so, that he absolutely will not ask nor follow any persons advice except yours. This is the work of my God, I see it, and I believe it."[22] She generally placed her most important communications in the postscripts. These usually contained some remark about her husband which she wished to be kept secret: "I wish your Excellency would do one thing for me before I go to Italy, which is to get from Mr Paradise a promise that he will let me in the Spring Summer and Autumn manage his affairs. For to tell you the truth in confidence he is not able hardly at those seasons of the year to write a common Not[e]."[23] Poor Mrs. Paradise! it was by stratagems such as these, which proved her own incompetence, that she sought to gain control of the property which her husband was hardly more capable of managing than she was. Five more communications besides this one she addressed to Jefferson in the three weeks preceding her departure for Italy.[24] In one of them she informed him that her husband had also neglected to write an important letter to their London merchant, Mr. Anderson: "You may suppose Mr Paradise has, from his Conversation written to England. He has not, and at his house when alone with me, he appears not to seem inclined to write."[25] It seems incredible that even Jefferson could have borne all this with tolerance and good humor and yet there is every evidence that he did. On the eve of their departure, when it was discovered that their resources had sunk to fifty pounds, he uncomplainingly advanced them eighty more.[26]

At the last minute, Short, who had for some time been planning a tour through southern France and Italy, decided to leave at the same time as the Paradises and Jefferson requested them to allow him to travel post-chaise with them. They gladly consented. "Will your Excellency have the goodness to tell Mr Short," Mrs. Paradise wrote, "that he will make us very very happy to go with us, and therefore, I shall be greatly obliged, if he will send his Trunk to me on Monday morning."[27] Jefferson was certainly not without guile in effecting this arrangement. His relationship with Mr. and Mrs. Paradise had by now become so complicated that he scarcely knew where he or they stood. He astutely realized that the conduct of both husband and wife was affected by the desire of each to hold his good opinion. It would be extremely helpful in his dealings with them if he could learn from a keen observer like Short just how they behaved when no longer under the influence of his presence. He did not suggest that Short should play the spy but he well knew that Short would not be able to resist such opportunities as would be offered his powers of witty analysis on a journey with Mr. and Mrs. Paradise. On the seventeenth of September he bade them Godspeed.

Short's first letter reached him within about ten days; it was written from the chateau of Jefferson's friend M. de. L'Aye near Villefranche, where Short was

spending some time before he should join Shippen and
Rutledge for a visit to Italy.

Au Chateau de L'Aye Sep. 24. 1788

Dear Sir

I came here yesterday evening from Villefranche
where I parted with my traveling companions. It is
now early in the morning & M. de L'Aye being engaged in writing by the post of the day, I have only as
yet seen the inside of the Chateau—with it, as well as
my reception both by the master & mistress I am perfectly content.—I hope I shall continue to be as well
pleased with what is to follow & that I shall be able to
pick up information that may be useful to me one day
or other in my own country.

You will perhaps wish to know something of our
journey thus far relative to M^r and Mrs Paradise—
Every thing went on exceedingly well as far as Villefranche for wch Paradise considered himself indebted
to the fear his wife had of shewing herself openly
before a person in correspondence with you & perhaps
there was something in it; but on the whole her
conduct was much more moderate than I had any
reason to expect. indeed our journey went on so smooth-
ly that it was scarcely possible to be in an ill humour—
there was a manifest disposition in Madame to quarrel
with the postilions as well as the tavern keepers but as
she had given up these departments to me before leaving Paris I insisted on her not interfering & succeeded
pretty well, owing probably & as Paradise thought
certainly, to the desire she had to preserve your good
opinion—we with difficulty passed the Pontneuf on
account of the mob assembled there, & who stopped
several carriages & endeavoured to exact of us money
to purchase [fusees] we got only as far as Villejuif that
night, because Mrs Paradise insisted on staying there—
we breakfasted the next morning at Fontainebleau,
visited the Chateau & Park, & slept that night at

Fossard[?] the next night at Auxerre, the next at Vitteaux, & the day after we dined & slept at Dijon—I called for Irish potatoes wch they gave us. they were excellent but I have seen much better beyond the blue ridge—we were at the same hotel with you.—Paradise and myself walked over the principal streets and ramparts—it is certainly much the cleanest town I have ever seen in France.

The next morning we went to Beaune—I wished to spend that day there—the first thing I did was to go to Tarent's. unfortunately he was gone some distance from home—a heavy rain was falling, but still his wife insisted on sending for him—on our return to the tavern we found Mrs Paradise in a fever to be gone—we dined & finding that Tarent did not arrive & that her fever increased we ordered the postchaise, after being aprised [sic] by two Benedictines, who were at the tavern & who had come there to superintend the making their wine, that even if Tarent sh^{d} arrive he w^{d} not be able to shew us what we wished to see as the vintage was finished, & there were no considerable cellars in Beaune —these Benedictines themselves were setting off for Chalons because the business of wine making was finished—after the posthorses were put to & we in the carriage Tarent arrived—he assured us the contrary & said he sh^{d} have been able to have shewn us several cellars where the wine was still making—it was now too late, & we were obliged to go on—

I saw with a great deal of pleasure Volnais [Volnay], Meursault, & Montraché [Montrachet]—I paid with sincerity my tribute of gratitude to the two last for the many glasses of fine wine they have given me, by gazing at them as we passed & by never quitting them with my eyes as long as we remained within sight of them. They made us pay at the tavern at Beaune three livres for a bottle of Volnais—I did not however think it equal to a wine we had at Auxerre for the same price & which I think was made in the neighborhood—it was of the year 84—& that at Beaune much newer—I learned with pleasure from Tarent that this year would be still better for wine than that of 84—he begged me to assure you of his zeal for your service & the fidelity with which he w^d continue to furnish you. I ate of the grape of wch the Volnais is made—I was struck with its resemblance to some of our wild grapes in Virginia & particularly some that grow in Surry on my fathers estate—the shape of the bunch, the size & color, & still more the taste of the grape, so absolutely the same, that I think it w^d be impossible to distinguish one from the other—the vine at my fathers grew on an oak tree which stood in an old field quite separate from any other—so that the sun acted on it with its full force. I could wish much to see a fair experiment made on the grapes of that tree. I recollect my father made one year by way of experiment some wine, of what grapes however I know not— the wine was very agreeable to my taste, but not at all resembling the Volnay.

We slept that night at Chalons—& the next at Villefranche—we stopped in the evening at the pavillon of M. de l'Aye—where we learned he was at Lyons—our intention was to go & sleep at Villefranche from whence I was to write to him my arrival there—luckily we met him as we entered Villefranche on his return from Lyons—he invited the company to his house wch was declined. We took leave to meet the next morning —he was obliged to come & dine at Villefranche the next day with the Chancellor of the Duke of Orleans who arrived there. he came to the tavern where we were & it was agreed he sh^d call on me after dinner to bring me to his house in his carriage.

M^r. & Mrs Paradise set off about 11 o'clock—before their departure we settled all accounts—their expenses were twenty eight guineas, mine five—they had remaining on hand twenty two only so that it was determined by both of them to receive the whole amount of the letter of credit wch was accordingly endorsed to them—

the postilions who set out with them from Villefranche
returned there before I left it & told me they had gone
on well & safely the first post—I sh^d not have entered
into all of these details about myself & my companions
with any other than yourself, Sir, because few would
have the goodness to excuse it, but as I know you will
I do not make an apology.

I have not time to tell you how certainly & with how
much pleasure I experience that I can quit Paris without regret, notwithstanding what you think to the contrary—I am told that my letter must be finished on the
instant as it is the last moment of the post—when I say
I do not regret Paris I hope you will remember that
I mean, Paris without any person from America in it.

Be so good Sir as present my most respectful compliments to the amiable & agreeable part of your family
at Panthemont, & yet I can hardly flatter myself that
they will be received by the two little prudes. Adieu
my dear Sir—sh^d you think of it, let Pio know I will
write him as I promised & that I intended it today, but
was prevented by hearing the departure of the post—
beleive me with the greatest sincerity

Y^r friend & servant

W Short[28]

Short did not see the Paradises again until he arrived
at Bergamo a little more than a month later, but he
kept his ears open for news about them, partly to satisfy his own curiosity and partly to be able to send word
to Jefferson. He remained at the Chateau de L'Aye for
a week and then traveled to Lyons along the River
Saone by water diligence. He was much impressed
with the scenery along the banks of the Saone and received a most "sensible impression" from Mont d'Or
because it recalled to his mind "at every instant, & in
every direction in which it was presented to us, some

part or other of the rich mountains of Albemarle or
Amherst."[29] The hotel in Lyons recommended by Jefferson was the Palais Royal, but Short discovered that
the Paradises had lodged next door at the Hotel
d'Artois. "I have done the same," he wrote Jefferson,
"that I might learn with greater certainty in what
manner Paradise arrived and set off from hence. . .
The Landlady here tells me that P. staid from tuesday
to thursday—that he set out in good health & in a good
way for Turin, having employed a Voiturier to transport him thither—she says she found him *un peu
chicaneur*, & what astonishes me still more is that she is
perfectly content with Madame."[30] Evidently Paradise's bungling, inexperienced attempts at being economical were, not unnaturally, misunderstood by the
landlady of the Hotel Artois. He was in reality the
most honest of men, as even Mrs. Paradise was forced
to admit in her most complaining moments.

Short's letters to Jefferson give a detailed, enthusiastic account of his journey. He had a particular reason
for wishing to convince his patron of his enjoyment of
it, for Jefferson had warned him that he was becoming
more fond of the society and gaieties of Paris than was
proper in a young American republican. Short had
been profoundly disturbed, and in an effort to convince
Jefferson that he was mistaken, he devoted whole days
to gaining information about the methods of farming,
of wine-making, the manufacture of cheese, etc. which
he thought would be useful for America, information
which he retailed to Jefferson in proof of his sincerity.
He also made observations upon manners and customs,
with remarks calculated to throw a favorable light on
American simplicity. He told Jefferson that at the

Chateau de L'Aye "They frequently drank & made me drink to your health, & with an air of so much sincerity, that I c^d not help giving full faith to it—& the more so as we were in a plain kind of dining room as different from a *salle à manger* in Paris, as the table of some of our Albemarle friends is from that of a rich financier in Philadelphia—one circumstance wch had weight with me will very probably appear to you trivial—it is that whilst we were dining in one end of the room there were women sewing & employed in domestic works in the other—having seen this nowhere but in a country where I have been accustomed in my early days to see so much sincerity, I c^d not help by a kind of association of ideas to consider as pure & sincere everything wch I heard there. . ."[31] Emotional thinking such as this on the subjects of simple manners, liberty, and "natural" goodness was accepted at its face value by even so practical a philosopher as Jefferson. The corruptness of European society and the comparative innocence of American were the unquestioned premises of much of the political thinking of the day.

The classics and the sacred soil of Greece and Rome were another of the few subjects on which a man might with impunity permit himself to show "enthusiasm." "The present letter," Jefferson wrote Short in December, "will probably reach you amidst the classical enjoyments of Rome. I feel myself kindle at the reflection, to make that journey."[32] Meanwhile at Lyons Short had procured the services of a *valet de place* to show him over the Roman ruins there: "We have held a counsel & I find I shall with difficulty confine him to a small number of chosen objects—he seems much more fond of paintings than the remains of Roman antiqui-

ties which are in the suburbs & wch I am panting after—
having as yet seen nothing of the kind—Is not the
Rhone a fine noble river? I remember well having
read of it as well as the Arar in Cæsar's commentaries—Paradise & myself have agreed to read over
together when we meet in Italy this excellent author &
some of the chosen epistles of Horace—The views of
these two rivers, & of a city founded by the Romans
makes me impatient to begin the execution of our
agreement—he has thoughts of leaving Madame with
her daughter & going with me to Rome."[33]

From Lyons Short proceeded to Geneva and thence
by way of Turin to Milan; he followed exactly the
same route which the Paradises had taken eight days
before. The journey from Geneva to Turin, although
short in distance required four and a half days to make
because here occurred that perilous passage of the Alps,
so much dreaded by eighteenth century travelers not
only because of the steepness and primitive condition
of the roads and the resulting probability of an over-
turned carriage, but also because bands of Italian
banditti were known to operate here in actuality as well
as in the pages of Mrs. Radcliffe's popular romances.
The mental dangers were almost as great as the physical ones, for the wild mountain scenery of the Alpine
passes was then regarded not with rapture but with
positive terror; women were sometimes stricken with
hysterics or fainting-fits at the mere sight of the dizzy
cliffs and precipices near which they passed. The men
were hardly less affected. Not to make this part of the
journey with Mr. and Mrs. Paradise and study their
reactions must have been a disappointment to Short; it
was a subject to which his pen could have done full

justice. As it was, his only adventure on the Mont Cenis pass was to be enveloped in rain and fog for twenty-four hours; the only bandit he encountered was his own *voiturier*, who took advantage of his being alone and cheated him outrageously.[34]

In both Geneva and Turin Short was disappointed in his expectations of meeting his two friends, Rutledge and Shippen. In each instance they had left, Short discovered to his indignation, about a week before his arrival even though he had let them know that he was on his way. In Turin he wrote Jefferson that he believed their hurry was occasioned by a desire to overtake Mr. and Mrs. Paradise, and Shippen's diary reveals that this guess was correct. Shippen and Rutledge were having the time of their lives on their "grand tour" of Europe; both of them were high-spirited, young, and ready for any sort of fun that came their way. As soon as they learned from Short's letter that the Paradises were just ahead of them they began to give chase, hoping, for one thing, to be included in their highly diverting company and for another to save expenses by combining forces and perhaps by wangling an invitation to visit the Barzizas in Bergamo. Shippen as usual was very short of funds and the only hope he had of remaining longer in Italy was from the hospitality of these friends. In Turin they discovered that the Paradises had left only a few hours before they arrived and in Milan that they were already in Bergamo.[35] Shippen, who in reality was overflowing with eagerness to see his flighty young cousin in the rôle of the Countess Barziza, wrote at once, intimating that he would like to visit them there. Before an answer could be received, however, a letter from his father reached

him in which it was distinctly pointed out that he was
spending too much money and that it was his duty to be
in London in time for the November term of the law
courts.[36] This meant starting back at once—no visit to
the Paradises, no more good times in the gay society of
Milan with the Count Castiglione for a cicerone, and
above all no more larks and adventures with his boon
companion Johnny Rutledge. Both shed involuntary
tears on parting, Shippen confided to his diary; it was
their farewell to a happy time.[37]

Short arrived the next day. The letter which he
wrote Jefferson soon afterwards is an eloquent reflection of the interests and the point of view of many of
the Americans who traveled in Europe at this time and
of others who, like the Paradises, had identified themselves with America. The friends of Jefferson, especially, were inspired to observe keenly such foreign practices and customs as might conceivably be put to use
in the new country, to note down the details and communicate them to him. Many valuable ideas, as well
as many which later proved to be impractical, were in
this way disseminated among American scientists and
agriculturists, especially in Virginia.

Milan Oct. 28. 1788

Dear Sir—My last was from Turin & being now able
to ascertain my route with more precision & finding it
will be doubtful whether your letter w^d overtake me on
the road, I am to beg you to do me the favor to write
to me poste restante a Roma.—I came here on Wednesday the 22^d & found Rutledge. Shippen had gone 24.
hours before my arrival, for Genoa, in order to return
to England by the way of France—Rutledge was waiting for me as he says we have agreed to pursue our
journey together—the letter you had given him for

Dal Verme & his acquaintance with Castiglione however have rendered Milan so agreeable to him, that I
do not think he was much disposed to quit it—I must
return you also for my thanks for your letter to Count
Dal Verme—his civilities so far as I have been able to
make use of them & still more his cordial offers of them
have been useful & agreeable—he is at present in the
country but desired I w^d not fail to return you his
thanks for your remembrance of him & for the constitution. Count Castiglione also, who out of gratitude for
his treatment in America, seems attached to all Americans, desired I will recall him to your remembrance &
assures me of his respect & friendship for you—He
carried Rutledge & myself the day before yesterday to
see some country houses in the environs & among others
to Montbello where we dined—this is the seat of his
brother's father in law—the improvements are less
magnificent than two others we saw, but as to situation,
it is superior to anything I ever beheld in Europe—it
stands on a rising ground about 9. miles from Milan—
it is on that ascent which begins but a few miles distant
from the town & continues to the Lake Como—its
gradual rise & its commanding & varied views form an
ensemble equal to anything that can be imagined—the
horizon by which it is bounded, is by the Appenines—
or the Alps—some of the last covered with eternal
snows—in many parts the horizon is boundless—What
added to the pleasure of our trip was the plain &
friendly reception which we met—notwithstanding the
family is ancient, noble & rich, & surrounded with a
numerous train of servants, they live in the simplicity
of manner & harmony of a good American family—our
intention was to dine only—it was impossible not to
yield to their cordial & pressing invitation to pass the
night—the Brother of Count Castiglione seems one of
the best & most friendly men I ever saw—he is a
zealous botanist & seems as much attached to American
plants & trees as the Count is to Americans themselves

—they both have a pépinière to which they pay great attention—the plants are for the most part American, but there are others also—I saw the Mimosa arborea, I think it is called—it pleased me & the brother insisted on my taking some of the seed for you—I did it to please him, but suppose it may be easily got from the King's garden at Paris.

As far as I have gone yet in Italy it seems the richest country I have ever beheld—cultivation is also in many respects in great perfection particularly whatever is connected with the uses made of water—I need not tell you, who have gone through this country that water is reduced here to a regular property, & is sold out in parcels like land or any thing else.—It is impossible for a person as he goes through the country, cursorily to examine these matters in detail—but I sh^d imagine a man of an agricultural turn might pass some time in Piedmont & Lombardy to great advantage—we went yesterday to see a dairy where Parmesan cheese is made —we saw whatever could be seen except the operation itself—we were there at 1. o'clock which we had been assured was the hour of making, but on arrival found it was not made till the evening—the hour varies according to the weather—This shews among many other things how critical an operation it is.—I found there two cows who had the distemper, I think certainly the same which has done so much mischief in Virginia— I am well acquainted with its symptoms, & effects—the stock in heads reduced from between eighty & ninety to 58.—the distemper was brought there by a cow purchased at some distance off—it is an agreeable kind of farming & particularly here where it is so valuable— it will be a long time however I imagine before we shall be able to consider a dairy as a part of our revenue in Virginia—I was too late in Piedmont for the rice— it was cut & trod out before my arrival there—the zeal of the gentleman to whom Mr Cleves had recommended me, & who came to meet me at Vercelli was such as to

carry me by the ricemill on the road to Novarre without thinking of it—I was sorry but it was impossible to
be angry—it was at Novarre only that I learned the
accident.

I saw at Aiguebelle in Savoy a turnspit of a kind
which they told me was common in that part of the
country but which I have met with no where since—it
is put in motion by the smoke & is so simple that I who
know nothing of these matters could easily describe it
to a workman so as to have it made—I made a kind of
drawing of it which suffices for me, but which w^d convey no idea to any body else.

The edict concerning the manner of cultivating silk
in Piedmont was given to me at Novarre by a gentleman who told me it was almost impossible to be had—
it was forbidden to be printed lest it should teach
foreigners the same art—I have not read it, & if I had
sh^d be able to say nothing more about it—You must
have observed the vines were cultivated differently here
from France—I have also found a little treatise on that
subject which perhaps may be useful. I have no doubt
we shall find it proper to cultivate the vine in America,
at least for a part of our own consumption.

I shall set off tomorrow for Bergamo—Rutledge will
join me there in some days & then we proceed for Rome
with all the expedition we can—I am in hopes to find
at Count Barziza's some new information respecting
the metairie—in the Milanois it is less complicated in
one respect than in France, & of course better for the
genius of the negroes.—I am to brush up my classics
with Paradise also—this was our agreement but I fear
my short stay will not allow me to make great improvement in that branch. I received here a letter from him
& Mrs P.—it was some days old—they were then well
at Alsano the seat of C^t Barziza—

I am very desirous my dear Sir to hear from you &
I hope I shall at the same time learn something further
of what is going on in America—your last was of the

26. 7^{br} rec^d at Geneva. I have examined myself often on the subject on which your opinion alarmed me, because I have been so little accustomed to find you mistaken—I mean that wch made you suppose I had rec^d impressions from my stay in Paris wch would diminish my happiness in America—I have satisfied myself fully that I have nothing to apprehend from an absence from Paris—my happiness in America or elsewhere depends so much on others & on circumstances of which I shall probably never be the master that it is impossible for me to say what degree I shall probably enjoy—still I can ascertain with precision that my stay in no part of Europe will have any influence on the happiness which I shall be capable of enjoying in my own country—I feel this moment & I feel it whenever my thoughts are in that chanel which is perhaps too often, that if there was a prospect of my returning to America in the manner I sh^d wish, I would be as impatient for the moment of my departure from Europe as I was for that of my landing in it after a wearisome, sick & disagreeable passage—let me beg you then my dear Sir to change that opinion which you had formed of me—you cannot doubt that it is your suffrage which I value above that of all others, & that without it all places must have for me few charms.

I have to beg one thing more & that is that you will be so good as to preserve me always a place in your remembrance & in your friendship—& that you will never doubt of the unutterable attachment of your friend & servant

                                    W. Short[38]

The carefully ambiguous wording of the latter part of this letter is almost certainly due to Short's wish to conceal from all but the knowing eyes of Jefferson that he was referring to his love affair with the Duchesse de la Rochefoucauld. This lady had been married to her uncle, a man who was twenty years her senior.

Short was at this time much in love with her, although
she had not yet shown as much return for his affection
as she later was to do. Jefferson of course realized that
such an apparently hopeless affection might prove
ruinous to his young friend's career and attempted to
persuade Short to return with him to America in 1789
in spite of having previously desired to make him his
successor in Paris. The affair continued, however, for
some years until the death of the Duc de la Rochefoucauld, whereupon his widow, now free to do as she
chose, from some over-developed sense of duty to her
mother-in-law, (who was also her grandmother!) refused to marry the man she loved with such unquestion-
able ardor. They remained friends and correspondents
for more than fifty years, until Short's death. He never
married.[39]

Mr. and Mrs. Paradise had lost no time in informing
Jefferson of their safe arrival:

My dearest Sir,

Permit me once more to repeat my sincere thanks for
the singular favours, which you have conferred upon
me and my family; favours which have added affection
to respect; and which shall ever be acknowledged by
us with the highest gratitude. Our journey hither has
been very prosperous, and we have had the satisfaction
of finding our friends in perfect health and completely
happy. We wait with impatience for the arrival of M^r
Short, who has been extremely kind to us, and who, I
am certain, will make a very good use of his travels.
As I have been under a necessity of using Mr Grand's
letter to the banker at Lyons, I am accountable to your
excellency on demand for the sum of thirty Louis d'or.
My wife and children join with me in wishing you and

your truly amiable family every felicity which this world can bestow, and I have the honour to be your excellency's most faithful friend

and most obliged h^{ble} serv^t

John Paradise.[40]

Mrs. Paradise, unable to bear the comparative anonymity of mere inclusion in a letter of her husband's, added to it one of her favorite postscripts in her own handwriting:

P. S.

I have only time to return your Excellency my Grateful thanks for all your good offices, as the post is just a going to set out. Next week I shall write you a long Letter. The Count my daughter and Mr Paradise and myself anxiously wait for the arrival of Mr Short. If he comes here, he will learn things from the Count that will be of great service to Virginia. I beg you will make my affectionate Love to your dear Daughters If your Excellency should have received Letters for Mr Paradise and myself, I beg you will take the trouble to make them in a packet and send them to us under cover to his Excellency Count Antonio Barziza Bergamo par Milan Italy

I am with Great Gratitude
Your Excellencies Most
Obliged Humb^l Servant
and Friend   Lucy Paradise

Bergamo Octr 10th [18?] 1788

Short went to Bergamo the day after writing to Jefferson, and the account of his visit is given in Mrs. Paradise's promised letter to Jefferson:

Dear Sir

On the 29th of October our dear friend Mr Short Came to us on the 1st of Novr he was taken Ill with a

Cold and fever which has continued upon him until
now. Every care and attention is paid to him and we
hope that he will soon be well. We have beged of him
not to continue his journey but return with us to Paris,
as we propose, as soon, as Mr Paradise hears from M^r
Anderson to return to Paris. We are very greatly afraid
that our friend Mr Shorts Constitution is not so strong,
as he, himself thinks it: Indeed the Physician has told
M^r P and myself in private that he thinks Mr Short is
in a slow Consumption. Inclosed I take the liberty to
send your Excellency a Letter for our friend Dr Bancroft, which we beg of you first to read and after seal it,
and send it to him, that we may receive his answer on
our arrival at Paris. The Count our Daughter M^r
Paradise and myself join in every good wish for your
Excellencies health and happiness.

> I am
> Your Excellencies
> Grateful friend
> and Hum^b Servt
>
> Lucy Paradise[41]

P. S
Give Mr P. and my, tender love to your dear Daughters. Tell Miss Jefferson I hope I shall hear her sing
and speak Italian at our return. We shall not expect
an answer to this Letter here as we shall be gone. M^r
Short desired me to beg your Excellency will write to
him to Milan Post restent instead of to Rome. should
the influenza which has indisposed him for ten days
quit him so as to permit him to leave this neighbour-
hood before the arrival of your letter he will leave
directions at the post office at Milan for them to be sent
to him. Our friend at this moment with us [is] not able
in our opinion to take any journey. We are beging him
to return with us, and the reason is, that he should be
with you. He is now with his friends who all love him
and we are anxious for him to continue with them. He

says in answer to our prayers that as soon as he is well
he is resolved to go to Milan, to join Mr Rutledge to
continue their journey, this however, is not in the
opinion of a[ny] of his friends here, a wise resolution.
I have [not] read this Letter to him as, we thought it
proper you should know the State of his health, therefore we beg your Excellency will not g[ive] him the
least hint of anything we have commun[ica]ted to you
concerning him.

Bergamo
Novr the 10th 1788
His Excellency Mr Jefferson

Jefferson received these sensational disclosures about
Short with equanimity. In spite of the Italian doctor's
gloomy opinion, he realized that his friend was normally healthy (incidentally, Short lived to be ninety) and
moreover he was by now accustomed to Mrs. Paradise's
exaggerations and "secret" communications. He begged Short to accept his sincere "condoleances" and
advised him not to proceed on his travels too soon and
to begin by "small journies." He did not hesitate to
reveal that he had heard of his illness from Mrs.
Paradise, despite that lady's excited injunctions to keep
her letter a secret.[42] To Paradise he wrote at the same
time a letter which reveals his continued friendliness,
although he had just learned, probably on the very day
he wrote the letter, that a draft of Paradise's on London, submitted in partial payment of the money Jefferson had lent him, was uncollectable. The American
painter John Trumbull, through whom he had conducted the matter, wrote that not only was the merchant
Anderson without funds belonging to Paradise but that
he was without any expectation of them until the fol-

lowing April. He would pay Jefferson's draft then, provided, as Trumbull wrote, the dividends from the Bank of England "should not be otherwise appropriated."[43] This undoubtedly meant that Paradise's creditors were threatening to attach his income. On all this, Jefferson, from motives that can only be construed as kindly, was silent.

Paris Nov. 22 1788.

Dear Sir

I had duly received yours and mrs Paradise's favor of Oct. 10. and yours of Oct. 20. a throng of work which held me till yesterday, did not admit a possibility of writing a single letter to any body while it lasted. I was just sitting down to write to yourself and mr Short yesterday, when I received mrs Paradise's favor of the 10th inst. informing me you proposed to leave Bergamo for Paris as soon as you should receive a letter from mr Anderson, and desiring me not to write an answer as you would probably be on the road. I disobey her however, because it is possible that waiting for Anderson's letter, or other accidental causes may detain you longer than you expect, and because I wish to prove to you that I seize with pleasure the first moment it has been possible for me to write you a line. the letter to Dr Bancroft will go off by tomorrow's post, and you will probably receive the answer after your arrival here. the news from America is that they are beginning their elections. mr Morris and a mr McCay are chosen senators for Pennsylvania. this is the only election I have heard of. the king of England has been for some time at death's door of a hydrocephalus, which threatens either death or perpetual insanity. the parliament was to meet the day before yesterday. it is thought they will establish a regency. the Notables are in session. they have proved themselves a meer combination of priests and Nobles against the people. the court wished to give to the tiers etat as many deputies as the other two orders should have jointly in the states general. one bureau decided in favor of it by a majority of one voice; the other five bureaux against it by almost an unanimity.

I am in hopes from mrs Paradise's letter, of seeing you here immediately. present me to her in the most respectful terms, and be assured yourself of the sincerity & attachment with which I have the honor to be Dear Sir

Your friend & Serv[t]

M[r] Paradise   Th: Jefferson[44]

William Short had had reason to be disappointed in the lack of excitement hitherto provided by his eccentric friends; but before he left Bergamo his highest expectations were to be fulfilled. The influence of Mr. Jefferson and the restraining presence of Short himself had combined to hold Mrs. Paradise in what was for her a surprisingly conventional course of behavior. Afterwards, the prospect of seeing her daughter in her new surroundings and the subsequent arrival at Bergamo were sufficiently diverting to satisfy her craving for emotional adventure. By the time of Short's recovery from his attack of influenza, that is about the twentieth of November, an outburst was long overdue and to a shrewd observer like Short it was apparent that the first occasion would bring it on. The occasion, as usual, was provided in part by the weakness and almost criminal impracticality of her husband. After stupendous efforts and much delay he had at length been brought to write the letter to Dr. Bancroft confirming the arrangement, which was certainly the best that could have been effected. It was clear that if they followed out the course of action prescribed, the debts would be paid

in a few years' time and that they could take their
former position in London, with a good income and
easy minds. The intervening lean years of subsistence
for himself and his wife on an income of £400 had all
but melted out of his consciousness, and once more
Paradise was, in his his own sanguine imagination, a
gentleman of fortune, able to indulge his most generous
and extravagant impulses. It was in this vulnerable
state of mind that he arrived at the home of his son-in-
law. Count Barziza had always been dissatisfied with
the financial arrangements made at the time of his
marriage. He saw now his opportunity for correcting
them. Paradise, pleased no doubt at being made a
grandfather, and delighted at the unexpected state of
happiness which his daughter seemed to enjoy in her
marriage, was easily persuaded by her husband to settle
on her a yearly income of £150, entirely oblivious, it
would seem, of the contract drawn up by Jefferson and
signed by himself which had so strictly limited the
income he was able to draw until the debts were paid.
It was useless for Mrs. Paradise to refuse her consent,
for legally her husband could do as he chose.[45] She did
not, however, withhold her resentment, although she
managed to suppress it until an occasion arose which
caused her to burst out with more violence than she
had ever shown before.

Short's recovery again brought up the question of his
itinerary for the remainder of his journey through
Italy. Rutledge had waited for him in Milan during
his illness and was now eager to proceed. It was at this
point that Barziza made the suggestion that precipitated the crisis. This was that Barziza and Paradise
should accompany Short and Rutledge as far as Venice,

where the party would remain for a time as Barziza's guests in his palace there, meanwhile leaving Mrs. Paradise and her daughter at Bergamo. This to Mrs. Paradise was the final straw. In the presence of them all she gave vent to the most violent outburst of anger she had ever shown. No longer in love with her husband, she was still violently jealous of him and her distorted conceptions of what might take place in Venice in the encouraging presence of two lively young men like Short and Rutledge was undoubtedly one of the strongest incentives to her fury. As always, it happened with dramatic suddenness. One moment she was the well-bred lady of fashion with a gracious manner and a well-modulated voice. The next she was transformed into a small dynamo of vindictive ire, lashing out blindly at every object within her path. To Short, who was at first an unparticipating observer, it was not without its comedy, this sight of an anger so great in a body so elegant and small. Her first victim was her husband whom she accused of extravagance, neglect, and even brutality. Next she turned on Barziza, bitterly reproaching him for his cupidity in having persuaded the weak Paradise to sign away her income. She painted in lively colors the poverty she should now be forced to endure—alone, of course, since for the hundredth time she had declared her intention of leaving her husband. This naturally provoked a counter-attack from her daughter, the Countess, who was put in the unhappy position of taking the side of her husband and her father against her mother. At this Mrs. Paradise's anger increased to such a degree that even Short was awed. Let Paradise's account of his wife's conduct appear ever so exaggerated, he told

Jefferson, "you may give full faith to it. I saw what I had supposed it impossible to be done even by her." She turned on Short himself. Mistakenly supposing that it was he who had proposed the jaunt to Venice she abused him roundly for it, declaring with a meaning look in his direction that when she got to Paris she would "paint everybody in their true colors to Mr. Jefferson." Nothing was able to restrain her fury. At length, in the midst of it all, the post arrived and in it the long-awaited letter from the London merchant, Anderson. The news it contained was the worst possible. The creditors had banded together and were demanding immediate payment of the debts. There were papers for Paradise to sign. But he had taken refuge in his only recourse, a gloomy and despairing stubbornness. He refused to sign anything until he had returned to Paris and consulted with Jefferson. "I left him," wrote Short, "really the most wretched man I ever saw—& half distracted—but still determined to sign no papers—he has since yielded. . ."[46]

No one of course could withstand Mrs. Paradise when she was aroused to the pitch at which she was at present. In a few days they set out for Paris, but not alone. Count Barziza, obliged to advance the money for their journey, traveled with them. In Paris he would persuade Mr. Jefferson to see that his money was returned and the settlement enforced. In Paris, Mrs. Paradise would persuade Mr. Jefferson to agree to her separation from her husband and see that a separate maintenance was provided. As for Paradise, he would do whatever Jefferson said—except live with his wife. Barziza carried in his pocket a letter to Mr. Jefferson from the Countess, imploring him to bring about some sort of a reconciliation between her father, her mother, her husband, and herself. In Paris, Mr. Jefferson, Minister Plenipotentiary from the United States of America to the Court of Versailles, unknowingly awaited the destiny that was traveling toward him in a postchaise along the road from Italy. As for Short, he joined Rutledge in Milan and together they began their long-interrupted journey to the classic soil of Rome. He never saw Mrs. Paradise again.

CHAPTER XV

Public Enemy and Private Friend

AT Auteuil about the first of December, 1784, Mr. and Mrs. John Adams, who had arrived in France six months before, felt impelled to repay some of their social obligations by giving a dinner. The principal guests were Baron de Geer, the Swedish Ambassador, and Baron de Waltersdorff, his Secretary. Dr. Franklin and Mr. Jefferson were invited, but were both ill and unable to attend. Among the remaining guests were Col. David Humphreys, secretary to the American Commissioners; Mr. William Short, secretary to Mr. Jefferson; Mr. and Mrs. William Bingham of Philadelphia; the "Chevalier" John Paul Jones; and Dr. Edward Bancroft, of Massachusetts, Dutch Guiana, London, and Paris. "Dr. Bancroft is a native of America; he may be thirty or forty years old. His first appearance is not agreeable, but he has a smile which is of vast advantage to his features, enlightening them and dispelling the scowl which appears upon his brow. He is pleasant and entertaining in conversation; a man of literature and good sense; you know he is said to be the author of Charles Wentworth."[1] The pleasant thrill of excitement at playing hostess to the author of so wicked a book, notorious for its attack on Christianity, would have been changed to horror if Mrs. Adams could have known the full truth about her guest. But that truth was destined to remain a state secret for more than a hundred years. While he lived, Dr. Bancroft walked the earth in full respect-

ability, honored with the friendship of such men as
Benjamin Franklin, John Paul Jones, John Adams,
Thomas Jefferson, and many other leading American
patriots. Clever, sensible, industrious, extremely able
in affairs, his nature was kindly and lovable, and when
the occasion arose he could prove himself a charitable,
loyal friend. He was born in Westfield, Massachusetts
on January 9, 1744, and after an irregular schooling
went to England where he studied medicine and received an M. D. degree. Several years of travel and
adventure followed, and then he settled for a time in
Dutch Guiana. Returning to England, he remained
there and began to write articles on American subjects
for the *Monthly Review*. In 1769 he published *An
Essay on the Natural History of Guiana* and also an
able defense of the liberty of the American Colonies
entitled *Remarks on the Review of the Controversy
between Great Britain and Her Colonies*. The next
year appeared anonymously *The History of Charles
Wentworth*. Meanwhile he had become a member of
the College of Physicians and a Fellow of the Royal
Society. Through his double interest in science and
American politics, he made the acquaintance and won
the friendship of Joseph Priestley and Benjamin
Franklin.[2] It was also at this time that he first became
acquainted with John Paradise.

In 1776 Bancroft began a career of double-dealing
which was to remain undetected until he had been in
his grave for more than sixty years. The first of the
American commissioners to arrive in Paris was Silas
Deane. He brought with him a letter of introduction
to Bancroft from Benjamin Franklin, whose friend and
valued correspondent Bancroft was. In the summer of

that year Bancroft joined Deane in Paris as secretary
of the Commissioners on a salary which continued to
be paid until the end of the Revolution.³ For this salary
he was not only expected to carry on the duties of a
secretary, but from his knowledge of England and his
correspondence with friends there to supply the Americans with valuable information not otherwise obtainable.

In December, 1776, the very month in which Franklin arrived in Paris, Bancroft received an offer of a
salary to perform the same service for the British.
This offer was made through the British spy Paul
Wentworth, also American-born. Bancroft accepted,
retaining of course his position as secretary and in-
former to the American commissioners as well as the
salary they paid him. The document by which his
agreement was made was kept secret by the British
Foreign Office until 1890, when it was allowed to be
reproduced in the B. F. Stevens *Facsimiles.* Bancroft
was to be known to his British correspondents as B.
Edwards, a reversal of his real name; he was to supply
information to Wentworth and Lord Stormont, Ambassador to France, on the following subjects: the
progress of the American treaty with France, the
names of American commercial agents in foreign
"islands," America's means of obtaining credit, Franklin's and Deane's correspondence with Congress, all
possible facts concerning American ships in European
waters, and lists of captures by American privateers
together with information as to how these captives were
disposed of.⁴ For this he received from the British
government a salary of £500 a year which was later
raised to 1,000.⁵ So well did he perform his services
that in the opinion of modern historians he did more

damage to the American cause, especially to American shipping, than any other individual whatsoever—far more than Benedict Arnold.[6]

The directions for conveying the information, preserved in Wentworth's handwriting, read like the records of a schoolboys' secret society. They were to be directed to "Mr. Richardson" and were to be written on the subject of gallantry; that is, love. The real messages were to be written in invisible ink on the covers and other blank parts of the paper; Lord Stormont was provided with a wash to make the writing appear. "Mr Jeans will call every Tuesday Evening after half past nine, at the Tree pointed out on the S^o Terrace of the Tuilleries & take from the Hole at the root—the Bottle containing a Letter:—

"and place under the Box-Tree agreed on, a bottle containing any Communications from Lord Stormont to Dr Edwards. All Letters to be numbered with white Ink.

"The bottle to be sealed—& tyed by the Neck with a common twyne, about half a yard in length—the other end of which to be fastened to a peg of wood, split at top to receive a very small piece of a Card—the bottle to be thrust under the Tree, & the Peg into the ground on the west side."[7]

To divert the attention of the Americans from these activities Bancroft supplied them with sufficient information about British secrets; once he allowed himself to be arrested by the British as an American spy. Among the few persons aware of the arrangement was George III, who at one time suspected Bancroft or "Edwards" as he knew him, of acting more in the interests of America than of Great Britain. The reverse

has later been proven true; Bancroft was honest at least
to the extent that he gave far more information to the
side which gave him the most money—or rather which
promised him the most money. For there exists in
Bancroft's handwriting a "Memorial" to the Marquis
of Caermarthen protesting bitterly that he had not
received all that was due him and enumerating in a
rather too boastful way the services that he performed.[8]

Bancroft deceived absolutely everyone whom he
wished to deceive, with the one notable exception of
Arthur Lee, who attempted to prove to an incredulous
world not only that Bancroft was an English spy, but
that Franklin, his friend and employer, was aware of it.
Silas Deane's confession of his own duplicity, and the
fact that he was so closely associated with both Franklin
and Bancroft lent some credibility to Lee's accusations
but not enough to win them serious consideration.
Lee's hatred for Franklin was so vindictive that he
was still trying to prove his case as late as 1787, when
Franklin was in virtual retirement in Philadelphia and
Deane a destitute pauper in London. In July of that
year he wrote his nephew Thomas Lee Shippen in
London "From many circumstances I am strongly inclined to believe, that Silas Deane receives a pension
from Dr Franklin & Robert Morris, as hush money.
Will it be impracticable for you to find this out? Perhaps Paradise might extract it from Bancroft with
whom I think you say he is intimate. The payments, if
any, will be made thro the house of Tireau & Grand
in Amsterdam, or Grand or le Couteulx in Paris, or
brokers in London. It may happen that periodical bills
are negociated by S. D. on some of those houses which
will be in the knowledge of some mercantile people

from whom you may learn it. The evidence which he
must have of the frauds & wickedness of these two men
is such as would ruin them: & I cannot think he would
spare them if he were not bribed to it. For money is
his God. Keep this matter in mind & accident may
perhaps lead you to what you may not be able to obtain
otherwise."[9] Nothing remains to indicate that Shippen,
either through Paradise or otherwise, discovered what
his uncle wanted to know; however, by a singular
coincidence, Bancroft himself in a letter to Jefferson
mainly on the subject of Paradise's affairs reveals that
at the time in question he was the trustee of a "charitable fund" for Silas Deane, which he administered at
his own discretion since Deane was too improvident to
be trusted with large sums of money.[10]

The question of Bancroft's double spying, chiefly
because of its bearing on Franklin himself, has been
discussed by historians ever since. Francis Wharton,
writing in 1889, gave a very thorough canvassing of the
facts that were then known, ending with a burst of
rhetoric for which he was to receive poetical justice in
a very short time:

To believe him [Bancroft] guilty of such atrocious
and yet exquisitely subtle perfidy we must believe that,
ingenuous, simple-hearted, and credulous as he appeared to the general observer, occupying to Franklin and
to America a position not unlike what Boswell did to
Johnson and Corsica, though with certain scientific
aptitudes to which Boswell laid no claim and with an
apparent occasional heroism of which Boswell was incapable, he was, nevertheless, a dissembler so artful as
to defy the scrutiny of Franklin, with whom he was in
constant intercourse; an intriguer so skillful as, without
money or power, to deceive Vergennes and the multi-

tudinous police with which Vergennes encircled him;
a villain so profoundly wary as to win the confidence of
Paul Jones, professedly aiding him in desperate secret
raids on the British coast, and yet, by an art almost
unfathomable, reserving the disclosure of these secrets
to British officials until a future day which never came;
a double traitor, whose duplicity was so masterly as to
be unsuspected by the British court, which held him to
be a rebel; and by such men as La Fayette, as John
Adams, as Jefferson, who regarded him as a true friend.
This amusing combination of apparently absolutely inconsistent characteristics may exist in bewildering
harmony in the character of Edward Bancroft; but
such a phenomenon should not be believed to exist
without strong proof.[11]

The very year that this was written the proofs of
Bancroft's duplicity began to appear. They are overwhelming.

Such was the man whom Mrs. Adams entertained at
dinner at Auteuil and many times afterwards in London; such was the man who, after Thomas Jefferson,
performed more devoted and unselfish services for
John and Lucy Paradise than anyone else. The acquaintance between Bancroft and Paradise which began before the Revolution soon became a friendship
after Bancroft's permanent return to London in 1783.
The two men had seen each other at intervals on the
several occasions of Paradise's visits to Franklin at
Passy. It was through the intercession of Bancroft that
Jefferson had first become interested in Paradise's
affairs, and it was probably through Bancroft's introduction that Paradise became personally acquainted
with Jefferson on his visit to London. Since then

Bancroft had remained an understanding and trust-
worthy friend and it was to him that Jefferson had
naturally turned for coöperation in the latter part of
1788 when the Paradises' affairs had reached another
crisis.

The plan set forth by Jefferson to Bancroft had met
with unqualified approval;[12] but first owing to Paradise's delay in confirming it and later to difficulty with
the creditors themselves, it had been impossible to put
it into operation. It was not until more than a month
after the return of the Paradises to Paris from Italy
that any definite developments took place. On January
26, Jefferson wrote to Bancroft again, putting him *en
rapport* of what had meanwhile occurred regarding
their friends:

A word now on Mr. Paradise's affairs: you were
informed at the time of the arrangement they had
established in their affairs, to wit. reserving 400£ a
year for their subsistence, abandoning the rest of their
income, about 400£ more, all their credits (one of
which is 800£ from an individual and another is
1000£ from the state) and the cutting of a valuable
wood, to their creditors. Their whole debts amounting
but to 2300£, the term of paiment cannot be long, if
this arrangement can be preserved. I had hoped that
the journey to Italy would have fixed Mrs. Paradise
with her daughter and left him free to travel or tarry
where he liked best, but this journey has been a burthen
instead of a relief to their affairs. In fact it is evident
to me that the society of England is necessary for the
happiness of Mrs. Paradise, and is perhaps the most
agreeable to Mr. Paradise also. It is become an object
therefore to obtain the concurrence of their creditors in
the arrangements taken. The inducement to be proposed to them is Mrs. Paradise's joining in a deed in

which these dispositions shall be stipulated (which by
the laws of Virginia will bind her property there) so
that the creditors will be secured of their debts in the
event of Mr. Paradise's death. The inducement of Mr.
& Mrs. Paradise is that their persons & property shall
be free from molestation & their substance not consumed at law.

We suppose that the creditors will name one trustee
& Mr. Paradise another (yourself) fully & solely
authorized to receive all remittances from America, to
pay to them first their subsistence money & the rest to
the creditors till they are fully paid.

Mrs. Paradise will set out in a few days for London
to set her hand to this accommodation; in the meantime
they hope you will prepare the ground by negociating
the settlement with the creditors; as far as I have any
influence with Mr. or Mrs. Paradise I have used it &
shall use it for the joint interests of their creditors &
themselves. For I view it as clearly their interest to
reduce themselves to as moderate an expense as possible
till their debts are paid. If this can be effected before
my departure in April I will not only aid it here, but
have any thing done which may be necessary in Virginia when I go there, such as the recording the deed,
&c. This journey of Mrs. Paradise will also be an
experiment whether their distresses will not be lighter
when separate than while together.[13]

The discreet Jefferson did not of course in his letter
give Bancroft anything like a full impression of all
that had transpired between himself and the Paradises
during the month since their return. He had found
himself dealing with two people who in all practical
matters were as good as mad. The scene through which
they had passed on the eve of their departure from
Bergamo, the added complication of Count Barziza's
demands for a settlement on their daughter, and the

realization that the long-expected climax with their
English creditors had finally been reached had reduced
poor Paradise to a state of nerveless inactivity and had
elevated his wife to such a pitch of incoherent excitability as only she was capable. First of all, the demands of the Barzizas had to be settled. For the
Paradises to pay the annual settlement of £150 to their
daughter was at this time out of the question. In an
admirably tactful and diplomatic letter to the Countess,
Jefferson said as much, giving her at the same time the
most amiable reassurances of her parents' continued
affection and of their determination to begin the payments as soon as their debts should be paid.[14] With this
arrangement the Count also was obliged to be satisfied[15]
The next problem was a much more difficult one. It
concerned the personal relations of Mr. and Mrs.
Paradise, both of whom had returned from Italy in the
determination that they must live apart. Individually
they appealed to Jefferson to arrange the terms of their
separation and in this also he obligingly undertook to
aid them. Meanwhile, although they continued to live
together at the Hotel d'Angleterre, they found it impossible to discuss their affairs with one another; their
only communications on the subject were through
Jefferson. The interviews which Paradise held with
him were reported to Mrs. Paradise in letters, to each
of which she wrote two, sometimes three replies. One
of her letters to Jefferson contained a proposal that was
in the highest degree embarrassing:

My Dear Sir
    I was in hopes my future Letters would have been
Letters of amusement, and not of Grief—Your very
great Goodness over powers me, so that I am confound-

ed and struck with it—To say, I shall ever be able to return all your extraordinary attentions is more then I am able at this moment to say. Thus far, I declare, that should any thing happen to put it in my power to shew you my heart, I will shew you my Gratitude in the fullest manner. I am now in a very disagreeable situation, and I call upon your Excellency for your advice, and beg, and pray, you will with out reserve, openly give it to me. I am able to teach the English Language, I would willingly undertake to teach it, to young ladies of good families. If this you do not approve, I think the next thing I ought to do, is to go to Virginia and could I go with you, and your family, I should be happy—.For to go on in the present situation I am in, I cannot. I should not wish to go to Virginia before Mr Paradise and myself had Settled the affairs of our Daughter, as that is an absolute Duty on my part. Mr Paradise will then in the case of my going with your Excellency to Virginia have only himself to provide for—. I will follow your advice in every thing whether I go with you to Verginia or stay here. I will continue in your family in Virginia if you will permit me—or I will live with my Steward. For to speak openly, I am afraid I am not able to undertake housekeeping in Virginia Pray my dear Sir let me receive your Answer soon I am not anxious for you to keep this a secret from Mr Paradise, on the contrary I wi[sh] you to tell him if you think proper. I shall not myself speak to him, until, I know you hav[e]

I am
Your Excellencies
Most Grateful Humb^l and
obedient Servant

Paris
Lucy Paradise[16]
Hotel d Angleterre
Jany the 4th 1789
His Excellency Thom^s Jefferson

It must by now have become clear to Jefferson, as it apparently was to Mrs. Paradise, that she was in love with him, and this letter with its frank proposal called for prompt action. Jefferson was far from being in love with her, and it was only his friendship for her husband which had prompted the kindness and respectful consideration on which she had built her pathetic, far-fetched hopes. Jefferson acted at once. In what must have been a kindly, tactful letter, now unfortunately lost, followed by an interview in the presence of her husband at which the poor lady wept bitterly and uncontrollably, he persuaded her to leave without her husband for London where she would assist Dr. Bancroft in dealing with the creditors.[17] Meanwhile a deed of trust was to be drawn up in which she contracted in the event of Mr. Paradise's death to pay the debts in the same manner as if he had been still alive, but only on the conditions that Paradise would formally make over to her a half of the income reserved for their joint use and also that he should sign a statement that he would "live within his Income, and not exceed it." Nothing, she contended bitterly, would induce her to pay any debts made by Mr. Paradise after the deed of trust was executed. It was Mr. Paradise, she avowed to Jefferson, who was of such an extravagant nature; as for her, she could live in the simplest style, as she had living witnesses to prove. Meanwhile how was she to get to England without money to pay the traveling expenses of herself and her maid? Would Mr. Jefferson kindly settle that?[18]

Mr. Jefferson did settle it. By the end of January all arrangements for her departure were made. Jefferson effected a tentative reconciliation between the

husband and wife, inducing them to consider her going
as an "experiment," so he wrote Short, "whether they
can live asunder."[19] To this Short replied: "I wish
[they] may be able to live asunder—for I am sure they
were never meant to live together. . ."[20] On February
1st Jefferson invited them both to dinner and a few
days later Mrs. Paradise and her maid set off for
London by way of Calais—on cash supplied by Jefferson. What could have been Jefferson's feelings when
he wrote and Short's when he received the communication of a week later: "mrs. Paradise is gone to
England to aid in settling their affairs. mr. Paradise is
here, absolutely inconsolable on her departure. . ."[21]

In London Mrs. Paradise was received by Dr.
Bancroft and his wife at N° 21 Charlotte Street, Rathbone Place, only a short way off from the house in
which she had been married exactly twenty years
before. Dr. Bancroft was almost as kind as Mr. Jefferson had been. He set to work at once to make arrangements about the deed. First he engaged Paradise's
former attorney, a Mr. Young, to represent him. He
then dispatched letters to all the creditors, requesting
them to attend a meeting. With Young and Mrs.
Paradise he discussed the endless details of the affair,
all of which he promptly and fully communicated to
Jefferson. It was necessary for Mr. Paradise to name
three trustees. Mrs. Paradise reiterated her determination to have nothing to do with the deed unless her
husband would sign over to her a half of the joint
income they would be allowed and also agree to exempt
her from responsibility in all future debts he should
contract. On her arrival Mrs. Paradise engaged a house
at No. 15 Margaret Street, Cavendish Square—a good

enough situation to indicate that her ideas of economy were not very far advanced. An application to Anderson for an advance of funds, however, was absolutely refused. He would advance her no money until the deed was signed. Dr. Bancroft came to the rescue and advanced enough money to establish her there. "I will not let her want," he wrote Jefferson.[22]

At the meeting the creditors were encouraged by the consent of Mrs. Paradise to take responsibility in case of her husband's death and all went well. It looked as if the deed would be drawn up and signed within a month. "Tell M^r P not to be uneasy," Lucy wrote to Jefferson, "but let him kneel down and thank his God that he has raised up to him and myself two such friends as your Excellency and the D^r My tears pour from my Eyes so that I can hardly continue to write. The Bell rings which obliges me to bid you adieu and to your Dear Children and Love to Mr P. . . ."[23]

In Paris Jefferson was obliged to carry the full load of the responsibility, Paradise being either unwilling or unable to write more than a very occasional letter on the subject of business. It is difficult to say which had the worst of it—Jefferson or Dr. Bancroft. Although Paradise was passive and willing to agree to anything that was suggested, he soon began to chafe under his long absence from London and once more had fallen into the habit of immoderate drinking. On the other hand, Mrs. Paradise's efforts to assist Bancroft were, owing to her nervous excitability and her impracticality, far more of a hindrance than a help. Jefferson continued to go through the form of consulting his friend on all the steps that were taken, as his letters to Bancroft show.

Paris Mar. 1. 1789.

Dear Sir

Your favor of Feb. 20 came to hand by the last post and I have this day had a consultation with mr Paradise on the articles which concern him. with respect to the naming three trustees, all among his friends, and also the omitting to convey the money in the funds to the trustees, we both agree in sentiment with you, if the creditors will consent to it. it was the fear of their dissent which had at first suggested a different proposition. he also agrees that 200£ a year shall be paid to mrs Paradise separately and independantly of him. so that all seem to be agreed on one side, and I hope you will be able to obtain a like concurrence among the other parties. mr Paradise lives with all possible oeconomy. but he had unavoidably contracted some debts for his journey from Bergamo & his subsistance here before mrs Paradise left him. these could not be paid out of his allowance, and therefore should be provided for before the operation of the deed. both he and mrs Paradise should receive their allowances clear of incumbrance. present me in the most friendly terms to mrs Paradise and be assured of the esteem & attachment with which I am Dr Sir

Your most obed^t humble serv^t

Th: Jefferson[24]

Dr Bancroft

Something of the truth about Mrs. Paradise's unhappy situation had become known among their friends in London and many of them began to pay her kind and sympathetic attention on her arrival with calls and invitations to dinner and proffers of assistance. Count Zenobio, to whom Paradise was indebted to the extent of £30 a year out of his income from the funds, at once stepped forward and waived his claims in favor of the creditors. He had for years shown himself a generous and understanding friend to Paradise. Another foreign friend whose kindness Mrs. Paradise was never tired of acknowledging was the Chevalier de Freire, now *chargé d'affaires* from Portugal to England in the absence of the Minister, Louis de Pinto. His attentions to Mrs. Paradise were perhaps not unmixed with a hope that she would use her influence with Jefferson to get him appointed Minister to the United States; and in this he was not to be disappointed. John Trumbull, the American painter, was another to whom Mrs. Paradise was grateful for "remarkable attentions," and also to Lord and Lady Hawke—the former the son of the great admiral; to Joseph Planta, the Librarian of the British Museum and friend of Dr. Johnson; and to the merchant, Mr. Anderson, who, in spite of having refused to advance her money, frequently invited her to dine.[25] Early in March Mrs. Paradise received a visit from young Shippen, now dutifully engaged in his studies at the Inner Temple. "I passed an hour with Madame yesterday," he wrote his father; "she has a vast deal to say about America, and is at least as mad as before she had traveled; she seems in love with every thing and every body she has seen except my Uncle William—He has offended her prodigiously, and she does not spare him. I remonstrated with her on the subject and begged her to recollect that she was abusing a very near & dear relation of mine, and that I could not suffer it. She said he was no relation of mine, or at least so distant that I could not have any thing to say to her who was so much nearer a relation—She was not enough acquainted with the table of consanguinity [to know] that an uncle is a degree nearer to his nephew than one cousin to another. Now & then there is some reason in her madness, but she is altogether the strangest woman without doubt that God ever formed. . ."[26]

Meanwhile Bancroft's efforts to have the deed executed had met with what was destined to be the first of many checks. For one thing Paradise, in giving his consent to the appointment of three trustees, had, characteristically, forgotten to name any. This entailed a delay of sufficient length to allow two letters to pass between London and Paris. The other was more serious. Ibbitson, Barlow, & Co., a firm of mercers, after long consideration, finally declined to put their signature to the deed. Bancroft at once perceived their motive, which was to force a private settlement more to their advantage than a general agreement would have been.[27] But although he saw through their design he was powerless to prevent it. An appeal to Jefferson for advice brought the usual well-considered advice:

Paris Mar. 15. 1789.

Dear Sir

Your favor of the 10th is just now received, and as the refusal of one of mr Paradise's creditors to accede to the deed of trust, will occasion some change in mr Paradise's plan. this again will require that the whole be dispatched. as the post goes out in the morning, and his lodgings are very distant from me I cannot consult him expressly on the occasion, but many conversations have put me so fully in possession of his desires & designs that I can venture to write as if I had consulted him. in the first place I am clear that no private agreement nor separate terms whatever should be entered into with any of the creditors, but that the agreement should be carried into effect honestly & honorably: I would advise that the deed of trust be executed immediately with the consenting creditors, and that an opening be left for any others to come in within two or three weeks, and that time being passed, that it be carried on exclusively for the subscribing creditors. mr Paradise had intended to have gone to England, for a few days, to return here & go with me to America. but if any one of the creditors refuses to accede to the deed, he must dispense with his trip to England, & go out with me to America, where he will stay till all his debts are paid. you will see at once that this arrangement requires an immediate dispatch of the deed, which on his behalf I take the liberty of pressing on you. indeed I do not think the consent of a single creditor is worth detaining [?] the deed an hour. the laws of Virginia will support the [deed] exclusively for the parties acceding to it, and any redress [which] a dissenting creditor might seek under the same laws against the person of mr Paradise or his portion of subsistence money must wait operations; before which are terminated, the purposes of the deed will have been fully effect[ed]. mr Paradise wishes you would be so good as to be one of his trustees, and I think he would approve of any other two whom yourself & mrs Paradise should propose. be so good as to present my compliments to her. I have received her letters and should have done myself the honour of writing to her but for an excess of business. be so good as to add to her that mr Trumbul is furnished with money to pay for Pinelli's books.

I thank you for the information relative to D. I dare say you are right in supposing no such other volumes exist as Poulloy pretended to me. he has probably some design in what he told me: but your information places my mind at ease.—how much are we to believe of the king's re-establishment? I will write you hereafter on Admiral Jones's affairs. I am with very great esteem Dr Sir your friend & serv^t

Th: Jefferson[28]

Dr Bancroft

When Bancroft communicated the contents of this letter to Mrs. Paradise, she professed to be delighted at Paradise's plan for going to America with Jefferson. Her kindly feelings toward him on her first arrival in London were beginning to undergo another change, in consequence of rumors which had reached her concerning his insobriety. "Was I Mr P.," she wrote, "I should think myself in Duty bound to go again to Virginia and try, all, I could, to send over as fast as I could things that would pay all the Creditors and have a little ready Money left in case of Sickness &c Indeed his going with your Excellency would be a very great Service to him, as from your Example, he would learn to live regularly, and Soberly. For me I can have no objection, as I am certain he will be happy to be always near you. But the Subject is so very delicate for me to determine, that whatever your Excellency shall think proper for him to do, will be well done. If we could get the Money Norton owes us, and if Virginia would, or could pay us what is in their Funds Clear. I am Certain the Debts would easely be paid. By the Depreciation we have lost Virginia Money £26300 which brought into Sterling is almost £1500 besides our Negroes . . . but it was for my Countries glory and I therefore submit."[29] The money had in truth been lost, as well as the slaves; nor is there any reason to doubt the sincerity of Mrs. Paradise's renunciation of her loss. In all their vacillations neither she nor Paradise ever swerved in their loyalty to America.

Bancroft was skeptical of Paradise's intention of going to America. He knew how easily his friend was swept away by the enthusiasm of the moment. He also knew how deep was his attachment to London. "I received great Satisfaction," he wrote Jefferson, "at learning that it was your intention to take Mr Paradise with you to America, being persuaded that your Presence would operate as a very Salutary restraint upon him, and Cure him of some bad habits as well as give him good ones, both which I think highly necessary to his future Success & Happiness in Life, if there be still room to hope for these. But from a Letter which he wrote me the 18th in^st I fear you will find it difficult when the time comes to perswade him to make this Salutary Voyage, because I find his desires & purposes are all directed to this Country. . ."[30]

Acting on Jefferson's advice Bancroft at once began to push a settlement of the deed. This was further complicated, however, by the insistence of some of the consenting creditors that instead of allowing Mr. and Mrs. Paradise a clear £400 a year, the arrangement should be altered so that the creditors should receive the money from the funds and in addition one-third of the income from Virginia. In this they were actuated by the fear that there would not be sufficient income to pay the allowance to the Paradises and leave enough over for the debts. On being consulted as to this, Jefferson was obliged to give reluctant consent:

Paris Mar. 30. 1789.

Dear Sir

Mr Paradise writes to you by this post on the subject of the proposition made to him by the Creditors to take the money in the funds & a third of his Virginia income instead of £400 a year. I think with him that he should accept it. my greatest objection is that it will not admit of a plain and unsuspicious execution. for it will be a question pretty difficult to decide in England, and

which the inexactitude of those who remit will often
bring on, Whether a Remittance be of the debts due to
the estate or of it's annual profits? however it must be
accepted, even under this unpromising appearance;
because, to be in England, is a first·requisite to his
happiness. he mentions to you the necessity that the
debts contracted for the daily subsistance of himself &
mrs Paradise must first be paid: this is rational, because, reduced to a moderate pittance, that pittance
should be clear of previous debts. and this ought to
come out of the first monies to be received, before the
deed begins it's operation. as he does not tell you how
much these debts are, I must supply the omission. my
advances for him have been 30. Louis on his journey
to Bergamo, 30. Louis more in January for the subsistance of himself & mrs Paradise, 20. Louis to mrs
Paradise for her journey to London, & 18. Louis since
her departure to mr Paradise for his subsistance, in all
98. Louis. this with the proceeds of his chariot cleared
off all scores here to the 1st or 2^{d} week of this month.
to that you must add half a guinea a day nearly from
that time till he shall go away, and ten guineas for his
journey. what mrs Paradise's necessities may have
called for in London you will know, so that putting
both together you may satisfy the creditors by naming
a definite sum, as I suppose they would not accede to a
vaghe proposition to pay his debts of subsistance, the
amount of which they can know nothing about. I am
sorry to be obliged to let my advances be named on this
occasion. but on my approaching return to America
I must settle my publick accounts, and from the statement I have made of them I shall be in want of this
sum, as well as others which I had advanced in the
same way, to make up my balance, a balance which, not
made up, would affect my reputation as a public man.
my manner of living here, however regular, has never
permitted me a copper of savings out of which I could
assist my countrymen who have been here in distress.

I have been obliged then to anticipate, trusting to their honour to replace it, and when they have failed, which has happened too often, I bear the loss, besides in the present case, it is only a question between mr Paradise's creditors & me, which of us shall lie out of this money. they have had advantages in their dealings with mr Paradise which decide the question fairly against them. —pardon, my dear Sir, this momentary attention to my own affairs, which I have been forced to make & believe me to be with great affection to mrs Paradise & yourself

Your most obed^t humble serv^t

Dr Bancroft   Th: Jefferson[31]

Jefferson was also obliged to acknowledge to Bancroft in the preceding letter as well as in the next his realization that Paradise could not be induced to settle permanently out of England:

Paris Apr. 9. 1789.

Dear Sir

Your favor of the 27th has been duly received, and in answer to the information relative to D[eane]. I can only beg the favor of you to avail yourself of any moment which may occur wherein principles either of fidelity or venality might induce him to give up the books, for the U. S. I will answer the price as far as 12. or 15. guineas for that containing his correspondence from Aug. 1777. to Mar. *1788.* (I presume you mean *1778*)

Mr Paradise's impatience to return to England is such that he has seriously proposed to go & deliver himself up to his creditors rather than stay away longer. I have put him off that by making him expect the deed every post. should it not be ready, it would be highly expedient to put it into the hands of some one who will draw it in the instant. the deed of settlement of his estate may be best done by the attorney acquainted with his affairs; but the deed for the creditors seems to require no such knowledge, and therefore may be written by any one who will write it first. I cannot but recommend to you to have it drawn, executed and sent here without a moment's delay. tho' I have not yet received my congé, I hold myself in readiness to depart within a week after receiving it. I can at no time count than on more than a week. I am with very perfect esteem Dear Sir

Your most obed^t humb^l ser^t

Dr Bancroft   Th: Jefferson[32]

Bancroft, thoroughly aroused at the urgency of this appeal, did all that was in his power to hasten the execution of the deed. By means of much difficulty and many consultations he persuaded the silk mercers to enter into the agreement, and finally all of the creditors but one, a man named Bettsworth whose debt was only £15, had consented to the arrangement. The new difficulty was with the attorney, Mr. Young, who either through neglect or through the pressure of other business continued to postpone the drawing of the important document in spite of all the Doctor's efforts to spur him to action. All of this was recounted to Jefferson in the greatest detail; Bancroft wished to make it clear that he himself was not dilatory in the matter.[33] Meanwhile Paradise, in his eagerness to have things settled so that he might return, made new concessions which Jefferson communicated in his next.

Paris Apr. 24. 1787. [1789]

Dear Sir

I have duly received your favor of the 14th [really the 17th] and communicated it to mr Paradise, who desires me to observe that, after retaining a very moderate subsistance for himself & mrs Paradise (as that of

£200 a year apiece which has been proposed) his first
and ruling object is to pay his debts: that therefore
instead of desiring a full third of all remittances from
Virginia, including debts, he would wish that whenever
these remittances are such as that his third added to the
money in the funds would exceed 400£ for himself and
mrs Paradise, the surplus should be paid to his creditors. and he would rather have it so settled in the deed.
he concurs in the idea of letting the deed commence it's
operation on the produce of the present year, so that
with the crop of the last year he may pay the debts
contracted for his subsistance before the [illegible] of
the deed. as the expectation of my congé leaves me
never sure of being here more than ten days, I think it
would serve the interests of all parties to enable me to
convey the deed to Virginia and have it recorded there.
this is essential to it's validity. I inclose for mrs Paradise a letter which came to me thro' the *post office*. I
mention this to account for the marks of violation on it.
with respectful compliments to her, I am with great
esteem D[r] Sir your most obed[t] humble serv[t]

Th: Jefferson[34]

D[r] Bancroft.

Paradise's rash suggestion that he should go to London before the signing of the deed was the cause of
great anxiety to all his friends, since it meant that it
would be in the power of any one of the creditors to
have him arrested and thrown in the King's Bench
Prison. While most of the creditors were tolerant, being by now impressed by the sincerity of his good
intentions regarding his debts, Bancroft on inquiry had
been informed by one of the most friendly of them that
there was another member of the group who would
certainly take advantage of Paradise's arrival in London to have him arrested, either out of resentment or

else from the hope of extorting, in advance of the
rest, the sum that was due him.[35] At this point Mrs.
Paradise received a letter from her husband announcing that he was determined to come and deliver himself
up. She wrote to Jefferson at once to implore him to
prevent it. If her "unthinking Husband" should take
such a step it would mean the ruination of them all.
Not only would he be ruined himself, he would drag
her and their daughter down with him. He was, she
declared dramatically, a "second Sr John Brute."[36]
Shortly after writing this she heard rumors from Paris
that prompted another and even wilder outburst to her
unwilling confidant: "I have just heard that Mr P. is
often drunk and he has Said it is my Letters that makes
him drink. I am certain it is false, as your Excellency,
must have Seen every Letter, I have written to him.
I am resolved my Letters shall never make him drunk
any more, as he never shall receive another from me.
He Supposes I am the cause of his not being able to
return here, it is false as Dr Bancroft knows. It is M^r
Young his Attoney who has not yet finished the Deed
and until the Deed is properly Signed by all his Creditors he must have patience, or he will most certainly be
carried to the Kings Bench, this is the truth, as D^r
Bancroft knowes. I should be happy to have him with
me, if he will act with prudence, and be Sober. I hear
he exposes himself at Paris to every person he see[s]
and tells them, that any thing that troubles him, makes
him drink. Why do not, I drink? and thousands besides? that is only an excuse. What is he not to feel pain
and trouble, then he might have a voided it, by not
spending his money and time with a Women this I
know he did to my certain knowledge, and I suppose

he must wish to see them greatly. A man has a right to ammuse himself, but he has No right to bring his Wife to want, and his Children also—*I am not the object of M*^{r}* P affect*^{t}. Pray my Dear Sir remember my Sex [when] you go to Virginia, and introduce [a] Marriage Settlemen[t] for to [pr]eserve my Sex from want in case of the Bad behaviour of their husbands."[37]

Protection of women's property rights, especially her own, was a subject on which she often wrote to Jefferson: "I am not the first Woman, that has been cursed with a Drunkard I know your Excellency will Say. I acknowledge it; but then, those Women, may have had friends that took them Under their Protection. I stand a lone, the greater My Misfortune. What, I would beg of your Excellency is, to assist me with your advice from time to time and to write to General W[ashington] and tell him what my Situation is, and to see, after the Debts are paid if I could take Possession of all My Property in Virginia during the Life of Mr P. If that can be contrived, I am safe, and then, shall be happy. Something of this Sort ought to be done and that as soon as possible. This is the Protection, I want from your Excellency and My Country. Every person that comes from Paris talk about his Drinking and that every person there laughs at him— I pray God to preserve my Dear Friends the Miss Jeffersons from Such a Husband."[38]

The weeks of delay about the deed dragged on into months. By the middle of April all parties were prepared to sign, and yet no efforts on the part of Bancroft or anyone else could induce the procrastinating Young to draw it up, and it was still unfinished at the end of June. Meanwhile the pressure on Jefferson from

Paradise and that on Bancroft from Mrs. Paradise must have been terrific. "I have never done any thing," said Mrs. Paradise, "without consulting, and following the advice of my Dear friend Dr Bancroft, as I well knew, I was not Wise enough to conduct myself." Dr. Bancroft was all kindness and industry, but he was subject to nervous headaches (natural enough to one who was in the daily company of Mrs. Paradise) which prevented him from attending important meetings of the creditors and sometimes from writing letters that were pressing. The chief cause of the delay, however, was the Attorney; Bancroft apparently lacked the forcefulness to move him to action.[39]

During all this time Mrs. Paradise continued to favor her beloved Mr. Jefferson with letters. Any subject would do so long as it gave her an opportunity of conversing with him. A favorite theme was Freire, to whom she was devoted and whom she ardently desired to have appointed as minister from Portugal when diplomatic relations with the United States should be established. She deplored the 25 per cent duty imposed by America on Madeira wine as unfair to a country which, she mistakenly contended, had been helpful in the time of distress. *"I own I love Portugal because of their attention to us."* She retailed to Jefferson all the bits of news which she received from America and elsewhere. Mrs. Washington had written her that the new constitution would certainly be received without tumult or disorder—a knowledge of which Jefferson had been master months before she wrote of it; General Washington had sent his compliments to "Mr. P." On May 5th, she had just heard that Lord Dunmore had been recalled from India; she prays that this is true, as

the Virginia papers had said that he was trying to
raise the Indians to cut the white men's throats. The
King of England had recovered from his madness but
later, she wrote, he had been afflicted "with a Dropsey."
She had heard a great noise about the fly that was
spoiling American wheat. She conjectured that it was
the "Wevil" and sent Jefferson directions for combat-
ing it. She took a pathetic pleasure in a commission
which Jefferson gave her to buy some books for him at
a sale and wrote to him voluminously on details concerning prices, octavo and quarto editions. The correct
spelling of the Latin and Italian titles was far beyond
her powers and Jefferson must have many times re-
gretted making the request, if indeed he ever labored
through her pages of all but indecipherable script.
Every letter had for its beginning, middle, and end her
protestations of gratitude to himself and Dr. Bancroft.
"Dr Bancroft behaves to Me with the greatest kindness;
Indeed I am over-powered, and tears falls from my
Eyes when I think of Your and the D^{rs} goodness to Me.
But how, I shall ever return such God-like Goodness,
I know Not."[40]

All through this long series of letters, to only the last
of which she received an answer, ran the theme of her
devotion to Jefferson. There can be no doubt that she
loved him tenderly. She is even jealous of him. In
London Jefferson had been attracted to Mrs. Maria
Cosway. He had carried on a lively and entirely innocent correspondence with her ever since. One of Jefferson's letters contained the famous dialogue of the Head
and the Heart, to which Mrs. Paradise refers as
"verses," although it is in rather flat-footed prose. "I
have not seen Mrs Cosway since my return," she wrote

with considerable venom, "but, I have been told that your Excellencies Verses, you sent her, and your Letters were like yourself well done—Indeed She shews your Letters to every body. I feel myself greatly honoured and flatered when ever I receive a Letter from you, but, I do not make them a show to any person."[41]

At the end of June it seemed probable that Jefferson, after so much delay, was at last going to leave for America. Mrs. Paradise wrote him a farewell letter, once more overwhelming him with protestations of undying gratitude. She loaded him with messages of affection to the dear Miss Jeffersons and with greetings for all her friends in America—General and Mrs. Washington, the Knoxes, the John Adamses, all the Lee connection except William, the Burwells, the Grymeses, Dr. Franklin and his daughter and many others. The main part of the letter was entirely without any indiscretions, although apparently from habit she urged him not to tell anybody that he had received it. But the wistful postscript gave away her true feelings: "I wish I was agoing with you to Virginia. It cannot be, therefore whatever is, is right."[42] An unkind fate had given her a husband whose gentle, sensitive nature her own corrosive violence had been able to destroy, and then turned it upon herself. Who knows what unfulfilled destiny might have been hers if she had been linked to a man who was strong enough to withstand her passionate will—a man whom she could respect as well as love? Poor, distracted Lucy Paradise, comforting herself with the stale crumbs of a philosophy which was as outmoded as the age which gave expression to it.

By the middle of June, Young's neglect of the deed

had become so exasperating that even Jefferson, with all his prudence, was beginning to lose patience and he allowed Bancroft to see it:

Paris June 15. 1789.

Dear Sir

Mr Paradise calls on me in the moment of the departure of the post, decided to set out to London immediately. I have however prevailed on him to agree to stay to the 29th instant, when, if his deed is not arrived, he is decided to go and see his creditors openly, and I am not to offer a persuasion to the contrary, even should I be here. indeed I could offer him no good reason, because the indolence of mr Young would not be a good one, as it may last to his death. I have not a moment to add another word but to assure you of the sincere esteem & respect of Dr Sir

Your most obed^t
& most humble serv^t

Dr Bancroft   Th: Jefferson[43]

Bancroft replied promptly:

Dear Sir

I have just received your favour of the 15th ins^t as I had before done that of a former date—I fully intended writing you a long Letter by Mr Cutting [but] I did not know of his departure until the preceding day when I had engaged Company to dine with me, from whom I could not disengage myself until midnight, and the next day I was unfortunately attacked by one of my Nervous Headachs which rendered all writing insupportably painful—That disorder, though abated, has not left me, and therefore I can only say, that after a multitude of efforts to engage Mr Young to finish Mr Paradise's Deed and a multitude of fruitless Promises which were from time to time made until I had determined to employ another Attorney, Mr Young on Tuesday last brought me a rough Draft of the Deed which we examined together, and after some amendments he took it away to get it transcribed for the inspection of M[r] Barlow the Trustee of the Creditors, after which it is to be engrossed, & the Creditors called together in order to have it signed. This I hope may be done in the course of the next week; but as many of them probably will not attend any general meeting, some days will afterwards be required to call on them separately for their Signatures. It is thought that M[r] Paradise may as well come here to sign the Deed, and if you should have left Paris it may be sent to you in Virginia or elsewhere directly from hence, properly authenticated—Should M[r] Paradise leave Paris as you mention on the 29th ins[t] I should hope and believe that all the Creditors will have been induced to sign before his arrival; and if so no harm will ensue—It would however doubtless be safest for him to be certain of their having signed before his arrival—but if his impatience to return will not admit of this I shall only advise that he come so as to be able to keep his arrival a Secret for a few days, in case it should through unforeseen difficulties or delay, be necessary.

I have the honor to be with the sincerest respect & attachment Dear Sir

Your most faithful
& Devoted Humble Servant

Charlotte Street Edw[d] Bancroft[44]
June 19th 1789.

By the 29th no further word had been received from Bancroft and yet it was decided that Paradise should remain in Paris for two more weeks in the hope that by then he could go to London without danger of arrest. Jefferson meanwhile had had no further news from America concerning his *congé*. On July 4th, Paradise and a group of prominent Americans in Paris drew up and presented to Jefferson a formal and elaborate testimonial of the services he had performed for America during his ministership. Paradise and Haskell called on Gouverneur Morris and invited him to be one of the signers, but he declined.[45] The style of the document is very similar to that of Paradise in his letters. This and the fact that his is the first signature make it seem very probable that the paper was composed by him.

> To his Excellency Thomas Jefferson Esquire
> Minister Plenipotentiary from the United States
> to the Court of Versailles

Sir

Your intention of withdrawing awhile from this court on a visit to our happy country offers an occasion which we cannot resist of testifying those sentiments of gratitude and attachment which your conduct has taught us to realise, as the emotions of ingenuous minds towards an illustrious Benefactor.

As citizens of the United States we feel a laudable pride in joining the general voice of our country and of that of the age in which we live in rendering the sincerest tribute of respect to a compatriot so distinguished for his exertions in favour of that country and for the general happiness of mankind; but as temporary residents in a foreign kingdom, a situation in which the grateful heart becomes more susceptible and good actions recieve an additional merit, you will pardon our zeal if it assumes a language which in other circumstances it might be unbecoming the dignity of a Republican Patriot to receive. Praise is honorable only in proportion to the freedom and information of the persons from whom it arises; from a depressed subject it is a proof of power and of meanness; from an enlightened freeman, of merit and of gratitude. It is the application of this principle which alone can render

public testimonials of this kind acceptable to such
minds as have the goodness to deserve them.

During your residence in this kingdom your particular kindness and attention to every American who has
fallen in your way have endeared you to their hearts;
and we are sure, as we speak the language which they
have often uttered on this subject, that were they all
present they would join in this our most cordial ac-
knowledgement. But your conduct in this respect,
though in the highest degree noble and generous, makes
but a part of the motives of our love and admiration.
The benefits resulting to the United States from your
various negotiations in Europe excite in us a gratitude
of a more extensive and patriotic nature. In these
negotiations, your comprehensive views & minute attentions to every interest of every part of the country
you represent, at the same time that your policy is
directed to the general harmony and happiness of all
nations, render you the proper minister of that enlightened people whose cause is the cause of humanity, and
whose example we trust will greatly benefit mankind.

As this is the anniversary of our Independence our
sensations of pleasure are much increased from the idea
that we are addressing ourselves to a man who sustained
so conspicuous a part in the immortal transactions of
that day—whose dignity energy & elegance of thought
and expression added a peculiar lustre to that declara-
tory act which announced to the world the existence of
an empire. Be pleased, Sir, to accept our congratulations on the return of this day: a day which we hope
arises with peculiar glory on our hemisphere, as it finds
an extensive people happily united under the organization of a new government which promises the most
lasting advantages. May your visit to that country
afford you a noble and endearing satisfaction, both as to
the prosperity of your particular connextions and
affairs, and as it may give you an opportunity of rendering new services by your information and advice to that

illustrious band of your fellow patriots who must welcome you with every token of respect.

While those of us who remain longer in France shall have reason to regret your absence, yet we cannot but rejoice with you on its occasion, and sincerely wish you a prosperous & happy voyage.

With every sentiment of gratitude and respect we have the honor to be, Sir,

Paris   your most obedient
July 4th, 1789   and very humble servants

John Paradise	Philip Mazzei
Samuel Blackden	E. Haskell
Joel Barlow	Th. Appleton
Jams Swan	Benjn Jarvis[46]

Paradise's gratitude to Jefferson was also evidenced in a letter which he wrote to his manager in Virginia the day before his departure from Paris:

Paris July 11th 1789.

My dear Mr Wilkinson

The purport of this letter is to inform you that I have drawn a bill upon Dr Bancroft for one hundred and seventy six pounds sterling, money which Mr Jefferson has had the generosity to advance me for my support. I desire you, therefore, to reimburse this sum to him immediately, and take the bill for your voucher—Had it not been for the unparalled kindness of this invaluable man, I most certainly must have starved; but as the Jeffersons are scarce, very scarce indeed in this world, I must desire you, my friend, for the future to be a little more regular in your remittances. To-morrow I shall set off for London, from whence I shall write to you a long letter. In the mean while I beg my best compliments to your good-mother and our other friends in Virginia, and am sincerely

Yrs

John Par[adise][47]

Paradise set off for London on the 12th, arriving on the 16th. He carried with him a letter from Jefferson to Thomas Paine containing Jefferson's enthusiastic approval of Paine's idea for a "geometrical wheelbarrow," and also a long and sympathetic account of the proceedings of the Estates General. "Mr. Paradise is the bearer of this letter," Jefferson wrote. "He can supply those details which it would be too tedious to write."[48] The day following Jefferson wrote to Bancroft concerning the bill, or draft, which he had reluctantly been obliged to ask Paradise to give him:

Paris July 12. 1789.

Dear Sir

Mr Paradise will be arrived in London before this reaches you. he could not determine to await the Deed any longer, but he proposed to land at your house in order to know in the first moment whether it was signed. he left in my hands a bill on you for £176 sterling which I had advanced for him & mrs Paradise [illegible]. [this] was part of a sum of money which I was to have paid in London before the last day of June. having failed to do this, I have received a letter on the subject which gives me uneasiness. I postpone answering it till I can hear from you what provision was made or left open by the deed for reimbursing this. my situation here leaves me no other resource: but if the first remittance due from mr Paradise's estate will be free, I think there is no [illegible]. I will thank you for an answer by return of post. I have not yet received my permission to go to America, nor heard any news about it. I begin to suspect they prefer my being abroad during the winter, rather than the summer. I am with very great esteem Dear Sir

Your most obedient
& most humble serv^t

Doct^r Bancroft.   Th: Jefferson[49]

Jefferson now found an opportunity of answering Mrs. Paradise's long series of communications of the past three months, in a letter written the day before the fall of the Bastille:

Paris July 13. 1789.

Dear Madam

I have been long without acknoleging the receipt of your favors of June the 2^d & 30th I expected every post would bring the deed which was to enable mr Paradise to go to London. before you receive this he will be arrived there: and he will be surprised to be told that the evening before he left Paris, mr Necker was dismissed from office and went off to Geneva. Monsieur de Montmorin resigned. it is said the Baron de Breteuil is taken into the ministry; but I am not yet sure of this last. there were great tumults in Paris last night, and engagements between the mob, and some of the foreign troops.—I have not yet received my Congé but am still expecting it, and still hoping that I am on the point of my departure. however I begin to see a possibility that I may not go till the fall. I shall still think it my duty to endeavour to have your affairs there rendered as energetic as possible. with respect to the particular proposition in your two last letters [ref. to Mrs. P on women's property rights], I suppose it to be impossible. there was never yet an example of it, and the laws are entirely against it. I have the honor to be with very great esteem Dear Madam

Your most obed^t humble serv^t

Mrs Paradise   Th: Jefferson[50]

Mrs. Paradise replied in eager haste:

Dear Sir

I received your affectionate and kind Letter of the 13th on the 17th the Day after the arrival of Mr Paradise. His arrival gave me an uneasiness for fear of an arrest, as the Deed is not yet finished. His appearance, speaks the great care, your Excellency has done him the Honour to shew him. He is very sensible of it. He has great reason so to be. For myself, I look up to you, as to an Angel sent from Heaven, to see justice done Me, and my only child. Indeed My Dear Sir the Moment I can say, the Debts are all paid, and I have an Hundred, or Two Pound in my Pocket Clear, I shall begin to feel rest, as it will inable me, to shew my Gratitude to My Friends. All, I find, is in Confusion where you are, and without a better Head to set their government right it will be worse. This Country trembles, when they even suppose that France will be as Free as themselves; because should they put their Funds upon the same plan as these, here, this Country will feel it very severely. It will give a stab that no time can cure. I shall be sorry for it. But if it makes the People more Virtuous (altho' I find them better then in the Countries I have seen) I shall be happy. I have just finished the Reign of Lewis the 14th He knew by the advice of Madame de Maintenon how to be a King, but his obstanicy was so great as often to hinder him from acting Right. God send peace all over France. Some of their Customs I like, that particularly which concerns Husbands and Wifes. They want the sincerity of us Americans. This Letter will be delivered to your Excellency, I hope by Count Soderini who is on his way to Venice. He is a Gentleman worthy to be known to your Excellency. [Note: Mrs. P has forgotten that she entertained Soderini and Jefferson together at dinner in 1786.] The wheather is very bad as it rains several times in a Day. The King is perfectly recovered. Dr Bancroft appears not to be tired in his acts of Friendship. I wish this Gentleman was a Minister here. Think of me when you are in Virginia and do me One Great Favour which is to examine my Property nicely and let me know what, I may shortly expect. I shall esteem it a favour if your Excellency will do me the Honour to present my affec^t Love to the Dear Miss Jeffersons, and my very best compt^s to Mr Short. I beg you will be so good as to tell him I wish him to be as happy as his Heart Could wish. To Col^o Blagden and Lady I return them thanks for their kind attentions to Mr Paradise, and my best Compt^s to them and all the Americans I know, and all other persons of my acquaintances

> I have the Honour to be
> Dear Sir
> Your Excellencies Most
> Grateful Humble Servant
> and Affec^t Friend

London
Margaret Street N° 15   L Paradise[51]
Cavendish Square
Saturday July ye 18th 1789

On receiving word from Bancroft that the proposed deed would not apply to Paradise's income of the present year and would consequently allow the debt to him to be paid, Jefferson replied with evident relief. The duns from his unknown London creditor had been extremely upsetting to him.

> Paris Aug. 5. 1789.

Dear Sir

I am now to acknolege the receipt of your favor of July 21. the measure adopted for reimbursing us will doubtless be effectual. I mentioned to you that my advance had put it out of my power to pay a sum of money in London which I was highly bound to pay. it brought on me a letter from the creditor which permitted me no longer to delay sending him mr Paradise's bill on you. this I did by the last post. but I informed him you were only the trustee, not the debtor of mr Paradise, and expressly desired no protest might be taken for delay of paiment but that his correspondent in London might be only instructed to receive the money when mr Anderson or yourself should be ready to pay it. I mentioned your expectations that a bill of lading would arrive this month. without troubling you further on this subject, I will trust to your delivering me from the future sollicitations of the person to whom I owe the money, as soon as you can.—quiet is so well established here that I think there is nothing further to be apprehended. the harvest is so near that there is nothing to fear from the want of bread. the National assembly are wise, firm & moderate. they will establish the English constitution, purged of it's numerous & capital defects. I am with very great esteem & respect Dear Sir your most obed^t humble serv^t

Th: Jefferson[52]

Dr Bancroft.

Throughout August and the early part of September, letters from Bancroft and Mrs. Paradise kept Jefferson informed of the progress, or rather the lack of progress of the deed. On the night of Paradise's arrival in London, Bancroft spirited him out of town to the house of a friend ten miles in the country. The difficulty now was that when it came to the actual point of signing the deed several of the creditors refused, giving very implausible reasons. It was obvious that they hoped individually to extract the money owing them, or a part of it, sooner than would be possible by collective action. This meant that any one of the protesting creditors would, the instant he heard of Paradise's arrival in London, have him arrested and thrown into prison. Consequently, to his great mortification he was obliged to remain in hiding at his friend's house for a month. So depressed were his spirits at this unlooked for continuation of his troubles that he was as usual reduced to complete inactivity and felt unable to write even to

Jefferson. Bancroft and Mrs. Paradise were obliged to
convey his messages of gratitude and to excuse him as
best they could for not writing himself. "He says, your
Excellency knows him very well, and he is certain you
will excuse it," wrote Mrs. Paradise.[53] At the end of
a month, about August 20th, several of the creditors
had been persuaded to sign and Bancroft considered it
was safe for Paradise to join his wife in Margaret
Street—but of course he was obliged to remain in the
strictest secrecy.[54] At the beginning of September Jefferson finally received his *congé*, and thereupon wrote
an answer to the several letters of farewell which Mrs.
Paradise had written him at various times when she
had heard rumors that he was about to depart.

Paris Sep. 10. 1789.
Dear Madam
    I am to acknolege the receipt of your favor of July
18, and that by the last post. having now received my
leave of absence I wait for nothing but a vessel bound
from some convenient port in France to some convenient one in America. I trust such a one will occur by
the end of the equinox which is as soon as I would wish
to be at sea. my baggage is already gone off for Havre.
on my arrival in Virginia I will pay all possible attention to obtain the information you desire relative to
your affairs. tranquillity is pretty generally restored in
this country, & the National assembly are going on well
in forming their constitution. it will be difficult for
them to form one which will appear the best possible
to every mind but they will form a good one, in which
liberty and prosperity will probably be placed on a
surer footing than they are in England. I imagine they
will still be two or three months engaged in this business.—incertain of the precise moment of my departure,
I take the liberty of making this a letter of Adieu for

my daughters and myself, & to their assurances of affectionate attachment to mr Paradise & yourself to add those also of Dear Madam your most obed^t & most humble serv^t

Th: Jefferson[55]

Mrs Paradise.

It was not until he had been in England for two months that Paradise, who to the continually reiterated surprise of his wife had remained entirely sober throughout that time, found himself able to write a letter to Jefferson, to whom by now he owed his very existence.

London Sepr 16th 1789

Dear Sir,

Our valuable friend doctor Bancroft and Mrs Paradise have already acquainted you with the reason which has hitherto prevented me from writing to you. As the deed in question is not yet finished, and I am still obliged in a manner to lurk, the dejection of my spirits still continues, and my seemingly culpable silence would have of course still have continued, had not Mr Trumbull informed me that you are not well. This has roused me from the torpor which my disgraceful situation has brought upon me, and I eagerly take up my pen, not, however, to express my gratitude for the unparallelled favours you have conferred upon me and my family; for what words can express it? but most earnestly to entreat you to let me know by return of the post how you are since no one can possibly be more deeply interested in your welfare than I am, and Mr Trumbull's intelligence has alarmed me beyond expression. On my arrival hither I found a letter from the inestimable M^r [George] Wythe, by which he informs me that in consequence of a late act of our general assembly he re[mains] the sole judge of the high court of chancery. I also found one from Mr Burwell, who does not mention a word about remittances. I hope, however, that the Planter, which is now daily expected, will bring them. As to my debt to you, I refer you to doctor Bancroft's letter. Mr Ledlier is certainly dead, but I have the satisfaction to find from the newspapers that the report of Major Langborn's death was groundless. Mrs Paradise joins me in every good wish to you and your amiable family. I beg my best compliments to Mr Short, and have the honour to be with a due sense of gratitude Your Excellency's

Most faithful friend and
obliged humble servant

John Paradise[56]

The incorruptibly friendly Jefferson soon reassured him:

Paris Sep. 25. 1789.

Dear Sir

My occupations prevented my acknoleging by the last post the receipt of your letter and returning you my thanks for your kind enquiries after my health which is perfectly reestablished. I am in expectation of receiving by tomorrow's post a letter from mr Trumbull announcing an opportunity of getting to America, & shall be ready to leave this place in the same instant. if by that or any other vessel I can be landed at Hampton, I shall be able to give to your affairs the spur which may be necessary, & to you some account of them. I inclose you a letter which was mislaid while you were here. hurry obliges me to conclude here with respects to mrs Paradise & assurances to you both of those sentiments of esteem & attachment with which I am Dear Sir

Your sincere friend & serv^t

Mr Paradise   Th: Jefferson[57]

At the same time Bancroft received the last letter which Jefferson was to write him on the subject of the Paradises:

Paris Sep. 25. 1789.

Dear Sir

Expecting to receive by tomorrow's post a letter from mr Trumbull announcing an occasion of getting to America, & that I must leave this place in the same instant I have only time to acknolege the receipt of yours of Aug. 21. in due time after it's date, to recommend to you the saving my credit as to the bill I drew on you, whenever mr Paradise's remittances shall put it in your power and to assure you that I shall be happy in every occasion of rendering you service & of proving to you those sentiments of esteem & respect with which I am Dear Sir

Your most obed^t

& most humble serv^t

Dr Bancroft.   Th: Jefferson[58]

Jefferson's departure from Europe, which did not actually take place until October 22, 1789, (owing to "contrary" winds which detained his vessel at Cowes for fourteen days,) did not bring to an end his activities on behalf of his unfortunate friends, although his correspondence with them from this time was nothing like so active as before. This was due, not to any falling off in his friendship and kind assistance, but rather to the tremendous activity in public life which began with his unwilling assumption of the Secretaryship of State. The services which he continued to render to the Paradises and their descendants ended only with his own death in 1826. On arriving in Virginia he carried out his promise of attempting to give a "spur" to their affairs there and in the early part of January, 1790, wrote Paradise a detailed account of what had been done:

Monticello Jan. 6. 1790.

Dear Sir

On my arrival in Williamsburg I had a meeting with Col⁰ Burwell & Mʳ Wilkinson on your affairs. the state of them here as given us by Mʳ Wilkinson is as follows.

Crop of Tobacco of the growth of 1788. this being 28 hogsheads has been sent you by the Planter. you have more here of an earlier growth as you had supposed.—

Crop of the growth of 1789. there will be 18 hogsheads of tobacco & a good crop of Corn. I pressed the remitting this to you as early as possible for your present relief, presuming that the 28 hogsheads sent by the planter would not more than replace anticipations.

Your chariot, when it shall be sold with the private debts due to you, will much about pay the debts due from you and your estate in this County.

But Norton's debt is not meant to be included in the preceding article. this cannot be counted on with certainty till Feb. 1791. by which time he will have exhausted all the delays allowed by the Law; this will be about £800. currency. On the other hand the debt of £300 your estate owes to Lee, & not included in the preceding article must be paid out of Norton's money, so that there will be a balance of £500 currency, not quite £400. sterling to be remitted to the creditors in the Spring of the next year.

About the same time they will receive the proceeds of the crop which shall be made in the present year, which being the first after the date of the Deed, is apprehended to be the first on which that operates. Mr Wilkinson's opinion of what may be expected annually on an average is as follows.

With the tobaccoes he thinks he can pay the taxes and expenses of the estate and your £200 Sterl
from corn he counts on   £300
The mill about   100
firewood about   100

making in all about   £500 currency

which when exchange is at par makes £375. Sterl. so that the creditors may count on certainly enough is about £750 Sterl in the Spring of 1791. & £375 annually afterwards.

Besides these there are two other resources which may be hoped productive.

1. The debt due you from this State, about £800 Sterling. The measures taken for buying up this kind of Stock, will probably raise it so near par as to enable you to sell out with very little loss, but within what time I cannot say.

2. The cutting of your wood at Chippoaks. Mr Wilkinson did not seem at first to view this as a resource worth attention. but I thought that never having been engaged in the sale of timber, he underestimated what he had not as yet had occasion to understand. I told him however that the circumstances under which Mrs Paradise & yourself are placed left the futurity [?] of that wood for no object at all; that the main object was to relieve you for the present, and that whether it would yield little or much it must be disposed of for the paiment of your debts. On this representation he entered chearfully & fully into my wishes [?], & it was concluded between Col° Burwell & him that they would hire some hands to cut it down, & that in addition to the sale of the timber the fine tobacco lands which would be thereby cleared would enlarge the

annual produce of that article, so that when you will begin to receive benefit from this wood and to what degree I cannot say.

I must here do justice to Mr Wilkinson against myself. my experience of the people called Stewards, had made me fear you placed too much confidence in yours. but what I hear and what I see of him removes all my apprehensions. he is really a man of another [omission] than that in which he is chosen. his skill and his integrity merit all confidence. You are equally fortunate in the person to whom he is submitted here. Col° Burwell is an excellent manager, clear in his own affairs and zealous in yours. You owe him abundance of thanks. This my dear Sir, is as full & faithful an account of your affairs as I am able to collect. I write it for you, for Mrs Paradise, for Dr Bancroft, & for your creditors, & I hope you will communicate it accordingly, the short time I am permitted to stay here not allowing me avocation enough from my own affairs to send different letters on the subject of the present one. Wishing therefore all possible happiness to yourself & Mrs Paradise, I have the honor to renew you assurances of the esteem & respect with which I am Dear Sir

her and your sincere friend
& humble Servant

Mr Paradise   Th Jefferson[59]

Fortunately, soon after Jefferson's departure in the autumn of 1789, Paradise had received from Virginia a shipment of tobacco which enabled him to pay not only what he owed to Jefferson but also to repay in part that which Bancroft had advanced for Mrs. Paradise's subsistence in London.[60]

Despite Dr. Bancroft's ugly record as a double-dealing, unscrupulous spy, he proved himself to be a loyal friend to John and Lucy Paradise. As their near neighbor in London he continued to keep in almost daily intercourse with them. The deed was delayed for many additional months, and it was not until February 16, 1790, that the Paradises were able to affix their signatures to it—an occasion for the greatest rejoicing.[61] Relieved though they were from the fear of immediate ruin, they were far from being relieved of the debts themselves, which hung like a cloud over the heads of them both, and after Paradise's death over that of his wife. The restriction of their income by the terms of the deed made it necessary for them to appeal again and again to Dr. Bancroft, who continued to be loyal and kind. He assisted them not only by advice and competent management of their business affairs but also by further loans of money—secured, however, by the English bonds which had been given to Paradise by his father. Bancroft seems to have been actuated by no ulterior motive. Perhaps he felt that by his kindness to this pair of enthusiastic Americans, he was in some degree expiating his crimes against the country itself.

CHAPTER XVI

John Paradise — Lost

ON the Saturday afternoon of June 12, 1790, James Boswell sat alone in the study of his house in Queen Anne Street, dull, listless, lost—the most unhappy human being whose innermost thoughts and feelings have ever been revealed.[1] The rudderless year spent in London since the death of his wife had brought him to a full realization of his misery, the depth of which his private journal sets forth in such inordinate abundance of detail. Unable to read, unable to think any thoughts except those of torturing self-analysis, he rose and left the house. He was in no condition to join Malone for a "revise" of his life of Johnson, so he spent a desultory hour with Sir Joshua Reynolds and then rapped languidly and without anticipation at the residence of the President of the Royal Society. Here he knew he would find company that in a happier mood would have supplied the nourishment that his social nature craved—a company of philosophers, scientists, and above all men of literature; for Saturday was the regular afternoon for Sir Joseph Banks's teas, or "conversations," a general occasion at which any reputable man of intellect was made to feel welcome. The company did not disappoint Boswell; literary men were present in abundance, but as he had dreaded, their conversation failed to rouse him to animation. He was too low today. From the eyes of one man, however, there shone a sympathetic gleam. This was John Paradise. Instinctively

apprehending in his glance the kindness of a fellow
feeling, Boswell approached him and the two men
entered into conversation. They had not met for some
years, but they were old acquaintances with a common
bond in their friendship for Dr. Johnson. Boswell
recalled the comfort and pleasure that had been afforded the old lexicographer in his last years by the generosity of the man who stood before him. He remembered too the losses which Paradise had suffered since that
time—loss of fortune, the loss of his younger daughter,
and above all the loss of health. It was at their last
meeting late in June of 1786 that Boswell himself had
discovered that Paradise was a fellow sufferer.

"One of the days of last week," he records in his
Journal, "when very dejected, I visited Mr. Paradise,
with whom I talked freely; and I found that though
then pretty well, he suffered severely from Hypochondria, and used to take to his bed. We consoled one
another. . ."[2] Here, amidst the chatter of Sir Joseph's
"Conversation" party, they consoled one another again.
A far better listener than he was a talker, Paradise
allowed Boswell to have most of the talk and Boswell,
assured of the attention of a man naturally sympathetic
and made the more so by having himself endured the
mental agonies of the disease, launched into an account
of his symptoms with lingering attention to detail.

He had been a victim of hypochondria from his
youth, he reminded Paradise, and lately the attacks had
increased in sharpness and in frequency, especially in
the last year. Perhaps Mr. Paradise recalled his essays
in *The London Magazine* under the general heading of
"The Hypochondriack," in which he had several times
described the symptoms of the malady. But what of

the remedy, what treatment had Dr. Warren prescribed, Boswell inquired, for it appeared that he and
Paradise employed the same physician. Without waiting for an answer he plunged into an account of his own
experience with the fashionable doctor. "Dr. Warren,"
he confided, "some months ago told me that a change
of spirits would come, and cautioned me against
imagining that I never could be well again. But alas!
as I then told him, that very thought is the worst part
of the disease. I could not conceive at present how
mankind in any situation could for a moment be de-
luded into a feeling of happiness, or even of quiet."
Lately, Boswell continued, he had learned that Sir
Joshua Reynolds and Lord Eliot and a number of
other acquaintances were also sufferers from hypochondria. Lord Eliot said that his attacks chiefly took
the form of sleeplessness, and that he had found opium
to be an excellent remedy. It could easily be left off
after the necessity for its use had passed. But Dr.
Warren had in the most insistent manner prescribed an
abundance of wine. Wine, the doctor had asserted, was
less harmful than beneficial in its effects. Less wine of
course must be consumed after the attack had passed,
but it must be drunk in sufficient quantity to keep the
spirits elevated. What did Mr. Paradise think? Had
he tried Warren's prescription, and was it efficacious?
There was no hesitation in the reply. It was expressed
simply, but firmly and impressively. Yes, Paradise
agreed, he had tried that prescription; he had for a
time drunk wine to great excess. However, it had made
him worse and he had abandoned it. He was now much
better, he concluded, and counseled his friend "not to
seek relief from excess of wine, as he had done." He

Μήπερ ἀπολείπῃς, ὦ φίλτατε· νῦν γὰρ
μαλίστα τῆς σῆς ἐπικυρίας χρείαν ἔχω.
ἐπεί ἡ μέθη τὰς ἐμὰς φρένας παντελῶς
κατέστρεψε, καὶ ἀληθῶς ὀλοφυρτέος
τυγχάνω. ἐλθὲ τοίνυν πρὸς ἐμέ ὡς
τάχιστα· φοβοῦμαι γάρ, ναὶ νὴ Δία, λίαν
λίαν φοβοῦμαι ὑπὲρ τῆς τῶν φρενῶμεν
καταστάσεως.

The affair concerning the trust is
settled — I only wish to see you for
my health — For the love of
heaven do not forsake me;
for I really am in a most deplorable
situation — If you are tired of

me and abandon me, I am a lost
man. I am
Yr most gratefully
John Parad[ise]

LETTER FROM JOHN PARADISE TO DR. WARREN.
Physician to Dr. Johnson, Boswell and Paradise.
Courtesy of the late Mr. Burton Paradise of Yale University.

had, he said, "found a moderate use of it much more efficacious."[3] The speaker's manner was earnest and the simple directness of his statement was impressive. No doubt Boswell's question recalled sharply those desperate months before the deed was signed, during which he was obeying his physician's orders most unwisely well. The letter which he then wrote to Dr. Warren, half in Greek and half in English, bespeaks a mind almost upon the verge of ruin: "Do not leave me, dearest friend, for now especially I have need of your help, since wine has upset my mind completely and truly I am in a lamentable state. Therefore come to me as quickly as possible for I am afraid, yes by Zeus I am very much afraid about the state of my mind. The affair concerning the trust is settled—I only wish to see you for my health—For the love of heaven do not forsake me; for I really am in a most deplorable situation—If you are tired of me and abandon me, I am a lost man."[4]

On many occasions during the next few years on which the fellow-sufferers met to compare notes. Dr. Johnson's case among others was discussed between them. "He once told me," confided Paradise, "that he was sometimes so languid and inefficient, that he could not distinguish the hour upon the town-clock."[5] Boswell had mentally noted this down for inclusion in his "Life," where he intended to give full emphasis to the symptoms of his eminent friend's disease.

"Hypochondria," Boswell had written, "brings on such an extreme degree of languor, that the patient has a reluctance to every species of exertion. The uneasiness occasioned by this state, is owing to a vivacity of imagination, presenting, at the same time, ideas of activity; so that a comparison is made between what is, and what should be. . . To be therefore overpowered with languor, must make a man very unhappy; he is tantalized with a thousand ineffectual wishes which he cannot realize. For as Tantalus is fabled to have been tormented by the objects of his desire being ever in his near view, yet ever receding from his touch as he endeavoured to approach them, the languid Hypochondriac has the sad mortification of being disappointed of realizing any wish, by the wretched defect of his own activity. While in that situation, time passes over him, only to be loaded with regrets. The important duties of life, the benevolent offices of friendship are neglected, though he is sensible that he shall upbraid himself for that neglect till he is glad to take shelter under the cover of disease. I indeed know an instance of a man of excellent understanding, fine taste, and nobleness of heart, who though admired in social intercourse, and distinguished in the highest publick appearances, is subject occasionally to fits of languor; but he has a singular felicity of acquiescence in that state while it lasts, and although his friends are uneasy, he himself suffers no pain. He has, to be sure, an uncommon sweetness of disposition; and his rank and fortune place him above all dependance, while his friends depend upon him. . ."[6] It was ideas such as these, communicated in their conversations, that made Paradise exclaim on one occasion that Boswell had described the disease perfectly.[7]

Among the many treatments suggested—wine, opium, physical exercise, country life, etc.—there was one which worked so remarkable a cure that the fame of it was echoed across the Atlantic in faraway Virginia.

A London correspondent wrote to the *Virginia Gazette* in Williamsburg: "We hear that a Gentleman of sedentary life, who has been long indisposed with indigestion and the hypochondriack passion, tried riding and several other sorts of exercises, but with little effect, was at last prevailed upon, by the advice of an eminent physician, to try being tossed in a blanket, which was accordingly performed every other morning for a fortnight, and has been attended with the greatest success, the Gentleman being now much better than he has been for two years past."

The friendship which was now renewed between Boswell and Paradise had commenced fifteen years before in Edinburgh. In the late summer of 1775, Mr. and Mrs. Paradise having decided to "go a jaunt" into Scotland, they were supplied with letters of introduction to Boswell by Bennett Langton and Sir John Pringle, then President of the Royal Society. Boswell was spending "two flat months," fitfully enlivened by flirtations with Mrs. Grant, (his wife and children having been left behind at Auchinleck), in attendance at the Court of Session in Edinburgh.[8] Although extremely bored himself with this city which was not London, he was nevertheless eager to show his visitors, (who included besides the Paradises an English clergyman named Gosset and a young Parisian, M. de Clere de Sept Chenes,) that the capital city of Scotland possessed social and cultural advantages of which he need not be ashamed. Anglophile though he was, he always maintained a certain dubious pride in Scotland and in this he resembled his fellow-countryman, Sir John Pringle. Sir John in his letter of acknowledgment after the Paradises' return, wrote: "Many thanks to you for the civilities shewn to M. de Sêptchenes, who forgot none of them more than Mr. Paradise. They both praised the *politesse* and the hospitality of those they had been recommended to. It is one circumstance in which we excel the English; but then as you observe, I believe all that parade of ours is only for a spirt, and I question much whether any foreigner that lives a twelve month with us will part with us with the same sentiments that he is disposed to do when he has only been once or twice in our company. . ."⁹

The acquaintance which was begun in Edinburgh was continued in London. The two men frequently met in the company of Johnson during Boswell's spring visits, and although Boswell found little to record in Paradise's conversation yet he liked and respected him and on one occasion defended him against the sharp tongue of Mrs. Thrale. "I never heard him say anything, but, My fader vos not a Greek, but my moder vos a Greek," she said. In recording the remark in his commonplace-book, Boswell says, "Young Burke and I thought her too severe. But, said Burke, 'it seems she does not find the Tree of Knowledge in Paradise.'"¹⁰

Boswell's friendship with Arthur Lee, who had been his fellow student at Edinburgh, and his slight acquaintance with Alderman William Lee were still other points of contact with the Paradises. Another had been Boswell's sympathetic attitude toward the American colonies. It was of special significance to Paradise that a confirmed Tory like Boswell should be able to see the merits of a cause in which he himself was so much interested. From the beginning Boswell had made no secret of his feelings. "I am growing more and more an American," he said to Temple in one of

several-letters on the subject of 1775. "I see the un-
reasonableness of taxing them without the consent of
their Assemblies. I think our Ministry are mad in
undertaking this desperate war."[11] Nor was his opinion
changed by subsequent events. ". . . amidst all the
sanguinary zeal of my countrymen," he wrote to
Edmund Burke in 1778, "I have professed myself a
friend to our fellow-subjects in America, so far as they
claim an exemption from being taxed by the representatives of the king's British subjects."[12] Such an attitude
as this was all the more appealing to Paradise because
it was, like his own, maintained in the heavily-charged
atmosphere of Dr. Johnson's violent prejudice.

After Dr. Johnson's death the man in whose company
Boswell and Paradise met most frequently was Bennet
Langton. Here scholarship was the common bond.
Boswell fancied himself as a man of learning and he
loved to develop his powers and exhibit his erudition
in the company of the two famous scholars. During his
long visit to London in 1785 Boswell spent many after-
noons and evenings in their joint society, with such men
as Taylor, the Greek teacher, or Shaw, "the Erse man,"
as a fourth or fifth.[13] The Essex Head Club had provided, and now after the renewal of their friendship
continued to provide, a meeting-place. Boswell, in the
lonesome latter years of his life, scarcely ever failed to
attend a meeting of the "demi-wits," as he called them,
where he enjoyed the society of Daines Barrington,
Dr. Brocklesby, Sastres, (the Italian master), Paradise,
and other old friends. Like Johnson he had cause to
thank them for many a cheerful Wednesday evening
that would otherwise have been empty and dull.

Paradise's life after his return from Paris, as Boswell

had an opportunity to judge it, was but a poor reflection of what it was before he had gone to America. His sufferings had left their mark upon him, and although he for a time enjoyed comparatively good health, and, as Mrs. Paradise insisted on telling everyone, had been perfectly sober ever since his return, he had lost his zest for the very things that had formerly been his greatest pleasure. His domestic life had been unhappy for many years; now, as even the slightest acquaintance might observe, all semblance of accord between him and his wife was given up. They lived together not because they wanted to but because their limited income forced them to, and Mrs. Paradise in her voluble way made it clear to Boswell and all who knew her that her husband was no longer the object of her affections. As for Paradise, his love, or infatuation, had out-lasted hers by many years, but now in the face of her continued disapproval it altogether ceased. His attitude toward her became one of forced reconciliation, calm where hers was violent. Even her fits of outrageous temper, which were growing ever more violent, ceased to disturb him—at least outwardly. He no longer feared the censure of the world, for the world had been too long aware of his wife's tantrums to give them much attention. He either remained silent, or if convenient left the house, and whenever possible paid protracted visits to friends who lived outside of London. Paradise's taste for literary and scholarly society was even more developed than Boswell's and through the Royal Society, the Essex Head Club, as well as through old friends like Langton, William Windham, Dr. Joddrell and half a dozen others he could indulge himself in it. But Boswell did not have to be told in their mutually consolatory conversations that the life of John Paradise had fallen into the sere and yellow leaf and that even hosts of friends were powerless to make it green again. A heavy weight of hours and adverse circumstance had bowed his fragile will. Life was now only so many years to be lived, years which held no prospect of happiness and but little alleviation from pain of heart and mind.

With Mrs. Paradise it was of course entirely different, for she lived her life from without rather than within and happiness for her was chiefly a matter of having enough money. The year's suspense in the settling of their affairs had made her desperately unhappy while it lasted—an unhappiness which she had been at little pains to conceal from the world. But once the deed had been signed and there was a fair prospect of the debt's being paid off in a few years, the winter of her discontent was past, her spirits rose, and her pent-up energies burst forth in a perfect exuberance of letter-writing to the man whom she found it impossible to forget—Thomas Jefferson. Between the first and the twenty-fourth of March she favored him with no less than five letters—three of them extremely long ones— none of which he "did himself the honor" to acknowledge.[14] She had already written to him in February to commiserate with him over the "horrid accident" of his cabin being burnt while his ship was anchored in Hampton Roads, to inform him a second time that the money which they owed him had been paid, and that

Mr. Paradise had been entirely sober since his return to England.[15] The main revelation of the letter, however, was a vain delusion which she cherished of persuading Mr. Jefferson to do something handsome for Mr. Paradise in the way of a foreign appointment. In this, she had convinced herself on the slenderest of evidence, she would have the powerful backing of President Washington. Since their visit to Mount Vernon she had become a correspondent of Martha Washington, whom she looked on as a friend. The circumstance that had inspired her fantastic request to Jefferson had been an interchange of letters between her and the General himself. On hearing of his election to the Presidency she had written him a letter:

London
May 12, 1789

Sir,

Give me leave as a Fellow Citizen to congratulate you on the Honour you have done us, in accepting to be our President for this, our New Federal Constitution—Long may your Excellency be Blessed with every happiness that this World can give, and that you may live, to see our Country flourish from your Wise and Good Councils, Is the Sincere Prayer of—

Sir
Your Excellencies
Most Obedient and Most
Grateful Humble Servant

Lucy Paradise[16]

The months of delay in receiving an answer were forgotten when the answer finally came. It was as dignified and non-committal as only Washington could be:

New York
November 23, 1789
Madam,

Your letter of the 12th of May has reached my hands
and I beg you to accept my sincere thanks for the con-
gratulation which you offer upon my election to the
office of President of the United States—and your good
wishes for my personal happiness.—

I have the honour to be,
Madam
Your most Obed[t] Serv[t]

George Washington[17]

There was surely nothing in the austere phrases of
this note to give encouragement to a person of normal
feelings. She was now elevated far above reason, and
allowed the fact of her having received any letter at
all from the man whom all the world revered to blind
her to its containing not one comma which could be
interpreted as personal. Thus she was inspired to write
to Jefferson the results of her wishful thinking—
oblivious of the fact that she had for a year bombarded
her husband with abuse, that he was still in the toils of
debt, and that Jefferson knew as well as she that he was
entirely incapable of conducting his own affairs, much
less those of the United States: "Should you think M[r]
Paradise worthy of your attention and our President,
General Washington also, I should esteem it a favour
when Ministers are appointed to remember him. I now
will take upon myself to Answer for his doing every
thing in his power to discharge such a trust properly.
England is the Country I wish, but, I am not to chuse.
I flatter myself our Country would Not be loosers by
such an appointment—I have just received a Letter
from Our Presedent. . ."[18] This request was repeated in

stronger terms in three subsequent letters each of which was almost a word for word repetition of the first. Although every one of them actually reached their destination, Mrs. Paradise was in an agony of fear that they should go astray and this in part accounts for her having written so often:

Dear Sir,

I did myself the honour of writing to your Excellency last Month by the New York Capt Domenick and sent it to the Care of Mr John Beckley. The purport of my first Letter was to Congratulate you and the Dear Miss Jefferson's on their Safe Arrival to their Native Land. I beg your Excellency to accept my grateful thanks for the many, and great acts of friendship and humanity you were pleased to shew to Mr Paradise, and myself during our Stay at Paris. I wish, I had it in my power to prove to you by my Actions the Sentiments of my Heart, but my distressed Situation is such at present, as not to inable me to prove to your Excellency the Sense, I have of your past favours by any Mark whatever, except but by my Letters.

On my arrival in this Country last Year, I thought it my Duty to write to Congratulate General Washington on his being Chosen our President, and he, in return, very politely has Answered it. I beg you will have the goodness to present Mr Paradises and my most respectful Comp^{ts} to the President his Lady and family, and tell them We ever remember with gratitude their attentions to us during our Short Stay with them at Mount Vernon. I would have sent you in this Letter a Copy of the the Ministers Portugal sends to the different Courts in Europe, which our good friend Chev^r de Freire, the Chergé des affaires of Portugal was so good as to give to Mr Paradise to Send to you, but the postage was the reason, as every Single Letter is a Shilling but, I shall send the first Copy by a Ship going directly to

New York, and the Second to Virginia to the Care of either Col° N Burwell or our Steward.

Chev' de Freire presents his respectful Compliments to you. This Gen' has the highest respect for you. He is a most Excellent, good, upright Man, and he would be happy to receive a Letter from you, and it is my wish you would write to him about M' P. I have the pleasure to acquaint your Excellency that M' Paradise is perfectly Sober, and has been so, ever since his return to this Country, as Chev' de Freire, and D' Bancroft can say is true, as they are the most intimate friends we have in this Country, and who, are almost, every day with Us. The Royal Society have chosen M' P as one of their Council.

Our friends wish, that he may be employed by our Country in Europe and they have desired him, to write. But he s[aid] the Subject was of such a delicate Nature he could not, and he said, that if his friends in America, thought him worthy they would employ him without any solicitations [from] him. He desired me to assure your Excellency [he] would do himself the Honour to Write to you very soon.

In my last Letter, I acquainted you that the Money you had the goodness to advance to M' Paradise at Paris, your Agent here had recv'd an order on our Merch' M' Anderson to pay it with Interest from the Twenty Eight Hog' of Tobacco Sent by our Steward last Autom; as also D' Bancroft who had advanced me Money for my Subsistance the time M' [P] was in Paris to pay him, and with Interest:—When We have Honestly and thankfully paid these two Debts, I wish, crave, you My Dear Sir to judge, the little very little we shall have left to live upon until our Steward shall think proper to make us a good remittance. Could your Excellency and our truly good President employ M' Paradise here so as to get a Salary to assist us until all the Debts are paid, it would make me the happiest of Women. And if in Heaven it is possible to see what

Mortals do on Earth, My Dear Father Col° Ludwell would certainly be rejoiced to See, that his only surviving Child was protected by that Country to which he him-self and His Ancestors had rendered great Services. Had I been a Man, I would have done the Same, but *I am a poor helpless Woman.* My present Melancholy Situation has obliged me to make this request and I hope it will not be without effect, as, I am anxious to see every person paid as soon as possible.

On Tuesday Febr^y ye 16th 1790 and not before Mr Paradise and Myself signed the Deed. The Creditors tell me they are obliged to me, for my having bound myself to pay their Debts in Case of the Death of M^r P; that Gent, is now, in a better State of health, then when we were first Married. I have followed your advice in every thing since my return to this Country, and, I shall ever continue to do so, to the end of my Life, provided, you will have the goodness to give it me Unasked from time, to time.

I shall be ever grateful to you Sir, if you will take the trouble to write as soon as it is Convenient to you, to Col° Nat^h Burwell and desire he will get the Debts of Lord Dunmore clearly made out, what the Debt was for, and also, Strongly attested, that the people here shall not have a word to say, to the justness of the Sum and If I pay the English their Debts, the English ought to pay mine. I have another favour to ask of you, which is to have the kindness to tell me who are to pay me for the Negroes the English took from my Estate in the time of the War. It would be doing me a great favour to let me know what I am to expect from the Loan office, as in the Year 1784 our Steward wrote to us he had long before that Year put into the Loan Office £26309. 8 paper Curr^y of Virginia. I am induced to make the above requests, as you were so good as to write to me from Paris, that you would do all in your power to give me a clear insight into all my affairs on your Arrival in America.

I put my Whole trust in you, and our Great Friend, [to] every thing I have desired, and may God bless you for this great act of humanity.

I wish greatly to have all my Estates devided into farms and be let at [illegible] dollars an hundred acres Virginia Money, and a proper person at a Salary of £100 Virginia Curr^y a year for to get the rents in, which Rents, to be paid every Three Months. My houses in Willi^{ms}burg want great attention to be paid them.

I shall never trouble your Excellency with such a long Letter again, but a thing once well done, is twice done. The Estates to be devided into farms of 500 acres and let for Five or Seven years, this is the way they do in England; and the other the reason is, that we should be able to know exactly what our income would be for Certain a Year, I have a fine Estate and was it properly Managed, We should have a very handsome fortune to live upon, I am certain if your Excellency will have the humanity to take upon you this. I have desired, that through you, and Col^o Nath Burwell, I shall have my Estates of all kinds in Virginia put into the regular order my heart wishes. I am fearful of having given your Excellency a great deal of trouble therefore enough for the present.

On the Tuesday the 2^d of March is a General Call of the House of Lords, and Commons, concerning the Test Act, it is thought it will be carried through the House of Commons, but will be thrown out in the House of Lords. The Presbyterians are all anxious to see what will be the end of this business.—

Mr St Andreé presents his respectful Compt^s to you. Mrs Cosway has desired her best Comp^{ts} also. This Lady is with child for the first-time. She has been extremely Ill, but is now perfectly recovered and expects in a few Months to Lyin.—

The Weather is, and has been all the Winter extremely Mild. All your Friends, (for you have not an enemy, I am certain in the World) grieve for your absence, and none more So then Mr Paradise and myself who Love you with Sincerity. We join in affec^t Love to our dear friends the Miss Jefferson's. Adieu My Dear Sir and believe me to be with Great Gratitude

	Your Most Humble
London	Servant, and Sincere
March	*Friend Lucy Paradise.*[19]
the 2^d 1790	
His Excellency Thomas	
Jefferson Esqr	

In the three letters that follow this one—on the 5th, the 20th, and the 24th of March—the frantic state of Mrs. Paradise's mind is revealed. She refers to letters which apparently she never wrote, to lists which in one letter she says she has not sent and in the next asserts she has. The elaborate instructions she gives Jefferson about the care of her estate are so conflicting with one another that he could not possibly have carried them out. In short it must have become clear to Jefferson that the lady was, for the time being at least, as good as mad. Her demands that her husband be appointed United States Minister to England or to some court in Europe continued, as did also her attempts to show Freire in a favorable light. At length in June Jefferson capitulated to the bombardment in a letter that was as kind as it was wise. It was clear that he could not continue to act as Secretary of State and also as the correspondent and agent of Mrs. Paradise and this he conveyed to her with his usual tact, but also with firmness.

New York June 23. 1790.

Dear Madam

I have to acknolege from you a long list of letters, towit, Octob. 7. Feb. 2. Mar. 2. 20. 24. and Apr. 5. [a mistake for March 5.] my apology must be a great throng of my own business during the two months I was at Monticello, and a long illness since my arrival here as well as a great throng of public business, which bids fair indeed, in my present situation, to suppress my private correspondencies. I made it my duty however to write you very fully from Monticello the 6th of January, with a comprehensive view of your affairs in Virginia. yet I perceive by your letters you have not received mine of that date. it was inclosed in one to Dr Bancroft. that was put un[der] cover to mr Anderson, & the whole under cover to mr Wilkins with a request to send it by some sure conveyance. I am mortified at it's miscarriage as it may have excited suspicions of inattention, of which, in a matter of business, I am incapable. I now send a copy of that letter, & will send a third by another conveiance. I hope it will satisfy you of my zeal to serve mr Paradise & yourself in any way in my power. in the way you point out in some of your late letters, it is not in my power. we shall have very few missions to Europe: and the public opinion requires that they should be filled by veterans in the public service who having long been proved on the theatre of business here, have acquired the confidence & affection of their country in general. nobody would have merited this more than the person you point out. the opportunity alone has been wanting. my return to Europe is very unexpectedly prevented, by an appointment which has no charms for me, more than that had; but in which it is said my agency may be more useful. it will close the chapter of my political history, and will not be a long one. I have no wish but for retirement to my own home and own family. present me most affectionately to mr Paradise and assure him of

my constant wishes to be useful to him, tho' my present
occupations will hardly permit me to repeat either to
him or you the assurances of it. my daughters were
well when I last heard from them. the elder one [is]
married to young mr Randolph of Tuckahoe, perfectly
to my mind. both of them recollect you with affection,
and ask a place in yours as the only return they could
ever wish or think of. I am with great esteem Dear
Madam

Your most obedient humble serv^t

Mrs Paradise   Th: Jefferson[20]

The above letter did not reach Mrs. Paradise until
the end of August. Meanwhile she kept on writing.
The most important news which she communicated in
the summer was that the Chevalier of Freire had been
appointed Minister Resident to the United States, just
as she had so much desired.[21] He had first been appointed to a European court, but Her Most Faithful
Majesty the Queen of Portugal, out of consideration
for his being well known to both Adams and Jefferson,
had, on the advice of de Pinto, altered this arrangement
in favor of America. Mrs. Paradise was jubilant, and
evidently considered that her insistence to Jefferson had
had its weight, as indeed it may have had. The appointment of Freire aroused considerable interest in
America, as it marked the first official recognition by
Portugal of the new republic, and it was with much
pride that Mrs. Paradise announced the news of it to
Jefferson, many months before it was communicated
through the regular channels.

It was in a letter from Mrs. Paradise that Mrs. John
Adams also was first informed of the event. To one
who had been a rival, if friendly, hostess in London,

she triumphantly proclaimed the success of her protegé and former dancing-partner. But Mrs. Paradise's confidences did not end there. Mrs. Adams was now the wife of the vice-President and as such might have considerable influence in the appointment she so ardently desired her husband to have as Minister to England, and so with disarming naïveté she informed her that Mr. Paradise had now entirely deserted the bottle. Moreover, remembering that Mrs. Adams had been on the scene at the time of her daughter's elopement and hasty marriage, she further informed her that the Countess Barziza had another son, was vastly happy, and was much beloved by her husband. Mrs. Adams, who was not aware of artful design in this elaborate frankness, merely dismissed the letter in a remark to her daughter: "It was all in the true style of Mrs. P——."[22]

The Chevalier Freire and his wife certainly owed the cordiality of their reception in America in great part to the Paradises. Mrs. Paradise enlisted the services of the ever-courteous Jefferson in obtaining a house for them and in advising them about business and other details. She also recommended them to the particular consideration of Mrs. Washington. They were soon received into the inner circle of the American capital's society and the Chevalier promptly lost his regret at having to leave England. Madame Freire, "brilliant with diamonds," was accounted "a truly elegant woman" by Mrs. William Cushing, wife of the Supreme Court Judge, with whom she often graced the dinner parties of "Lady" Washington.[23]

Mrs. Paradise's elevation of spirits over Freire's appointment was completely lost when she finally received the polite words from Jefferson which showed that he had not the slightest intention of appointing Mr. Paradise, much as he liked him, to a responsible office in the foreign service. The answer which she now wrote, besides containing more than a suggestion of madness, shows her in the worst possible light. For months now, the burden of her letters to Jefferson had been the sobriety, good health, and general fitness of her husband for the post which she, and not he, had requested Jefferson to give him. She flatteringly attributed the change in him to Jefferson's influence and declared over and over again that she was entirely assured it would continue. As soon, however, as she discovered that Jefferson would certainly never appoint him, she reverted to the same sort of abuse of him as she had indulged in before. Jefferson, with his affection for Paradise and his appreciation of all that was fine in him, could but have been disgusted when he received the letter in which she fully revealed her selfishness and treachery. It was fifteen years before he wrote to her again.

Dear Sir

I have been honoured by your very polite and friendly Letter of, June the 23^d on August the 31st 1790. It brings me an Account of my Estates &c. in Virginia. I have received your first, and Answered it. In that Letter, I trouble you with my Grateful thanks—I now repeat the Same, and wish sincerely I had it in my power by some Means to convince your Excellency of the Sincerity of my heart—I beg you will not take up your precious time in writing a third Letter on that Subject.

I am perfectly sensible of the Zeal you have to Serve Mr Paradise and Myself, but be assured My dear Sir,

I have not the least wish to make my appearance on the Great and fatiguen theatre of the World. My Wish is to live honestly, quiet, retired, without Shew, and with all the Comforts of Life. The Person who wishes for a Publick Station ought first to know how to make a tender affectionate Husband, Father, and Friend, and if such a person only knows the Name without the meaning, they little know their duty in a publick Life Many who think themselves calculated for a Minister were they to be put into such a Station, instead of being respected might bring upon themselves the Laughter of the whole World, which would be no pleasing Sight for their near Relations. Mr Paradise has been out of London Six Week on a visit to One of his Learned Friends. He writes to me, and says he is in perfect health. At his return to London I will shew him your Excellencies kind Letter. I have found London too dear a Place to live in; therefore, I have proposed to Mr Paradise and Dr Bancroft, for Us to go and Lodge and Board at Bath for a little time, as I find it is the most certain Method to live within our Income. Dr Bancroft is always the same tender, sincere friend. Indeed, *I* owe him very Great Gratitude and shall, if, I live, take one of his Daughters to live with me. This I cannot do until all the Debts are paid. I have one favour to beg of your Excellency which is to have the goodness to be my Friend and protector and to write to *Me* Once a Year at least. For when some persons See *I am* protected by my Friends in America they will be affraid (altho they will not say it) to use me unhandsomely for fear I should write.

I earnestly beg of your Excellency to preserve your health as it is of the greatest importance to our Country and to me more then any American.

I am happy to hear My Dear Mrs Randolph has married to your entire satisfaction. I hope Miss Jefferson will follow her example and that you will be blessed in the Winter of Life. Be pleased to present my affec^t Love to Mrs Randolph and Miss Jefferson. I am with the greatest esteem

Dear Sir

Your Excellencies
Most Grateful Humb^{le}
Servant

London   Lucy Paradise[24]
Sep^t ye 26th 1790

Be pleased to send your Letters to Mr Anderson.

P. S.

I have hear that our good and great President is very ill. God preserve his Life, but should any accident happen to him I will Mourn as deep as for My Father, which is Six Months in Bombasin. Three Months in Black Silk and love Ribbons and the other Three in Black Silk and white Ribbons. Bishop Maddison brings this Letter—

His Excellency Thomas Jefferson Esqr

It is easy to see, from Mrs. Paradise's own words to Jefferson, that the idea of Paradise's being appointed an American minister in Europe was one that was hatched and kept alive by her alone and that Paradise himself had refused to have anything to do with it. Even if he had not been one of the most modest of men, he possessed enough common sense to realize that such a proposal could never come to fruition. In April, 1790, at the very time when she was most violently agitating the question, he wrote a letter to Washington and one to Jefferson, both of which indicate how reluctant he would have been to force himself upon their attention. The immediate purpose of these letters was to introduce his young Italian friend, Count Andriani, a man of republican views and great personal attractiveness. Paradise's undated letter to Washington reached its destination in June, 1790:

[London]

Sir,

I avail myself of the opportunity afforded me by my friend Count Andriani, of conveying to you an Ode which Count Alfieri, the author of it, desired me long ago to convey to you. The rambling, and of course unsettled condition, I have been in since my return to Europe, has entirely put it out of my power to comply sooner with Count Alfieri's request; and this unpleasant condition, added to an apprehension of being troublesome, has likewise deprived me of the satisfaction of joining my most sincere congratulations with those of my fellow-citizens, on the auspicious event which has placed you, the object of our veneration, love, confidence, and gratitude, at the helm of our Government. That you may long, Sir, live to make our country prosper, is, I can assure you, the most ardent wish, not only of us Americans, but of all those Europeans also, who, sensible of the value of liberty, know how much indebted they are to the example, which the glorious cause you have so nobly defended, has given to the world, for the rapid and successful strides that are now making in a considerable part of Europe, towards the attainment of that invaluable blessing.

There is not a more popular man in France, than our gallant Marquis, your pupil; nor indeed can popularity be more justly merited. His actions are directed by the purest views, and his glory consists in doing good to mankind. May his labors, therefore, be crowned with success! Count Andriani is a nobleman from Milan, highly distinguished by every valuable endowment, and deserving of the honor of being presented to you. As he is thoroughly acquainted with the affairs of

Europe, I have nothing further to say at present, than to offer my most respectful compliments to Mrs. Washington, and subscribe myself with the greatest respect, Sir, your most obliged, and

Most obedient, humble servant,

John Paradise.[25]

The letter to Jefferson was evidently written on or about the same date;

London April 2[d] 1790.

Dear Sir,

With pleasure I embrace the opportunity that my friend Count Andriani offers me of congratulating your excellency on your safe return to your native country. The unparalleled favours you have, ever since I have had the happiness of knowing you, so kindly conferred upon me and my family will to the very last moment of my life, be remembered by me with the deepest sense of gratitude; and you may rest assured, my dearest Sir, that I shall always be ready cheerfully to use the utmost exertion of my best services on every occasion wherein you may think it proper to command me. Many and very important events have happened in Europe since you left it; but as Count Andriani is thoroughly acquainted with them, I will refer you to him, who will, without any prejudice, fully satisfy you upon every particular, and whom I take the liberty to recommend to your excellency in the strongest terms, confident that you will find him in every respect worthy of those civilities which I know it is your delight to shew to men of merit. Nor will I trouble you at present with my own affairs, as by the next packet I shall be able to give you a more accurate account of them. Most sincerely, therefore, wishing you, and those true models of virtue and filial piety, your two amiable daughters,

every felicity which this world can afford I remain
with the greatest respect,

My dearest Sir,
Your most faithful friend, and most obliged humble
servant,

John Paradise.[26]

One more service was to be performed for Paradise,
before he died, by the indefatiguable Jefferson. It was
after more than a year of silence that he addressed his
final letter to his friend:

Philadelphia
August 26, 1791

Dear Sir,—Tho' the incessant drudgery of my office
puts it out of my power to write letters of mere correspondence, yet I do not permit them to suspend the offices
of friendship, where these may effect the interests of
my friends. You have in the funds of Virginia in loan
office certificates reduced to specie value £905.17-6½
and in final settlement £62-8. These are of the description allowed by the general government to be transferred to their funds, if subscribed to them before the
last day of next month. If so transferred, four ninths of
them would now sell for about 22/6 the pound, or
would bear an interest of 6. per cent paid regularly:
two ninths would bear an interest of 3. per cent paid
regularly, & sell for 12/6 the pound. I wrote Mr.
Burwell to know if any orders were given him on this
subject, & he answers me in the negative. Supposing
this has proceeded from your being unable at such a
distance to judge the expediency of transferring the
debt from the state to the general government, I have
taken the liberty this day to advise him to do it, because
if not done before the last day of next month it can
never be done afterwards. Observe that since Congress
has said it would assume all these debts, where the
parties should chuse it, the states have repealed their

provision for paiment, & the moment the time is out for transferring them, their value will sink to nothing almost. Tho' I advise Mr. Burwell to transfer them to the United States, so as to secure them, yet I advise him also to let them lie there, & not to sell them till orders come [from] England because I do not foresee any loss from waiting a while for orders. I would certainly advise orders to be given to him to sell the 6. per cents, when he finds a favorable occasion; I believe they may rise to 24/ the pound, which will be making them nearly as much sterling as they are currency. This might enable a remittance immediately to your creditors of about 500l. It might be well to authorize him also to do as to the 3. per cents, & the deferred part, what occurrences shall render expedient. It is impossible to foresee what will happen, & therefore power had better be given where there may be a full reliance in the discretion of the person.

Be so good as to present my respects to Mrs. Paradise, to convey to her my acknoledgment of the receipt of her favor of Mar. 1, & to pray her to consider this as intended for her as well as yourself. I am with the greatest esteem of her & yourself Dear Sir your friend & serv[t]

Th: Jefferson[27]

The five years of life that remained to Paradise after his return to London were spent in attempting to renew, as well as comparative poverty and ill health would allow, his rôle as a scholarly gentleman of leisure. Although his own low spirits and the exasperation of having to live with a half-mad wife robbed him of much of the pleasure of such an existence, he was still possessed of a group of friends whose loyalty is a tribute to his own personal charm and worth. The friendship between him and Boswell grew apace and by the beginning of 1791 developed into an intimacy which included their two households. Mrs. Paradise in her impulsive way had taken a fancy to Boswell's two elder daughters, Veronica and Euphemia. Veronica was just at the coming-out age, not very much younger than Philippa Paradise would have been if she had lived, and Mrs. Paradise found some consolation in doing for her what she might have done for her own daughter. Boswell was happy enough to have assistance; he owned that he was but a sorry parent, and toward Euphemia in particular he was impatient and lacking in understanding. He fell more and more into the habit of dining, or supping, or having tea at the Paradise's house, sometimes in company with his daughters, sometimes alone.[28] When Langton was in town, the three friends would occasionally talk a night away much as in the old days. One December evening in 1793, Boswell, as was now so often the case, found himself dining too well at the house of a friend. "Was too forward in drinking," he observes in his Journal, "which I fear was observed. Was somewhat intoxicated." The fact that there were clergymen present caused him to be more prudent than was his wont and he left the company as soon as he could. His refuge for the evening was the house of Paradise: "Found Mr. and Mrs. Paradise by themselves; eat a bit of cold veal and drank some Mountain."[29] And so to bed.

Another friendship which Paradise renewed in these latter days was that with William Windham. Windham was a restless soul who spent as much time out of England as in it; even in London he was something of a wanderer, drifting in and out of the lives of his varied assortment of friends, but always assured of a welcome

by his wit and charm. One July evening he sauntered
out with his son Robert, fresh from Eton, and elected
to call at Paradise's. Here he found Count Zenobio,
whose wanderings about the globe rivalled his own.[30]
The pleasant evening which he spent encouraged him
to accept an invitation to return two days later when
there would be a larger company. About ten o'clock in
the evening, having dined at Lord Loughborough's, he
set out to keep his engagement. On the street he ran
into the unhappy Boswell, "absurdly wandering" as he
frequently accused himself of doing. It was easy to
persuade him to go along to Paradise's. But an entertainment at the Paradise's house in Margaret Street
was not what it had been in the former days at Charles
Street, Cavendish Square. Their rooms were crowded,
it was true—Count Woronzow, Matsante, Zenobio,
Knox and others were present; but it was obvious that
his old friend's circumstances were reduced. There
were not even enough servants to serve the guests
properly and the Hon. William Windham was obliged
to wait an unconscionable time for his refreshment,
which was merely tea, and probably he would not have
even got that had not Boswell fetched it for him.[31]

Three years later the Paradises were obliged to move
to an even more inexpensive house at 87 Great Titchfield Street. Here, on June 24, 1794, Windham was
invited to a dinner which they were giving for Mr. Jay,
the envoy newly arrived to assist the American Minister, Thomas Pinckney, in the negotiation of the famous
treaty. But the Hon. Mr. Windham "for some reason
felt no great inclination to go" and accordingly dined
at his Club.[32]

Diversion was sometimes created among the London

scholars during this time by Dr. Parr's occasional visits
to town. A few days after the beheading of Louis XVI
in 1793, Paradise and two other friends, Sir James
Macintosh and T. G. Street, accompanied Dr. Parr to
hear Bishop Horsley deliver a sermon before the
House of Peers on the martyrdom of Charles I. This
group of rabid Whigs could not have gone to hear a
sermon from such a Tory as Dr. Horsley with any other
intention than to scoff, and it was soon obvious that this
was the purpose for which they remained. The story is
told by Street: "We took our station in the aisle, and
Dr. Parr fronted the Bishop, who frequently cast a
glance at him, as he proceeded in his sermon. Dr. Parr
(we must remember that he was a clergyman himself)
became restless and indignant during its progress. It
concluded with these expressions.—'Let us pray that the
thoughts of their hearts may be forgiven them.' Dr.
Parr instantly exclaimed: 'Damnable doctrine! Master Horsley, damnable doctrine!' Many persons around
us could hear those expressions. The Doctor then turned to Mr. Paradise, and continued his angry comments
in Greek."[33] The fact that Dr. Horsley was an esteemed
personal friend of Paradise's could not have allowed
him to be very happy as a participant in such a scene.

Paradise's remarkable linguistic powers were often
called into use by his friends. Late in December, 1794,
Frederick North, a younger son of the Prime Minister
who later became Earl of Guilford, gave a "collation"
for the Turkish Secretary of the Embassy and his staff.
North had always been greatly interested in Eastern
affairs; he had traveled extensively in Greece as a
young man and had actually embraced the Orthodox
Catholic faith. Paradise, who was present, was entirely

at home in the four languages in which the guests principally conversed—Greek, Turkish, Italian, and English—and was able to be of assistance to the Englishmen present, most of whom could speak no language but their own. Lord Glenbervie, a brother-in-law of Frederick North and a tremendous swell, was one of those who depended on Paradise's assistance, and at his request Paradise accompanied him on the morrow to act as his interpreter during an hour's visit to the Turkish Ambassador.[34]

It was through his wife that Paradise had made the useful acquaintance of Frederick North, who was a man of urbane, pleasant manners, was something of a wit and very much an "original." He was filled with the enterprising energy which was so lacking in Paradise and when the two men had met in Paris they had taken an instant liking to one another, attracted no doubt by the law of opposites. Some years after their meeting it developed that the authorities in Venice required further proof of Paradise's respectability and position than was contained in Jefferson's statement, before they would consent to enroll the Countess Barziza in the Golden Book. Frederick North was appealed to. He secured a statement from his father, Lord North, who was now Governor of the Right Worshipful Levant Company, and another from the Duke of Leeds, a descendant of the founder of the Company. He accompanied Paradise to the Doctors Commons and to the Prerogative Court of Canterbury and altogether amassed an impressive pile of affidavits asserting among other things that John Paradise was "in the Rank and Situation of a Gentleman" and that "his alliance would be esteemed as honourable in this country." These documents were dispatched to Venice, and Mrs. Paradise, for her own unfathomable reasons, sent copies of them to Jefferson in America, among whose papers they were carefully preserved.[35]

The Paradises' personal and financial troubles affected them in ways as different as their natures were opposite. Paradise, always shy and reserved, shrank more than ever from general society. In the company of any but his most intimate and congenial friends he was painfully conscious of their depleted condition and of the mortification he felt in being obliged to accept pecuniary assistance. His mental anguish before long began to affect his physical health, and it became more and more apparent that he was in a weakened and dangerous condition. Lucy remained insensible to what was happening, or if she observed it, she was indifferent. Ruled now more than ever by a selfish concern for her own interests and by an increasing sense of the wrongs she suffered, she paid little attention to the man for whom she had long since ceased to profess either love or respect. If he erred in reticence and reserve, she went even further in the other direction. With her to think was to speak, and as she constantly thought about her wrongs and her woes, she incessantly complained about them. The most private affairs of her husband and herself were broadcast indifferently in whatever society she found herself at the moment she felt impelled to speak. People were at first amused and diverted by such incredible lack of reticence, but soon they became tired of it and before long Mrs. Paradise, once a commanding and attractive figure in London society, became little more than an obnoxious bore. "One of my dinners, since my going out," wrote Dr.

Burney to Madame D'Arblay in May, 1795, "was at Charlotte's, with the good Hooles. After dinner Mr. Cumberland came in, and was extremely courteous, and seemingly friendly, about you and your piece. He took me aside from Mrs. Paradise, who had fastened on me and held me tight by an account of her own and Mr. Paradise's complaints, so circumstantially narrated, that not a stop so short as a comma occurred in more than an hour, while I was civilly waiting for a full period."[36] Fanny, out of her old dislike of Mrs. Paradise, was delighted and replied that his account had captured "the very woman."[37] Such scenes as this, and far worse ones when his unhappy wife's bad temper got out of control, made Paradise more and more reluctant to appear in company with her. His own bad health, now steadily growing worse, was another cause which forced on him a seclusion which was calculated to increase his hypochondrical malady.

The year 1795 witnessed the death of three of his contemporaries, with whom he had been very closely associated. Early in the spring word reached London of the sudden and totally unexpected death in India of Sir William Jones on the very eve of his departure for England. Jones had expected to retire and to carry on in England the linguistic researches for which he had been gathering material while in India. Although he and Paradise had long since quarreled, they had each of them been for many years the most intimate friend that the other possessed. The news must have been shocking and discouraging. In May, Boswell sickened and died in his house around the corner in Queen Anne Street. The attack which carried him off was also a sudden one and his death was a shock to all his friends

—to none more than Paradise, whose companion in misery he had been for the past five years. A few months later an announcement arrived from Virginia of another death, which, while it could have brought no sense of personal loss, added to the general gloom of his own increasing illness of mind and body. His cantankerous brother-in-law, William Lee, lonely and blind although not very old, had settled his final account at Green Spring. Up till the end he had worried over financial problems, which could not have been very serious ones considering the large estate he left. Francis Lightfoot, a philosopher and a charming gentleman, had remonstrated with him: "You will at all events leave a sufficiency to your children, to make them happy, unless they are wanting in themselves; in which case millions would be insufficient."[38] Poor William Lee! millions would have indeed been insufficient to satisfy that craving for possession which had ruled him all his days.

On Saturday, December 12, 1795, John Paradise's unhappy struggle with life came to an end. It could have occasioned no very great regret among the friends who knew and loved him well, for it was only too evident that the cord of his earthly happiness had long since loosened and sagged. A notice of his death was written for the *Gentleman's Magazine* by an understanding hand: "In Titchfield-street, [died] John Paradise, esq. L. L. D. of the University of Oxford, and F. R. S. He was born at Salonichi, brought up at Padua, and by far the greatest part of his life resided at London; was passionately fond of learned men, and opened his house to all descriptions of them. He was naturally silent and reserved in conversation, owing to an excess of modesty, which made him pay greater deference to the opinions of others than his own. He spoke many languages with facility, the modern Greek, Latin, Turkish, French, Italian, and English; and was as amiable in his manners as he was eminent in his literature. It has been said of him, by a distinguished person, *c'est la probité même*; to which may be added, *revetue des formes douces de la sensibilité.*"[39]

EPILOGUE

The Paradise House in Williamsburg

ON Tuesday, August 27, 1805, the merchant ship *Planter* sailed into Hampton Roads and docked at Norfolk.[1] She was a ship which for almost half a century had been weaving the shuttle of trade between Virginia and England, a ship which John and Lucy Paradise, and latterly Lucy Paradise alone, had awaited many times in London with anxious hearts, for as often as not, she had borne in her hold the tobacco from the Ludwell plantations that for them meant wealth or poverty for the ensuing year. Today she carried as a passenger Lucy Ludwell Paradise herself, and as a part of her cargo all of that lady's portable worldly goods. At last, almost ten years after her husband's death, Mrs. Paradise had been able to make the break with London and was returning home to Virginia to end her days there. Nothing, apparently, had been left behind, from her piano forte to her four-wheeled carriage, painted black and trimmed in yellow, with silver horse's heads for ornaments, and a little flight of steps which could be let down for her convenience in mounting and dismounting.[2] Her household furniture included two mahogany "sophas," a portable writing-desk, two curtained bedsteads, several wash-hand-stands, and even three "closed night chairs." There was also the mahogany table, laden with associations, at which she had presided with so many notable people as her guests, from Thomas Jefferson to Samuel Johnson. There was her table silver, including fish knives, salt ladles, candlesticks, sugar tongs, a mustard pot, a tea strainer, and labels for the decanters. There were her silver spectacles, and the gold mourning-ring which William Lee had given her on the death of her sister; there was a pair of gold bracelets, one of gold ear drops, her silver thimble, and her gold chain with its two crosses. There were her portraits and pictures: a large portrait of Thomas Jefferson and one of Peter Paradise; a large painting entitled "America"; two smaller portraits, one of George Washington and the other of Lord Hawke, who had died of gout early that spring. There was even a "gold picture," (no doubt a miniature,) of her husband.[3]

It was with no sense of defeat that she was returning to Virginia. The pride of family and place, and the obstinate, violent will that had traveled to England in the breast of that nine-year-old child of 1760 had remained unconquered in that breast by all the tragedies of half a century. A Virginia Ludwell still, she was returning home to claim the prestige of that great colonial name which she was the last to have borne—to a Virginia, which, although it had vanished in reality, still existed in her uncapitulating mind.

There is something almost symbolic in her departure from Virginia at the height of the great colonial flowering and her return to it forty-five years later. That so much could have happened in so few years almost makes a mockery of time. The Indian Wars of her father's day had been terminated; the Revolution had been kindled and had flamed into a seven year's war for Independence; seven additional painful, growing years had passed under the Articles of Confederation and then Virginia and the other States had bound them-

selves together for better or for worse in the bonds of
the Federal Constitution. The nation that was then
born had grown into maturity. Two presidents, both of
whom she had known well, had served their time, and
now a third, who twenty years ago had been her most
beloved friend, was at the beginning of his second term.
As to the Virginia of her childhood, it had vanished
almost as completely as if it had never been, and the
glory of the name of Ludwell had departed even as the
name itself. Even now, with ten years of her life still
ahead of her, Lucy Paradise must have appeared to
others as a ghost revisiting the scenes of a former life,
claiming old rights and prerogatives which had long
since ceased to exist, warming over old friendships and
old kinships which had been cold these many years.
But as for her, her possessive spirit had kept these
things alive. She knew, even if nobody else was willing
to remember, what it had meant to be a Ludwell of
Virginia. She knew, too, that her wide experience "on
the great and fatiguen theatre of this world" would
give her a social advantage over the provincial ladies
who were her friends and kinswomen and among whom
she intended to live out her life. She still retained the
airs and graces of the cosmopolitan world in which she
had lived. She would not abandon them in republican
America. She was on her way to Williamsburg to
become a *grande dame*.

Her first act on landing on American soil was to
write a letter to "Thomas Jefferson Presedent of the
United States of North America." She had arrived in
Norfolk that very day, she informed him, having come
back to spend her remaining years "in the Bosom of
[her] Native Country and Friends." She would not

have stayed in England for one month after her husband's death had not one illness after another prevented her from leaving. "M^r B Waller has written to me he has taken a house for me in the City of Williamsburg as I desired him. All my Children are Dead and Mr Paradise. I now am only Left. The honour of paying my Respects to your Excellency and your Amiable Daughter and her family will make [me] happy. . ."[4]

Mr. Jefferson's response was formal and forbidding. The incentive that had made him for years so assiduous a friend had been taken away by the death of her husband—he had never really cared for her—and moreover, his duties as President could not possibly allow him to give her affairs the time and attention which he knew she would demand. It would be better to make this clear at once:

Th: Jefferson presents his congratulations to Mrs. Paradise on her safe return to her native country after an absence of so great a portion of her life. if habits formed to the comforts & accommodations of a country so much more advanced in the arts than this, are not too firmly established, he has little doubt she will enjoy more security & tranquility here, where her fortune will place her at her ease, and the society of her relations & neighbors supply that of strangers. he prays her to accept his friendly salutations & assurances of respect.

Monticello Sep. 19. 05.[5]

The "comforts and accommodations" of London had grown less and less during the ten years she had remained there. Not only had the old debts continued to harrass her but also the new ones which in her imprudent, unprovidential way she continued to contract. After John Paradise's death, most of his friends had fallen away and she was obliged to depend on the few, who, through pity or through less disinterested motives, could be induced to tolerate her vagaries and show her kindness. As to the many illnesses of which she spoke to Jefferson, it is impossible to know with certainty what they were, although it seems likely that they were mental rather than physical. Her temper had continued to grow more and more irritable—even irascible—and her correspondence and her conversation became more and more filled with those non sequiturs which bespoke a total lapse of reason. Gossipy Matilda Hawkins gives an illuminating glimpse of her during this time: "My younger brother remembers to have met Mrs. Paradise one day at dinner at Mrs. Welch's; her personal attractions were at that time much on the decline, and her countenance retained little other expression but that of extreme irritability. She then resided at one of the villages in the neighborhood of London, and regretting that there was no stage-coach from her village, which would convey her to that part of London to which her business occasionally called her, he suggested that the deficiency might be supplied by availing herself of another conveyance, to take her to her place of destination, when she quitted the stage. Upon which, turning to him, with a most emphatical look and tone of voice, she said, 'Lord! Sir, you might as well advise me to cut off my nose to improve my face.' My brother was astonished, and could not perceive any connection between the two propositions."[6]

The inscrutable Dr. Bancroft continued to aid her

with her business affairs. As well he might, for John
Paradise, with rare foresight, had bequeathed to him
in his will "Three hundred pounds over and above
what may be due from me to him"[7]—doubtless for this
very purpose. In 1801, when Bancroft was considering
a journey to America, Mrs. Paradise was in despair;
she could not bear to "loose" her old friend, she declared, "if it is but for a day."[8] A bequest of a hundred
pounds had been made to the Reverend Mr. Smarnove,
Chaplain of the Legation of her Imperial Majesty of
all the Russias. "This Legacy," Paradise had stated in
his will, "though the same proceeds from my Will and
intention I must do my Wife the Justice to observe she
most earnestly desired me to remember our ffriend the
Legatee of it."[9] The Rev. Mr. Smarnove, whom Mrs.
Paradise became accustomed to refer to as her "priest,"
officiated at the Greek Orthodox church in Welbeck
Street which also served as the chapel of the Russian
Embassy. Mrs. Paradise, a convert to Orthodox Catho-
licism, had become increasingly ardent as life had
heaped more and more ills upon her ever-troubled
spirit, and like so many other women she discovered in
religion a consolation and a cure for the mental dis-
turbances which seized her at this critical stage of her
existence. "With the Blessing of God I am now in
good health," she stated at the age of fifty-four, "and
with My Priests Blessing and command who is the
Revd Mr Smirnove."[10]

Another old friend who behaved to her "with the
greatest attention and politeness" during her widow-
hood was Count Semen de Woronzow, who for many
years had been the Russian Ambassador to England

and, with his charming wife, an intimate frequenter of the "levée Paradisiac" of happier days. A man distinguished for his liberal political views, Count Woronzow was a sympathizer with the revolutionists in France and did much to mitigate the harshness of the English attitude toward them in the crucial year of 1793. In the early part of the next century he returned to Russia for a time, where he was prominent in forming the third coalition under Alexander I. A confirmed Anglophile, he received permission to return to London and continued to reside there until his death in 1832.[11] It was at the Paradise house in Charles Street that Woronzow made the acquaintance of Thomas Jefferson, who won his lasting admiration. He was in the group of legatees, which included Jefferson, Bishop Horsley, William Windham, Count Woronzow, Frederick North, Isaac Hawkins Browne, Richard Warburton Lytton, Col. Nathaniel Burwell of Virginia, and Bennet Langton, who each received from Paradise the sum of sixteen pounds with which to buy a mourning-ring.[12]

Excepting for friends like these and a very few others, Lucy Paradise was completely alone in the world. After the visit to Italy in 1789, a coolness seems to have developed between Count Barziza and the Paradises and neither John nor Lucy ever saw their daughter again. No doubt the cause was a disagreement over money matters, for Count Barziza, always an avaricious man, had pressed his wife's parents for payment of their obligation to him at the time when their London creditors were driving them into bankruptcy. By insisting on a strict fulfillment of the terms

of his marriage contract, he had finally succeeded in
laying his hands on every penny of the money which
John Paradise had inherited from his father, thus leaving his wife's parents entirely dependent upon their
income from Virginia. John Paradise's violent objection to the match was at length tragically justified, even
in the eyes of his wife. "On August the Second [1800],"
Mrs. Paradise told Jefferson, "My only child Died at
Her artful wicked husbands house at venice after loos-
ing half her Nose and the roof of her Mouth."[13] She
left behind two young sons, John and Philip Ignatius;
her two eldest children had died in early infancy. Mrs.
Paradise never saw either of her grandchildren, and it
was not until after her death that they seem to have
made any effort to communicate with England or
America.

After the death of her daughter Mrs. Paradise's
thoughts turned more and more to Virginia. She began
to communicate with her nieces and her nephew, the
children of William Lee. It was to William Ludwell
Lee, now the master of Green Spring, that she turned
for assistance when the death of her manager, William
Wilkinson, occurred in 1800. She transferred her
power of attorney from Thomas Jefferson, who had
begged to be excused, to him, and it was under his
authority that William Coleman of James City County,
recommended by Bishop Madison as a man of "perfect
integrity & capacity for Business," was appointed the
new manager.[14] Cornelia, the eldest child of William
Lee, had been married to John Hopkins, and her sister,
Portia, to William Hodgson. It was to Mrs. Hodgson
that Mrs. Paradise addressed one of the more remarkable of her effusions:

London No 29 Howland Street, Fitzroy Square.
My Dear Niece,

I hope you will have received my last letter. It is a long time I have not received a letter from you. If Mr. Hodgson would write to me and send a Letter to his nearest relations to pay me a visit that would get us acquainted. It would make me happy [words obliterated] United well always prosper. My affectionate [regards to] Cornelia and tell her she should write me and tell me the news of all our Relations and who is Married, Born and Died. I have altered my intention of going home for some time and for that reason I have taken the house No 29 Howland Street Fitzroy Square London. I read in the newspapers of June the 30th that Mrs Martha Washington the Wife of our great and Good General and President Washington was Dead. let me know if it is true and tell me the month and her age and what was the illness which was the cause of her Death. I went directly into Mourning and I shall continue in Mourning 6 months. If you and all my numerous Relations and acquaintance was to get into the habit of Writing it would make me happy. I hope Mr Hodgson and yourself and children are well. Present my affectionate compliments to Mr Hodgson and all my relations. In your answer to this Letter please tell me if the City of Washington is finished. Accept my blessings and my best wishes attend you all

Your Affectionate Aunt

July 31, 1802   Lucy Ludwell Paradise[15]

P. S. Please to tell me if the Congress is held in the City of Washington. Send me an answer soon. I love the three children of my dear sister.

Two years after this letter was written, William Ludwell Lee died. There was now no one in Virginia to whom she could turn. Her two nieces, so she complained to Jefferson, had responded little or not at all to her appeals for friendship and affection. There was nothing to do but take the long-deferred step of return-ing to Virginia to live and there to manage her affairs herself as well as she was capable of doing. By the beginning of 1805 she was mentally resolved to go, but as always there was the question of money. She was entirely without funds, and there were still "very Great Debts to pay." At length she appealed to Littleton Waller Tazewell, a particular friend of her nephew. "I have not the honour of knowing you only by name therefore I am a Stranger in my native Country," she wrote him with characteristic disregard of gram-mar and logic.[16] Stranger though he was, Tazewell came effectually to her assistance with a remittance which enabled her to pay her debts in London and to buy a passage to Virginia for herself, her coach, and her household furniture. Benjamin Waller had rented for her from one of her nieces the brick house on the Duke of Gloucester Street which had formerly be-longed to her father and her grandfather.[17] This was the house that forever after was destined to be famous as the "Paradise House," from which for the next seven years she ruled, or attempted to rule, the social life of her native town.

The Williamsburg legend of "Madam Paradise," sometimes also referred to as "Lady Paradise," is to this very day one of the livest in a town which has always cherished its legends. To her contemporaries there she appeared as a lady of somewhat foreign man-ners with remarkably good taste, who was fascinating but very peculiar. It is easy to read between the lines of the stories about her that, while she was laughed at by many as an eccentric and dreaded as a bore, she was respected and even feared by the ladies of the community as a tyrannical arbitress of elegance who knew the ways of the great world and was determined to enforce them upon the little city which she had condescended to make her home.

The fact that her family had for three generations been the greatest landowner in the vicinity of Williamsburg encouraged her to affect the rôle of lady of the manor, an attitude which could hardly have been pleasing to the citizens of a country so lately become republican. One of her first public appearances was at Sunday morning service in Bruton Parish Church. We can well imagine the astonishment of her fellow parishoners when Madam Paradise, dressed no doubt in the extreme height of the fashion, marched sedately to her pew, preceded by a turbanned black boy who bore her prayer-book and her hymnal upon a cushion held at arm's length in front of him.

She gave entertainments on a grand scale and with a condescension toward her fellow townsmen that was by no means unnoted by them. "Mrs Paradise is making great preparations for the 4th of July, at the Rawleigh Tavern," wrote the sixteen-year-old Eliza Prentis to her brother. "On that day she gives a Dinner to the Light Horsemen and the gentlemen of the town, and at night she gives a Ball to the inhabitants. I suppose she thinks these *great actions* will immortalize the name of Col^l Ludwell's Daughter. Papa received a Card from her yesterday, soliciting his company to Dinner, and himself and family to the Ball."[18]

Another of the few authenticated stories about her

Williamsburg life is concerned with an episode in the life of James Monroe, who not many years afterwards became the fifth President of the United States. On December 18, 1807, Col. Monroe arrived in Norfolk from a mission abroad. He was accompanied by his wife and children. Incidentally, Maria Monroe seems at this time to have introduced a new style of dress for American children which lasted for many years. "She was dressed in a short frock, that reached about half way between her knees & ankles, under which she displayed a long pair of loose pantaloons, wide enough for the foot to pass through with ease, frilled round with the same stuff as her frock & pantaloons. I was so pleased with it & so persuaded you would immediately adopt it for Fannilia & Lisba," wrote the Hon. St. George Tucker to his daughter, "that I took more than ordinary notice of it. The little monkey did not fail to evince the advantages of her dress. She had a small Spaniel dog, with whom she was continually engaged in a trial of skill, & the general opinion seemed to be that she turned & twisted about more than the Spaniel. At intervals when she had tired the dog, she was bestriding, first her Mama's, then her sister's, then her Papa's knee & then again the Spaniel, till we left the room. I must recommend her dress for my dear brats..."

The scene of this incident was an evening party in Williamsburg which had been arranged for Monroe by the gentlemen of the town when he passed through on his way to Washington. When the party was at its height, Madam Paradise made one of her dramatic entrances. She flew up to Mrs. Monroe and embraced her, and then turning to little Maria she almost stifled her with kisses. Lastly, she seized the hands of the

Colonel and, after bidding him welcome to Virginia with great *empressement*, she added with conviction, "Sir, we have determined to make you President."[19]

As the years passed on Mrs. Paradise's peculiarities grew upon her to an alarming degree. It became more and more evident that she was mentally far from normal. Her friends and neighbors, partly through kindliness and partly through some latent sense of awe which her presence still demanded, humored her in her fancies, accepting her as a community burden to be borne with local pride. There were some who rebelled. Frances Bland Coalter told her father as a sort of climax to her account of her loneliness in faraway Staunton that she would be glad "even to see Mrs Paradise."[20]

Among the stories which have come down about her is one concerning the obsession that she had for borrowing and wearing the new clothes of her friends. "It began to be whispered about that things lent in this way were not promptly returned, and, above all, not returned in their original purity and freshness. It was perilous to lend and equally perilous to refuse. . . A stylish lady received from foreign parts a very handsome bonnet. She wore it in anxious triumph, and in a few days the inevitable message came from Mrs. P. The turbaned damsel gave 'Missus' compliments, and she would take it very kind if that there new bonnet war lent her.' The bonnet was sent, and in the evening and for some successive evenings it was sent for and the answer returned: 'Missus hasn't quite done with it.' At last the bonnet was returned utterly dilapidated and the woman confessed not only that 'missus' had worn it all day, but that she had worn it all night; in point of fact, had made a night-cap of it!"[21]

It must have been about the end of her seventh year in Williamsburg that there occurred an incident which even her most tolerant and respectful neighbors could not overlook. Some friends of Mrs. Paradise were invited to take a drive with her in her coach. When they arrived, they were politely escorted by their hostess to the carriage-house and requested to enter the carriage, to which no horses had as yet been hitched. After some moments, the Negro servant, Henry, entered and at Mrs. Paradise's command began to draw the carriage back and forth along the floor. An hour of this solemn ritual elapsed before Mrs. Paradise announced that the drive was over and permitted her guests to dismount.

It could not have been very long after this that they moved her away from the "Paradise House" to another house, a larger one not far away on Francis [?] Street. This was the Eastern State Hospital for the Insane. On January 29, 1812, a committee of three aldermen having examined her and declared her to be insane, William McCandlish as her "friend" was appointed to manage her estate, and William Coleman, Bishop Madison, W. L. Harris, and J. A. Deneufville acknowledged bond as his sureties in penalty of $65,000.[22] She remained there for more than two years before she died, on April 24, 1814.

The litigation over her estate, which began at once, continued for twenty-three years.[23] Her natural heirs were her grandchildren, the two sons of the Countess Barziza. There was no question as to their legal right to her personal estate, but the real estate, which formed

WEST VIEW

EASTERN LUNATIC ASYLUM

EASTERN LUNATIC ASYLUM, WILLIAMSBURG, VIRGINIA.
America's first hospital for the insane, where Mrs. Paradise died.
Courtesy of Dr. G. W. Brown, Superintendent Eastern State Hospital, Williamsburg.

the bulk of her property, was at once claimed and taken
possession of by the two daughters of William Lee, on
the grounds that persons of alien birth and citizenship
could not inherit land in America. Early in 1815,
Philip Ignatius Barziza, then a lad of eighteen, arrived
in Virginia to take possession of his grandmother's
personal property and to lay claim to the real estate
which had already been seized by Mrs. Hopkins and
Mrs. Hodgson. He at once fell into Mrs. Paradise's
habit of writing letters to Thomas Jefferson, who sym-
pathized with his cause and did everything in his power
to help him win the succession of law-suits that now
began. He even entertained him at Monticello.[24] At
length in 1826, the case was decided against him in the
Virginia Supreme Court. Meanwhile he had become
an American citizen and a resident of Williamsburg,
where, in accordance with the sanguine example of his
grandparents, he amassed a substantial pile of debts on
the prospect of his inheritance. Twice during the next
twenty years he was obliged to have recourse to the
Bankruptcy Act; it was not until 1858 that the Virginia
court records become clear of lawsuits in which his
name appears as the plaintiff or the defendant, almost
invariably unsuccessful. Among the several occupations by which he attempted to earn a living for himself and his family was that of a keeper at the asylum
which had harbored Madam Paradise.[25] However, in
a town which has been described by its own inhabitants
as a place "where the lazy take care of the crazy," this
is scarcely surprising.

Viscount Philip Barziza, as he had the right to be
called until he renounced his Venetian citizenship, was
married to Cecile Belette, that very "houri" whom he

had been so surprised to see emerging from one of the Williamsburg "hovels." In fairly rapid order, she presented him with the following children: Francis Travis, William Lee, Edgar Athling, Philip Ignatius, Philippa Ludwell, Edgar Antonio, John Paradise, James Lee, and Lucy Ludwell.[26] Not long after the arrival of Lucy another child was born. In announcing its birth to a friend, the Viscount acknowledged that he was at a loss for a name. "How many had you already?" he was asked. "Nine," was the reply. "Boy or girl?" "Boy." "Then, damn it all, Barziza, name him Decimus Ultimus." Thus it was, according to a vigorous Williamsburg legend, that the most distinguished of the Barziza children, who after the War between the States became a prominent lawyer in Texas, received his name.

What could have been the vagrant thoughts and fancies that flitted across the crazy brain of Lucy Ludwell Paradise during the last two blank years of her life? Did her consciousness continue to be governed by Don Quixote dreams of former worldly splendor? Or was she at the last sentenced to perceive the reality of her own self-seeking nature? No doubt, if there were rational moments, her mind dwelt on her carefree childhood at Green Spring and those early years in London when her father, by indulging every wish, had taught her such deceptive expectations of life. She remembered too the time when those expectations had been in part fulfilled, when the tobacco had flowed in abundance from Virginia, permitting her husband and herself to play the rôles for which nature and environment had fitted them. Which of those great men did she most often recall, for whom she had played the part of hostess and her husband that of friend? Not Dr. Johnson; she had never really liked him, had only taken a certain pride in her husband's friendship with the great celebrity of the day. Not Sir William Jones, nor Bennet Langton, nor Dr. Parr, nor even Boswell; such men were scholars, or thinkers, or mere talkers, and were uncongenial to her practical nature. There can be little doubt that of all her husband's friends the one most often in her thoughts was Thomas Jefferson. Him she had admired and loved. She remembered him for the order which he had brought into her husband's life, and consequently into her own; she remembered him for his forthright power of acting, when action was demanded, for his years of kindness and under-standing toward herself, and for his formal but undevi-ating courtesy. With a bitter pang of jealousy she remembered Maria Cosway, to whom Jefferson had long ago addressed a few sentimental letters such as she had never been able to elicit for herself. At times too her now defenseless consciousness must have been mocked by thoughts of what might have been had a kinder fate presented her with Thomas Jefferson, and not John Paradise, for a husband. Perhaps in the un-bounded freedom of fancy that only lunacy can bestow she could visualize herself as the Lady of the White House, administering to Americans at home the hospi-tality she had so often in reality delighted to dispense to them abroad.

And what of John Paradise? The image of this gentle, sensitive man who had been her most inadequate husband must often have obtruded itself upon her consciousness. She must have thought a little of the days when their love was new and untried and in consequence unruptured. Even the insensitive Lucy Paradise must have realized at last that she had been his ruin—he, for whom things had been ideas, while for her ideas had been things. John Paradise! man of feeling, man of sensibility, man of his age—beloved of Samuel Johnson and of Thomas Jefferson and of almost all who knew him, excepting her to whom an ironic fate had bound him with bonds which only death, not he, was strong enough to break.

Notes
on the Family Connections

OF

LUCY LUDWELL PARADISE,

DAUGHTER OF

PHILIP LUDWELL, III.

NOTES ON THE FAMILY CONNECTIONS

1.

THE LUDWELL–Higginson LINE
of Philip Ludwell I.

Thomas Ludwell of Discoe, Bruton, Somerset, England. d. 1657. ═ Jane Cottington, daughter of James Cottington of Discoe, Bruton, Somerset, England.

PHILIP LUDWELL I of Green Spring in Virginia. b. [?] at Bruton, Somerset, Eng., came to Va., 1660. d. 1716 in England, buried at Church of St. Mary, Stratford-le-Bow, Middlesex, England. Member of the Council. Married (2nd) Frances Culpeper, widow of (1st) Col. Samuel Stevens and (2nd) Sir William Berkeley, royal governor of Va., of Bruton, England and Green Spring; from whom Philip I inherited Greenspring and Chippokes.

═ **LUCY HIGGINSON** m. 1667 [?]. Daughter of Capt. Robert Higginson of the Middle Plantation. b. [?]. d. 1675. Widow of (1st) Maj. Lewis Burwell, (2nd) Col. William Bernard. From her marriage to Lewis Burwell were descended the line of Lewis, Nathaniel and Carter Burwells.

Thomas of Rich Neck. Secretary of State for Virginia. Left Rich Neck to his brother, Philip I.

Rebecca, daughter of Lewis Burwell III was Thomas Jefferson's "Belinda."

Jane Cottington, who married Col. Daniel Parke, Jr., governor of the Leeward Islands, and, as aide to Marlborough, bearer of the news of Blenheim to Queen Anne; mother of Lucy, who married Col. William Byrd of Westover; grandmother of Daniel Parke Custis, who married Martha Dandridge, later Mrs. Washington.

PHILIP II of Greenspring.

2.

THE LUDWELL–Harrison LINE
of Philip Ludwell II.

Benjamin Harrison II═══Hannah
of Wakefield (1645-
1712).
Member of the Council.

PHILIP LUDWELL II ══HANNAH	Sarah,
of Green Spring.	who married James Blair,
b. 1672 at Carter's Creek.	the Commissary of Va.,
d. 1726/7.	and 1st President of the
President of the Council.	College of William and

PHILIP LUDWELL II ══*HANNAH*
of Green Spring.   m. 1697.
b. 1672 at Carter's Creek. b. 1678.
d. 1726/7.   d. 1731.
President of the Council.

Sarah,
who married James Blair,
the Commissary of Va.,
and 1st President of the
College of William and
Mary; mother of John,
President of the Council.

Hannah Philippa,
who married in 1722
at Green Spring,
Thomas Lee of Stratford,
President of the Council;
mother of
Philip Ludwell Lee
of Stratford,
Thomas Ludwell Lee
of Belleview,
Richard Henry Lee
of Chantilly,
Francis Lightfoot Lee
of Menokin,
William Lee
of Greenspring,
Arthur Lee
of Lansdown,
Hannah Lee,
wife of Gawin Corbin II
of Peckatone,
Alice Lee,
who married in 1762 in
London, Dr. William
Shippen, Jr.
of Philadelphia;
mother of
Thomas Lee Shippen.

Lucy,
who married in 1715
at Green Spring, John
Grymes II of Brandon
on the Rappahannock,
member of the Council;
mother of Lucy, wife of
Carter Burwell of Carter's
Grove (half-brother of
Robert Carter Nicholas, Treas.
of Va., and exec. of Est.
of Philip Ludwell III); and also
of Philip Grymes of Brandon,
member of the Council and His
Majesty's Receiver-General, who was
father of Mary, wife of Thomas
Nelson of Yorktown, Governor
of Va., and of Susannah, wife
of Nathaniel Burwell of Carter's
Grove and Carter Hall.

PHILIP III
of Green Spring.

3.

THE LUDWELL–Grymes LINE
of Philip Ludwell III.

Henry Corbin, of Peckatone, (1629-1675), came to Va., 1654, member of the Council; father of Laetitia, wife of Richard Lee of Mt. Pleasant and mother of Thomas Lee of Stratford; of Richard Corbin of Laneville, President of the Council, exec. of Est. of Philip Ludwell III, (whose son, John Tayloe Corbin, married Mary, daughter of Benjamin Waller, exec. of Est. of Philip Ludwell III); and of

Edmund Jenings (1659-1727)══Frances
of Ripon, Yorkshire,
Eng. Attorney General of
Va., and President of
the Council.

Charles Grymes ══Frances   Elizabeth,
of Morattico.   mother of
(1697 [?]-1743).   Beilby Porteous,
Brother of John   Bishop of
Grymes II of   Chester and
Brandon; member   London.
of the Council.

PHILIP LUDWELL III ══FRANCES   Lucy,
of Green Spring.   "the Lowland Beauty"
b. 1716 at Green Spring.   m. 1737.   of Gen. Washington,
d. 1767 at London,   b. 1717 at Morattico.   who married in 1753
buried at the Church of   d. 1753 at Green Spring.   at Green Spring, Henry
St. Mary, Stratford-le-Bow.   Lee of Leesylvania;
Member of the Council.   mother of "Lighthorse
                                 Harry" Lee, and
                                 grandmother of Robert
                                 Edward Lee.

Hannah Philippa   ══William Lee   Frances   LUCY
b. 1737 at Green Spring.   m. 1769 in London.   b. 1750
d. 1784 at Ostend,   Son of Thomas Lee   at Green Spring,
buried at the Church of   of Stratford.   d. 1768
St. Mary, Stratford-le-Bow.   b. 1739 at Stratford.   at London,
Inherited Green Spring in   d. 1795 at Green Spring.   buried at Church
division of her father's   Sheriff and alderman   of St. Mary, Strat-
estate; mother of William   of the City of London.   ford-le-Bow.
Ludwell Lee (1775-1803);
Portia Lee (1777-1840),
wife of William Hodgson; Cornelia Lee (1780-1815), wife of John Hopkins, counsel for Aaron Burr. William inherited Green Spring, and left it to his sisters who also claimed the estate of Lucy Ludwell Paradise on the grounds that her Italian grandchildren could not inherit Virginia real property.

4.

THE LUDWELL–PARADISE LINE
of Lucy Ludwell Paradise.

Ludville ══ a Greek lady
Philip Lodvill [?],
divine of Oxfordshire,
Eng. Translator (1762)
of "The Orthodox Con-
fession of the Catholic
and Apostolic Eastern
Church."
d. 1767, buried at the
Church of St. Mary,
Stratford-le-Bow.

Peter Paradise ══a daughter
(1704-1779)
British consul
at Salonica.
Exec. of Est. of
Philip Ludwell III

LUCY LUDWELL ══JOHN PARADISE
b. 1751 at Green Spring.   m. 1769 in London.
d. 1814 at Williamsburg.   b. 1743 at Salonica.
Inherited Rich Neck and   d. 1795 at London.
Chippokes in division of   Fellow of the Royal Society
her father's estate.   of London. Exec. of Est.
                            of Philip Ludwell III.

LUCY ══COUNT ANTONIO BARZIZA   Philippa
b. 1771 at London. of Venice, m. 1787   b. 1774 at London.
d. 1800 at Venice. in London.   d. 1787 at London.

Count Giovanni   VISCOUNT FILIPPO IGNACIO ══CECILE BELETTE
b. 1789 at Venice. b. 1796 at Venice.   of Williamsburg.
d. [?].   Came to Va. 1815.
                    d. after 1858.

Philip Ignatius Barziza
Edgar Antonio
Frances Travis
Philippa Ludwell
Edgar Athling
James Lee
William Lee
Lucy Ludwell
John Paradise
Decimus Ultimus

ACKNOWLEDGMENTS

THE genius of John Paradise for attracting friends and of Lucy Paradise for stimulating interest has carried over from the eighteenth to the twentieth century and many persons and institutions have in a variety of ways contributed assistance to this book about them.

It was Mrs. Helen Bullock who, as Archivist of Colonial Williamsburg, first began to collect the widely scattered material about the Paradises, and it was she whose contagious enthusiasm first aroused that of many of the people connected with this book, including my own. I have the pleasant duty of thanking her not only for generously turning over the material which she had collected, but also for her continued interest and able practical assistance during the long period in which this book was in the making.

My thanks are also due to Philippa Alexander Bruce Shepperson for extensive assistance in the collecting of material, especially about the Ludwell family, for the preparation of the Notes on the Family Connections of Lucy Paradise, for assembling the illustrations, and for seeing the book through the press.

I am indebted to a number of individuals who have kindly permitted the use of letters and other documents from their private collections: Dr. Lloyd P. Shippen, M. D., of Washington, D. C. for access to the Shippen Papers; Franklin Bache, Esq., of West Chester, Pa. for several letters from Sir William Jones to Benjamin Franklin and for his able assistance in identifying the persons alluded to in these letters; Mr. and Mrs. Victor

W. Stewart, the present owners of Chippokes, for permission to use the photograph of that plantation, and especially to Mrs. Stewart for material on the history of Chippokes; Miss Lucy Vaiden of Williamsburg, Va., for the passport of Viscount Philip Ignatius Barziza and other family documents; Mrs. George Coleman of Williamsburg, Va., for letters from the Tucker collection in her possession; Robert Henning Webb, Esq., of the University of Virginia for a letter from the Prentis collection; Mrs. Edward H. Cofer of Smithfield, Va., for items from the account book of W. M. Jones, storekeeper of Surry, Va.; Mrs. John T. Daniel of Cape Charles, Va., for information about the Barziza family; and the late Burton Paradise, Esq., of Yale University for a letter from John Paradise to Dr. Warren.

I wish to thank the Civici Musei ed Istituti d'Arte e di Storia of Venice, Italy for transcribing material from their archives; and the Institute of Historical Research of the University of London for transcribing material from the British Museum, the Prerogative Court of Canterbury, the Public Record Office, the archives of the Royal Society of London and of the Royal Society Club, and the Registers of the Church of St. Mary, Stratford-le-Bow, and to thank these institutions for permission to use this material. I am also indebted to Miss Mary Grigsby Shepperson for assistance in transcribing material from the Virginia Historical Society. The Index is the professional work of Miss Genevieve Yost of Williamsburg, Virginia.

The following institutions have permitted the use of manuscripts from their various collections and this permission is hereby gratefully acknowledged: Colonial Williamsburg, the Library of Congress, the Virginia

Historical Society, the American Philosophical Society, the Massachusetts Historical Society, Harvard College Library, the Library of the College of William and Mary, the New York Public Library, the Library of the University of Pennsylvania, the Yale University Library, and the Alderman Memorial Library of the University of Virginia. To the staffs of these various institutions I am extremely grateful, especially to that of the Yale Library, where I worked for almost a year, and to that of the Alderman Memorial Library for assistance far beyond the range of ordinary duties.

I am particularly indebted to the Viking Press, Inc. for permission to quote from the Isham Collection of Boswell Papers from Malahide Castle now in the course of publication by the Viking Press, Inc., under the editorship of Professor Frederick A. Pottle.

Fortunately most of the manuscripts quoted were photographed before war conditions made it necessary to remove them from their usual repositories. My thanks are due to Mrs. Dan S. Norton for aid in rechecking this material. However, certain manuscripts were not photographed and hence it was impossible for them to be rechecked for accuracy. These include: all papers from the Shippen MSS, Library of Congress; three letters from John Paradise to Jefferson: those of May 23, 1786, of November 10, 1786, and of June 27, 1786; also one letter from Jefferson to John Paradise of August 26, 1791.

The Sterling Fellowship Committee of Yale University awarded me a Fellowship, for which I am duly grateful, as I am also to the General Education Board for a generous grant of money. I wish also to acknowledge the financial assistance of the Committee on

Research at the University of Virginia and to thank
the President and the Board of Visitors for granting
me a year's leave of absence.

ARCHIBALD B. SHEPPERSON.

University of Virginia,
August 7, 1942.

SELECTIVE BIBLIOGRAPHY

MANUSCRIPTS

American Philosophical Society: Franklin Manuscripts.

British Museum: Additional Manuscripts.

Civici Musei ed Istituti d'Arte e di Storia, Venice, Italy. Archives.

Colonial Williamsburg, Inc.: Manuscripts in Office of Archivist.

Library of Congress: Franklin Papers. Jefferson Papers. Shippen Papers. (Used by permission.) Short Papers. Washington Papers.

Massachusetts Historical Society: Jefferson Manuscripts. Jefferson's Garden Book, 1766-1826.* Jefferson's Account Book, 1783-1790.*

New York Public Library: Lee Manuscripts.

University of Pennsylvania Library: Franklin Manuscripts.

Prerogative Court of Canterbury: Records in Somerset House, London.

Public Record Office, London: Account Books of the Levant Company, 1722-1744. Chancery Register of the Levant Company, 1746-1757. Executive Journals of the Colonial Council of Virginia.*

Royal Society of London: Manuscript Records of the Royal Society Menu Book of the Royal Society Club.

University of Virginia, Alderman Memorial Library: Jefferson Manuscripts. Lee Manuscripts.

Virginia Historical Society: Lee Manuscripts; Ludwell Manuscripts.

Library of the College of William and Mary: Southall Papers.

The following individuals have kindly permitted the use of manuscripts from their private collections: Franklin Bache, Esq.; Mrs. Edward H. Cofer; Mrs. George Coleman; the late Burton Paradise, Esq.; Miss Lucy Vaiden; and Robert Henning Webb, Esq.

*Photostatic copy in the Alderman Memorial Library, University of Virginia.

PERIODICALS

American Historical Review. New York and Lancaster, Pennsylvania.

Columbian Centinel. Boston.

Gentleman's Magazine. London.

London Chronicle. London.

London Evening Post. London.

New England Historical and Genealogical Register. Boston.

New York Times. New York.

North American Review. Boston and New York.

Phi Beta Bappa Key. New York.

Public Advertiser and Literary Gazette. London.

St. James's Chronicle. London.

Virginia Gazette. Williamsburg.

Virginia Magazine of History and Biography. Richmond.

William and Mary Quarterly. Williamsburg.

BOOKS

Adams, Mrs. Abigail: *Letters of Mrs. Adams, the Wife of John Adams.* Edited by Charles Francis Adams. 4th edition. Boston. 1848.

Adams, Miss Abigail: *Correspondence of Miss Adams.* New York. 1842.

Adams, Miss Abigail: *Journal and Correspondence of—.* New York and London. 1841.

Adams, John: *The Works of . . . with a Life of the Author*. Edited by Charles Francis Adams. Boston. 1850-1856. 10 vols.

d'Arblay, Madame: *Diary and Letters of—*. London. 1854. 7 vols

d'Arblay, Madame: *The Early Diary of Frances Burney, 1768-1778*. Edited by Anne Raine Ellis. London. 1907. 2 vols.

Armes, Ethel: *Stratford Hall: The Great House of the Lees*. Richmond. 1936.

Beaven, The Rev. Alfred B.: *The Aldermen of the City of London*. London. 1908. 2 vols.

Bemiss, Samuel Flagg: *The Diplomacy of the American Revolution*. New York and London. 1935.

Best, Henry Digby: *Personal and Literary Memorials*. London. 1829.

Boswell, James: *Boswelliana, the Commonplace Book of—*. Edited by the Rev. Charles Rogers. London. 1876.

Boswell, James: *The Hypochondriack*. Edited by Margery Bailey. Stanford University. 1928. 2 vols.

Boswell, James: *The Letters of—*. Edited by C. B. Tinker. Oxford. 1924. 2 vols.

Boswell, James: *Private Papers of . . . from Malahide Castle*; in the Collection of Lt.-Col. Ralph Heyward Isham. Edited by Geoffrey Scott and Frederick A. Pottle. Mount Vernon, N. Y. 1928-1934. 18 vols.

Burke, Edmund: *Correspondence of the Right Honourable—*. Edited by Earl Fitzwilliam and Sir Richard Bourke. London. 1844. 2 vols.

Burnaby, The Rev. Andrew: *Travels through North America*. New York. 1904.

Burnett, Edmund C., ed.: *Letters of the Members of the Continental Congress*. Washington. 1921-1936. 8 vols.

Cary, Wilson Miles: *Sally Cary, A Long Hidden Romance of Washington's Life. With Notes by Another Hand*. New York. 1916.

Chancellor, E. Beresford: *History of the Squares of London*. London. 1907.

Chancellor, E. Beresford: *Wanderings in Marylebone*. London. 1926.

Church, George: *Marylebone and St. Pancras*. London. 1890.

Dampier-Smith, J. L.: *Who's Who in Boswell*. Oxford. 1935.

Davis, John: *Travels of Four Years and a Half in the United States of North America During 1798, 1799, 1800, 1801, and 1802*. New York. 1909.

Dictionary of American Biography. Edited by Allen Johnson and Dumas Malone. New York. 1928-1936. 20 vols. and supplement.

Dictionary of National Biography. Edited by Leslie Stephen and Sidney Lee. London. 1885-1901. 60 vols. and supplement.

Dinwiddie, Robert: *The Official Records of—*. Edited by R. A. Brock. Richmond. 1883. 2 vols.

Douglas, Sylvester, Lord Glenbervie: *The Diaries of—*. Edited by Francis Bickley. London. 1928. 2 vols.

Eastern State Hospital of Virginia: *The One Hundred and Fifty-Eighth Report of—*. Richmond. 1931.

Enciclopedia Universal Illustrada. Bilboa, Madrid, and Barcelona. 1905-1933. 70 vols. and supplement.

Fox, Robert Hingston: *Dr. Fothergill and His Friends*. London. 1919.

Franklin, Benjamin: *Benjamin Franklin*. By Carl Van Doren. New York. 1938.

Franklin, Benjamin: *. . . and His Circle. A Catalogue of an Exhibition*. By R. T. H. Halsey. New York. 1936.

Franklin, Benjamin: *The Complete Works of—*. Edited by John Bigelow. New York and London. 1887-1889. 10 vols.

Franklin, Benjamin: *Franklin in France.* By Edward E. Hale and Edward E. Hale, Jr. Boston. 1888. 2 vols.

Franklin, Benjamin: *Memoirs of the Life and Writings of*—. By William Temple Franklin. London. 1818. 2 vols.

Franklin, Benjamin: *The Works of*—. Edited by Jared Sparks. Boston. 1840. 10 vols.

Franklin, Benjamin: *The Writings of*—. Edited by Alfred Henry Smyth. New York. 1905-1907. 10 vols.

Fry, Katherine: *A History of the Parishes of East and West Ham.* London. 1888.

George III: *The Letters of King*—. Edited by Bonamy Dobrée. London, Toronto, Melbourne, and Sydney. 1935.

Great Britain: *Reports of the Historical Manuscripts Commission of*—.

Griswold, Rufus Wilmot: *The Republican Court.* New York. 1855.

Hawkins, Laetitia Matilda: *Memoirs, Anecdotes, Facts and Opinions.* London. 1824. 2 vols.

Hill, Constance: *The House in St. Martin's Street.* London and New York. 1907.

Inchbald, Elizabeth: *Memoirs of Mrs. Inchbald.* By James Boaden. London. 1833. 2 vols.

Jay, John: *Correspondence and Public Papers of*—. Edited by Henry P. Johnston. New York and London. 1890. 4 vols.

Jay, John: *Diary of*—, *as Written During the Peace Negociations of 1782.* Edited by Frank Monaghan. New Haven. 1934.

Jefferson, Thomas: *The Domestic Life of*—. By Sarah N. Randolph. New York. 1871.

Jefferson, Thomas: *The Life of*—. By Henry S. Randall. New York. 1858. 3 vols.

Jefferson, Thomas: *Memoir, Correspondence, and Miscellanies, from the Papers of*—. By Thomas Jefferson Randolph. Boston and New York. 1830.

Jefferson, Thomas: *The Relation of . . . to American Foreign Policy, 1783-1793.* By William Kirk Woolery. Baltimore. 1927.

Jefferson, Thomas: *The Works of*—. Edited by Paul Leicester Ford. New York and London. 1904-1905. 12 vols.

Jefferson, Thomas: *The Writings of*—. Edited by Andrew A. Lipscomb and Albert Ellery Bergh. Washington. 1904. 20 vols.

Jefferson, Thomas: *The Writings of*—. Edited by H. A. Washington. Washington. 1853-1854. 9 vols.

Johnson, Samuel: *Johnsonian Miscellanies.* Edited by George Birkbeck Hill. Oxford. 1897. 2 vols.

Johnson, Samuel: *Johnsoniana.* Edited by Robina Napier. London. 1884.

Johnson, Samuel: *Letters of*—. Edited by George Birkbeck Hill. New York. 1892. 2 vols.

Johnson, Samuel: *The Life of*—. By James Boswell. Edited by John Wilson Croker. New York. 1843. 2 vols.

Johnson, Samuel: *The Life of*—. By James Boswell. Edited by George Birkbeck Hill. Revised and enlarged edition by L. F. Powell. Oxford. 1934. Vols. 1-4.

Johnson, Samuel: *The Life of*—. By Sir John Hawkins. Dublin. 1787.

Johnson, Samuel: *A Poetical Review of the Literary and Moral Character of the late . . . L.L.D.* London. 1786.

Jones, Sir William: *Memoirs of the Life, Writings, and Correspondence of*—. By Lord Teignmouth. Philadelphia. 1805.

La Rochefoucauld Liancourt, François Alexandre Frédéric, Duc de: *Travels through the United States of North America, the Country of the Iroquois and Upper Canada in the years 1795, 1796, and 1797.* London. 1799. 2 vols.

Larpent, Sir George, ed.: *Turkey, its History and Progress, from the Letter-books of Sir James Porter.* London. 1854. 2 vols.

Lee, Arthur: *Life of—.* By Richard Henry Lee. Boston. 1829. 2 Parts.

Lee, Edmund Jenings: *Lee of Virginia, 1642-1892.* Philadelphia. 1895.

Lee, Richard Henry: *Letters of—.* Edited by James Curtis Ballagh. New York. 1911-1914. 2 vols.

Lee, William: *The Letters of—.* Edited by Worthington C. Ford. Brooklyn. 1891. 3 vols.

Lysons, Daniel: *The Environs of London.* London. 1795. 3 vols.

Madison, James: *The Writings of—.* Edited by Gaillard Hunt. New York and London. 1904. 9 vols.

Mason, Frances: *John Norton and Sons.* Richmond. 1937.

Massachusetts Historical Society: *Collections of the—.* Seventh Series. Volume 1. Boston. 1900.

Meade, The Rev. William: *Old Churches, Ministers, and Families of Virginia.* Philadelphia. 1857. 2 vols.

Mereness, Newton D., ed.: *Travels in the American Colonies, 1690-1783.* New York. 1916.

Morris, Gouverneur: *A Diary of the French Revolution.* Edited by Beatrix Cary Davenport. Boston. 1939. 2 vols.

Nollekens, Joseph: *Nollekens and His Times;* By John Thomas Smith. Edited by Wilfred Whitten. London. n.d. 2 vols.

Orr, Lucinda Lee: *Journal of a Young Lady of Virginia 1782.* Baltimore. 1871.

Oxford, University of: *Alumni Oxonienses.* Later Series. By Joseph Foster. 1887-1891. 4 vols.

Oxford, University of: *A Catalogue of all the Graduates in Divinity, Law, Medicine, Arts and Music* (proceeded or created) *in—, 1659-1850.* Oxford. 1851.

Parr, Samuel: *Memoirs of the Life, Writings, and Opinions of the Rev.—* By William Field. London. 1828. 2 vols.

Parr, Samuel: *Parriana, or Notices of the Rev.—.* By E. H. Barker. London. 1828. 2 vols.

Parr, Samuel: *The Works of—, with Memoirs of his Life and Writings and a Selection from his Correspondence.* By John Johnstone. London. 1828. 8 vols.

Porteous, The Rt. Rev. Beilby: *The Works of . . . with his Life.* By the Rev. Robert Hodgson. London. 1823. 6 vols.

Price, Richard: *Memoirs of the Life of The Rev.—.* By William Morgan. London. 1815.

Priestley, Joseph: *An Appeal to the Public on the Subject of the Riots in Birmingham, Part II.* London. 1792.

Reynolds, Sir Joshua: *Life and Times of—.* By C. R. Leslie and Tom Taylor. London. 1865. 2 vols.

Roof, Katharine: *Colonel William Smith and Lady.* Boston. 1929.

Royal Society of London: *History of the—, from its institutions to the end of the Eighteenth Century.* By Thomas Thomson. London. 1812.

Royal Society of London: *A History of—.* By Charles Richard Weld. London. 1848. 2 vols.

Royal Society of London: *The Philosophical Transactions of—, from 1665 to 1800.* London. 1809. 18 vols.

Royal Society Club: *Annals of the—.* By Sir Archibald Geikie. London. 1917.

Small, Miriam Rossiter: *Charlotte Ramsay Lennox, An Eighteenth Century Woman of Letters.* New Haven and London. 1935.

Smith, John Thomas: *A Book for a Rainy Day.* London. 1905.

Smollett, Tobias: *The Expedition of Humphry Clinker.* Philadelphia. 1902.

Sonneck, Oscar G.: *Francis Hopkinson and James Lyon.* Washington. 1905.

Sparks, Jared, ed.: *Correspondence of the American Revolution.* Boston. 1853. 4 vols.

Stevens, B. F.: *Facsimiles of Manuscripts in European Archives Relating to America.* London. 1890.

Virginia: *The ... Historical Register.* Edited by William Maxwell. Richmond. 1848-1853. 6 vols.

Virginia: *Journal of the House of Delegates of the Commonwealth of—,* (5 May, 1777-18 October, 1780.) Richmond. 1827-1828.

Virginia: *The Proceedings of the Convention of Delegates for the Counties and Corporation in the Colony of—, March 20, 1775-July 5, 1776.* Richmond. 1816.

Virginia: *The Statutes at Large; being a Collection of all the Laws of—, from the First Sessions of the Legislature in the year 1619.* Richmond. 1821. 13 vols.

Virginia Historical Society: *Collections of the—.* Edited by R. A. Brock. Richmond. 1892.

Wallace, D. D.: *The Life of Henry Laurens.* New York. 1915.

Wansey, Henry: *Journal of an Excursion to the United States of North America in the Summer of 1794.* Salisbury (Eng.). 1796.

Washington, George: *The Diaries of—, 1748-1799.* Edited by John C. Fitzpatrick. Boston and New York. 1925. 4 vols.

Washington, George: *Letters to—.* Edited by S. M. Hamilton. Boston and New York. 1898-1902. 5 vols.

Wharton, Francis, ed.: *The Revolutionary and Diplomatic Correspondence of the United States.* Washington. 1889. 6 vols.

Windham, William: *Diary of the Right Honourable—, 1784-1810.* Edited by Mrs. Henry Baring. London. 1866.

Wood, Alfred C.: *A History of the Levant Company.* London and New York. 1935.

CHAPTER REFERENCES

PROLOGUE
A BRIDGE BETWEEN TWO WORLDS

1 William Lee's account of his family, quoted in Meade, II, 139.
2 *New England Historical and Genealogical Register*, XL, 179, "Papers in Egerton MS. 2395."
3 *Virginia Magazine of History and Biography*, XVIII, 1-24, "The Randolph Manuscript."
4 Lysons, III, 495.
5 *Lee of Virginia*, 128.

CHAPTER I
COLONIALS AT "HOME"

1 *London Chronicle*, May 18-20, 1769.
2 Foster, III, 1064. Paradise received his degree on April 14, 1769.
3 *Dictionary of National Biography*, sub Philip Lodvill.
4 This account of Green Spring and the Ludwell plantations is based chiefly upon letters and inventories in the Lee and Ludwell MSS at the Virginia Historical Society.
5 See Appendix I of present volume.
6 *Virginia Gazette*, January 25, 1752.
7 *Ibid.*, November 30, 1759.
8 Prerogative Court of Canterbury, Legard 183, Will of Philip Ludwell. Two incomplete versions of this will have been published in the *Virginia Magazine of History and Biography*.
9 MS of Jefferson's Garden Book, sub March 9-14, 1778.
10 *William and Mary Quarterly*, 1st series, VII, 153, "Diary of John Blair [for 1751]," sub March.

11 *Ballagh*, I, 48, Richard Henry Lee to William Lee, July 7, 1770.
12 *Virginia Gazette*, October 10, 1771.
13 *Dictionary of American Biography*, sub Philip Ludwell.
14 The principal source for this fact and others concerning Philip Ludwell III is the *Virginia Magazine of History and Biography*. Other sources are the Ludwell MSS at the library of the Virginia Historical Society, the *William and Mary Quarterly*, the *Virginia Gazette*, and E. J. Lee's *Lee of Virginia*.
15 *Virginia Gazette*, October 29-November 5, 1736.
16 *Ibid.*, July 22-29, 1737: "Williamsburg, July 29 . . . we are inform'd, That *Philip Ludwell*, Esq; only Son and Heir of Hon. *Philip Ludwell*, Esq; deceas'd, late One of His Majesty's Council of this Colony, was married to Miss *Fanney Grymes*, eldest Daughter of Col. *Charles Grymes*, a young Lady of great Merit, and Fortune." Also *Lee of Virginia*, 128. The date of the birth of Hannah Philippa Ludwell, their first child, is here given as December 21, 1737.
17 See Note 10, *supra*, sub November 8.
18 *Virginia Gazette*, May 24, 1751.
19 *Ibid.*, August 16, 1751.
20 See Note 10, *supra*, sub November 20 and 21.
21 *Official Records of Robert Dinwiddie*, II, 24-27.
22 *Ibid.*, I, 189-190 and note. Dinwiddie to George Washington, June 2, [1754].

23 *Ibid.*, II, 419-421. Dinwiddie to the Earl of Loudon, May 24, 1756; also *Executive Journals of the Colonial Council of Virginia, sub* September 3, 1756.

24 Hamilton, *Letters to Washington,* I, 76-77.

25 Ludwell MSS, Virginia Historical Society.

26 While it is not possible to prove finally that Alice Lee accompanied the Ludwells, she is known to have sailed to England in the spring of 1760 and to have been a member of her uncle's household in London.

27 Hamilton, *Letters to Washington,* III, 214. The Rev. Andrew Burnaby to Washington, April 14, 1761.

28 The family of Beilby Porteous, Bishop of London, moved from Virginia to York, England, in 1720 to procure a better education for their children, of whom Beilby was the youngest of nineteen. The Bishop was a cousin of Lucy Ludwell Paradise through her mother. See Hodgson, *Works of the Right Reverend Beilby Porteous.*

29 Thomson, Appendix IV, *sub* John Paradise.

30 Dampier-Smith, *sub* John Paradise. Quoted from Rogers, *Boswelliana.*

31 Public Record Office, MS of the Account Book of the Levant Co., 1732-1744. S.P.105/202; also *ibid.,* MS of the Chancery Register of the Levant Co., 1746-1757. S.P.105/183.

32 Wood, 7.

33 Foster, III, 1064, *sub* John Paradise.

34 Prerogative Court of Canterbury, Harris 213, Will of John Paradise.

35 Records of Westmoreland County, 1751-1764, Court Orders. Quoted in Armes, 100.

36 Shippen MSS, Library of Congress. Statement of the curate of St. Mary le Strand Church [London], dated April 3, 1762.

37 Fry, 231; also Fox, 169.

38 The notice of Philip Ludwell's death in *St. James's Chronicle,* March 26-28, 1767, and in several other London newspapers gives his residence as "near St. James's." His daughter, Hannah Philippa, was married two years later from her residence in Cecil Street (*London Chronicle,* March 7-9, 1769). His will shows that he resided in the Parish of St. Martin's-in-the Fields.

39 Halsey, 14 and 32.

40 Franklin MSS, American Philosophical Society. Franklin to Dr. John Pringle and William Strahan, February 22, 1763.

41 Ludwell MSS, Virginia Historical Society. Philip Ludwell to [Emmanuel] Jones, November 8, 1760.

42 See note 38, *supra.*

43 Will of Philip Ludwell, see note 8, *supra.*

CHAPTER II
Non Incautus Futuri

1 Lee MSS, Virginia Historical Society. Col. Richard Corbin to Mrs. Hannah Philippa Lee, June 10, 1769.

2 Beaven, I, 307.

3 Mason, 104. William Nelson to John Norton and Sons, August 15, 1769.

4 *Ibid.,* 112. George Flowerdewe Norton to John Hatley Norton, November 10, 1769.

5 See note 2, *supra,* I, 14 and 308; also III, xxxviii, 135 and 211.

6 Lee, *Life of Arthur Lee,* I, 126. Arthur Lee to Richard Henry Lee, March 23, 1769.

7 Lee MSS, Virginia Historical Society. William Lee to the Hon. Richard Corbin, March 10, 1769.

8 *Ibid.* William Lee to Richard Henry and Francis Lightfoot Lee, March 15, 1769.

9 *Ibid.* William and Hannah Ludwell Lee to Richard Corbin, Robert Carter Nicholas, Benjamin Waller and John Wayles, Esqrs., March 14, 1769; also William Lee to Robert Carter Nicholas, March 14, 1769; also William Lee to Richard Henry and Francis Lightfoot Lee, March 15, 1769.

10 *Ibid.* William Lee to Richard Henry and Francis Lightfoot Lee, February 5, 1770.

11 *Ibid.* William Lee to Benjamin Waller, March 31, 1770; to John Wayles, March 31, 1770; and to Richard Corbin, April 2, 1770.

12 MS letter in the New York Public Library from Francis Lightfoot Lee to William Lee, November 10, 1769.

13 See note 11, *supra.*

14 Lee MSS, Virginia Historical Society. William Lee to Richard Henry and Francis Lightfoot Lee, April 4, 1770.

15 Ballagh, I, 46. Richard Henry Lee to William Lee, July 7, 1770.

16 See note 15, *supra.*

17 Ballagh I, 77. Richard Henry Lee to William Lee, October 23, 1772.

18 Lee MSS, Virginia Historical Society. William Lee to Robert Carter Nicholas, March 20, 1773.

19 *Ibid.* William Lee to Richard Henry and Francis Lightfoot Lee, February 20, 1773; and to Robert Carter Nicholas, March 20, 1773.

20 *Ibid.* Richard Henry Lee to William Lee, July 4, 1773; also Robert Carter Nicholas to William Lee, July 31, 1773.

21 Ballagh, I, 39-41. Richard Henry Lee to William Lee, dated December 17 and 20, 1769.

22 Lee MSS, Virginia Historical Society. Richard Henry Lee to William Lee, May 3, 1770.

23 *Ibid.* William Lee to Robert Carter Nicholas, February 5, 1770; and to Richard Henry and Francis Lightfoot Lee, February 5, 1770.

24 *Ibid.* Philip Ludwell Lee to William Lee, January 21, 1771.

25 *Ibid.* William Lee to Cary Wilkinson, March 20, 1771.

26 *Ibid.* William Lee to Cary Wilkinson, May 22, 1771.

27 *Ibid.* Cary Wilkinson to William Lee, May 26, 1771.

28 *Ibid.* William Lee to Richard Henry and Francis Lightfoot Lee, August 9, 1771. Nicholas's letter of resignation is not preserved, but the letter just cited refers to it.

29 See note 28, *supra.*

30 Lee MSS, Virginia Historical Society. William Lee to Richard Henry and Francis Lightfoot Lee, March 7, 1771.

31 *Ibid.* William Lee to Richard Henry and Francis Lightfoot Lee, August 9, 1771.

32 *Ibid.* William Lee to Robert Carter Nicholas, January 20, 1772.

33 *Ibid.* William Lee to Cary Wilkinson, February 15, 1772.

34 *Ibid.* William Lee to Cary Wilkinson, April 22, 1772.

35 *Ibid.* William Lee to Richard Henry Lee, August 20, 1772.

36 *Ibid.* William Lee to Richard Henry and Francis Lightfoot Lee, February 20, 1773.

37 *Ibid.* William Lee to Richard Lee, February 10, 1775.

38 MS letter in the New York Public Library from Richard Henry Lee to William Lee, September 5, 1775.

39 *Virginia Gazette,* June 28, 1776.

CHAPTER III

THE PARADISE HOUSE IN LONDON

1 Shippen MSS, Library of Congress. Thomas Lee Shippen's Account Book.

2 Chancellor, *History of the Squares of London,* Chap. II, "Cavendish Square"; also Chancellor, *Wanderings in Marylebone;* also Church, *Marylebone and St. Pancras;* also Smith, *A Book for a Rainy Day.*

3 Smollett, *Humphry Clinker,* 130-131.

4 Chancellor, *Wanderings in Marylebone,* 56.

5 Chancellor, *History of the Squares of London,* 48.

6 Smith, *Nollekens and His Times,* II, 108.

7 Hawkins, *Memoirs, Anecdotes, Facts and Opinions,* I, 63-64. Quoted in Small, 46.

8 *Dictionary of National Biography,* sub Joseph Nollekens.

9 Smith, *Nollekens and His Times,* I, 81.

10 See note 9, *supra.*

11 Smith, *Nollekens and His Times,* I, 90.

12 *Journal of Susanna Burney,* sub March 9, 1780. Quoted in Constance Hill, 199-202.

13 *Diary and Letters of Madame d'Arblay,* II, 89ff. Miss F. Burney to Mrs. Phillips (née Susanna Burney); letter dated 1782—early in the year, probably February.

14 *Ibid.,* II, 172, sub Monday, [December 23, 1782].

15 Hawkins, *Memoirs, Anecdotes, Facts and Opinions,* I, 72.

16 See note 15, *supra.*

17 See note 15, *supra.*

18 Ellis, *The Early Diary of Frances Burney,* II, 313-316. Charlotte Burney to Mrs. Phillips (Susanna Burney), endorsed January 16, 1784.

CHAPTER IV

SCHOLARSHIP FOR DELIGHT

1 John Paradise's certificate of membership in the unpublished records of the Royal Society; also Thomson, *History of the Royal Society,* Appendix IV.

2 Foster, III, 1064; also *A Catalogue of all the Graduates . . . in the University of Oxford 1659-1850,* sub John Paradise.

3 *Dictionary of National Biography,* sub Sir James Porter; also Larpent, *Turkey, its History and Progress.*

4 *Dictionary of National Biography,* sub Anthony Askew; also Barker, 428.

5 *Ibid.,* sub Swithin Adee.

6 *Ibid.,* sub Isaac Hawkins Browne, the Younger.

7 Van Doren, 170.

8 *Philosophical Transactions of the Royal Society,* LXIX, Part ii, 337, and LXX, Part i, 163.

9 G. B. Hill, *Boswell's Life of Johnson,* IV, 364, note 2.

10 Weld, II, 94-102.

11 W. T. Franklin, *Memoirs of Benjamin Franklin,* II, 87.

12 Smyth, *Writings of Franklin,* X, 350-351. Sir Joseph Banks to Franklin, August 13, 1784.

13 *Columbian Centinel,* May 13, 1795; for Kippis' retraction, see *Gentleman's Magazine,* September, 1795, LXV, Part ii, 715.

14 Geikie, *Annals of the Royal Society Club.*

15 MS menu-book of the Royal Society Club.

16 Weld, II, 15, note.

17 Geikie, 169-171.

18. *Ibid.*, 201.

19 *Journal and Correspondence of Miss* [Abigail] *Adams*, 83.

20 Franklin MSS, American Philosophical Society. William Temple Franklin to Franklin, October 12, 1784.

21 Geikie, 148.

22 Boaden, I, 258 and 291.

23 Morgan, 76-80.

24 Charles Francis Adams, *Letters of Mrs. Adams*, 289. Mrs. Adams to Mrs. Cranch, May 21, 1786.

25 Van Doren, 420-422.

26 Bigelow, *Works of Franklin*, IX, 46-48. Franklin to Richard Price, August 16, 1784.

27 Van Doren, 718.

28 Fox, 179.

29 *Dictionary of National Biography*, *sub* William Hodgson.

30 Jefferson MSS, Library of Congress. Lucy Paradise to Jefferson, March 2, 1790.

CHAPTER V

THE VAST PRESENCE OF DR. JOHNSON

1 G. B. Hill, *Letters of Johnson*, I, 314. Johnson to Mrs. Thrale, April 1, 1775.

2 *Ibid.*, II, 2. Johnson to Mrs. Thrale, January 15, 1777.

3 G. B. Hill, *Boswell's Life of Johnson*, III, 68.

4 *Ibid.*, IV, 18.

5 Field, I, 161.

6 Barker, I, 321.

7 Johnstone, I, 93-94. Bennet Langton to Parr, February 5, 1777.

8 G. B. Hill, *Boswell's Life of Johnson*, IV, 238.

9 *Gentleman's Magazine*, March, 1795, LXV, Part i, 179. Parr to "Sylvanus Urbanus."

10 Joseph Priestley, *An Appeal to the Public on the Subject of the Riots in Birmingham*, Part II, 103.

11 Croker, *Boswell's Life of Johnson*, II, 348.

12 G. B. Hill, *Boswell's Life of Johnson*, III, 390.

13 Boswell, *Private Papers*, XIII, 233, "Boswell's Journal," *sub* April 24, 1779.

14 *Diary and Letters of Madame d'Arblay*, I, 353. Fanny Burney to Mrs. Thrale, July 8, 1780.

15 G. B. Hill, *Johnson's Letters*, II, 183. Johnson to Mrs. Thrale, July 4, 1780.

16 Constance Hill, 294. Quoted from Susanna Burney's journal of circa 1780.

17 Ellis, *The Early Diary of Frances Burney*, lxxxviii. Quoted from Susanna Burney's journal.

18 *Diary and Letters of Madame d'Arblay*, I, 123.

19 Smith, *Nollekens and His Times*, I, 280-281.

20 G. B. Hill, *Johnsonian Miscellanies*, I, 105. Quoted from Dr. Johnson's *Prayers and Meditations*.

21 G. B. Hill, *Boswell's Life of Johnson*, IV, 228-233; also G. B. Hill, *Johnson's Letters*, II, 301. Johnson to Mrs. Thrale, June 19, 1783.

22 G. B. Hill, *Johnson's Letters*, II, 305. Johnson to Mrs. Thrale, June 21, 1783.

23 *Ibid.*, II, 325. Johnson to Mrs. Thrale, August 13, 1783.

24 Sir John Hawkins, *Life of Johnson*, 502.

25 Leslie and Taylor, *Life of Reynolds*, II, 455.

26 Hawkins, *Memoirs, Anecdotes, Facts and Opinions*, II, 104.

27 G. B. Hill, *Boswell's Life of Johnson*, IV, 293 and 503, Appendix D.

28 G. B. Hill, *Johnson's Letters*, II, 434.

CHAPTER VI
ACCOMPLISHED JONES

1 The only biography of him is the *Memoirs of the Life, Writings, and Correspondence of Sir William Jones,* by Lord Teignmouth, published in 1805.
2 Franklin MSS, American Philosophical Society. William Hodgson to Franklin, May 8, 1781.
3 Teignmouth, 385, note.
4 *New York Times,* July 24, 1938, Sec. IV, p. 4, col. 3.
5 Teignmouth, 410-411.
6 Napier, 185. Article entitled "A Biographical Sketch of Dr. Samuel Johnson," by Thomas Tyers.
7 Johnstone, I, 477.
8 Courtenay, *A Poetical Review of the Literary and Moral Character of the late Samuel Johnson, LL.D.*
9 Teignmouth, 20, note.
10 Barker, I, 429-430, note.
11 Teignmouth, 21.
12 *Ibid.,* 19-20.
13 Johnstone, I, 136-137.
14 Barker, I, 317-318.
15 Johnstone, I, 147.
16 See note 15, *supra.*
17 Best, *Personal and Literary Memorials.*
18 Johnstone, I, 69-74.
19 Best, 62.
20 G. B. Hill, *Boswell's Life of Johnson,* I, 291-292.
21 See note 17, *supra.*
22 Teignmouth, 166.
23 G. B. Hill, *Boswell's Life of Johnson,* III, 365, note 4.
24 *Ibid.,* III, 361.
25 G. B. Hill, *Johnson's Letters,* II, 71. Johnson to Mrs. Thrale, October 15, 1778.

26 Johnstone, I, 108. Bennet Langton to Parr, August 28, 1778.
27 *Ibid.,* I, 109. William Jones to Parr, October 22, 1778.
28 Teignmouth, 92-93.
29 *Proceedings of Delegates of Colony of Virginia,* 49.
30 Lipscomb and Bergh, *Writings of Thomas Jefferson,* XIX, 31-32. Jefferson to James Madison, April 25, 1786.
31 Hening, IX, 377-380.
32 Maxwell, I, 179. Richard Henry Lee to Patrick Henry, January 25, 1778.
33 *Journal of House of Delegates of Virginia* (5 May, 1777-18 October, 1780).
34 Lee MSS, Virginia Historical Society. William and Hannah Philippa Lee to Robert Carter Nicholas, Richard Henry Lee, Francis Lightfoot Lee, and Richard Lee, October 15, 1778.
35 *Ibid.* William Lee to Francis Lightfoot Lee, October 15, 1778; William Lee to Richard Henry Lee, October 15, 1778; William and Hannah Philippa Lee to Robert Carter Nicholas, Richard Henry Lee, Francis Lightfoot Lee, and Richard Lee, October 15, 1778; and William Lee and Hannah Philippa Lee to Richard Henry Lee and Francis Lightfoot Lee, October 15, 1778.
36 *Ibid.* Richard Henry Lee to William Lee, July 15, 1781; and Ralph Izard to Mrs. Izard enclosed in a letter from Mrs. Izard to Hannah Philippa Lee, October 30, 1781.
37 Lee, *Life of Arthur Lee,* II, 342. William Jones to Arthur Lee, June 29, 1778.
38 *Gentleman's Magazine,* February, 1779, LIX, 103.
39 Sparks, *Works of Franklin,* VIII, 366, note.

CHAPTER VII
CITIZEN PARADISE

1 Van Doren, 576 and 635-636.
2 W. T. Franklin, *Memoirs of Benjamin Franklin*, II, 263-265. Joseph Priestly to the Editor of the *Monthly Magazine*, November 10, 1782.
3 Johnstone, I, 109-111. William Jones to Parr, July 19, 1779.
4 MS letter in the possession of Franklin Bache, Esq. William Jones to Benjamin Franklin, September 17, 1781.
5 Sparks, *Works of Franklin*, VIII, 365-366 and note.
6 Smyth, *Writings of Franklin*, IX, 646-647. Franklin to Madame Helvetius, April 23, 1788.
7 Charles Francis Adams, *Letters of Mrs. Adams*, 199. Mrs. Adams to Miss Lucy Cranch, September 5, 1784.
8 *Journal and Correspondence of Miss* [Abigail] *Adams*, 74.
9 This letter seems not to have survived but it is referred to by Franklin in his letter to Jefferson of May 6, 1781. The letter is among the Franklin MSS, Library of Congress.
10 Ford, *Works of Jefferson*, II, 182, note; also Hening, X, 66.
11 Sparks, *Works of Franklin*, VIII, 366, note. John Paradise and William Jones to Franklin, June 1, 1779; and John Paradise and William Jones to Franklin, June 5, 1779; also University of Pennsylvania MSS, Count de Vergennes to Franklin, June 1, 1779.
12 See note 3, *supra*.
13 *Journal of House of Delegates of Virginia*, 25.
14 Southall Papers, Library of the College of William and Mary, MS transcripts from the York, James City, and Surry County records (originals destroyed) concerning escheats of the various parcels of the Paradises' property.
15 *Journal of House of Delegates of Virginia*, November 16, 1779.
16 MS letter in the possession of Franklin Bache, Esq. William Jones to Franklin, November 15, 1782.
17 Johnstone, I, 476-477.
18 Franklin MSS, American Philosophical Society.
19 Sparks, *Works of Franklin*, VIII, 505. Franklin to the Rev. Richard Price, October 9, 1780.
20 Franklin MSS, Library of Congress. Franklin to Thomas Jefferson, May 6, 1781.
21 MS letter in the possession of Franklin Bache, Esq. William Jones to Franklin, September 17, 1781.
22 W. C. Ford, *Letters of William Lee*, III, 891. William Lee to Arthur Lee, November 20, 1782.
23 Lee MSS, Virginia Historical Society. William Lee to John Paradise, March 8, 1780.
24 MS letter in the possession of Franklin Bache, Esq. William Jones to Franklin, March 5, 1782.
25 Fitzwilliam and Bourke, *Correspondence of Burke*, II, 487-490. William Jones to Burke, May 7, 1782.

CHAPTER VIII
AN INTERNATIONAL ACCIDENT

1 Monaghan, *Diary of Jay, loc. cit.*
2 Bemiss, 191-192.
3 *Ibid.*, 193, note; also Dobrée, 154-155 and 169.
4 W. T. Franklin, *Memoir of Benjamin Franklin*, II, 127.
5 Bemiss, 190.
6 *Ibid.*, 194.
7 See note 1, *supra*.

8   Johnston, *Correspondence of Jay,*
    II, 316. Jay to the Count de
    Montmorin, June 26, 1782.

9   See note 1, *supra.*

10 Johnston, *Correspondence of Jay,*
    II, 319. Jay to Robert R. Liv-
    ingston, June 28, 1782.

11 *Public Advertizer* [London], June
    26, 1782.

12 Johnston, *Correspondence of Jay,*
    II, 367-370. Jay to Robert R.
    Livingston, November 17, 1782.

13 Franklin MSS, University of
    Pennsylvania. William Jones
    and John Paradise to Franklin,
    July 15, 1782.

14 Johnston, *Correspondence of Jay,*
    II, 370-371. Jay to Robert Liv-
    ingston, November 17, 1782.

15 Bemiss, 230-231.

16 *Ibid.,* Chap. XVI, "The Point of
    Independence," especially 226-
    227 and 230-231.

17 Hale and Hale, Jr., II, 328.

18 *Ibid.,* II, 214.

19 Fitzwilliam and Bourke, *Corres-*
    pondence of Burke, III, 4-6.
    William Jones to Burke, Octo-
    ber 8, 1782.

20 Lee MSS, Virginia Historical So-
    ciety. William Lee to Arthur
    Lee, August 6, 1777.

21 MS letter in the possession of
    Franklin Bache, Esq. William
    Jones to Franklin, August 5,
    1782.

22 See note 19, *supra.*

23 G. B. Hill, *Boswell's Life of*
    Johnson, II, 438.

24 See note 19, *supra.*

25 Jones's version of what transpired
    in Nantes is given in a number
    of his letters: 2 MS letters to
    Franklin, one on August 5, 1782
    and the other on November 15,
    1782 (both letters in the posses-
    sion of Franklin Bache, Esq.);
    to the Bishop of St. Asaph on
    September 13, 1782 (Teign-
    mouth, 218-220); to Baron

Eyre on October 2, 1782
(Teignmouth, 220-221); and to
Edmund Burke on October 8,
1782 (Fitzwilliam and Bourke,
Correspondence of Burke, III,
4-6).

26 Wallace, 395.

27 See note 21, *supra.*

28 See note 25, *supra.*

29 Teignmouth, 225-226. Georgiana,
    Duchess of Devonshire, to
    Jones, October 28, 1782.

30 *Historical Manuscripts Commis-*
    sion, Report XIV, Appendix IV,
    514-515. Sir William Jones to
    Lord Kenyon, Attorney General
    of England, January 27, 1783.

31 Fitzwilliam and Bourke, *Corres-*
    pondence of Burke, III, 30-32.
    Sir William Jones to Burke,
    April 13, 1784.

32 Lee, *Life of Arthur Lee,* II, 344.
    Sir William Jones to Arthur
    Lee, September 28, 1788.

CHAPTER IX
Levée Paradisiac

1   MS letter in the possession of
    Franklin Bache, Esq. Sir Will-
    iam Jones to Franklin, Novem-
    ber 15, 1782.

2   Franklin MSS, American Philo-
    sophical Society. The Rev.
    Richard Price to Franklin,
    April 6, 1784.

3   Smyth, *Writings of Franklin,* IX,
    256-257. Franklin to the Rev.
    Richard Price, August 16, 1784.

4   Jefferson MSS, Library of Con-
    gress. Edward Bancroft to
    Jefferson, November 18, 1785.

5   Shippen MSS, Library of Con-
    gress. Arthur Lee to Thomas
    Lee Shippen, January 30,
    [1787].

6   *Ibid.* Thomas Lee Shippen to
    William Shippen, February 2,
    1787.

7   See note 6, *supra.*

8 Roof, 151. Quoted from the *Journal and Correspondence of Miss* [Abigail] *Adams.*

9 *Ibid.*, 174. Quoted from the *Journal and Correspondence of Miss* [Abigail] *Adams.* William Smith to Abigail Adams Smith, June 10, 1787.

10 *Ibid.*, 150-151. Quoted from the *Journal and Correspondence of Miss* [Abigail] *Adams.*

11 Charles Francis Adams, *Letter of Mrs. Adams,* 312. Mrs. Adams to Mrs. Richard Cranch, January 20, 1787.

12 Burnaby, 197-213.

13 Charles Francis Adams, *Letters of Mrs. Adams,* 314-315. Mrs. Adams to Mrs. Richard Cranch, January 20, 1787.

CHAPTER X

EXCELLENCY MEETS MAJESTY

1 Charles Francis Adams, *Letters of Mrs. Adams,* 268. Mrs. Adams to John Quincy Adams, September 6, 1785.

2 *William and Mary Quarterly,* 2nd series, XI, 336. Jefferson to William Short, March 28, 1786.

3 *London Chronicle,* March 18-21, 1786.

4 Charles Francis Adams, *Works of John Adams,* I, 420; also Randall, I, 445, note 2.

5 Lipscomb and Bergh, *Writings of Jefferson,* I, 94-95.

6 Woolery, 70.

7 Lipscomb and Bergh, *Writings of Jefferson,* VIII, 73-76. Jefferson to Louis de Pinto, August 7, 1790; also *ibid.*, 132, same to same, February 21, 1791.

8 Roof, 129. Quoted from the *Journal and Correspondence of Miss* [Abigail] *Adams.* Miss Adams to John Quincy Adams, February 25, 1786.

9 Randolph, *Memoir of Jefferson,* I, 446. Jefferson to Rayneval, March 3, 1786.

10 *Collections of the Massachusetts Historical Society,* 7th series, I, 17-21. Jefferson to William Stephens Smith, July 9, 1786.

11 Ford, *Writings of Jefferson,* IV, 208-209. Jefferson to Anne Scott Randolph Jefferson, April 22, 1786.

12 Lipscomb and Bergh, *Writings of Jefferson,* V, 294-295. Jefferson to Charles Thomson, April 22, 1786.

13 Randolph, *Domestic Life of Jefferson,* 95-96. Jefferson to James Madison, January 30, 1787.

14 *William and Mary Quarterly,* 2nd series, XI, 336-337. Jefferson to William Short, March 28, 1786; also *ibid.*, same to same, April 3, 1786.

15 Charles Francis Adams, *Works of John Adams,* III, 394.

16 Washington, *Writings of Jefferson,* IX, 368, "A Tour to Some Gardens of England."

17 See note 16, *supra.*

18 Charles Francis Adams, *Works of John Adams,* III, 395, "Diary."

19 *Ibid.*, III, 397.

20 Ford, *Writings of Jefferson,* IV, 213. Jefferson to John Page, May 4, 1786.

21 Charles Francis Adams, *Works of John Adams,* III, 393, "Diary."

22 Jefferson MSS, Library of Congress. Lucy Paradise to Jefferson, May 5, 1786.

23 Charles Francis Adams, *Letters of Mrs. Adams,* 280-281. Mrs. Adams to Miss E. Cranch, April 2, 1786.

24 *London Chronicle,* April 1-4, 1786.

25 Charles Francis Adams, *Letters of Mrs. Adams,* 284. Mrs. Adams to Miss Lucy Cranch, April 2, 1786.

26 See note 21 *supra.*

27 Jefferson MSS, Library of Congress. Edward Bancroft to Jefferson, November 18, 1785.

28 *Ibid.* Edward Bancroft to Jefferson, February 13, 1786.

29 *Ibid.* Jefferson to James Madison, February 9, 1786.

30 Lipscomb and Bergh, *Writings of Jefferson,* XIX, 31-32. Jefferson to James Madison, April 25, 1786.

31 Jefferson's Account Book, *loc. cit.*

32 Jefferson MSS, Library of Congress.

33 *Ibid.*

CHAPTER XI

A HARPSICHORD FOR MONTICELLO

1 Jefferson MSS, Library of Congress.

2 *Ibid.*

3 Ford, *Writings of Jefferson,* IV, 444-445. Jefferson to George Wythe, September 16, 1787.

4 Jefferson MSS, Library of Congress.

5 Sonneck, 68. Jefferson to Francis Hopkinson, May 9, 1786.

6 See note 5, *supra.*

7 Jefferson MSS, Library of Congress.

8 *Ibid.*

9 *Ibid.*

10 Roof, 138-139. Jefferson to William Stephens Smith, December 20, 1786.

11 Jefferson MSS, Library of Congress.

12 *Ibid.*

13 Randolph, *Domestic Life of Jefferson,* 117. Martha Jefferson to Jefferson, April 9, 1787.

14 *Ibid.,* 121. Jefferson to Martha Jefferson, May 5, 1787.

15 *Ibid.,* 121. Jefferson to Martha Jefferson, May 27, 1787.

16 *Ibid.,* 123. Jefferson to Martha Jefferson, June 1, 1787.

17 Roof, 144-145. Jefferson to William Stephens Smith, August 31, 1787.

18 Lipscomb and Bergh, *Writings of Jefferson,* VII, 299. Jefferson to Francis Hopkinson, March 13, 1789.

19 Jefferson MSS, Library of Congress.

20 *Ibid.*

21 *Ibid.*

22 *Ibid.*

23 *Ibid.*

24 *Ibid.*

25 *Collections of the Massachusetts Historical Society,* 7th series, I, 21. William Stephens Smith to Jefferson, July 18, 1786.

26 Jefferson MSS, Library of Congress.

27 *Ibid.*

28 Lee MSS, Virginia Historical Society. William Lee to A. Donald, April 5, 1786; to the same, April 13, 1786; to John Paradise, May 6, 1786; to Capt. Wallace of the "George," May 6, 1786; and to Messrs. Donald and Burton, May 6, 1786.

29 Jefferson MSS, Library of Congress.

30 Ford, *Writings of Jefferson,* IV, 288.

CHAPTER XII

ELOPEMENT À LA MODE

1 Shippen MSS, Library of Congress. Thomas Lee Shippen to William Shippen, April 1, 1787.

2 See Chap. II, note 36.

3 Charles Francis Adams, *Letters of Mrs. Adams,* 325. Mrs. Adams to Mrs. Warren, May 14, 1787.

4 Shippen MSS, Library of Congress. Thomas Lee Shippen to William Shippen, October 30, 1786.

5 *Ibid.* Thomas Lee Shippen to William Shippen, March 2, 1789.

6 *Ibid.* Thomas Lee Shippen to Anne Shippen Livingston, February 26, 1787.

7 *Ibid.* Thomas Lee Shippen to William Shippen, October 30, 1786.

8 *Ibid.* Account Book of Thomas Lee Shippen.

9 *Ibid.* Thomas Lee Shippen to William Shippen, February 2, 1787.

10 *Ibid.* Thomas Lee Shippen to William Shippen, April 1, 1787.

11 *Ibid.* Diary of Thomas Lee Shippen.

12 See note 10, *supra.*

13 See note 10, *supra.*

14 Shippen MSS, Library of Congress. Diary of Thomas Lee Shippen.

15 See note 14, *supra.*

16 Hawkins, *Memoirs, Anecdotes, Facts and Opinions,* I, 73-74.

17 Jefferson MSS, Library of Congress.

18 *London Chronicle,* April 10-12, 1787.

19 Shippen MSS, Library of Congress. William Shippen to Thomas Lee Shippen, June 19, 1787.

20 *Ibid.* William Lee to Thomas Lee Shippen, May 28, 1787.

21 *Ibid.* Arthur Lee to Thomas Lee Shippen, January 2-6, 1787. This letter is printed in E. J. Lee's *Lee of Virginia,* 278.

22 *Ibid.* Arthur Lee to Thomas Lee Shippen, August 1, 1787. This letter is printed in E. J. Lee's *Lee of Virginia,* 283-284.

23 Jefferson MSS, Library of Congress.

CHAPTER XIII
A PASSAGE THROUGH AMERICA

1 Hawkins, *Memoirs, Anecdotes, Facts and Opinions,* I, 73-74.

2 *Gentleman's Magazine,* LVII, Part i, 1030, *sub* November 4, [1787]; also *London Evening Post,* November 3-6, 1787.

3 Jefferson MSS, Library of Congress. Lucy Paradise to Jefferson, November 22, 1787.

4 See note 3, *supra.*

5 Mereness, *Travels in the American Colonies;* also John Davis, *Travels in the United States;* also Wansey, *Journal of an Excursion to the U. S.*

6 Information supplied to the author in a letter from Mrs. John T. Daniel of Cape Charles, Va., a descendant of Viscount Philip Ignatius Barziza.

7 La Rochefoucauld Liancourt, II, 24.

8 *Ibid.,* II, 117.

9 Lee MSS, Virginia Historical Society. Ralph Izard to Mrs. Ralph Izard, October 30, 1781.

10 See note 3, *supra.*

11 Jefferson MSS, Library of Congress, John Page to Jefferson, March 7, 1788.

12 *William and Mary Quarterly,* 2nd series, V, 7. Article entitled "Charles Bellini, First Professor of Modern Languages in an American College." Charles Bellini to Jefferson, dated May 29, 1786, but this is evidently a mistake for 1788. Letter transcribed by N. G. Nardini.

13 *Ibid.,* 2nd series, V, 92. Article entitled "Letters of the Rev. James Madison, President of William and Mary College, to Thomas Jefferson." Madison to Jefferson, February 10, 1789.

14 Jefferson MSS, Library of Congress. Letter of Jefferson introducing Lucy Paradise, July 6, 1788.

15 See note 11, *supra.*

16 *Virginia Gazette,* May 13, 1773.

17 British Museum, Add. MSS 33978.

18 Short MSS, Library of Congress. William Nelson, Jr. to William Short, July 12, 1788.

19 *Ibid.* William Nelson, Jr. to William Short, March 20, 1789.

20 Orr, 41-43.

21 Lee MSS, Virginia Historical Society. William Lee to Col. Thomas Ludwell Lee, January 25, 1788.

22 Fitzpatrick, *Diaries of Washington, sub* [December] 30, [1787]; [December] 31, [1787]; [January] 1, [1788]; and [January] 2, [1788].

23 Short MSS, Library of Congress. William Short to Fulwar Skipwith, June 8, 1788.

24 Fitzpatrick, *Diaries of Washington, sub* [January] 2, [1788].

25 See note 21, *supra.*

26 Shippen MSS, Library of Congress. Thomas Lee Shippen to William Shippen, November 13, 1787.

27 See note 2, *supra.*

28 See note 18, *supra.*

29 *Correspondence of Miss* [Abigail] *Adams,* 75. Mrs. Abigail Adams Smith (née Abigail Adams) to Mrs. John Adams, May 20, 1788.

30 Shippen MSS, Library of Congress. Thomas Lee Shippen to William Shippen, March 2, 1789

31 *Ibid.* William Short to Thomas Lee Shippen, May 31, 1788.

32 Van Doren, 759.

33 Franklin MSS, American Philosophical Society. William Temple Franklin to Franklin, September 7, 1784.

34 *Ibid.* William Temple Franklin to Franklin, October 12, 1784.

35 Sparks, *Works of Franklin,* X, 321-322. The Rev. Richard Price to Franklin, September 26, 1787.

36 Van Doren, 770.

37 Franklin MSS, American Philosophical Society. John Ingenhousz to Franklin, August 9, 1788.

38 Smyth, *Writings of Franklin,* IX, 647. Franklin to Madame Helvetius, April 23, 1788.

39 *Ibid.,* IX, 503-504. Franklin to the Abbé de la Roche, April, 1786.

40 Franklin MSS, Library of Congress. William Nelson, Jr. to Franklin, July 20, 1789; also Franklin to William Nelson, Jr., August 3, 1789.

41 Shippen MSS, Library of Congress. William Shippen to Thomas Lee Shippen, March 2, 1788.

42 Griswold, 92.

43 Hunt, *Writings of Madison,* V, 120 and 123. Madison to Jefferson, April 22, 1788.

44 See note 43, *supra;* also Burnett, VIII, 731.

45 See Chap. XVII, note 31.

46 Griswold, 172.

47 Brock, *Proceedings of Virginia Historical Society.* New Series, XI. Article entitled "Orderly Book of Major William Heth of the 3rd Virginia Regiment."

48 Ford, *Writings of Jefferson,* V, 26. Jefferson to William Carmichael, June 3, 1788.

49 Griswold, 102, note 1.

50 See note 29, *supra.*

CHAPTER XIV

MR. JEFFERSON'S GREAT YOUNG MAN

1 Shippen MSS, Library of Congress. Thomas Lee Shippen to William Shippen, June 9, 1788.

2 *Phi Beta Kappa Key,* I, No. 7, 34.

3 Short MSS, Library of Congress. William Short to William Nelson, Jr., May 30, 1788.

4 See note 1, *supra.*

5 Short MSS, Library of Congress. William Short to Thomas Lee Shippen, May 31, 1788.

6 *Ibid.* William Short to Fulwar Skipwith, June 8, 1788.

7 *Ibid.* Fulwar Skipwith to William Short, June 14, 1788.

8 *Ibid.* William Short to Fulwar Skipwith, July 10, 1788.

9 *Ibid.* William Short to Thomas Lee Shippen, July 11, 1788.

10 Jefferson MSS, Library of Congress. Jefferson to John Paradise, July 16, 1788.

11 *Ibid.* Jefferson to John Paradise, July 17, 1788.

12 *Ibid.* Count Antonio Barziza to Jefferson, March 18, 1788. The letter from the Countess Barziza seems not to have survived.

13 Jefferson MSS, Massachusetts Historical Society. John Paradise to Jefferson. Letter undated but evidently written about June 30, 1788.

14 Jefferson MSS, Library of Congress. Jefferson to Count Barziza, July 8, 1788.

15 Lipscomb and Bergh, *Writings of Jefferson,* XIX, 45-46. Jefferson to the Countess Barziza, July 8, 1788.

16 Original in the possession of Miss Philippa Ludwell Barziza of Texas. A duplicate in Jefferson's handwriting exists among the Jefferson MSS, Library of Congress.

17 MS of Jefferson's Account Book, *sub* July 16, 1788.

18 Jefferson MSS, Library of Congress. Lucy Paradise to Jefferson, August 2, 1788.

19 *Ibid.* Jefferson to Edward Bancroft, August 24, 1788.

20 *Ibid.* Jefferson to Col. Nathaniel Burwell, September 6, 1788; also Paradise's Power of Attorney to Burwell, in Jefferson's hand.

21 *Ibid.* Lucy Paradise to Jefferson, August 17, 1788.

22 See note 21, *supra.*

23 See note 21, *supra.*

24 Jefferson MSS, Library of Congress. Five letters from Lucy Paradise to Jefferson on August 21, 1788; on September 11, 1788; on September 12, 1788; on September 13, 1788; and a letter undated but evidently written about September 18, 1788.

25 *Ibid.* Lucy Paradise to Jefferson, September 11, 1788.

26 *Ibid.* Lucy Paradise to Jefferson, September 13, 1788.

27 *Ibid.* Lucy Paradise to Jefferson, about September 18, 1788.

28 *Ibid.* William Short to Jefferson, September 24, 1788.

29 *Ibid.* William Short to Jefferson, October 2, 1788.

30 See note 29, *supra.*

31 See note 29, *supra.*

32 Lipscomb and Bergh, *Writings of Jefferson,* VII, 235. Jefferson to William Short, December 8, 1788.

33 See note 29, *supra.*

34 See note 33, *supra.*

35 Shippen MSS, Library of Congress. Thomas Lee Shippen's Diary, *sub* October 16, 1788.

36 *Ibid.* Thomas Lee Shippen to William Shippen, September 25, 1788.

37 *Ibid.* Thomas Lee Shippen's Diary *sub* October 21, 1788.

38 Jefferson MSS, Library of Congress. William Short to Jefferson, October 28, 1788.

39 *North American Review*, CCXXIII, 471-486. Article entitled "William Short: Jefferson's Only 'Son,'" by Marie Kimball.

40 Jefferson MSS, Library of Congress. John Paradise to Jefferson, October 10, 1788.

41 *Ibid.* Lucy Paradise to Jefferson, November 10, 1788.

42 *William and Mary Quarterly*, 2nd series, XII, 145. Jefferson to William Short, November 21, 1788.

43 Jefferson MSS, Library of Congress. John Trumbull to Jefferson, November 18, 1788; also Grand & Co. to Jefferson, June 7, 1788.

44 *Ibid.* Jefferson to John Paradise, November 22, 1788.

45 *Ibid.* Jefferson to the Countess Barziza, December 24, 1788.

46 *Ibid.* William Short to Jefferson, November 29, 1788.

CHAPTER XV

PUBLIC ENEMY AND PRIVATE FRIEND

1 Charles Francis Adams, *Letters of Mrs. Adams,* 207-208. Mrs. Adams to Miss Elizabeth Cranch, December 2, 1784.

2 *Dictionary of American Biography* and *Dictionary of National Biography,* sub Edward Bancroft.

3 Van Doren, 580 ff.

4 Stevens, *Facsimiles of Manuscripts in European Archives Relating to America,* No. 235.

5 *American Historical Review,* XXIX, 494. Article by Samuel Flagg Bemiss, "British Secret Service and the French-American Alliance," quoting Edward Bancroft's Memorial to the Marquis of Carmarthen, September 17, 1784.

6 *Dictionary of American Biography,* sub Edward Bancroft.

7 See note 4, *supra.*

8 *American Historical Review,* XXIX, 492-495. Article by S. F. Bemiss entitled, "British Secret Service and the French-American Alliance."

9 Shippen MSS, Library of Congress. Arthur Lee to Thomas Lee Shippen, July 30, 1787. (Date within letter; letter not dated at heading.)

10 Jefferson MSS, Library of Congress. Edward Bancroft to Jefferson, March 10, 1789.

11 Wharton, I, 641.

12 Jefferson MSS, Library of Congress. Jefferson to Edward Bancroft, August 24, 1788.

13 Ford, *Writings of Jefferson,* V, 66. Jefferson to Edward Bancroft, January 29, 178[9] (misdated 1788).

14 Jefferson MSS, Library of Congress. Jefferson to the Countess Barziza, December 24, 1788.

15 *Ibid.* Count Antonio Barziza to Jefferson, January 11, 1789.

16 *Ibid.* Lucy Paradise to Jefferson, January 4, 1789.

17 *Ibid.* Lucy Paradise to Jefferson, January 29, 1789; same to same, January 15, 1789; and same to same, January 18, 1789.

18 See note 17, *supra.*

19 *William and Mary Quarterly,* 2nd series, XII, 148. Jefferson to William Short, January 22, 1789.

20 Jefferson MSS, Library of Congress. William Short to Jefferson, February 11, 1789.

21 *William and Mary Quarterly,* 2nd series, XII, 150. Jefferson to William Short, February 9, 1789.

22 Jefferson MSS, Library of Congress. Edward Bancroft to Jefferson, February 20, 1789.

23 *Ibid.* Lucy Paradise to Jefferson, February 27, 1789.

24 *Ibid.* Jefferson to Edward Bancroft, March 1, 1789.

25 *Ibid.* Lucy Paradise to Jefferson, May 15, 1789.

26 Shippen MSS, Library of Congress. Thomas Lee Shippen to William Shippen, March 2, 1789.

27 See note 10, *supra.*

28 Jefferson MSS, Library of Congress. Jefferson to Edward Bancroft, March 15, 1789.

29 *Ibid.* Lucy Paradise to Jefferson, March 31, 1789. Mrs. Paradise's mention of £26,300 is either a mistake or a gross exaggeration. It is possible she meant to write £2,630.

30 *Ibid.* Edward Bancroft to Jefferson, March 27, 1789.

31 *Ibid.* Jefferson to Edward Bancroft, March 30, 1789.

32 *Ibid.* Jefferson to Edward Bancroft, April 9, 1789.

33 *Ibid.* Edward Bancroft to Jefferson, April 17, 1789.

34 *Ibid.* Jefferson to Edward Bancroft, April 24, 178[9]. (Misdated 1787.)

35 *Ibid.* Edward Bancroft to Jefferson, April 23, 1789.

36 *Ibid.* Lucy Paradise to Jefferson, April 14, 1789.

37 *Ibid.* Lucy Paradise to Jefferson, May 5, 1789.

38 *Ibid.* Lucy Paradise to Jefferson, June 2, 1789.

39 See note 37, *supra.*

40 Jefferson MSS, Library of Congress. Seven letters from Lucy Paradise to Jefferson on April 14, 1789; on May 5, 1789; on May 15, 1789; on May 26, 1789; on June 2, 1789; on June 30, 1789; and on July 18, 1789.

41 See note 37, *supra.*

42 Jefferson MSS, Library of Congress. Lucy Paradise to Jefferson, June 30, 1789.

43 *Ibid.* Jefferson to Edward Bancroft, June 15, 1789.

44 *Ibid.* Edward Bancroft to Jefferson, June 19, 1789.

45 Morris, I, 127-128.

46 Jefferson MSS, Library of Congress. John Paradise, Samuel Blackden, Joel Barlow, James Swan, Philip Mazzei, E. Haskell, Thomas Appleton, Benjamin Jarvis to Jefferson, July 4, 1789.

47 *Ibid.* John Paradise to William Wilkinson, July 11, 1789.

48 Randolph, *Memoir of Jefferson,* II, 496. Jefferson to Thomas Paine, July 11, 1789.

49 Jefferson MSS, Library of Congress. Jefferson to Edward Bancroft, July 12, 1789.

50 *Ibid.* Jefferson to Lucy Paradise, July 13, 1789.

51 *Ibid.* Lucy Paradise to Jefferson, July 18, 1789.

52 *Ibid.* Jefferson to Edward Bancroft, August 5, 1789.

53 *Ibid.* Lucy Paradise to Jefferson, August 18, 1789.

54 *Ibid.* Edward Bancroft to Jefferson, August 21, 1789.

55 *Ibid.* Jefferson to Lucy Paradise, September 10, 1789.

56 *Ibid.* John Paradise to Jefferson, September 16, 1789.

57 *Ibid.* Jefferson to John Paradise, September 25, 1789.

58 *Ibid.* Jefferson to Edward Bancroft, September 25, 1789.

59 Jefferson MSS, Massachusetts Historical Society. Jefferson to John Paradise, January 6, 1790.

60 Jefferson MSS, Library of Congress. Lucy Paradise to Jefferson, February 2, 1790.

61 *Ibid.* Lucy Paradise to Jefferson, March 2, 1790.

CHAPTER XVI

JOHN PARADISE—LOST

1 Boswell, *Private Papers,* XVIII, 86.

2 *Ibid.,* XVI, 200.

3 *Ibid.,* XVIII, 46.

4 MS letter, undated, from Paradise to Dr. Warren, lent by the late Burton Paradise.

5 G. B. Hill, *Boswell's Life of Johnson,* I, 64.

6 Boswell, *Hypochondriak,* I, 144-146.

7 Boswell, *Private Papers,* XVIII, 101.

8 *Ibid.,* X, 228.

9 *Ibid.,* X, 277. Sir John Pringle to Boswell, October 17, 1775.

10 Dampier-Smith, 245. Quoted from *Boswelliana* by the Rev. Charles Rogers.

11 Tinker, *Letters of Boswell,* I, 239. Boswell to the Rev. William Temple, August 12, 1775.

12 Fitzwilliam and Bourke, *Correspondence of Burke,* II, 209. James Boswell to Burke, March 3, 1778.

13 Boswell, *Private Papers,* XVI, 111.

14 Jefferson MSS, Library of Congress. Five letters from Lucy Paradise to Jefferson, on March 1, 1790; on March 2, 1790; on March 5, 1790; on March 20, 1790; and on March 24, 1790.

15 *Ibid.* Lucy Paradise to Jefferson, February 2, 1790.

16 Washington MSS, Library of Congress. Lucy Paradise to Washington, May 12, 1789.

17 *Ibid.* Washington to Lucy Paradise, November 23, 1789.

18 See note 15, *supra.*

19 Jefferson MSS, Library of Congress. Lucy Paradise to Jefferson, March 2, 1790.

20 *Ibid.* Jefferson to Lucy Paradise, June 23, 1790.

21 *Ibid.* Lucy Paradise to Jefferson, July 20, 1790.

22 Charles Francis Adams, *Letters of Mrs. Adams,* 353-354. Mrs. Adams to Mrs. [A. A.] Smith, January 25, 1791.

23 Griswold, 331-332.

24 Jefferson MSS, Library of Congress. Lucy Paradise to Jefferson, September 26, 1790.

25 Sparks, *Correspondence of the American Revolution,* IV, 342-343. John Paradise to George Washington. Letter not dated but marked received by Washington in June, 1790. It is impossible to say which of the five odes written by Alfieri on the subject of American freedom is referred to here.

26 Jefferson MSS, Massachusetts Historical Society. John Paradise to Jefferson, April 2, 1790.

27 Jefferson MSS, Library of Congress. Jefferson to John Paradise, August 26, 1791.

28 Boswell, *Private Papers,* XVIII, 176, 179, 228 and 248.

29 *Ibid.,* XVIII, 243.

30 Baring, *Diary of Windham,* 233.

31 See note 30, *supra.*

32 Baring, *Diary of Windham,* 313.

33 Barker, I, 497-498.

34 Bickley, *Diaries of Lord Glenbervie,* I, 31, *sub* December 27 and December 30, 1794.

35 Jefferson MSS, Library of Congress. Papers enclosed in a letter from Lucy Paradise to Jefferson, May 29, 1790.

36 *Diary and Letters of Madame d'Arblay*, VI, 30-31. Dr. Charles Burney to Mme. d'Arblay, May 7, 1795.

37 *Ibid.*, VI, 33. Mme. d'Arblay to Dr. Charles Burney, May 13, 1795.

38 Armes, 189. Francis Lightfoot Lee to William Lee, April 30, 1795.

39 *Gentleman's Magazine*, LXV, Part ii, 1059, *sub* "Obituary of Remarkable Persons with Biographical Anecdotes," December 12, [1795].

EPILOGUE

THE PARADISE HOUSE IN WILLIAMSBURG

1 Jefferson MSS, Massachusetts Historical Society. Lucy Paradise to Jefferson, August 27, 1805.

2 This carriage is preserved in the coach house at "Chippokes," Surry County, Virginia, in the possession of Mr. and Mrs. Victor Stewart. It is unquestionably of late eighteenth century manufacture, and there seems to be no reason to doubt that it is the one which was brought to Virginia by Mrs. Paradise in 1805.

3 Ludwell MSS, Virginia Historical Society. "An Inventory of the Negroes and Household furniture belonging to L. L. Paradise at her House in the City of Williamsburg taken by the Subscribers January 23d 1812."

4 See note 1, *supra*.

5 Jefferson MSS, Massachusetts Historical Society. Jefferson to Lucy Paradise, September 19, 1805.

6 Hawkins, *Memoirs, Anecdotes, Facts and Opinions*, I, 72.

7 Prerogative Court of Canterbury, Harris, 213. Will of John Paradise.

8 Jefferson MSS, Massachusetts Historical Society. Lucy Paradise to Jefferson, January 31, 1801.

9 See note 7, *supra*.

10 Jefferson MSS, Massachusetts Historical Society. Lucy Paradise to Jefferson, August 27, 1805.

11 *Enciclopedia Universal Illustrada,* *sub* Voronzof, Conde Semen.

12 See note 7, *supra*.

13 Jefferson MSS, Massachusetts Historical Society. Lucy Paradise to Jefferson, January 31, 1801.

14 *Ibid.* Lucy Paradise to Jefferson, January 31, 1801; also same to same July 31, 1802; also *William and Mary Quarterly*, 2nd series, V, 149. [The Rev.] James Madison to Jefferson, November 1, 1800 [?].

15 *Virginia Magazine of History and Biography*, XXIII, 369. Lucy Paradise to Mrs. William Hodgson, July 31, 1802.

16 MS letter in the possession of Colonial Williamsburg, Inc. Lucy Paradise to Littleton Waller Tazewell, February 24, 1805.

17 See note 1, *supra*.

18 MS letter from Eliza B. Prentis to Joseph Prentis, Jr., June 28, 1807. Quoted with the kind permission of its owner, Robert H. Webb, Esq.

19 MS letter in the possession of Mrs. George Coleman from Mrs. L. [St. George] Tucker to Mrs. Frances Coalter, December 18, 1807. P. S. written by the Hon. St. George Tucker.

20 *Ibid.* Mrs. Frances Bland [Tucker] Coalter to the Hon. St. George Tucker, April 11, 1806.

21 Cary, Appendix II, 77.

22 Southall Papers, Folder 297, Library of the College of William and Mary. Copy of the paper appointing a lunacy commission for Lucy Paradise.

23 *Ibid.,* Folder 297; also *Barziza vs. Hopkins and Hodgson,* Randolph Reports, 23 Virginia, II, 276-293; also *McCandlish vs. Hopkins and Hodgson,* Call, VI, 208; also *College of William and Mary vs. Hodgson and Hopkins,* Munford, VI, 163.

24 *William and Mary Quarterly,* 2nd series, V, 29.

25 *The One Hundred and Fifty-Eighth Annual Report of the Eastern State Hospital of Virginia,* 31. Also passport and other papers of the Viscount Philip Ignatius Barziza in the possession of Miss Lucy Vaiden of Williamsburg, Va.

26 Information supplied to the author in a letter from Mrs. John T. Daniel, of Cape Charles, Va., a descendant of Viscount Philip Ignatius Barziza.

INDEX

Abdrahaman, minister from Tripoli, 198-99.
Adams, Abigail, *see* Smith, Abigail (Adams).
  Abigail, 95-96, 145, 189, 190-93, 195, 204, 205, 248, 249, 260, 351, 357, 379, 416-17.
  John, 119, 141, 160, 260, 290, 357, 379, 416.
    in England, 93, 95, 187, 189, 191, 196-206.
    in France, 351-52.
Adee, Dr. Swithin, 82.
Adhemar, Count d', 203.
Aiguebelle, 339.
Ailsbury, Lord, 71.
Alcaic ode to Liberty, 125.
Aldgate ward, 40.
Alexander I, 439.
Alexandria, 290, 292, 297.
Alfieri, Count, 93, 116, 421.
Allanby, Capt. John, 274.
Allen, Mr. and Mrs., 33.
Althorpe, Lord, 125, 177.
Alzano, 269, 339.
America, 2-5, 142, 155, 195, 236, 368, 369, 385, 390, 392, 393, 413.
  Englishman's ideas about, 171-73.
"America" (painting), 434.
America Square, 241.
American revolution, 7, 36, 40, 46, 58, 59, 79, 80, 85, 95, 96, 97, 98, 120, 125, 127, 130, 133, 228-29, 276, 277, 283, 434.
Amsterdam, 355.
Amusements, 51, 131, 202, 286-87.
Anderson, Mr., 319, 321, 323, 326, 343, 344, 349, 364, 366, 389, 411, 415, 420.
Andriani, Count, 93, 420-21, 422.
Angel Inn, 262, 263, 264.
"Answer to the resolutions and address of the American Congress," 3.
Antiquarianism, 27.
Appeal to the Public, 106.
Appleton, Thomas, 235, 384.

Arabic language, 89, 120, 131.
Arblay, Madame d', *see* Burney, Fanny.
Archer, Lady, 72.
Archer's Hope, 44, 276.
Architecture, styles of, 15, 201, 202.
Ariosto, 108.
Arnold, Benedict, 353.
"Artaxerxes", 71.
Articles of Confederation, 434.
Ashburnham, Lord, 71.
Askew, Dr. Anthony, 82.
Association, 53.
Athens, 82.
Auchinleck, 403.
Aubert, Mr., 92.
Austen, Jane, 70.
Auteuil, 144, 351, 357.
Auxerre, 329.
Aviaries, 299.
l'Aye, Mons. de, 327, 328, 330, 331, 332, 333.

Back-scratchers, 68.
Bacon, Francis, 39.
  Nathaniel, 7-8, 14.
Bacon's castle, 15.
Baker, William, 40.
Balloon ascensions, 128.
Balls, 275.
Bancroft, Edward, 184, 200, 204, 207-08, 241, 415.
  advances money, 184, 364, 384, 396, 411.
  aids Paradise, 207-08, 227-38, 256, 260, 271, 272, 273, 284, 325, 343-46, 357-59, 362-65, 367-78, 380-81, 384-85, 387-92, 419, 437-38.
  friendship for Paradise, 396-97.
  letters to Jefferson, 265-66, 380-81.
  sketch of, 351-57.
Bank of England, 345.
Bankruptcy Act, 447.
Banks, Sir Joseph, 65, 88, 89, 92, 93, 283-84, 395, 399.
  Lady and Miss, 284.

Barbary Powers, 199.
Barber, Francis, 114.
Baretti, Giuseppi, 63, 67, 75, 108.
Barlow, Joel, 381, 384.
Baron Munchausen, 92.
Barrington, Daines, 405.
Barry, James, 62, 109, 116.
Bartram, John, 30, 97.
Barziza, Count, 246, 251-72, 315, 317,
   325, 335, 339, 342, 343, 456.
   accompanies Paradise, 347-49.
   demands marriage settlement,
   359-60.
   marriage, 251-272.
   quarrels with Paradises, 439-40.
Cecile (Belette), 447-48, 456.
John, 440, 456.
Lucy (Paradise), 60, 77, 154, 191,
   232-34, 456.
   children of, 311, 417, 440, 446.
   death, 439-440.
   in Golden Book, 315, 428.
   Jefferson's statement about, 318-
   19, 428.
   marriage of, 245-272.
   marriage settlement, 359-361.
Philip Ignatius, 275-76, 440, 446,
   456.
   children of, 448, 456.
Barziza family, 268-69.
Basil, Miss, 71.
Bastile, 209, 386.
Bath, 190-94, 419.
Beal, Mr., 287.
Bearcroft, Mr., 105.
Beauclerk, Topham, 65, 107, 129.
Beaune, 329-330.
Beckley, John, 410.
Belette, Cecile, see Barziza, Cecile
   (Belette).
Belgium, 40, 154, 174, 310.
Belleview, 288, 454.
Bellini, Charles, 282, 306.
Benedictine monks, 329.
Bengal, 179.
Bengali, 173.
Bennet, Dr. William, 123, 124.
Bentinck street, 62.
Benton, 261.
Bergamo, 272, 315, 331, 335, 339, 342,
   345, 346, 348, 365, 371.

Berkeley, Sir William, 7, 13, 14, 453.
   Lady, 14, 453.
Bernard, Col. William, 453.
Bertoni, 72.
Bettsworth, Mr., 373.
Bingham, William, 351.
Birds, 145, 275, 299.
Birmingham, 105, 106.
Blackden, Samuel, 384.
Blagden, Sir Charles, 78, 94, 298, 388.
Blair, James, 8, 454.
   John, 17, 19, 454.
   Sarah (Harrison), 454.
Bland, Giles, 7.
Blankets, 49, 53.
Blenheim, 115, 201.
Bligh, Capt., 92-93.
Bloomsbury, 107.
Board of Ordnance, 85-86.
Bodleian, 264.
Bois de Boulogne, 144.
Bolt court, 118.
Boston, 145, 167, 186, 192.
Boswell, Euphemia, 425.
   James, 6, 62, 65, 94, 95, 100, 106-07,
   111, 116-17, 118, 248, 356, 449.
   death of, 430-31.
   friendship with Paradise, 403-07,
   424-25.
   quoted, 3, 82, 83, 103, 104-05,
   106, 107, 114.
   Veronica, 425.
Botetourt, Lord, statue of, 279.
Bougainville, Mons., 92.
Bowdoin, Gov. James, 168-69, 302.
   Mrs., 169.
Boylston, John, 192, 193.
Brandon, 454, 455.
Breteuil, Baron de, 386.
Bridgen, Mr., 191.
Bridgport, 39.
British Foreign Office, 353.
British Museum, 89, 366.
Broadway, 301, 302, 303.
Broadwood, Mr., 219.
Brocklesby, Dr., 114, 405.
Bronze (serving maid), 68.
Browne, Isaac Hawkins, 439.
   Isaac Hawkins, jr., 82.
Brudenell, Mr., 72.
Brussels, 153.

Bruton parish church, 10, 18, 443.

Bryant, Jacob, 115.

Bull, Miss, 70.

Burke, Edmund, 6, 62, 65, 122, 129, 155, 170, 177, 178-79, 404, 405.

Burney, Dr. Charles, 65, 70, 71, 73, 107-09, 114, 213, 216, 220-21, 235, 430.
    letters, to Jefferson, 222-24.
    to Paradise, 217-18.
    Charlotte Ann, 70, 71, 75, 430.
    Fanny, 65, 69-75, 108-11, 216, 430.
    characteristics, 73-74.
    Susanna, 70, 71, 75, 108-09.

Burr, Aaron, 455.

Burwell, Carter, 453, 454.
    Lewis, 453.
    Lucy (Grymes), 454.
    Nathaniel, 322-25, 379, 391, 394-96, 411-13, 423, 424, 439, 453, 454.
    Rebecca, 453.
    Susan (Grymes), 454.

Bushfield, 287.

Byron, Lord, 216.

Byrd, Lucy (Parke), 453.
    William, 453.

Caermarthen, Marquis de, 198, 355.

Cagliostro, Count, 209.

Calais, 197, 209, 363.

Canada, 160, 166.

Canton, John, 97.

Capes Henry and Charles, 24, 274.

Capitol, 4, 278.

Card playing, 204, 205, 260, 287.

Carleton, Sir Guy, 160, 161.

Carli, Signor, 304.

Carmichael, William, 304.

Carter Hall, 454.

Carter's creek, 454.

Carter's Grove, 454.

Cary, Moorey and Welch, 15.

Castiglioni, Count, 336, 337.

Castle, Mr. and Mrs., 70, 108.

Castle street, 62.

Cavallo, Mr., 200, 210.

Cavendish, Hon. Henry, 90, 92.

Cavendish square, 60-63, 79, 100-01, 266, 293, 363, 388, 426.

Caversham, 201.

Cecil street, 30, 35, 41.

Celestini stop, 213, 217, 219, 221-23, 226.

Cerberus (dog), 67.

Chálons, 329, 330.

Chamberlain, Mason, 30.

Chamberlayne, Major, 289.

Champs Elysées, 235.

Chantilly, 288, 291, 454.

Chapone, Mrs., 74.

Charles I, 13, 427.

Charles II, 7, 69, 84.

Charles street, 60, 63, 67, 79, 94, 100, 124, 181, 186, 187, 188, 189, 196, 203, 229, 236, 242, 247, 250, 251, 253, 256, 258, 259, 260, 266, 293, 426, 439.
    hospital, 63.

Charlotte, queen of England, 93.

Charlotte street, 27, 61, 256, 260, 266, 363, 381.

Chaumont, Mons. de, 139.

Chelsea, 61.

Cherson, Archbishop of, 284.

Chester, Bishop of, 28, 455.

Child, Mr., 202.

Chippokes, 10, 14, 44, 45, 51, 152, 276, 308, 323, 395, 453, 456.

Choto, Emperor of, 20.

Chrisna Nagar, 179.

Christ church, 28, 262, 263.

Churchill, of Corpus Christi, 28.

Clarges, Lady and Miss, 70.

Cleaver, William, 28.

Clerc de Sept Chenes, Mons. de, 403-04.

Cleves, Mr., 338.

Clinton, Gov., 306.

Clothing, 15, 92, 205, 444, 445-46.

Cloyne, Bishop of, 123.

Coaches, 43, 74, 371, 394, 433, 442, 446.

Coalter, Frances Bland (Tucker), 445.

Cockfighting, 202, 287.

Colchester, 103, 127.

Coleman, William, 440, 446.

College of Physicians, 352.

Collinson, Peter, 97.

"Commentaries on Asiatick Poetry," 132.

Commissioners to Paris, 168, 352-57.

Congress of U. S., 88, 96, 135, 141, 160, 187, 283, 301, 302, 353, 389, 390, 423, 441.
Constantinople, 82, 216.
Constitution of U. S., 291, 301-02, 308, 311, 377, 389, 390, 435.
Constitutional convention, 291, 301-02.
Consuls, British, 25, 26, 250.
Cook, Capt., 87, 89, 92, 93.
Copy-press, 200, 210-11.
Corbin, Frances, see Jenings, Frances (Corbin).
   Gawin II, 454.
   Hannah (Lee), 454.
   Henry, 455.
   John Tayloe, 455.
   Laetitia see Lee, Laetitia (Corbin).
   Mary (Waller), 455.
   Richard, 34, 39, 41, 54, 455.
Corn, 15, 17, 50, 61, 394.
Cornwallis, Lord, 136, 280.
Corpus Christi, 28.
Corregio, 250-51.
Corsica, 248, 356.
Cosway, Maria, 190, 378-79, 413, 449.
   Richard, 190.
Cottington, James, 453.
   Jane see Ludwell, Jane (Cottington).
Cotton, 16, 26, 51.
Courtenay, John, 122.
Covent Garden, 116.
Cowes, 393.
Coxe, Rev. William, 71.
Cranch, Mrs., 191.
Crane court, 83.
Craven street, 30.
Crewe, Mrs., 70.
Crofts, Mr., 262.
Crowe, Mr., 262.
Crown and Anchor tavern, 89.
Culpeper, Frances see Ludwell, Frances (Culpeper) Berkeley.
Cumberland, Mr., 430.
Cushing, Mrs. William, 417.
Custis, Daniel Parke, 453.
Cutting, John Brown, 186, 260, 308, 380.

Deane, Silas, 141, 352-57, 368, 372.

Declaration of Independence, 3, 197, 218, 281, 288.
Den, Mrs., 78.
Deneufville, J. A., 446.
Deserted Village, 171-72.
Devonshire, Duchess of, 65, 70, 178.
Dew, experiments in, 283.
Dairies, 338.
Dal Verme, Count, 337.
Dampier, William, 35.
Dances, 48, 75, 204, 286.
"Dialogue of the Heart and the Head", 190, 378.
Digby, Admiral, 160.
Diggs, Edward, 51.
Dijon, 329.
Dilly, Mr., 101, 248.
Dinwiddie, Governor, 20-21.
"A Discourse on the late Fast, by Phileleutherus Norfolciensis", 124-25.
Distemper, 338.
Doctors Commons, 428.
Doctor's Riot, 304-06, 311.
Dodsley, Richard, 125.
Domenick, Capt., 410.
Donald and Burton, 240, 267.
Dorset, Duke of, 70.
Dover, 149, 157, 209.
Drake, Sir Frances, 26.
Drury Lane, 116.
Dryden, 40.
"The Duenna", 304.
Duer, President, 306.
Duke of Gloucester street, 4, 10, 442.
Dunbar, Dr., 108.
Dunmore, Lord, 132, 377-78, 412.
Dutch Guiana, 351, 352.
Dyer, George, 123.

East India company, 26, 108.
Eastern State Hospital, 446, 447.
Eccles, Miss, 304.
Eddington Hill, 262, 263.
Edgecumbe, Lady, 70.
Edgehill, 200-01.
Edinburgh, 248, 403, 404.
Edwards, B.. pseud. of Dr. Bancroft, 353.
Elector Palatine, 91.
Electricity, 83, 90, 142, 173.

Eliot, Lord, 400.
Elizabeth, queen of England, 26.
Ellis, Mr., 134.
England, 2, 5, 17, 23, 24, 26, 27, 142, 152, 155, 156, 177, 178, 188, 192, 193, 275, 294, 366, 368, 390.
Englefield, Sir Henry, 92.
English, 290.
English language, 25, 81, 120, 124, 155, 361, 428, 432.
Escheats and forfeitures, bill of, 146, 147.
An Essay on the Natural History of Guiana, 352.
Essex, 29.
Essex Head Club, 116, 117, 405, 406.
Essex street, 117.
Estates General, 385.
Eton, 426.
Evelina, 69, 72, 73, 110.
Eyre, Baron, 177.

Facsimiles of Manuscripts in European Archives, 353.
Fairfax, Lord, 192.
    George William, 192.
Falmouth, 294.
Faro, 204.
Farquhar, Mr., 294.
Faujas de Saint-Fond, 90-91.
Fauntleroy, Mr., 58.
Fauquier, Gov., 207.
The Federalist, 302.
"Fellow Remarkably Stupid", 115.
Ferries, 289, 297.
Fersen, Count, 92.
Festino Rooms, 248-49.
Fettercairn castle, 118.
Fielding, Henry, 66.
Fitzherbert, Mrs., 204.
Fitzroy square, 441.
Flags, British, 187.
Flax, 16, 51.
Fleet street, 83, 118.
Foley place, 62.
Fontainebleau, 328.
Fontana, Abbé, 83.
Foodstuffs, 15, 17, 53, 68, 89, 91, 204, 262, 287, 332, 338, 425.
Foote, Samuel, 128.

Fossard, 329.
Fothergill, Dr. John, 29, 97, 193.
Fourth of July, 312, 443.
Fragment of Polybius, 143-44, 159.
France, 130, 142, 158-61, 275, 295, 327, 336, 387, 390.
Francis street, 105.
Frankfurt-on-the-Main, 135.
Franklin, Miss, 379.
    Benjamin, 2, 3, 4, 5, 83, 90, 94, 193.
       aids Paradise, 30-31, 113, 138-55, 160-62, 165-66, 181-82, 299, 300.
       illness, 297-99.
       letters, to Gov. Bowdoin, 168-69.
         to Jefferson, 168.
       lightning conductors, 30, 84-88, 142, 172-73.
       member of Honest Whigs, 96-98, 120.
       of Royal Society, 83.
       opinion of Paradise, 182, 168-69, 307.
       portrait, 30.
       turns against Paradise, 176-77, 182.
       visited by Paradise, 87-88, 139-47, 149-51, 157-67, 179-80, 297-300.
    William Temple, 94, 139, 298.
Fraunces Tavern, 303.
Frederick the Great, 209.
Fredericksburg, 288, 297.
French, 21, 25, 26, 140, 162, 188, 224, 290.
French embassy, 204.
French language, 25, 81, 120, 124, 199, 432.
French revolution, 96, 98, 105, 169, 439.
Freire, Chavalier de, 75-78, 290, 366, 377, 410-11, 416-17.
    Madame, 417.
Furniture, 15, 128, 433, 442.
Fuseli, Henry, 69.

Gaelic dictionary, 115.
Gardens, 14, 17, 29-30, 201, 202, 299, 338.
Garrick, David, 65, 107, 122, 128.
Geer, Baron de, 351.

Geneva, 334, 335, 340, 386.
Genoa, 336.
Gentleman's Magazine, 105, 293, 431.
George II, 32, 33.
George III, 86, 87, 94, 98, 127, 142,
    158, 197-98, 216, 354, 378, 387.
Georgia, 171-72.
Germany, 40, 310, 315, 316.
Gibbon, Edward, 62, 65, 122.
Gibralter, 166.
Gideon, Lady, 71, 74.
Gist, Mr., 241, 242, 243.
Glenbervie, Lord, 428.
Golden Book of Venice, 269, 315, 318,
    428.
Goldsmith, Oliver, 65, 171-72.
Gooseley, Capt., 49, 52, 53.
Gosset, Rev., 403.
Governor's land, 54.
Governor's Palace, 278.
Grand, Mr., 313-14, 341, 355.
Grant, Mrs., 403.
Grapes, 330.
Gravesend, 15-16.
Great Portland street, 62.
Great Russell street, 107.
Great Titchfield street, 67, 426, 431.
Greaves, Samuel, 117.
Greece, 25, 26, 148, 189, 216, 224,
    333, 427.
Greek language, 25, 81, 120, 124, 128,
    129, 155, 178, 212, 215, 233,
    427, 428, 432.
Greek Orthodox Church, 438.
Green Spring, 6, 10, 17-18, 22, 42,
    44, 45, 49, 51, 53, 56, 58, 64,
    134, 247, 276, 280, 285, 286,
    288, 293, 431, 440, 448, 453,
    454, 455, 456.
    battle at, 136, 153, 280.
    description, 13-18.
    jail at, 14.
    Paradise visits, 276-86, 296-97.
Greenwich, 209.
Greenwich Observatory, 90.
Griffin, Cyrus, 302.
Grosvenor Square, 189, 202, 260.
Grymes, Alice, *see* Page, Alice
    (Grymes).
    Col. Charles, 19, 455.

Frances, *see* Ludwell, Frances
    (Grymes).
Frances (Jenings), 455.
John II, 454, 455.
Lucy, *see* Burwell, Lucy (Grymes).
Lucy, *see* Lee, Lucy (Grymes).
Lucy (Ludwell), 18, 454.
Mary, *see* Nelson, Mary (Grymes).
Philip, 318, 454.
Philip, 318-19.
Susannah, *see* Burwell, Susan
    (Grymes).
Guilford, Earl of, 427-28, 439.
Guinea coast, 169.
Gunpowder, 130.

Hackney, 95.
Hagley, 201.
Hague, 309.
Hales, Lady, 70.
Ham House, 29.
Hamilton, Lady, 62.
Hamilton, 94.
Hampstead, 63, 124.
Hampstead Heath, 60.
Hampton, 392.
Hampton Court, 202.
Hampton Roads, 24, 274, 407, 433.
Hanover Square, 248.
Harcourt, Earl of, 205.
Harley, Lord, 60.
Harley street, 61.
Harmonica, 225.
Harness, 15, 199.
Harpsichords, 212-13, 217-26, 233, 304.
Harris, Mr.,.71.
    W. L., 446.
Harrison, General, 245.
    Benjamin II, 454.
    Hannah, *see* Ludwell, Hannah
        (Harrison).
    Sarah, *see* Blair, Sarah (Harrison).
Harrow, 123, 124, 127.
Haskell, 382, 384.
Hastings, Warren, 178-79.
Hatsell, Mrs., 74.
Hatton, 127.
Hãvre, 390.
Hawke, Lord and Lady, 72, 366, 434.

Hawkins, Sir John, 68, 116, 117, 264, 273.
    Laetitia Matilda, 66, 74, 110, 117, 266-67, 437.
Hayes, Mrs., 71.
Haymarket, 70.
Heberden, Dr., 116.
Hebrides, 171, 248.
Helvetius, Madame, 144-45, 299.
Henley, 261.
Henry, Mrs., 304.
    Patrick, 134-35.
Henson, Mr., 53.
Higgins, Dr., 107.
Higginson, Lucy, see Ludwell, Lucy (Higginson) Burwell Bernard.
    Capt. Robert, 453.
High Wycombe, 201.
Highgate hills, 63.
History of Charles Wentworth, 351, 352.
Hodgson, Portia (Lee), 440-41, 447, 455.
    William, 98, 440-41, 455.
Hoes, 48-49, 54.
Holland, 160, 174, 310, 315, 316.
Home, Dr., 29.
    Anne, see Pringle, Anne (Home).
"Honest Whigs", 96-97, 120, 142.
Hoole, John, 108, 430.
Hopkins, Cornelia (Lee), 154, 440-41, 447, 455.
    John, 440, 455.
Hopkinson, Francis, 218-19, 226.
Horses and horse-racing, 16, 17, 18, 202, 287, 288.
Horsley, Bishop, 103, 427, 439.
Hose, 53.
Hotel d'Angleterre, 360, 361.
Hotel d'Artois, 332.
Hotel de Dannemore, 150, 151.
Hotel de Valentinoir, 139.
Hotel du Port Mahon, 138, 143.
Houris, of Williamsburg, 276, 447.
House of Commons, 158, 413.
House of Lords, 413, 427.
Howard of Effingham, Francis, 8.
Howland street, 441.
Humphreys, David, 93, 187-88, 292, 351.

Hungary, 82.
Hunter, Sir John, 29.
Hunting, 51, 286-87.
Hypochondria, 5, 399-403.
"The Hypochondriack", 399.

Ibbetson, Barlow & Co., 367.
Implements, agricultural, 15, 44, 57.
Inchbald, Mrs., 95.
Indemnities, 183-84.
India, 170-71, 173, 178-79, 377-78, 430.
Indians, 20, 21, 289.
Indigo, 15.
"Inflammable air", 142.
Influenza, 343, 346.
Ingenhousz, Dr., 86, 299, 312.
Inner Temple, 186, 247, 250, 253, 366.
Inns of Court, 29.
Italian language, 25, 81, 108, 120, 188, 199, 212, 343, 428, 432.
Italy, 25, 37, 82, 271, 275, 311, 320-21, 325-28, 334-44, 346-50, 358, 439.

Jackson, of Christ Church, 28.
James City county, 135, 147-48, 440.
James river, 14, 24, 42, 276.
Jamestown, 14.
Jarvis, Benjamin, 384.
Jay, John, 119, 160-67, 181, 305-06, 426.
    Sarah (L), 302.
Jefferson, Misses, 343, 376, 379, 388, 391, 410, 414, 419-20, 422, 436.
    Martha, see Randolph, Martha (Jefferson).
    Nancy, see Marks, Nancy (Jefferson).
    Thomas, 2, 3, 4, 5, 17, 90, 94, 119, 133, 145-46, 152, 160, 168, 173, 184, 186-87, 195-244, 265, 271, 273, 280, 283, 285, 290-92, 302, 308-50, 351, 352, 356, 357, 358-65, 367-96, 407-424, 428, 429, 433, 435, 439, 440, 441, 453.
    at ball, 203-06.
    books of, 199, 378.
    borrows umbrella, 311.
    buys furniture in England, 199-200.

Jefferson, Thomas (Continued)
  friendship with Paradise, 206-211.
  letters, to Bancroft, 322-24, 358-
    59, 365, 367-68, 370-74, 380,
    385, 388-89, 393.
    to Count Barziza, 315-16.
    to Countess Barziza, 316-17.
    to Burney, 219-20, 224-25.
    to Carmichael, 304-05.
    to John Paradise, 209-10, 212-
      14, 235, 238-39, 313-14, 345-
      46, 392, 394-96, 423-24.
    to Lucy Paradise, 230-31, 234-
      35, 242-43, 386, 390-91, 415-
      16, 436.
    to George Wythe, 215.
  Lucy Paradise's affection for, 312,
    362, 377, 378-79, 449.
  opinion of Paradise, 215, 319.
  orders harpsichord, 212-13, 217-
    26, 233.
  portrait, 434.
  presented to King George III,
    196-98.
  statement about Countess Barziza,
    318-19, 428.
  testimonial to, 382-84.
  visits London, 196-209.
  visits Paris, 209-254.
Jeffreys, Governor, 8.
Jenings, Edmund, 455.
  Elizabeth, 455.
  Frances, see Grymes, Frances (Jen-
    ings).
  Frances (Corbin), 455.
Jewelry, 205, 434.
Jodrell, Sir Paul, 112, 115, 293, 294,
  406.
  Richard Paul, 115, 256.
Johnson, Samuel, 2, 3-4, 5, 29, 65, 66,
  67, 71, 73, 79, 82, 94, 100-119,
  122, 127, 129, 130, 151, 171,
  216, 248, 356, 366, 398, 399,
  404, 405, 433, 449.
  comments on Lucy Paradise, 110-
    11, 112.
  death, 95, 117-18.
  Dictionary, 119.
  illness, 113-14, 118, 401.
  letter to Paradise, 118.
  momentoes, 118-19.

Johnson, Samuel (Continued)
  visits camp, 130-31.
Johnstone, Dr. John, 105, 122.
Jones, Anna Maria (Shipley), 173-74,
  178.
  Emmanuel, jr., 31.
  John Paul, 169, 351, 352, 357, 368.
  Sir William, 65, 89, 107, 120-179,
    293, 449.
    death, 178, 430.
    Franklin's recommendation of,
      168-69.
    Jay's opinion of, 161-67.
    letters, to Lee, 179.
      to Parr, 124-26, 149-50.
    poetry of, 126-27.
    scholarship of, 120-27.
    visits France with Paradise, 139-
      47, 149-51, 157-78.
"Junius Americanus", 101.

Kensington, 61.
Keppel, Lord, 156.
Kew, 202.
King's Bench prison, 374, 375.
King's Commissioners, 14.
Kippis, Dr. Andrew, 88.
Kirkman, 212-13, 217, 219, 220, 221,
  222.
Kirwans, Mrs., and Miss, 71, 75, 76.
Knight, Mr., 284.
Knightsbridge, 61.
Knox, Gen. Henry, 303-04, 379, 426.
  Mrs. Henry, 303-04, 379.

Lafayette, 136, 141, 165, 200, 310,
  312, 314, 357.
Lake Como, 337.
Lambs Building, 125.
Lamps, 200.
Laneville, 41, 455.
Langborn, Major, 392.
Langton, Bennet, 89, 100, 102-03, 107,
  114, 117, 124-25, 128, 131, 149,
  264, 273, 403, 405, 406, 425,
  439, 449.
Langton, 129.
Languages, 81, 115, 120-21, 124, 131,
  132, 155, 432.
Lansdown, 454.
Lansdowne, Marquis of, 205.

La Rochefoucauld-Liancourt, Duc and
    Duchess, 279, 340-41.
Latitudinarians, 104.
Laurens, Henry, 160, 176.
Leasowes, 201.
Le Couteulx, 355.
Ledlier, Mr., 392.
Lee, Alice, *see* Shippen, Alice (Lee).
    Arthur, 11, 28, 29, 39-41, 83, 101,
        137, 141, 153, 170, 179, 186,
        247, 267-68, 302, 355, 404, 454.
    Charles, 290, 292.
    Cornelia, *see* Hopkins, Cornelia
        (Hopkins).
    Francis Lightfoot, 43, 48, 55, 135,
        288 291, 431, 454.
    Hannah, *see* Corbin, Hannah (Lee).
    Hannah Philippa (Ludwell), 11,
        18, 19, 23, 24, 34-36, 41, 44-45,
        55, 136, 454, 455.
    Henry, 22-23, 134, 288, 455.
    Henry (Lighthorse Harry), 288,
        455.
    Laetitia (Corbin), 455.
    Lucinda, 288.
    Lucy (Grymes), 22-23, 455.
    Philip Ludwell, 11, 28, 48, 288,
        454.
    Portia, *see* Hodgson, Portia (Lee).
    Richard, 135, 288, 455.
    Richard Henry, 41, 43-48, 55, 58,
        134-35, 200, 288, 291, 302, 454.
    Robert E., 455.
    Thomas, 23, 28, 454, 455.
    Thomas Ludwell, 288, 454.
    William, 7, 28-29, 80, 101, 141,
        153, 154, 170, 247, 267-68, 288,
        291, 394, 404, 434, 440, 447,
        454, 455.
    alderman, 40, 58, 455.
    characteristics, 36-40, 56.
    death, 431.
    entertains Paradise at Green
        Spring, 276, 280, 285, 292.
    letters to Wilkinson, 48-53.
    manages wife's estate, 36-59, 134-
        36, 295-96.
    marriage, 11, 35, 36, 41-42.
    quarrels, with R. C. Nicholas,
        54-55.

Lee, William (Continued)
    with Paradise, 43-44, 239-40,
        267-68, 295-97, 366, 379.
    with Wilkinson, 47-59.
    wife owns "Paradise house", 4-5,
        42-45, 48, 135-36, 286, 442.
    William Ludwell, 247, 280, 440,
        441, 455.
Lee Hall, 288, 455.
Leeds, Duke of, 428.
Leesylvania, 288, 455.
Leghorn, 250.
Lennox, Charlotte, 67.
Le Picq, Mr., 75.
Lettsom, Dr., 283.
Levant, 25, 27, 269.
Levant company, 25-26, 27, 133, 428.
Lewknor, 115.
Libro d'Oro, *see* Golden Book of
    Venice.
Lichfield, 69, 113, 118.
Life of Johnson, Boswell, 62, 107
    Hawkins, 116.
Ligarius, 165.
Lightning conductors, 30, 84-87, 142,
    172-73.
Lincolnshire, 129, 130.
Linnaeus, 97.
Liquors, 15, 49, 62, 90, 92.
Lisbon, 66.
Literary Club, 216.
Littlepage, 300.
Lives of the Poets, 95.
Livestock, 16, 17-18, 44, 49, 51, 52.
Livingston, Robert R., 161.
Loan office, 412.
Locke, Mr. and Mrs., 70.
Lodvill, Philip, 12-13, 25, 26-27, 456.
Lombardy, 338.
London, Bishop of, 455.
London, Earl of, 21.
London, 21-23, 27-33, 39-40, 60-138,
    147-150, 181-90, 195-209, 245-
    72, 385-432.
London Chronicle, 11, 205.
London Coffee House, 96, 97.
London Magazine, 399.
Lords of Trade and Plantation, 8.
Loughborough, Lord, 426.
Louis XIV, 387.
Louis XVI, 143, 427.

Lover's Walk, 60.
Lowther, Margaret, see Page, Margaret (Lowther).
Ludgate hill, 96.
Ludville, see Lodvill.
Ludwell, Frances, 16, 19, 24, 34, 35, 42, 44, 45, 455.
    Frances (Culpeper) Berkeley, 14, 453.
    Frances (Grymes), 19-20, 455.
Ludwell, Hannah (Harrison), 18, 454.
    Hannah Philippa, see Lee, Hannah Philippa (Ludwell).
    Jane (Cottington), 453.
    Jane Cottington, see Parke, Jane Cottington (Ludwell).
    Lucy, see Grymes, Lucy (Ludwell).
    Lucy (Higginson) Burwell Bernard, 453.
    Philip I (?-1716), 6, 7-8, 13, 14, 18, 33-34, 318, 453.
    Philip II (1672-1726/7), 8, 14, 18, 33-34, 318, 453, 454.
    Philip III (1716-1767), 8-9, 12, 13, 15, 16, 17, 23, 28, 29, 36, 37, 47, 56, 138, 192, 318, 319, 412, 443, 454, 455.
        death, 33.
        letters, to Emmanual Jones, 31-33.
        to Henry Lee, 22-23.
        to Washington, 21-22.
        sketch of, 18-24.
        will of, 34-35, 44-45, 254-55.
    Thomas, 7, 453.
Ludwell estate, 13-18, 31, 35-59, 182-83.
    confiscated, 113, 132-33.
    division of, 34-35, 42-46.
    escheated, 133-38, 147-49, 163.
Ludwell-Paradise house, see "Paradise house".
Ludwell family, 13, 33-34.

McCandlish, William, 446.
McCay, Mr., 345.
Macedonia, 4, 12, 25, 26, 37.
Madison, Bishop James, 282, 283, 306, 420, 440, 446.
    James, 200, 208, 238, 239, 302, 306.
Madrid, 160, 182, 304.
Malone, Edmund, 62, 398.

Marchetti, 71.
Macintosh, Sir James, 427.
Magazines (powder), 84.
Maintenon, Madame de, 387.
March's Tavern, 261.
Margaret street, 61, 363, 388, 390, 426.
Marie Antoinette, 92.
Market square, 20.
Marks, Hastings, 200.
    Nancy (Jefferson), 200.
Marriage settlements, 376.
Marylebone Fields, 63.
Marylebone Gardens, 60.
Maskelyne, Rev. Nevil, 90, 92.
Mason, Mr., 71.
    George, 148.
Mataponi river, 289.
Matsante, 426.
Matthias, T. J., 94.
Maty, Dr. William Matthew, 97.
The Mausoleum of Julia, 72.
Mazzei, Philip, 384.
Menokin, 288, 454.
Merchants, 15, 39, 61, 195, 277, 278, 288, 319.
Metaire, 339.
Middle Temple, 132.
Middlesex, 29, 61.
Middlesex Hospital, 63, 89, 94.
Milan, 315, 336, 337, 342, 343, 347, 350, 422.
Mill Hill, 97.
Miller, Philip, 33.
Mills, 16, 339, 395.
Milton, 125, 126.
Minuets, 48, 109, 204, 205, 286.
Mitre Tavern, 89.
Monasteries, manuscripts from, 27.
Monroe, James, 444-45.
    Maria, 444.
Mont Cenis pass, 335.
Mont d'Or, 331.
Montague, Lady Mary Wortley, 27.
Montbello, 337.
Monthly Review, 352.
Monticello, 17, 415, 436, 447.
Montmorin, Mons. de, 386.
Moor Park, 202.
Morattico, 455.
Morris, Gouverneur, 382.
    Robert, 345, 355.

Mortimer street, 61, 67.
Morton, Dr. Charles, 89.
Moser, Mary, 69, 112.
Mota, 71.
"Mottoes for Alderman", 40.
Mount Athos, 27.
Mount Pleasant, 455.
Mount Vernon, 22, 289-92, 408, 410.
Mourning, 420, 441.
Murray, Mr., 191.
"My Mother bids me bind my hair", 29.

Nantes, 157, 165, 167, 169-70, 175.
Napkins, at Royal Society dinners, 91.
Necker, Mr.. 386.
Necks, Capt., 49.
Negroes, 49, 51-54, 57, 278, 289, 304, 339, 412.
Nelson, Mary (Grymes), 454.
  Thomas, 148, 284, 454.
  William, 29, 39, 51, 291, 309-10.
  William, jr., 284-85, 294, 300.
Nesting, 247.
New College chapel, 263.
New Jerusalem, 52.
New Light preachers, 51-52.
New York, 156, 167, 295, 297, 301-07.
Newgate, 98.
Newman street, 76.
Newmarket, 17.
Nicholas, George, 23.
  Robert Carter, 34, 37, 46, 48, 51, 52, 54-55, 135, 454.
Nicholson, Francis, 8.
Nicolaides, 128, 131.
Noel, Dr., 263-64.
Nollekens, Joseph, 66, 68, 69, 112, 190.
  Mary (Welch), 66, 67-69.
Norfolk, 274, 433, 435, 444.
North, Lord, 133, 158, 428.
  Frederick, see Guilford, Earl of
Northy, Mrs., 76.
Norton, George Flowerdewe, 29, 39, 323, 324, 369, 394.
Novarre, 339.
Nowell, Dr. Thomas, 28.

Ode in Imitation of Callistratus, 178.
Ode to Pyrrha, 125, 126.
Oedipus Tyrannus, 128.

Ogle, Mr., 70.
Ohio river, 21, 136.
Oil, spermaceti, 200.
Omai, Otaheitan chief, 92.
Onions, 57.
Opium, 402.
Orange, Va., 208, 238.
Oranges and orangeries, 17, 204.
Orchards, 17, 44, 51.
Ord, Mrs., 107-08.
Organs, 220, 221, 224.
L'Orient, 157.
Orléans, Duke of, 330.
"The Orthodox Confession of the Catholic and Apostolic Eastern Church", 456.
Osborne, Edward, 26.
Osterly, 202.
Oswold, Richard, 159-60, 166.
Oxford market, 62.
Oxford street, 60.
Oxford university, 5, 12, 27, 28, 81, 105, 115, 120, 131, 259, 261, 262, 263, 300, 431.

Pacchierotti, 70, 71, 72, 73.
Padua, 12, 431.
Page, of Christ Church, 28.
  Alice (Grymes), 282.
  John, 281, 282-83, 306.
  Margaret (Lowther), 282-83.
Paget, Richard, 129.
Paine, Thomas, 385.
Palais Royal, 332.
Pall Mall, 190.
Palmers, Miss, 71.
Pamunkey river, 289.
Panthemont, l'Abbaye de, 225, 331.
Pantheon, 64, 109.
Paoli, Gen., 78, 130.
Paradise, John,
  at Belleview, 288-89.
  at Green Spring, 276-86, 296-97.
  at Mount Vernon, 22, 289-92.
  characteristics, 5-6, 12, 36, 37-38, 59, 63-64, 74, 78,-79, 80-81, 113, 121-22, 227, 307, 313, 429, 449-50.
  children of, 60.
  death, 431-32.

Paradise, John (Continued)
drinking, 258, 259, 261, 364, 375, 376, 391, 406, 408, 411, 417.
executor of Ludwell, 35.
extravagance, 136-37, 184-85.
fear of thunder, 173, 213, 215, 230, 289.
financial troubles, 113, 423, 429, 312-14, 319-20, 362-90, 397, 429.
Franklin's letter of recommendation, 168-69.
Franklin's opinon of, 182, 307.
friendship, with Boswell, 403-07, 421-25.
with Franklin, 30-31, 113, 138-47, 149-52, 157, 161-65, 176-77, 181, 299-300.
with Hoole, 108.
with Jefferson, 206-11.
with Johnson, 100-119.
with Jones, 121-27, 131-32.
with Ludwell, 28, 35.
guardian of Lucy Ludwell, 12.
health of, 399, 406, 429, 430.
house and hospitality of, 60-63, 184-90.
in Alexandria, 292.
in Bath, 190-94.
in Nantes, 169-76.
in New York, 295, 301-06.
in Paris, 87-88, 139-47, 149-51, 157-65, 176, 179-80.
in Philadelphia, 297-301.
in Williamsburg, 276-85.
Jefferson's opinion of, 215, 319.
lack of business ability, 37-38, 59, 80.
Lee's opinion of, 186.
letters, to Banks, 284.
to Franklin, 150-51.
to Jefferson, 210-11, 221-22, 232-33, 236-37, 271-72, 315, 341-42, 391-92, 422-23.
to Washington, 421-22.
to Wilkinson, 384.
library, 241.
linguist, 5, 25, 26, 27, 81, 121, 163, 262, 427-28, 432.
marriage, 11, 12-13, 35-36, 42, 245-46.
member, of Honest Whigs, 96-97.

Paradise, John (Continued)
of Royal Society, 27, 81-99.
parents of, 25.
petition to Virginia Assembly, 147-48.
portrait, 434.
quarrel, with father, 13, 133.
with wife, 43-44, 181-82, 233, 257, 265-66, 273, 346-50, 406.
scholarship of, 26-28, 80-81.
sketch of, 25-28.
student, at Oxford, 22, 27-28, 431.
at Padua, 22.
table, 119, 433.
Visitor at College of William and Mary, 319.
will of, 438.
Lucy, see Barziza, Lucy (Paradise).
Lucy (Ludwell), borrows bonnet, 445-46.
characteristics, 6-7, 9-10, 12, 24, 63-64, 74-75, 78-79, 109-12, 203, 312, 429-30, 437.
childhood, 13-18, 23-24.
death, 446.
dress of, 205.
extravagance and debts, 136-37, 184-85, 436-37.
gives balls, at Raleigh Tavern, 443.
on Twelfth Night, 75-78.
guardian of, 12.
illness, 437, 445-46.
in Williamsburg, 276-85, 433-46.
Johnson's comment on, 110-11, 112.
letters, to Mrs. Hodgson, 441.
to Jefferson, 227-29, 231-32, 240-42, 271-72, 320-21, 342-44, 360-61, 386-88, 410-14, 418-20.
to Washington, 408.
love for Jefferson, 312, 362, 377, 378-79, 449.
marriage, 11, 12-13, 35-36, 41-42, 245-46.
marriage settlement, 254-55.
property, in Williamsburg, 44-45, 152, 265, 413.
religion, 438.

Paradise, John (Continued)
Lucy (Ludwell) (Continued)
social position and ambitions, 13,
33, 64, 69, 79, 186, 281, 435.
temper, 24, 406, 437.
see also Paradise, John.
Peter, 12, 25, 26, 27, 28, 35, 41, 63,
82, 132, 133, 138, 434, 456.
Philippa, 60, 273, 285, 293-95, 425,
456.
"Paradise house" (owned by Lee),
4-5, 10, 42-48, 135, 286, 436,
442, 446.
"Paradise's loss", 113.
Paris, 87, 97, 98, 138-51, 157-67, 176,
179-81, 196-98, 200, 209-43,
292, 308, 311-27, 331, 340, 349-
50, 353, 358-96, 410, 411.
Parliament, 39, 95, 142.
Parke, Col. Daniel, jr., 453.
Jane Cottington (Ludwell), 453.
Lucy, *see* Byrd, Lucy (Parke).
Parr, Dr. Samuel, 65, 100, 102-06,
108, 124, 126, 127-29, 131, 147,
149-50, 427, 449.
Passy, 138, 139, 140, 144, 150, 155,
161, 168, 299, 357.
Paynshill, 201.
Peckatone, 454, 455.
Peknah, 67.
Pembroke, 263.
Pennsylvania, 96, 105, 155, 345.
Pepys, Sir Lucas, 108.
The Persian Heroine, 115-16.
Phi Beta Kappa, 309.
Philadelphia, 29, 30, 187, 218, 247,
249, 283, 292, 297-301, 306,
333, 351, 355.
Philosophical Society, 299.
Transactions, 84, 85, 94.
Pianos, 220, 287, 433.
Pimlico, 61.
Pinckney, Thomas, 426.
Pindar, 128.
Pinelli, 368.
Pinto, Chevalier de, 198, 366, 416.
Pio, 331.
Piozzi, Gabriel, 71, 101.
Hester Lynch Thrale, *see* Thrale,
Mrs.
Planta, Joseph, 76, 366.

Plumer, Thomas, 129.
"Poem to the Happiness of America",
187.
The Poet's Fate, 123.
Poland, King of, 92.
Porteous, Beilby, 455.
Porter, Sir Joseph, 81-82.
Portugal, 198, 366, 410, 416.
Postal service, 374.
Poulloy, 368.
Poviatowski, Michael, 92.
Prentis, Eliza, 443.
Prerogative Court of Canterbury, 428.
Presbyterians, 193, 413.
Price, Dr. Richard, 6, 95-96, 98, 105,
138, 211, 231, 298.
opinion of Lucy Paradise, 182.
Priestley, Joseph, 6, 95, 96, 97, 98,
104, 105, 106, 138, 352.
Pringle, Anne (Home), 29.
Sir John, 29, 84, 86-87, 88, 89, 93,
142, 403.
Prussia, King of, 189, 209, 214.
trade agreement, 309.
Pulteney street, 258, 259.
Purfleet, 84.

Queen Anne street, 62, 398, 430.
Queen square, 273, 293.
Queens College, 263.
Quilling for harpsichord, 218-19, 225.

Radcliffe, Mrs., 334.
Rainfall, experiments in, 283.
Raleigh Tavern, 4, 443.
Ramsay, Miss, 191.
Randolph, Edmund, 292.
Martha (Jefferson), 225-26, 419-20.
Thomas Mann, 416.
Raphael, cartoon of, 129.
Raspe, Rudolf Eric, 92.
Rasselas, 67.
Rathbone place, 11, 27, 41, 63, 260,
266, 363.
Rauzzini, 70.
*Remarks on the Review of the Con-
troversy between Great Britain
and her Colonies*, 352.
Resin, 217, 219.
Reynolds, Frances, 108, 109.

Reynolds, Frances (Continued)
  Sir Joshua, 62, 65, 67, 71, 106, 107, 114, 116, 130, 398, 400.
  William, 29.
Rich Neck, 10, 14, 44, 45, 54, 152, 276, 286, 453, 456.
"Richardson, Mr.", 354.
Rinaldo, 70.
Rings, 19, 35, 434, 439.
Rochester, 114.
Rogers, Samuel, 105.
Rohan, Cardinal, 209, 214.
Rome, 25, 333, 334, 339, 343, 350.
Romney, George, 62.
Rosewell, 282.
Rowe, Mr., 31.
"Royal Philosophers", 91.
Royal Society, 5, 27, 29, 65, 81, 83, 85-99, 115, 120, 138, 142, 169, 172, 187, 203, 283-84, 298, 352, 398, 403, 406, 411, 456.
Royal Society club, 89-93, 95, 114.
Rucker, Mr. and Mrs., 189, 191, 249.
Rue Jacob, 138, 150, 151.
"Ruins of Palmyra", 145.
Rush, Dr. Benjamin, 283.
Russell, Dr. Patrick, 89.
Russia, 438, 439.
Rutledge, Gov., 187.
  John, 187, 310-11, 328, 335-37, 344, 347-48, 350.

Sackville street, 95.
St. Andreé, Mr., 413.
St. Helena, 90.
St. James church, 30.
St. James park, 204.
St. James, levee, 197.
St. Martin's street, 70.
St. Martins in the Fields, 30.
St. Mary Hall, 27, 28, 263.
St. Mary le Strand church, 29.
St. Mary, Stratford le Bow, 13, 35, 453, 455, 456.
St. Paul's cathedral, 85.
St. Peter's cathedral, 263.
Salonica, 12, 25, 26, 35, 431.
Salthill, 261.
Sampson, Sir, 71.
Saone river, 331.
Sastres, 71, 405.

Savoy, 339.
Say and Sele, Lord and Lady, 72-73.
"The School for Soldiers," 304.
Sheridan, Richard, 304.
Scotland, 101, 403.
Scott, Dr. William, 124.
Sea voyages, 171.
Searle, Mr., 150.
Seed, 33, 50-51.
Sequestration Act, 133-34, 136-37.
Serpentine walls, 14.
Seward, William, 78, 115, 184, 231.
Shakespeare, 200.
Shaw, 405.
Shelburne, Lord, 159, 160, 169, 173, 174.
Shergoure, Mr., 263.
Shipley, Anna M., *see* Jones, Anna M. (Shipley).
Shippen, Alice (Lee), 23, 28, 29, 246, 454.
(Shippen) Thomas Lee, in Bath, 191-94.
  in Europe, 300-01, 308, 328, 335-36.
  meets Paradise in London, 186, 188, 203, 355-56, 366.
  writes of Lucy Paradise's marriage, 246-64, 267-68.
  William, 29, 177, 246, 292, 300-01, 454.
  Mrs. William, 300.
Ships, 41, 50, 74, 89, 92, 93, 170, 178, 237, 240, 273, 392, 394, 410, 433.
Shirley, 247.
Short, William, 186, 285, 297, 308-350, 388, 392.
  letters to Jefferson, 328-31, 336-40.
Silk cultivation, 17, 57, 339.
Silver, 199, 433-34.
Skipwith, Fulwar, 311.
Slaves, 16-17, 44-45, 46, 53, 57, 169-70.
Slingsby Bethel, 40.
Small, William, 207.
Smarnove, Rev., 438.

Smith, Mr., 75-76.
  Abigail (Adams), 145, 187, 189-90, 191, 199, 206, 248, 295, 301, 304, 306.
  John Thomas, 68.
  William Stephens, 93, 187, 189-90, 191, 196, 200, 202, 204, 210-11, 222, 225, 226, 236, 249, 308.
Smollett, Tobias, 61, 193.
Sacchini, 70, 72.
Society for Advancement of Useful Knowledge, 283.
Society for Political Enquiries, 299.
Society of Antiquaries, 89.
Soderini, Count, 78, 93, 204, 259, 269, 290, 323, 387.
Solander, Dr. Daniel, 71, 89, 93.
Somerset house, 84.
Somerset Parish, 18.
Sophocles, 128.
South Sea Bubble, 60.
Spain, 130, 160, 161, 166.
Spencer, Lord and Lady, 131, 163.
Spilsby, 129.
Spotswood, Gov., 8.
Spring Garden, 308.
Stackhouse, Dr., 263.
Stamp Act, 39.
Stanmore, 124, 127.
State house, Jamestown, 7, 14.
Staunton, 445.
Steevens, 107, 116.
Sterne, Laurence, 209.
Stevens, B. F., 353.
  Col. Samuel, 453.
Stevenson, Mrs., 273, 293.
Steuben, Baron, 305, 306.
Stewards, on Paradise plantation, 58, 210, 228, 237, 265, 361, 396, 411, 412.
Stormont, Lord, 353, 354.
Strahan, William, 29.
Strand, 30, 84, 89.
Stratford-Langton, 29.
Stratford-upon-Avon, 200.
Stratford Hall, 11, 23, 28, 36, 57, 247, 288, 454, 455.
Streatfield, Miss, 70.
Streatham, 71, 113.
Streatham park, 101.

Street, T. G., 427.
Stuart, Mrs. David, 290.
  Nancy, 290.
Surry county, 18, 135, 148, 276, 308, 330.
Swan, James, 384.

Table, of Paradise, 119, 433.
Taliaferro, widow, 23.
Tarent, Mr., 329, 330.
Tasso, 108.
Taxation no Tyranny, 3.
Taxes and taxation, 50, 95.
Taylor, quack physician, 107.
  Greek teacher, 405.
Tazewell, L. W., 442.
Tea, 92, 204.
"Teacup, Mrs.", 76.
Teddington, 250.
Teignmouth, Lord, 122.
Temple, Sir John and Lady, 302, 404.
Tenducci, 71.
Test Act, 413.
Thackeray, Dr., 123.
Thames river, 30, 192.
Thessalonica, 148.
Thomson, Charles, 200.
Thrale, Mrs., 65, 73, 100, 101, 108, 110-11, 113, 114, 115, 117, 130, 404.
  Misses, 75.
  Queeney, 71.
Thunder, Paradise's tear of, 173, 213, 215, 230, 289.
Thurlow, Lord, 155, 178.
Timber, 44, 49, 50, 53, 395.
Tireau & Grand, 355.
Toano, 289.
Toasts, 91-92, 98.
Tobacco, 12, 15, 26, 27, 47, 52, 54, 58, 128, 183, 195, 237, 239-40, 241, 275, 276-77, 394, 395, 396, 411, 433, 448.
  merchants, 240, 241, 242, 243.
  shipping instructions, 50.
Tories, 86, 102, 119, 129, 133, 142, 216, 404.
Tower of London, 160, 176.
Trade, 26, 37, 132, 169, 183, 195, 276-77.

Treaty of Peace, *1783*, 158, 163, 166-67, 181, 182, 183, 195, 197, 309.
Tree of Knowledge, 404.
Trees, 17, 30, 53, 217, 275, 338.
Trenton, battle of, 303.
Tripoli, 198.
Tristram Shandy, 92.
Trumbull, John, 187, 235, 260, 344, 345, 366, 368, 391, 392, 393.
Tuckahoe, 416.
Tucker, St. George, 444.
Turin, 332, 334, 335, 336.
Turks and Turkey, 25, 26, 81, 169, 199, 216, 261-62, 427, 428.
Turkish language, 25, 81, 120, 262, 428, 432.
Turner, Sir Gregory Page, 73.
Turnspit, 339.
Tuscany, Grand Duke of, 83.
Twelfth Cake, 78.

Udny, John, 250-251.
University of Edinburgh, 28.
University of Leyden, 82.
University of Padua, 12.
University of Pennsylvania, 300.

Vauxhall, 64.
Venice and Venetians, 25, 269, 272, 316-17, 347-48, 387, 428, 429, 440.
Venetian blinds, 212, 217.
Venetian minister, 204.
Venus, 90, 201.
Vercelli, 338.
Vergennes, 166, 357.
Versailles, 318, 350.
Villefranche, 327, 328, 330, 331.
Virginia, 11, 12, 13, 15, 17, 18, 23, 24, 31, 34, 64, 132, 136, 145, 152, 159, 181, 192, 208, 393, 402, 435.
    debts of, 369.
    description of, 274-75, 276-77.
    society in, 306.
Virginia. Council, 18, 20, 134, 135, 192, 309, 318, 319.
    General Assembly, 14, 21, 22, 23, 132, 146, 147, 148, 192, 282, 283.
    Supreme Court, 447.

Virginia Gazette, 11, 58, 94, 403.
Voss, Mr., 241, 242, 243.

Wakefield, 454.
Wales, Prince of, 91, 190, 204.
Walker, Capt., 50.
    Mr., 213, 217, 218, 219, 221, 222, 223.
Wall street, 301, 302.
Wallace, Capt. Walter, 237.
Waller, Benjamin, 34, 436, 442, 455.
    Mary, *see* Corbin, Mary (Waller).
Walpole, Horace, 6, 65, 130.
Waltersdorff, Baron de, 351.
Warley Common, 130, 131.
Warren, Dr. Richard, 94-95, 184, 294, 400-01.
Washington, Corbin, 287.
    George, 21-22, 24, 126, 160, 187-88, 289-90, 291, 292, 303, 376, 379, 408, 409, 410, 420, 441, 455.
        letter to Lucy Paradise, 409.
        portrait, 434.
    Hannah, 287.
    Lund, 290.
    Martha (Dandridge) Custis, 289, 303, 304, 377, 379, 408, 417, 422, 441, 453.
Washington (city), 441.
Watson, Sir William, 90, 172.
    William, jr., 90.
Wayles, John, 34.
Weavils, 378.
Welbeck street, 438.
Welch, Mrs., 437.
    Anne, 66, 68.
    Mary, *see* Nollekens, Mary (Welch).
    Saunders, 66, 69.
Welsh harp, 131.
Wentworth, Paul, 353-54.
Wescot, Lord, 201.
West Point, 289.
Westminster, 61, 66.
Westminster Abbey, 117-18.
Westminster Hall, 156, 250.
Westover, 17, 247, 453.
Wharton, Francis, 356.
Whateley, 201.
Wheat, 15, 51, 378.
Wheel barrows, geometrical, 385.

Whigs, 4, 5, 39, 86, 95, 102, 104, 130, 133, 142, 143, 427.
White Conduit House, 302.
Whitefield, Rev. George, 60.
Whitefoord, Caleb, 69.
Wilkes, John, 8, 39, 65, 101, 106, 248.
Miss, 106.
Wilkins, Mr., 415.
Wilkinson, Cary, 32, 37, 47-56, 135, 147, 183.
William, 183, 384, 394, 395, 396, 415, 440.
William and Mary College, 8, 19, 31, 49, 119, 207, 214, 247, 278, 281, 282, 309, 318, 319.
Williams, Jonathan, 170.
William's ferry, 289.
Williamsburg, 11, 16, 17, 19, 20, 21, 29, 94, 119, 146, 206, 207, 214, 274, 283, 289, 308, 394, 403, 444.
ball in, 275.
description, 278-79.
in Revolution, 135, 278.
Wilson, Benjamin, 85-86.
Wilson, Richard, 62-63 .
Wilton, Mr., 67.
Wimpole street, 61, 189.
Winchester, 21.

Windham, Robert, 426.
William, 65, 116, 124, 406, 425-26, 439.
Wine, 15, 19, 49, 68-69, 91, 92, 128, 262, 263, 310, 329, 330, 332, 377, 402.
Woburn farm, 201.
Woffington, Peg, 109.
Women's property rights, 376.
Worcester, 200-01.
Woronzow, Count Semen de, 290, 426, 438-39.
Countess, 204.
Wren, Christopher, 63.
Wythe, George, 214-15, 247, 281-82, 283, 291, 306, 391.
Mrs. George, 215, 281.

York county, 135, 147-48.
York river, 289.
York street, 229.
Yorkshire, 192.
Yorktown, 20, 29, 51, 167, 187, 274, 278, 294, 295.
battle of, 142, 153, 158, 278, 303.
Young, Mr., 363, 373, 375, 376, 379-80.
Sir George, 205.

Zenobio, Count, 71, 93, 116, 117, 184, 191, 269, 321, 323, 365-66, 426.